QUAKER WOMEN, 1800–1920

❧ THE NEW HISTORY OF QUAKERISM

The first historical series in Quaker studies in over a century, these volumes offer a fresh, comprehensive, up-to-date treatment of the history of Quakerism from its seventeenth-century origins to the twenty-first century. Using critical methodologies, this limited series emphasizes key events and movements, examines all branches of Quakerism, and explores its global reach.

Quaker Women, 1800–1920

Studies of a Changing Landscape

Edited by Robynne Rogers Healey and Carole Dale Spencer

The Pennsylvania State University Press
University Park, Pennsylvania

Library of Congress Cataloging-in-Publication Data

Names: Healey, Robynne Rogers, 1964– editor. | Spencer, Carole Dale, editor.
Title: Quaker women, 1800–1920 : studies of a changing landscape / edited by Robynne Rogers Healey and Carole Dale Spencer.
Other titles: New history of Quakerism.
Description: University Park, Pennsylvania : The Pennsylvania State University Press, [2023] | Series: The new history of Quakerism | Includes bibliographical references and index.
Summary: "An interdisciplinary investigation of nineteenth-century Quaker women's cultural challenges, historical landmarks, and gender transgressions. Explores the dynamic ways that Quaker women were active agents of social and cultural change within multiple contexts"—Provided by publisher.
Identifiers: LCCN 2023022252 | ISBN 9780271095509 (hardback) | ISBN 9780271095516 (paper)
Subjects: LCSH: Quaker women—History—19th century. | Social change—Religious aspects—Society of Friends—History—19th century. | LCGFT: Essays.
Classification: LCC BX7748.W64 Q83 2023 | DDC 289.6—dc23/eng/20230616
LC record available at https://lccn.loc.gov/2023022252

Copyright © 2023 The Pennsylvania State University
All rights reserved
Printed in the United States of America
Published by The Pennsylvania State University Press,
University Park, PA 16802-1003

The Pennsylvania State University Press is a member of the Association of University Presses.

It is the policy of The Pennsylvania State University Press to use acid-free paper. Publications on uncoated stock satisfy the minimum requirements of American National Standard for Information Sciences—Permanence of Paper for Printed Library Material, ANSI Z39.48-1992.

To our granddaughters
Cadence, Lorelai, Sophia, Catherine, Saoirse, Ava, and Maeve
Kelsea, Ashlea, Grace, and Kaia

We analyze and write the past; you are the future.

CONTENTS

Foreword by Janet Scott xi
List of Illustrations xiii
Acknowledgments xv
List of Abbreviations xvii

Introduction 1
ROBYNNE ROGERS HEALEY AND
CAROLE DALE SPENCER

PART I: ENGAGING CONFLICT
AND SEPARATIONS

1 Hicksite Women in the Long Nineteenth Century 17
THOMAS D. HAMM

2 Elizabeth Robson, Transatlantic Women Ministers, and the Hicksite-Orthodox Schism 38
ROBYNNE ROGERS HEALEY

3 Women in the World of George W. Taylor: The Public and Private Worlds of Orthodox Quaker Women 57
JULIE L. HOLCOMB

PART 2: ENGAGING DIVERSITY

4 Vocation, Religious Identity, and the Abolitionist Networks of Sarah Mapps Douglass and Sojourner Truth   79
   STEPHEN W. ANGELL

5 "She Hath Done What She Could": The Charitable Antislavery Work of Eleanor Clark of Street   102
   ANNA VAUGHAN KETT

6 Ruth Esther Smith (1870–1947): Foremother to Friends in Central America   122
   JENNIFER M. BUCK

PART 3: ENGAGING SACRED AND SECULAR LITERATURE

7 An Unforeseen Consequence of the Orthodox-Hicksite Schism (1827–1828): The Fiction Writing of Amelia Opie, Helen Hunt Jackson, Mary Howitt, and Mary Hallock Foote   137
   ISABELLE COSGRAVE

8 A Friendly Daughter: Lucy Barton's (Ex-)Quaker Identity, Cultural Negotiations, and Authorial Inheritance   156
   NANCY JIWON CHO

9 The "Mystic Sense" of Scripture as Taught by Holiness Quaker Hannah Whitall Smith   178
   CAROLE DALE SPENCER

PART 4: ENGAGING THE WIDER SOCIAL AND CULTURAL WORLD

10 "Radicalism Within Boundaries": Excavating the Contribution of Women Quakers to Radical Reform in Britain and Their Transnational Networks in the Nineteenth Century   199
    JOAN ALLEN AND RICHARD C. ALLEN

11 "We Must Hope That the Moderates
    with Their Quiet Attire Are the Rising Section":
    British Women Friends' Relinquishment
    of Plain Dress   222
    HANNAH RUMBALL

12 "The Joy of Doing Right": The Humanitarian
    Work of Doctor Hilda Clark During the
    First World War   245
    LINDA PALFREEMAN

Afterword by Emma Lapsansky-Werner   265

Selected Bibliography   269

List of Contributors   277

Index   283

FOREWORD

JANET SCOTT

> Our lives are not private possessions but windows of grace, their possibility kindled by the tenderness of others.
> —*A Spirit-Led Church*, 3.4, Britain Yearly Meeting, 2015

In 1985, at the time of the sanctuary movement in the United States, a Friend in North Carolina said to me, "My meeting was part of the Underground Railroad, so of course we became a sanctuary meeting." It was the "of course" that particularly struck me, for it illustrates how the stories we tell in our communities shape our understanding not only of who we are but of who and how we are supposed to be. Common stories are one of the factors that hold communities together.

This is particularly true of those Quakers in the contemporary world who hold lightly to doctrine. The tender kindling of lives into windows of grace is encouraged by the accounts and testimonies of individuals and meetings who have struggled as we have and have found the spiritual power to live lives faithful to their call.

How stories are told is often a function of the time of their telling. L. V. Hodgkin's *Book of Quaker Saints*, a children's book published in 1917, verges, as the title suggests, on hagiography. But we live in times that are perhaps more cynical. We want, as Oliver Cromwell is reputed to have demanded, to be seen "warts and all." For these stories, we turn less to the preachers and teachers and more to the academics and researchers. The authors of the chapters in this volume have done remarkable work. They have brought before us some of the Quaker women who have mostly been neglected in previous histories and shown us how they negotiated lives of faith in changing and often difficult times.

The nineteenth century was a time of great change. Technical, economic, and political developments changed traditional ways of life. Colonization, slavery, and poverty oppressed people and led both to resistance and to campaigns for reform. Women's changing relationship to work outside the home, the development of the caring professions, and the increasing availability of education in schools and universities gave new opportunities to some women. As the surrounding cultures changed, they affected Quaker life and meetings. The century saw the gradual removal of the hedge of plain speech, plain dress, and regulation that separated Quakers from the outside world. By the end of the century, the separate business meetings for women that George Fox had set up had all but disappeared, as men's and women's meetings merged.

The research here shows us the formation of faith in meetings and families, in the reading of scripture, and in times of prayer. The women featured in this book, brought up to spiritual equality, had to negotiate social inequality in their meetings and their dealings with the world. They saw needs and set out to meet them, often at a personal cost. It is good to see how networks of women supported one another.

These stories illuminate different ways to be faithful, whether writing or teaching, campaigning, performing humanitarian work, or engaging in mission. Of course, they are only a selection, mainly of those women whose financial and family circumstances gave them the freedom to follow their call. We have yet to hear the voices of the poor and of the women whose work sustained more privileged lives. There are many stories yet to be told.

In our own difficult and troubled times, we need stories that are nuanced, that recognize the complexity of discipleship, of living within a faith tradition while challenging and sometimes transforming it. These chapters give the reader not only a greater knowledge of Quakers in the nineteenth century but also the material for a deeper perception of the many ways in which individuals have responded to the Spirit of God. Here we find evidence of Friends who have lived as "windows of grace" through whom divine light shines.

ILLUSTRATIONS

11.1　Photograph of Caroline Barrow, Ann Cash, and Elizabeth Petipher Cash, ca. 1860–65　229

11.2　Grecian-style aesthetic wedding gown worn by Geraldine Cadbury, 1891　233

11.3　Photograph of the wedding of Geraldine Southall and Barrow Cadbury, September 8, 1891　235

11.4　Fashionable wedding dress worn by the Quaker Lucretia Seebohm (née Anson Crouch), 1874　239

ACKNOWLEDGMENTS

Any work of scholarship represents a great deal of effort; an edited anthology like this one—especially one produced during a global pandemic—represents a great deal of work by many people. Thanks, therefore, are due to those who made this book possible. Our first thanks must go to the contributors who worked under challenging conditions, which included difficulty getting access to sources. They patiently and diligently participated in a long process of writing and consistently revising material. We learned a lot from one another in the process. The work of historians is impossible without the work of archivists. We are all grateful to the staff at many Quaker libraries: the Library of the Society of Friends at Friends House, London; Woodbrooke Quaker Study Centre, Birmingham; the Friends Historical Library at Swarthmore College, Swarthmore, Pennsylvania; and Haverford College Library Quaker and Special Collections, Haverford, Pennsylvania. Thanks also to archivists at the many other repositories that hold Quaker records around the world. The Conference of Quaker Historians and Archivists (CQHA), the Quaker Studies Research Association (QSRA), Friends Historical Society (FHS), Friends Historical Association (FHA), and the Quaker Studies Unit at the American Academy of Religion (AAR) have provided support in multiple ways. These organizations create space for the discussion of Quaker history; that space allows scholars at any stage of their careers to question accepted interpretations and offer potential revisions to how we understand the Quaker past. Many of the ideas presented in the pages that follow have benefited from presentations at the conferences hosted by these organizations. We are also grateful to the Gender Studies Institute at Trinity Western University for supporting this volume with a publishing subvention.

We are grateful to Dana Graham Lai, who created the initial bibliography for the project, and to Sydney Harker for preparing the index. The reviewers graciously helped sharpen our arguments considerably. We are particularly thankful to Penn State University Press for answering questions quickly and providing insights throughout the production process.

ROBYNNE ROGERS HEALEY AND CAROLE DALE SPENCER

ABBREVIATIONS

AGT Alfred Gillett Trust at C. & J. Clark in Street, England
BFASS British and Foreign Anti-Slavery Society
CYM California Yearly Meeting
FCCA Friends Collection and College Archives, Earlham College, Richmond, IN
FHLSC Friends Historical Library, Swarthmore College, Swarthmore, PA
FWVRC Friends' War Victims' Relief Committee
HCLQSC Haverford College Library Quaker and Special Collections, Haverford, PA
HCP Hilda Clark Papers
IYM Indiana Yearly Meeting
LSF Library of the Society of Friends, London, England
LYM London Yearly Meeting
NSWS National Society for Women's Suffrage
NYYM New York Yearly Meeting
PYM Philadelphia Yearly Meeting
TFP Taylor Family Papers

Introduction

ROBYNNE ROGERS HEALEY AND CAROLE DALE SPENCER

This is the fifth volume in Penn State University Press's New History of Quakerism series, a series that seeks to provide up-to-date analysis of Quaker history in accessible volumes. This book addresses constructions of gender, predominantly for women, in the long nineteenth century. It brings together an interdisciplinary body of writers who seek to reassess nineteenth-century Quaker women and the ways in which they engaged their intersecting worlds. With a focus on gender, the authors offer new findings and interpretations about Quaker women in four thematic sections: Engaging Conflict and Separations, Engaging Diversity, Engaging Sacred and Secular Literature, and Engaging the Wider Social and Cultural World. These essays analyze aspects of diverse nineteenth-century Quakerism, adding to volumes that touch on Quaker women and extending a gendered analysis to the century of first-wave feminism.[1] Our book draws on interdisciplinary scholarship in history, literature, material culture, and religious studies and foregrounds the experience of women in transatlantic and transnational contexts.

Given the dominance of Victorian separate-sphere ideology in the nineteenth century, this period is fertile ground for scholars interested in investigating the ways in which Quaker spiritual equality interacted with Victorian ideology and the changing nineteenth-century world. There is surprisingly little literature on nineteenth-century Quaker women compared to the amount of scholarship on seventeenth- and eighteenth-century Quaker women. Margaret Hope Bacon's pioneering work *Mothers of Feminism* was published more than thirty years ago. It covers a vast time line, demonstrating that Quaker women's feminist consciousness developed because each generation struggled for equality. Book-length studies have been dedicated to well-known nineteenth-century Quaker women like Lucretia Mott.[2] But there are only two recent monographs that focus on nineteenth-century Quaker women over the whole century. One is Jody Cross-Hansen's *The Contribution of Quaker Women to the Political Struggle for Abolition, Women's Rights, and Peace*, and the other is Sandra Stanley Holton's *Quaker Women: Personal Life, Memory, and Radicalism in the Lives of Women Friends, 1780–1930*. Both studies focus within national boundaries; the first concentrates on American women, the second on British women.

New research is beginning to illuminate the complexities of the Quaker testimonies on equality, slavery, and peace and the ways in which gender, race, ethnicity, and culture worked with these testimonies to shape Quaker women's lived experience. This work challenges views that Quaker women were always treated equally with Quaker men and that people of color were welcomed into White Quaker activities.

These essays interrogate stereotyped interpretations of Quaker women and their role in shaping or reinforcing cultures of dissent and conformity. Nineteenth-century Quakerism was far more diverse in its expressions than the Quakerism of the seventeenth and eighteenth centuries. This is reflected in the schisms that fragmented the Religious Society of Friends throughout the century. A central goal of this volume is to examine how diverse groups of Quaker women navigated the intersection of their theological positions and social conventions in various locations. The authors do not just ask how Quaker women challenged traditional ideals of gender, race, and class; they ask how Quaker women supported those ideals. Together, the essays highlight the complexity of nineteenth-century Quakerism and the ways in which Quaker women used their faith to expand or limit socially constructed identities. For instance, the chapter on Quaker missions to Central America places Quakers in colonial and imperial narratives as colonizers as well as progressive reformers.[3] The scholars represented here use varied disciplinary methodologies and a broad range of archival materials in the extensive collections available at Quaker and non-Quaker repositories.

Indeed, the interdisciplinary focus of the chapters that follow establishes the extent to which Quaker women challenged or endorsed the cultural and textual norms of the long nineteenth century.

Before summarizing the findings presented in this volume, it is important to provide some context for Quakerism through the long nineteenth century. Quakers at the beginning of the nineteenth century were a relatively united body. Over the course of the eighteenth century, they had become a highly organized sect, visibly and practically distinct from the societies in which they lived.[4] By 1920, Quakers were no longer united. Several nineteenth-century schisms, along with intellectual, cultural, and economic changes, transformed Quakers into a diverse religious group, with multiple branches of Friends all claiming to represent original Quakerism.

Theological conflict among Friends first appeared in the late 1790s, when Irish Friend Abraham Shackleton (1752–1818) and American Friend Hannah Jenkins Barnard (ca. 1754–1825) questioned whether a loving God would order the elimination of enemies as recorded in the Old Testament. Both were disowned by their meetings for challenging the accuracy of scripture, but such rifts were limited. There were other localized divisions in the early nineteenth century, such as the breakaway Children of Peace in Upper Canada (Ontario) and the New Light Movement in the New England Yearly Meeting (NEYM), but it was the acrimonious Hicksite separation of 1827–28 that tore the North American meetings apart and established a precedent for division as a mechanism for dealing with disagreement.

The Hicksite-Orthodox schism revolved around the Long Island minister Elias Hicks (1748–1830), "the most polarizing figure in American Quakerism between 1800 and 1850," as Thomas D. Hamm puts it.[5] Hicks had traveled extensively throughout the American meetings in the early nineteenth century, speaking out against what he saw as innovations in contemporary Quakerism, including the connections Friends had formed with non-Quakers through humanitarian reform activities. Especially troubling for extreme quietists like Hicks was the growing sway of evangelical doctrine. Early nineteenth-century British Quakerism had been markedly influenced by evangelicalism, but evangelical theology was also prevalent among some American Friends. These Quakers insisted on the authority of scripture over the Inward Light, the divinity of Christ, and salvation through Christ's atoning sacrifice. By 1820, Quakers were coalescing into opposing factions over Hicks's reservations about the authority of scripture and the divinity of the historical Jesus, and his rejection of the Trinity and the doctrine of atonement. At every level of the North American meetings, Hicksites challenged Orthodox Friends—those who upheld evangelical doctrine—over the importance of these beliefs for the Society. Although both sides agreed on several principles, the members of each faction claimed that *they* were the legitimate Friends and the others apostate.[6]

Open conflict emerged at the end of 1822, when Orthodox Philadelphia Friends publicly denounced the preaching of Hicks and Priscilla Hunt Cadwalader (1786–1859), a minister from the Indiana Yearly Meeting (IYM) who shared Hicks's views but had arrived at them independently.[7] More than four years of bitter debate ensued. Each side used every means at its disposal—pamphlets, letters, the traveling ministry, meeting governance and discipline—to oppose the other. The discord erupted in April 1827, when the Philadelphia Yearly Meeting (PYM) separated. By the fall of 1828, the New York, Baltimore, Ohio, and Indiana Yearly Meetings had also separated. Apart from two minor divisions in New Bedford and on Nantucket Island, the NEYM did not separate, nor did the Virginia and North Carolina Yearly Meetings. On the other side of the Atlantic, the London Yearly Meeting (LYM) and Dublin Yearly Meeting considered the Orthodox the legitimate Quaker bodies.

The Great Separation was not as simple as a dispute between liberal and evangelical Friends.[8] Besides theological differences, scholars have attributed the rupture to disparities between urban and rural Friends and divisions between wealthy Quakers who had embraced the changing American economy and those less wealthy and more bound to tradition.[9] Larry Ingle contends that Hicksites viewed their efforts as a reformation, an attempt to restore Quakerism to its primitive roots.[10] The lack of charity that attended the schism left a deep scar on Quakerism in Britain as well as in North America, although it was felt most keenly in the North American meetings, where bitter contests over meeting property and family allegiances followed the rupture. Further separations occurred among both the Hicksites and the Orthodox.[11]

After the schism, Hicksites disagreed about participation in radical reform movements, including abolition. Beginning in 1843, reform-minded Hicksites in New York, the Delaware Valley, Ohio, Indiana, Illinois, and Michigan left their meetings and formed yearly meetings of Congregational or Progressive Friends.[12] Orthodox Quakers in North America and the United Kingdom divided over Quaker evangelicalism as it was expressed by English minister Joseph John Gurney (1788–1847), brother of prison reformer Elizabeth Gurney Fry (1780–1845). Gurney advocated an evangelicalism close to the non-Quaker evangelicalism of the period. By 1860, evangelical North American Quakers were called Gurneyites. For some Orthodox Friends, Gurney was not evangelical enough. In Manchester, England, Isaac Crewdson (1780–1844) spoke for these Quakers in his 1835 pamphlet *A Beacon to the Society of Friends*, which rejected the idea of Inward Light and insisted on the Bible as the sole source of revelation. The Beaconite controversy that followed took its name from Crewdson's pamphlet.[13] When the LYM tried to silence Crewdson and his supporters, they formed their own body, called Evangelical Friends, a group, with its renunciation of women in ministry and its practice of physical baptism and communion, hardly distinguishable from other evangelicals. Quietist Orthodox Friends took a dim view of Gurney's evangelicalism. Gurney's fiercest critic was Rhode Island minister John Wilbur (1774–1856). The NEYM, which supported Gurney, forced Wilbur's disownment, which resulted in the Wilburite branch of Quakerism when Wilbur's supporters formed their own yearly meeting in 1845.[14] Similar separations followed in the New York (1846), Baltimore, Indiana, and Ohio Yearly Meetings (all 1854). By 1860, the Quaker tree had sprouted many branches.

Each Quaker branch underwent further transformation in the latter part of our period, including relaxing discipline regarding plainness and marriage to non-Quakers. The two dominant influences were the holiness movement and liberal Quakerism. By 1900, religious liberals dominated the Hicksites to the extent that, despite eschewing interactions with "the world" in the 1830s, they now openly identified with liberal Protestants.[15] The Orthodox underwent a holiness revival that fractured Gurneyite Friends. Revivalist Friends focused on holiness doctrine such as instantaneous sanctification as a "second work of grace," borrowed from the Methodist tradition; they also turned from traditional Quaker worship and adopted a pastoral system of ministry.[16] Gurneyite Friends in the New York, Indiana, Western, Iowa, Kansas, and North Carolina Yearly Meetings who opposed the revivalists separated and became known as Conservative Friends.[17] Liberal or modernist theology, with its endorsement of reason and science, transformed British and American Gurneyite Friends at the end of the long nineteenth century. Liberal Quakers, like John Wilhelm Rowntree in the United Kingdom and Rufus Jones in the United States, contended that religious and historical education was important for Quaker identity and for keeping abreast of developments in science (such as evolution), biblical studies (such as biblical criticism), and social science (such as ending poverty and war).[18] Modernist or liberal Quakerism "emphasized service as the fulfillment of Quaker religious life."[19] Diverse as they were, most nineteenth-century Quakers shared a commitment to missions at home and abroad.[20]

Wars of the long nineteenth century, including the American Civil War and especially the First World War, forced Friends to confront the way they interpreted and practiced their opposition to war. The yearly meetings were all officially pacifist during the First World War, but Quakers themselves reacted in different ways. Some became conscientious objectors, some performed alternative service, and a significant group (30 percent of eligible British Quakers and 50 percent of eligible American Quakers) enlisted in active service.[21] Friends' examination of war and peace during the war resulted in "a renewed commitment to peace and peacemaking and, for North American Friends, reconciliation among Quakers who had been divided in nineteenth-century separations. The peace testimony, which historically had been a testimony against war, became a pro-active testimony focused on opposition to war and commitment to facilitating the economic, social, and political conditions for a peaceful international world order."[22]

This collection is arranged thematically rather than chronologically to maximize interactions between chapters that share a similar focus.

PART I: ENGAGING CONFLICT AND SEPARATIONS

Quaker women were not innocent bystanders in the fracturing and restructuring of the nineteenth-century Quaker world. Part 1 explores the roles Quaker women played in the bitter schisms that transformed the Society of Friends and reshaped it into the branches and bodies that exist today. The three chapters examine how women responded to the deepening divisions among Friends by assuming new roles, engaging in doctrinal debates and radical reforms, and providing leadership that provoked and aided schism.

In chapter 1, Thomas D. Hamm surveys Hicksite women and concludes that while they were less visible than men in the controversies leading to schism, once the separation had taken place, women were among the most visible Hicksite leaders. This created tensions over the question of women's roles. Hicksite women themselves supported the notion of women's separate sphere throughout most of the century, despite their tradition of equality in ministry. But a faction of Hicksite women were theologically liberal and radically reform-oriented. Many, though embattled, persevered within their yearly meetings; others were disowned for their abolitionist activity; some resigned from Friends. Most leaders of the first women's rights convention were Hicksite Quakers. But these were the exception among Hicksite women, and it was not until late in the century that support for gender equality became common among Hicksite Friends.

Chapters 2 and 3 focus on lesser-known Quaker women who expanded gender roles for Orthodox/Gurneyite women. In chapter 2, Robynne Rogers Healey shows how British traveling women ministers tried to impose paternalistic Quakerism on American Quakers, at the same time reshaping gender stereotypes in a period when doctrinal instability created openings for women as leaders. She introduces the English minister Elizabeth Robson, one of the most widely traveled ministers of her day, who played a significant role in defending the Orthodox side of the schism. Healey argues that while Robson was theologically conservative, she was not a model of nineteenth-century middle-class domesticity and submissiveness.

In chapter 3, Julie L. Holcomb offers a case study of one network of the Orthodox/Gurneyite Quaker women in the world of George W. Taylor, a Philadelphia merchant and antislavery activist. Holcomb uncovers the activities of three generations of women and their friends who influenced and supported Taylor's reform work. Like Hamm, Holcomb explores how schism helped crack the boundaries between public and private among the Orthodox in a period of great social and religious change, opening new opportunities for reform activity.

PART 2: ENGAGING DIVERSITY

Although Quakers were evangelistic and mission-oriented from the beginning, the nineteenth century revitalized Friends and inspired them to reach beyond their own racial, ethnic, and class boundaries to bring Light, aid, and "uplift" to marginalized people both at home and abroad. Part 2 of the volume examines how White Quaker women began interacting with a more ethnically and racially diverse world while navigating their own privileged gender ideals within Quaker communities and abroad. The three chapters in this section examine the successes and failures of different ways of engagement with diverse cultures: the empowerment/disempowerment dance in the integration of African American women; the humanitarian work of British Quaker women in antislavery campaigns and aid to freed, impoverished Black Americans; and the evangelization of Hispanic cultures by Gurneyite women.

In chapter 4, Stephen W. Angell examines the lives of prominent nineteenth-century African American women who had significant interaction with Quakers, such as educator, artist, writer, and abolitionist Sarah Mapps Douglass, who identified as a Quaker but was compelled to sit in the Negro section and was never admitted to membership, despite attending meeting regularly. Sojourner Truth was strongly influenced by Quakers and joined Progressive Friends late in her life. Angell acknowledges that, while Quaker leaders were admired for upholding Friends' testimony to the spiritual equality of all people, many Quakers mirrored the paternalistic and condescending attitudes of the privileged White culture and harbored views of White superiority.

Anna Vaughan Kett, in chapter 5, explores the work of the network of Quaker women around Eleanor Stephens Clark, the wife of the English shoemaking pioneer James Clark. While Clark's philanthropic work has been well researched, the reform activity of the female members of his family has been largely ignored. Kett uncovers the extent and variety of their antislavery activity, which, along with Holcomb's work, demonstrates the transatlantic sisterhood of Quaker women's abolitionism and the effectiveness of the free-produce movement.

In chapter 6, Jennifer M. Buck examines Ruth Esther Smith, the pioneering holiness Quaker missionary in Central America who founded and helped shape Hispanic Friends churches worldwide. Buck contends that Smith's relationships across class and racial lines were boundary breaking for her day, as she modeled gender equality and empowered women and Indigenous leaders. Buck describes Smith's endeavors as contextualizing Quakerism in a new culture rather than importing White colonialism.

PART 3: ENGAGING SACRED AND SECULAR LITERATURE

Quaker women have a long tradition of writing and publishing from the sect's earliest period—tracts, journals, travel diaries, autobiographies, letters, even theological writings. But Quakers, like other religious groups in the early nineteenth century, had strong objections to the reading of fiction.

However, the nineteenth-century breakdown of Quaker sectarianism led to gradual assimilation to the wider culture, opening new avenues of literary genres for Quaker women.

Isabelle Cosgrave, in chapter 7, describes Quakers' unique theological objection to fiction as an approach to "truth," different from other religious traditions that also disapproved of fiction. She then examines how four women writers—British, American, Gurneyite, and Hicksite—navigated traditional Quaker resistance to the writing of fiction. Her work suggests that schism, geography, culture, and the changing nature of Quaker identity played a part in fiction's eventual acceptance by most Quakers by the end of the century.

The next two chapters examine female authors who pioneered in writing biblical exegesis, a new venture in religious writing for Quaker women. In chapter 8, Nancy Jiwon Cho details Lucy Barton's groundbreaking work of creating Bible literature for children. Cho explores the distinct theological features of Barton's work that reveal the influence of the Orthodox Quakerism of her upbringing as well as the emergent evangelical Quakerism and its focus on scripture. Cho's work is the first to assess the influence of Barton's Quakerism on the style and themes of her writing. This chapter and the next, on Hannah Whitall Smith, highlight the Quaker theology inherent in these women's writing and the fluidity of Quaker identity in this transitional century.

Carole Dale Spencer, in chapter 9, details Hannah Whitall Smith's use of Quaker experiential and mystical approaches to scripture in her popular books on Bible study for a broad evangelical audience. Like Barton, Smith was influenced by her Orthodox, quietist upbringing, and, as an adult, by the evangelical revival of the later nineteenth century that spurred her love of scripture. Smith contrasts the contemplative approach to scripture of her childhood with the more focused evangelical Bible study. Yet, unlike most evangelicals, she was not a biblicist or strict literalist and held some unorthodox views.

PART 4: ENGAGING THE WIDER SOCIAL AND CULTURAL WORLD

The first three parts of the book explore aspects of Quaker women's engagement with the broader culture through spaces opened by schism, by facing ethnic and racial diversity, and through literary expansion. The three chapters in part 4 detail how women discovered new identities through emergent professions and through greater freedom of expression in dress. They also document the boundaries women faced and the barriers that limited the extent of their social activism.

In chapter 10, Joan Allen and Richard C. Allen offer a broad overview of the nineteenth-century female reform activities of many lesser-known British Quaker radicals, many of whom contended with the disapproval of their religious communities. Humanitarian work, educational reform, and peace activism—esteemed Quaker engagements—were generally supported, but reform focused on suffrage and the political arena drew meeting censure like that experienced by women in North America. Many of these British women came from privileged backgrounds; they used their connections and credentials for women's rights, temperance, and antislavery in leading transatlantic women's networks and linking up with other reform-minded women around the world. Women activists were often forced to choose between faithfulness to their Quaker meetings and commitment to their radical causes. It was not until the end of the century that British Quakers adopted more enlightened attitudes toward women's roles.

Hannah Rumball uses the lens of material culture in chapter 11 to consider the distinctive dress styles of three high-profile British women after the testimony on plainness was relaxed. Rumball's three case studies illustrate the different choices available to women with greater freedom and means in reconciling different degrees of fashionability with their religious identity. These ranged from maintaining strict plainness while incorporating sumptuous fabrics, to freely adopting the latest Parisian fashions and accepting censure, to finding a new aesthetic borrowed from the Romantic movement's Grecian styles.

The final chapter, by Linda Palfreeman, moves into the end of the long nineteenth century with a case study of the humanitarian work of the pioneering doctor Hilda Clark during the First World War. Hilda's grandparents were James Clark and Eleanor Stephens Clark, profiled in chapter 5. This study reinforces how humanitarianism, social reform, and women's rights were passed down through Quaker families. Hilda and her three sisters all became suffragists. Hilda defied conventional gender expectations throughout her life. She never married, and she found her soulmate in another woman, Edith Pye, also a doctor and humanitarian of renown.

CONCLUSION

This study retrieves a number of underresearched and overlooked Quaker women who have left extensive archival materials and reexamines others whose contributions have been underappreciated, overshadowed by the patriarchal histories of Quaker men. These women, active between 1800 and 1920, a transformative time in the Society of Friends, found opportunities for expanding the Victorian feminine separate sphere of home and family into a "third sphere," translating their generations of administrative skills and female networks into home-based humanitarian organizations. As the century progressed and the rigid sectarian Quaker hedge began to crumble, they extended their activities into the public sphere.

This collection of interdisciplinary research demonstrates how Quaker women's faith—shaped by emerging evangelicalism, Romanticism, and liberalism—motivated their behavior, whether to preserve Quaker traditions or to expand Quaker ideals into more radical possibilities. Historians have long concluded that Quakerism in its origins had both conservative and radical characteristics, and developments in the long nineteenth century brought both impulses to new heights.

Some early studies of nineteenth-century Quaker women tended to elevate the feminist and egalitarian impulses in Quakerism, such as spiritual equality, independence in the traveling ministry, and relatively equal secondary education of girls and boys, in order to place the Society of Friends at the forefront of gender and racial equality in the nineteenth century. But this book demonstrates that, while these impulses contributed to the pioneering work of many Quaker women, the Society as a whole, whether Hicksite, Orthodox, or Gurneyite, only gradually accepted new roles for women. Conformity to religious and social customs remained strong barriers to innovation. Gender roles do not appear to be a factor in the schisms, but they became a divisive issue in the newly formed branches. Some women had to choose between accepting limitations along with commitment to their Quaker communities, or to endure censure and commit fully to their reform or professional work. And some chose—or were forced—to leave the Society and take their Quaker ideals into new communities.

The Society of Friends has been long admired for being at the forefront of breaking racial barriers in antislavery, abolition, and aid and education for racial minorities. While this study highlights some progressive women leaders who worked for abolition, racial equality, and the empowerment of minorities, most White Quaker meetings only grudgingly and gradually supported such work, while tacitly harboring racist and condescending attitudes toward other ethnic and racial groups.

In documenting the humanitarian activities of Quaker women in the long nineteenth century, this study reveals that a contributing factor to these women's leadership was the rising wealth of Quaker families, which provided the means for these women to engage in their public activities. What of working-class Quaker women in this transformative century of the Industrial Revolution? Likewise, while this volume touches on African American and Hispanic cultures, further research is needed in these areas and into Quaker engagement with other non-White, non-Western cultures. Although this volume touches on Helen Hunt Jackson's *Century of Dishonor*, which exposed the American government's mistreatment of Indigenous peoples, it was more common for Quakers to cooperate with federal initiatives to "civilize" Indigenous Americans. Moreover, assessing the contextualization of Western Quakerism in African, Asian, and Middle Eastern cultures, including the importation of White colonialism and paternalism through Quaker women's missionary, educational, and social endeavors, is beyond the scope of this volume. Clearly, there is much work still to be done.

The work presented here assesses the fluid nature of Quaker identity, as openings for interaction and cooperation with non-Quakers and other religious traditions, and exposure to the arts and material culture in the wider society, began to dilute Quaker "peculiarities." We hope it will stimulate further research and analysis of gender, literary, religious, cultural, ethnic, and diversity studies in this age of the evolution of Quakerism. We also hope that this work will encourage further interdisciplinary studies of the adaptation of the Religious Society of Friends to mainstream culture, and of how Quaker women, with their spiritual insights and practice of Quaker ideals, shaped the cultures in which they lived.

NOTES

1. An important book that examines women in the first 150 years of Quaker history is Michele Lise Tarter and Catie Gill, eds., *New Critical Studies on Early Quaker Women, 1650–1800* (Oxford: Oxford University Press, 2018).

2. See, for example, Carol Faulkner, *Lucretia Mott's Heresy: Abolition and Women's Rights in Nineteenth-Century America* (Philadelphia: University of Pennsylvania Press,

2011); Christopher Densmore, Carol Faulkner, Nancy Hewitt, and Beverly Wilson Palmer, eds., *Lucretia Mott Speaks: The Essential Speeches and Sermons* (Urbana: University of Illinois Press, 2017).

3. Initial plans for this volume included a chapter on Quaker missions to Indigenous American communities. Travel restrictions imposed by the pandemic made it impossible for that chapter to be completed in time for inclusion.

4. See Robynne Rogers Healey, ed., *Quakerism in the Atlantic World, 1690–1830* (University Park: Penn State University Press, 2021).

5. Thomas D. Hamm, *Liberal Quakerism in America in the Long Nineteenth Century, 1790–1920* (Leiden: Brill, 2020), 14.

6. H. Larry Ingle, *Quakers in Conflict: The Hicksite Reformation* (Knoxville: University of Tennessee Press, 1986; reprint, Wallingford, PA: Pendle Hill Publications, 1998), 10–13. Both sides agreed on "unprogrammed worship, nonpastoral ministry, plainness, pacifism, and the status of Friends as a 'peculiar people.'" Orthodox Friends remained committed to the Virgin birth, the atonement, and the Trinity. Hamm, *Liberal Quakerism in America*, 18.

7. Thomas D. Hamm, "Quakerism, Ministry, Marriage, and Divorce: The Ordeal of Priscilla Hunt Cadwalader," *Journal of the Early Republic* 28, no. 3 (2008): 412–13.

8. Hamm, *Liberal Quakerism in America*, 20.

9. See esp. Robert W. Doherty, *The Hicksite Separation: A Sociological Analysis of Religious Schism in Early Nineteenth Century America* (New Brunswick: Rutgers University Press, 1967).

10. Ingle, *Quakers in Conflict*, 38–61.

11. Thomas D. Hamm, *The Transformation of American Quakerism: Orthodox Friends, 1800–1907* (Bloomington: Indiana University Press, 1988); Hamm, *Liberal Quakerism in America*.

12. Thomas D. Hamm, "Conflict and Transformation, 1808–1920," in *The Cambridge Companion to Quakerism*, edited by Stephen W. Angell and Pink Dandelion (Cambridge: Cambridge University Press, 2018), 34.

13. Thomas D. Hamm, "Hicksite, Orthodox, and Evangelical Quakerism, 1805–1887," in *The Oxford Handbook of Quaker Studies*, edited by Stephen W. Angell and Pink Dandelion (Oxford: Oxford University Press, 2013), 70.

14. Hamm, "Conflict and Transformation," 35.

15. Hamm, *Liberal Quakerism in America*, 46.

16. Carole Dale Spencer, *Holiness: The Soul of Quakerism* (Colorado Springs: Paternoster, 2007), 161–93.

17. Hamm, *Liberal Quakerism in America*, 52.

18. Hamm, "Conflict and Transformation," 42–44; Hamm, *Liberal Quakerism in America*, 58–73; J. William Frost, "Modernist and Liberal Quakers, 1887–2010," in Angell and Dandelion, *Oxford Handbook of Quaker Studies*, 78–83.

19. Hamm, *Liberal Quakerism in America*, 69. See also Joanna Dales, *The Quaker Renaissance and Liberal Quakerism in Britain, 1895–1930: Seeking a Real Religion* (Leiden: Brill, 2020).

20. Jacalynn Stuckey Welling, "Mission," in Angell and Dandelion, *Oxford Handbook of Quaker Studies*, 309–17.

21. Margaret E. Hirst, *Quakers in Peace and War: An Account of Their Peace Principles and Practice* (London: Swarthmore Press, 1923), 372; Thomas D. Hamm, Margaret Marconi, Gretchen Kleinhen Salinas, and Benjamin Whitman, "The Decline of Quaker

Pacifism in the Twentieth Century: Indiana Yearly Meeting of Friends as a Case Study," *Indiana Magazine of History* 96, no. 1 (2000): 54.

22. Robynne Rogers Healey, "The Peace Testimony and the Crisis of World War I," in *The Creation of Modern Quaker Diversity, 1830–1937*, edited by Stephen W. Angell, Pink Dandelion, and David Harrington Watt (University Park: Penn State University Press, 2023), 214.

PART I

Engaging Conflict and Separations

CHAPTER 1

Hicksite Women in the Long Nineteenth Century

THOMAS D. HAMM

In 1843, an otherwise obscure Hicksite Friend, Mary Moore, rose to speak out of the silence in the Cherry Street Meeting in Philadelphia. As a hearer recorded, she "reminded the young women of their privileges, greater by far than exists in any other society; that they had the liberty of opening their mouths in public testimony, and in the congregation of the people, which they would not dare to do where the priests bear rule." In this, Mary Moore spoke for Friends male and female.[1] Two decades earlier, another minister, Joseph Foulke, had reached a similar conclusion. "Surely the Society of Friends have been eminently favoured above all the families of the Earth, and above all the Societies of Christendom in establishing women's m[ee]t[in]gs, and fully recognizing their gifts in the right exercise of the discipline, and in taking their part in the work of the Ministry, so that male and female are all one in the Church of Christ, and designed by their creator to be natural help mates to each other."[2]

The nineteenth century was one of divisions for American Friends, the first of which was the Hicksite separation of the 1820s. Women were less prominent than men in that controversy. Once the separation had taken place, however, women were among the most visible Hicksite leaders. By 1850, Lucretia Mott was arguably one of the two best-known Friends in the

United States (the poet John Greenleaf Whittier, an Orthodox Friend, was the other). As Hicksites divided into conservative and radical wings, the role of women in Quaker affairs became a source of contention. Some Hicksites, male and female, while affirming women's ministry, agreed with most of their non-Quaker neighbors that the primary role of woman was as wife and mother. But when the women's rights movement emerged in the United States between 1848 and 1860, seeking unprecedented public roles and legal rights for women, Hicksite women like Mott would provide much of its leadership. During the Civil War, Hicksite women threw themselves into varied activities, ranging from support of the Union to relief work for the freed people. After the war, Hicksite women helped open Swarthmore College and form a variety of new Quaker organizations. In the early twentieth century, Hicksites saw the increasing openness of other denominations to women's ministry and growing support for women's rights as proof of the truth of positions that Friends had long held.

WOMEN AND THE HICKSITE SEPARATION

Historians of the Hicksite separation agree that it was largely an affair of men, at least in its public controversies. True, visiting female ministers from the London Yearly Meeting, particularly Ann Jones, Anna Braithwaite, and Elizabeth Robson, were among the fiercest critics of Elias Hicks. But when Larry Ingle made a list of the American leaders of the two sides in the 1820s, it included only one woman. It was men who barricaded themselves into meetinghouses, led walkouts, and rioted. Certainly, women emerged at certain critical junctures. For example, it was an inquiry from the Long Island Orthodox elder Phebe Willis that led Elias Hicks to pen a letter that became one of the sources of division.[3]

One woman, Priscilla Coffin Hunt, whose remarriage in 1827 made her Priscilla Cadwalader, was an active proponent of Hicksite views and one of the chief targets of Orthodox ire. Born in North Carolina in 1786, she had been widowed at age twenty-six and had subsequently moved to Blue River Meeting in southern Indiana. Recorded a minister in 1817, she had embarked on a long trip east in 1821. By November 1822 she was within the bounds of the Philadelphia Yearly Meeting (PYM), where she encountered Elias Hicks, also traveling in the ministry there. We have no evidence of previous contacts between them, but the themes of their ministry were remarkably similar. She warned Orthodox leaders that they were persecutors who would "nail to the cross" true spiritual life. Predictably, Orthodox Friends were outraged, but supporters of Hicks were delighted. Back in Indiana, Priscilla defended Hicks's views on the authority of scripture and the divinity of Christ and denied the existence of Satan as a distinct being, arguing that the devil was simply the evil within each human being, released when they did not follow the Inward Light. When separation came to the Indiana Yearly Meeting (IYM) in 1828, a majority of Blue River Friends followed Priscilla into the Hicksite fold, even though Hicksites were a small minority in the IYM.[4]

Other women were active supporters of Elias Hicks, among them Lucretia Mott, Maria Imlay, Esther Moore, and Martha Smith in the PYM and Phebe Johnson in the New York Yearly Meeting (NYYM). But unless women were the authors of some of the anonymous pamphlets that were a prominent feature of the Great Separation, the most public actors were men.[5]

This does not mean that Hicksite women were simply following the lead of their husbands and fathers. We have numerous examples of women making up their own minds. In Clinton County, Ohio, Lydia Sabin wrote to her Orthodox family that "offend or please who it might she must say amen to Elias Hicks doctrine," according to a letter from Nathan Hunt.[6] For Rachel Hicks on Long Island, a decision came only after real agony of soul. "Among all the members of our Society, there was not another, who was tried as I was," she wrote in 1828. Rachel had good reason to feel torn. Her father, Gideon Seaman, was an Orthodox leader. But Rachel's husband, Abraham Hicks, was Elias's nephew. She found it impossible to believe that it was God's will to cause her father grief, but she was also convinced that Hicks's preaching was truth.[7] Notes made at the time of the separation by two Hicksites at Middletown Meeting in Delaware County, Pennsylvania, are revealing. These Hicksites visited each adult member, and their carefully compiled records show that they did not assume that husbands spoke for wives. Sarah Yarnall "after considerable conversation about the present controversy directed John Yarnall her son to put her name to our list she being an aged and infirm woman." Sarah Webster "subscribed her name without hesitation," and Jane Baker "wrote her own name and said she was not afraid of her friends." When the two men called on Frances Carr, she decided that she would side with the Hicksites, but she had reservations and wanted to read Hicks's published sermons more carefully.[8]

We have no reason to think that gender was an issue in the separation. Between 1830 and 1860, however, questions about the roles of women in the Society of Friends and the larger American society would divide Hicksites.

HICKSITE WOMEN AFTER THE SEPARATION

After 1830, and until the end of the nineteenth century, old currents retained life among Hicksite Friends. They were diverse. Many were traditionalists who saw Elias Hicks standing against Orthodox innovation. Others were probably following majority opinion in their meetings. Only a minority could be perceived as liberal in the sense of favoring innovation and openness to ideas taken from beyond the Quaker world.

It is thus unsurprising to find that traditionalism, particularly quietism, remained strong in Hicksite circles for another generation. Such Friends emphasized utter abnegation of self, fearful of doing anything that could be categorized as "creaturely activity," done according to human wisdom instead of divine direction. They reiterated Elias Hicks's reservations about Friends' forming ties with non-Quakers in philanthropic and reform organizations. And they were uncompromising in upholding testimonies against worldliness and deviations from plainness.[9]

Many Hicksite women strongly supported such an outlook. Ministers such as Rachel Hicks in the NYYM; Margaret Brown in the Genesee Yearly Meeting; Mary S. Lippincott, Mary Pike, and Susanna Jewett in the PYM; and Margaret Hatton in the IYM were unrelenting opponents of innovation. Typical is the language of Deborah Bringhurst from Wilmington, Delaware, in 1832: "The knowledge that I am a poor, short-sighted creature and know nothing rightly except 'as given from above,'—and that infinite Wisdom and Goodness dispose these events, has a tendency to silence *selfish* feelings, and to produce humble prostration of *our will* to the Divine Will. And in this passive state we are enabled to *obey* and to *resign*."[10] This outlook lingered in some places for the rest of the century. Thus Margaretta Walton, a minister from Fallowfield, Pennsylvania, could write in her diary early in 1878, "I went to Race S[tree]t Meeting this morning as an empty vessel and returned in peace." Quietists strove after emptiness as the state that God through the Holy Spirit was most likely to find acceptable.[11]

Many Hicksites saw women's domestic and social roles in terms that differed little from those of non-Quakers.[12] Ohio Friend Joseph B. Chapman recorded his desire that his daughters be "accustomed to industry and the active duties of housewifery."[13] Hicksite women embraced such views. Elizabeth Margaret Chandler, while winning public attention as an author, was blunt: "It is on all sides acknowledged, that the domestic circle is the proper sphere of woman."[14] Rachel Hicks, in a letter to Seneca women in upstate New York, described men as the "proper persons to administer ... civil affairs." Women were intended to be "faithful wives, wise mothers, and obedient daughters." Mothers should teach daughters "industry, economy and cleanliness in their persons and houses, encourage them to be cheerful and obliging in their deportment—to observe modesty and strict morality in their intercourse with others." Reared thus, they would "render home a happy retreat for their brothers and fathers."[15] In an epistle to the NYYM of Women Friends in 1850, Baltimore women urged wives and daughters to circumscribe "their wants within the bounds of circumstances; that husbands and fathers may be spared the temptation of engaging in business beyond their ability to manage," and to "move harmoniously under the guidance of a meek and quiet spirit."[16]

But even those who saw Quaker women called mainly to be wives and mothers embraced education for them. Samuel M. Janney urged fellow Virginians to emulate Friends: "If we wish to see woman become what she was designed to be, the true partner and helpmate of man, we must give her an education that will develop her intellectual powers, improve her native taste, and enable her to control her affections and place them upon worthy objects." This was consistent with conservative visions of women's roles, but Janney went so far as to argue that women should be educated for careers: "What would we think of a young man who should live in idleness and entirely dependent upon the bounty of some relative for support? Would we not consider him a useless drone, deficient in manly spirit and true dignity?" Janney asked. "Now, I can see no good reason, why young ladies should not endeavor to pursue some occupation, that would contribute to their happiness, and promote the welfare of society."[17] Janney himself conducted a school for girls. Perhaps the best-known and most influential such institution was the Sharon Hill Boarding School in Delaware County, Pennsylvania, headed by John Jackson, a much-loved minister, and his wife, Rachel.[18]

Other Hicksites thought of themselves as theological and social liberals, open to ideas from the larger world. One of the first post-separation manifestations came in proposals to give women Friends equal rights with men in administering the Discipline. Long-standing practice was that men and women Friends held separate meetings for business, and that action in most cases required the approval of both. But there were exceptions that galled some women Friends. Male Friends could receive or disown men without the unity of women Friends, whereas the reception into membership or disownment of a woman required the men's approval. Likewise, men could alter the Discipline without the approval of the women's yearly meeting. Critics appeared early, including one in 1830 who argued that "there can be no reasons offered against women participating equally in the administration of the discipline, which would not also justify the oppression of the slave-holder."[19]

Advocates of reform had limited success. By 1843, the New York, Genesee, and Ohio Yearly Meetings had approved allowing "women to have the same privileges as the men in receiving and disowning the members of their own sex & allow[ing] them a joint action in the formation of discipline."[20] The IYM, however, rejected a similar proposal.[21] Philadelphia likewise refused to move. Western and Caln quarterly meetings and Green Street Monthly Meeting in the city urged change, and discussions, extensive at times, took place between 1834 and 1847, but unity was not found, partly owing to opposition from conservative women.[22] "My Friends, a body with two heads, what an anomaly" was the reaction of Susannah Jewett to the proposals.[23] Mary S. Lippincott was of the same mind: "Men are the formers of discipline, and women can only strengthen their hands by prayer, and strengthening counsel!"[24]

Other Hicksite women advocated even more radical changes. Not long after the separation of 1827–28, controversies erupted in the NYYM and PYM. The focal point was the *Delaware Free Press*, a weekly newspaper edited by Benjamin Webb in Wilmington. Webb blended support for the reforming working men's movement, with its criticisms of the consequences for workers of unrestrained capitalism and industrialism, with denunciations of evangelical Christianity. Although Webb claimed that his ideas were perfectly consistent with those that Elias Hicks had embraced, most Hicksites thought that he had gone too far, and they disowned him.

Significantly, one of the points of criticism was support for Webb by Frances Wright, a radical English feminist and freethinker. A few women Friends were vocal supporters of Webb, including Phebe Johnson and Elizabeth M. Reeder, who disrupted Hicksite meetings with their uninhibited preaching. They were also disowned.[25]

This radical impulse petered out. But a more enduring one emerged in the 1830s, tied to the abolitionist and nonresistance movements. It found its most prominent proponent in Lucretia Coffin Mott, who would in turn link these movements with the foundations of the women's rights movement in the United States.

Lucretia Coffin was born on Nantucket in 1793. Educated at the Nine Partners School in New York, she met her husband, James Mott, there. After their marriage, they became residents of Philadelphia, where Lucretia was recorded a minister in 1821. She was not a major figure in the Hicksite separation. But afterward she became one of the most visible Hicksite Friends. When the American Anti-Slavery Society was organized in Philadelphia in December 1833, she was the only woman invited to address it. She was a founding member of the Philadelphia Female Anti-Slavery Society and presided over the first Anti-Slavery Convention of American Women in 1837. She also followed with interest the organization of the New England Non-Resistance Society in 1838 and spoke at its meetings.[26]

Antislavery was a venerable Quaker commitment, and nonresistance, which repudiated all human governments based on force, had obvious affinities with Quaker pacifism. Both movements drew significant support from Hicksites. But many traditionalist Hicksites looked askance at such activities. To their minds, when Friends joined non-Quakers in groups like antislavery societies, they risked eroding Quaker distinctiveness. Particularly suspect were the prominent roles of clerics in such groups, whom strict Friends saw as "hirelings." The most vocal advocate of such views was a minister from New York City, George Fox White. He denounced reformers as "traders in benevolence" and branded them as "more *degraded than the Devils in hell.*" While White was extreme, Hicksite yearly meetings cautioned members against joining in "the reforms of the day" and "mixed societies."[27]

Conservative Hicksite women endorsed these views. Consistent Friends, Mary Pike complained, "waited to know the mind of Truth," but reformers "sprang to action." White's complaints about reformers often had clear gendered allusions. A New York Friend in 1842 noted how White "in his public communications frequently aims blows at Lucretia Mott." Traveling in Chester County, Pennsylvania, where Hicksite sympathy for reform was strong, White was especially pointed: "'What did woman want in the name of rights, but liberty to roam over the country from Dan to Beersheba spurning the protection of man?' For himself, before he would submit to the dictation of an imperious woman, he would 'traverse the earth.'"[28]

Hicksite women reformers thus found themselves embattled, but most were undeterred. The most extreme reaction was to quit Quakerism. That was the decision of Abby Hopper Gibbons in New York City, after Friends there disowned her husband and father for their connections with the radical abolitionist weekly the *National Anti-Slavery Standard*.[29] In Rochester, New York, Amy Kirby Post, a reform stalwart, likewise resigned her membership in 1845.[30]

In other yearly meetings, reform-minded women joined separatist movements. One center was the Green Plain Monthly Meeting in Clark County, Ohio, and by 1848 radical reformers in the IYM had coalesced into what they called the Green Plain Yearly Meeting of Congregational Friends. In their opening statement, they attacked virtually every other organized church and affirmed the broadest liberty of individual opinion: "man should never concede to any combination or order of men, his *individual freedom*."[31] In the next few years, like-minded radicals separated from the Genesee, New York, Ohio, and Philadelphia Yearly Meetings. Originally, they labeled themselves "Congregational Friends," but by the 1850s "Progressive Friends" was the preferred name.[32] "We have adopted the name 'Progressive' to avoid being confused with other societies, and as an appropriate recognition of the truth that the law of progress is applicable alike to individuals and associations," the newly formed Ohio Yearly Meeting of Progressive Friends affirmed in 1852. Openness to change and innovation was fundamental for Progressive Friends.[33]

Women led in the formation of such groups. Nowhere was that more the case than in the Genesee Yearly Meeting, where reformers withdrew in 1848 to form the Waterloo Yearly Meeting. Amy Kirby Post joined this body, and other leaders included well-known Hicksite women like Rhoda DeGarmo, Mary Ann McClintock, and Margaret Prior. It was not coincidental that within weeks of the formation of the Waterloo Yearly Meeting, the first women's rights convention in American history was held in the nearby town of Seneca Falls, New York.[34]

Hicksite and Progressive Friends were central figures at the Seneca Falls Convention in July 1848. Of the five women who signed the call for the convention, four—Lucretia Mott, Martha Wright, Mary Ann McClintock, and Jane Hunt—were Hicksites or had strong Hicksite ties. The fifth, Elizabeth Cady Stanton, had met Mott when both attended the World Anti-Slavery Convention in London in 1840. She had never known a woman like Mott, comfortable speaking in public and arguing questions of reform and politics. Mott was, as Stanton put it, "an entire new revelation of womanhood." Other Waterloo Progressives, such as Amy Kirby Post, were also present. Ironically, none of the women felt capable of conducting such a large gathering, so James Mott presided.[35]

The Seneca Falls Convention issued a "Declaration of Rights and Sentiments," patterned on the Declaration of Independence, that detailed the legal and social oppression of women. It opened with the premise "that woman is man's equal—was intended to be so by the Creator, and the highest good of the race demands that she should be so recognized." It proceeded to demand full legal equality, including the right to vote and to pursue any career or calling for which women had the ability, including the ministry. The Seneca Falls Convention inspired similar gatherings in New England, New York, Ohio, and Indiana from 1848 to 1852. Hicksite women played leading roles, with Mott often in attendance.[36] The first in Ohio took place in Salem, a town where Hicksites were strong.[37] The first in Indiana was likewise in the Hicksite center of Wayne County.[38]

Unsurprisingly, Progressive Friends gave the movement enthusiastic support. Green Plain Yearly Meeting asserted in its opening statement of principles that in a truly just society, "all the rights which belong to our common nature, would be as freely conceded to woman as to man."[39] In 1850, Waterloo Progressive Friends hailed woman "as an intelligent moral agent, accountable to our common Father for the right occupancy of talents conferred" on her to "bless and humanize mankind." Instead, "by *man-enacted laws*, and by customs growing out of an unjust assumption of power ... she has been regarded as little more than as an appendage to man, only to minister to his comfort and gratification—a subordinate, dependent on him."[40] When the Pennsylvania Yearly Meeting of Progressive Friends organized in 1853, its first action was to call for woman to "be admitted to her rightful part with man in the administration of civil government."[41] Elizabeth Cady Stanton formally joined Waterloo Progressive Friends, while Susan B. Anthony, the most important feminist leader to emerge in the 1850s, was also a Progressive Friend.[42]

Hicksite feminists like Mott also called for women to have equal rights in education and the professions.[43] Men and women should "together tread the halls of learning," Waterloo Progressives resolved in 1850.[44] The PYM three years later demanded that women "must be rendered eligible to the professions and free to engage in the industrial pursuits of life."[45] Notable were efforts to bring women into the medical profession. In 1850, the Female Medical College of Pennsylvania opened in Philadelphia, led by Dr. Joseph S. Longshore and his brother, Thomas, both radical reformer Hicksites.[46] Among the students was Mary F. Thomas, a Hicksite who would become the first licensed female physician in Indiana and a leader in the state's women's rights movement.[47] The most important graduate in the first years, and a longtime faculty member, was Ann Preston. The daughter of Hicksite abolitionists in Chester County, Preston worked tirelessly to make a place for women in the medical profession. "Female Physicians are a want of the age which must and will be met and satisfied," she wrote in 1852.[48]

Not all Hicksites welcomed proposals for radical change in American society. "Women in their proper places are more useful and dignified in my eyes than men," wrote Joseph P. Plummer, an elder from Richmond, Indiana, in 1850, "but when they slide off of their true platform they sink perhaps too low in my estimation, they are so mischievous in that state."[49] Joseph Foulke, despite his support for women as ministers, was even more acerbic: "The Serpent in Eden was the first woman's rights advocate," he told a like-minded Friend.[50]

HICKSITE WOMEN AND THE CIVIL WAR

Hicksite women were interested, often worried, observers of the crisis of the Union in the 1850s. Many were enthusiastic supporters of the Republican Party, founded on opposition to the extension of slavery. One New Jersey Hicksite woman wrote that Republicans had "a noble cause at heart."[51] Some sympathized with John Brown, whose attempt to raise a slave revolt at Harper's Ferry, Virginia, in the autumn of 1859 sharpened sectional divisions. Lucretia Mott played host to Brown's wife, Mary Ann Brown, and called him "a moral hero."[52] Another Philadelphia-area Hicksite, Mary H. Child, was ambivalent. "Far be it from me to encourage in any way the spirit of war," she wrote to the governor of Virginia. But she warned that Brown's conduct had "created a sympathy for him, that our southern brethren are yet scarcely aware of. This has aroused an hatred of slavery and oppression in thousands of minds heretofore dead or lukewarm to this now all-absorbing subject."[53] By 1860, many Hicksite women felt that the signs of the times were ominous, among them Rachel Moore, a minister in the PYM. She told her hearers that in the United States "the greatest of all cruelties, human slavery, was not [merely] allowed but protected." Moore foresaw "great woes which would certainly follow."[54]

When the war came, Hicksites were one in their support of the Union. The overwhelming majority lived in Union territory, but a small group in Loudoun and Frederick Counties in Virginia found themselves in the Confederacy.[55] Many Hicksite women opposed attempts at compromise that made concessions to slavery. Among them was Lucretia Mott, who feared proposals that would "strengthen the pro-slavery parts of the Constitution & yield the claim to rob and murder by thous[an]ds—an infinitely greater number, than in any probable war, might be slain."[56] When "fratricidal war" did come, some Hicksites saw it as a fitting punishment for the nation's sins. "The cup of iniquity was filled to the brim," concluded Rachel Hicks.[57] Others temporized. "I do not approve of war and yet do not wonder the men feel so," one wrote in May 1861. "My own patriotic blood boils with indignation when I hear how the Southern Rebels are trying to insult our flag, destroy our freedom and ruin our government."[58] In Philadelphia, old abolitionist Sarah Hopper Palmer wrote to her sister, "I'm opposed to war—to cutting down men like grass—but if ever war was holy, this one, in favor of the most oppressed, the most forbearing, the most afflicted, down-trodden, insulted part of humanity, is a holy war."[59]

Hicksite women found many ways, short of fighting, to support the Union cause. In Waterford, Virginia, Lizzie and Lida Dutton and Sarah Steer published a small Unionist newspaper.[60] When Jubal Early's Confederate raiders arrived in Sandy Spring, Maryland, in 1864, Alice Stabler defied them. "You are a Yankee woman," they taunted her. "No, but I am a good Union woman," she answered.[61] Hicksite women joined "loyal leagues" and took part in soldier aid activities.[62] Some became army nurses. Cornelia Hancock of New Jersey was nationally known for her work.[63]

Many Hicksite women were especially drawn to work on behalf of the freed slaves in the South. Lucretia Mott noted that old fears of working with non-Friends were falling away.[64] Scores went south as teachers and nurses among the freed people.⁶⁵ Of these, probably the best known was Martha Schofield, who spent the rest of her life teaching in a Black school in South Carolina.⁶⁶

INTERNAL EQUALITY

Between 1865 and 1900, Hicksite women achieved full equality within the Society of Friends. All leadership positions became open to them, and women won equal rights in policymaking. Hicksites also moved to combine men's and women's meetings for business.

As noted above, some yearly meetings had acted earlier to give men's and women's meetings equal authority. The Baltimore and Indiana Yearly Meetings joined them in the 1860s, and the Illinois Yearly Meeting, formed in 1874, embraced such equality from the beginning.⁶⁷ Philadelphia accepted reform the same year.⁶⁸ Changes in Discipline now required the unity of both the men's and women's yearly meetings, and membership matters required the approval of both the men's and women's monthly meetings.⁶⁹ Another change allowed women to serve on the yearly meeting representative committees that functioned as executive committees. All the Hicksite yearly meetings had done so by 1877.⁷⁰

Even as yearly meetings revised their Disciplines to give women's monthly meetings equal rights, sentiment in favor of combining men's and women's meetings was growing. Arguments for the change were twofold. One was that many meetings were too small to hold separate meetings properly.⁷¹ The other was that the practice was simply outdated. One Friend asserted in 1875 that separating men and women was "all right in its day, but I am led to believe that its day is nearly over."⁷² Another thought that separate meetings were "attended with more or less inconvenience and confusion, while the object of each meeting is precisely the same."⁷³ Many Hicksites, however, had doubts. In 1874, some women argued that in united meetings, "women would not act independently in the presence of husbands and fathers, and that but a few years would elapse before they would cease to be consulted, and if they did express an opinion, it would avail nothing."⁷⁴ And sometimes women Friends dealt with subjects inappropriate to take up with men present. Phebe Earle Gibbons, the editor of a new periodical, the *Journal*, wrote in 1877, "Subjects of living value and importance are often discussed by the women of Philadelphia Yearly Meeting, concerning which not ten of them would feel as if they could speak at all were men present." She raised "licentious literature" as an example: "How painful it would be to a woman to discuss it in the presence of a large assembly of men."[75]

The innovators prevailed. As early as 1873, men and women at Marietta Monthly Meeting in Iowa met jointly, and in 1878 the NYYM approved joint meetings for small meetings.[76] By 1900, only the PYM maintained separate men's and women's yearly meetings, and it allowed joint meetings at lower levels.[77] Most Hicksites were apparently satisfied, although some fears proved justified. After yearly meetings combined sessions, clerks were much more likely to be men than women.[78]

Another indication of Hicksite commitment to women's rights is seen in the opening of Swarthmore College in 1869. Hicksites were so determined to have women serve on the board of trustees that they obtained a special act of the Pennsylvania legislature to authorize it.[79] In contrast to other eastern colleges, Swarthmore was coeducational from the beginning. While a few Hicksites had reservations, most were clear about what they saw as the advantages of educating men and women together. The board praised coeducation: "Character, refinement of manners, scholarship, culture in the best and highest sense, morals, all those things which go toward making life truer, nobler, purer, better and more worth the living, are developed and strengthened by it."[80]

It is indicative that in the organizations that Hicksites formed after 1865, initially First Day School conferences, then the Friends Union for Philanthropic Labor (FUPL), and finally Friends General Conference (FGC), no consideration was given to separation of the sexes. The assumption always was that men and women Friends would work together. But tensions sometimes arose. In 1890, twenty-seven of the forty-four representatives present at the biennial meeting of the FUPL were female.[81] But at other conferences, some women noted with dismay that men tended to dominate discussions.[82] Women did have leadership positions. After the FGC was organized, Jane P. Rushmore became a central figure in its office staff.[83] In 1916, forty-three of the 103 members of its central committee were women.[84]

"THE SWEET MINISTRY OF PHILANTHROPY"

Hicksite women's involvement in what one called "the sweet ministry of philanthropy"[85] went back before the separation of the 1820s, and it continued into the twentieth century. Particularly in cities, exclusively female groups like the Female Association of Philadelphia for the Relief of the Sick and Infirm Poor with Clothing provided relief to the "deserving poor."[86] After 1870, such groups expanded their activities. In 1892, Hicksite women in Baltimore not only distributed food, clothing, and fuel but also organized sewing circles, conducted kindergartens, and sent children to farms for the summer.[87] A few Hicksite women, like Cornelia Hancock, spent decades working in the Philadelphia slums. Symptomatic of a desire to confront the problems of poverty "systematically and scientifically" was the establishment of Friends Neighborhood Guild in 1901.[88] By 1900, Hicksite women in New York City were conducting "bazaars," purveying "fancy work, aprons, any and all kinds of handiwork, useful or artistic," along with jams, jellies, preserves, pies, and cakes to raise funds to aid the destitute.[89] "We cannot be true . . . to the tradition of Quakerism . . . unless we take upon our selves the responsibility for bettering our economic and social conditions," one wrote in 1916.[90]

Another cause that many Hicksite women embraced was peace. Here, they followed the lead of Lucretia Mott, who wrote in 1870, "Even the woman question, as far as voting goes, does not take hold of my every feeling as does war."[91] Between 1870 and 1920, Hicksite women attacked the "war spirit." An aged member of the Illinois Yearly Meeting, Elizabeth H. Coale, argued in 1900 that Quaker pacifism "should be brought to the front, and boldly pushed forward."[92] Women Friends criticized the Spanish-American and Boer Wars, urged international arbitration, and blasted military training in schools.[93] When the First World War came, Hicksite women first opposed American intervention and then supported conscientious objection and the League of Nations.[94] Brooklyn Friend Mary S. McDowell lost her public school teaching position because of her vocal pacifism.[95] From the 1890s on, Hannah Clothier Hull from the PYM was central to a number of pacifist organizations, including the Women's International League for Peace and Freedom.[96]

The literature from the period 1870–1920 shows that Hicksite women regarded alcohol as being as great a threat to civilization as war. "We are as one united band in the cause of Temperance," Baltimore Yearly Meeting women wrote in an 1880 epistle.[97] NYYM women thought that "upon our sex, in the varied relations we sustain, rests greatly the work of bringing about [this] much needed reform."[98] Hicksite women joined in the "woman's crusade" that gave rise to the Woman's Christian Temperance Union in

Ohio and Indiana in 1874.⁹⁹ By the late nineteenth century, one of the standard arguments for granting women voting rights was that it would bring about Prohibition. "We are accounted the weaker vessel, but I deny it," one Hicksite woman said in 1898. "If you will let us have a little chance we will see whether the law against saloons can't be put into effect, and carried out." Hicksite women joined men in hailing the Eighteenth Amendment as a triumph for Quaker principles.¹⁰⁰

TOWARD SUFFRAGE

Hicksite women continued to be highly visible in the movement for equal rights for women between 1865 and 1920. Lucretia Mott remained an iconic figure until her death in 1880. From the 1860s until her death, Susan B. Anthony (1820–1906), a Hicksite from Rochester, New York, was, with her close friend Elizabeth Cady Stanton, the most visible feminist in the United States. In 1901, Hicksites in Philadelphia organized the Friends Equal Rights Association to forward the cause. Their annual meetings featured non-Quaker suffragist leaders like Carrie Chapman Catt.¹⁰¹

Hicksite justifications for women's rights remained much the same as they had been earlier. Sometimes they reflected unpleasant trends in the larger society. A New Jersey Hicksite woman, for example, enumerated among the results of women's voting not only honest elections, Prohibition, compulsory education, and crackdowns on gambling but also "no emigration, no paupers to our shore."¹⁰² Hicksite women faced frustrations. At the FGC annual sessions in 1916, speakers noted that recent referenda in New York, Pennsylvania, and New Jersey had all rejected women's suffrage. Even worse, some of the biggest negative votes had come from places where Friends were numerous, such as Bucks County.¹⁰³

In the final push toward the Nineteenth Amendment, another Hicksite woman, Alice Paul (1885–1977), played a central role. A Swarthmore graduate from a long line of Quaker ancestors, Paul was deeply influenced by the confrontational approach of the English suffragette movement. Finding existing American suffrage organizations too conservative after she returned from England, Paul took the lead in organizing the National Woman's Party in 1916 to secure national women's suffrage through a constitutional amendment. Tactics like picketing the White House proved effective, forcing President Woodrow Wilson to endorse the cause. Approval of the amendment came in 1920. Paul promptly turned her attention to a new cause, an Equal Rights Amendment. Although Paul's radicalism made her relations with Friends uneasy at times, she "proudly claimed her Quaker heritage as motivation for her commitment to women's rights."[104]

CONCLUSION

By the early twentieth century, Hicksites concerned about declining membership were consoling themselves with the thought that non-Quakers were embracing many of their beliefs.[105] This was certainly the case with women's rights. No longer were Friends unique in recognizing women in the ministry. Causes that Quaker women had advocated, ranging from antislavery to assorted humanitarian issues, had either triumphed or become mainstream. Hicksite women had been central to the beginning of the women's rights movement in the United States. It was appropriate that a Hicksite woman would be a central figure in the ratification of the Nineteenth Amendment.

NOTES

1. William Adams, "Reminiscences. —No. 60," *Journal*, 3rd Mo. 31, 1875, 70. The *Journal*, published by Hicksite Friend Phebe Gibbons, eventually merged with the *Friends' Intelligencer*.

2. "Some Account of the Life, Travels, and Experiences of Joseph Foulke," typescript, p. 35, box 1, Foulke Family Papers, FHLSC.

3. H. Larry Ingle, *Quakers in Conflict: The Hicksite Reformation* (Knoxville: University of Tennessee Press, 1986), 63, 81–83.

4. Thomas D. Hamm, "Quakerism, Ministry, Marriage, and Divorce: The Ordeal of Priscilla Hunt Cadwalader," *Journal of the Early Republic* 28, no. 3 (2008): 410–20.

5. Ingle, *Quakers in Conflict*, 158, 161–62; Carol Faulkner, *Lucretia Mott's Heresy: Abolition and Women's Rights in Nineteenth-Century America* (Philadelphia: University of Pennsylvania Press, 2011), 41–59; *Letters of Martha Smith, with a Short Memoir of Her Life* (New York: Piercy and Reed, 1844).

6. Nathan Hunt to Nathan and Sarah Harlan, 4th Mo. 25, 1829, copy, Ann Jones Papers, FHLSC.

7. Rachel Hicks to Elias Hicks, 8th Mo. 25, 1828, box 24, Elias Hicks Papers, FHLSC; *Memoir of Rachel Hicks (Written by Herself)* [. . .] (New York: G. P. Putnam's Sons, 1880), 31–34.

8. "Notes Taken by Wm. P. Morgan and Minshall Painter When They Were Taking a List of the Members of Middletown Preparative Meeting to Assist Their Memory Respecting Each Case," 1827–28, box 37, Painter Family Papers, FHLSC.

9. Thomas D. Hamm, "Hicksite, Orthodox, and Evangelical Quakerism, 1805–1887," in *The Oxford Handbook of Quaker Studies*, edited by Stephen W. Angell and Pink Dandelion (Oxford: Oxford University Press, 2013), 65–69.

10. Deborah Bringhurst to Hannah Hurnard, 2nd Mo. 12, 1832, Hurnard Manuscripts, FHLSC.

11. Margaretta Walton diary, 1st Mo. 6, 1878, box 1, Margaretta Walton Papers, FHLSC.

12. The literature on women's roles and domesticity in nineteenth-century America is vast. See, for example, Anne M. Boylan, *The Origins of Women's Activism: New York and Boston, 1797–1840* (Chapel Hill: University of North Carolina Press, 2002); and Linda K. Kerber, "Separate Spheres, Female Worlds, Woman's Place: The Rhetoric of Women's History," *Journal of American History* 75, no. 1 (1988): 9–39. On reconciling domesticity and public action, see Julie Roy Jeffrey, "Permeable Boundaries: Abolitionist Women and Separate Spheres," *Journal of the Early Republic* 21, no. 1 (2001): 79–93.

13. "Letter from Joseph B. Chapman to His Children," *Friends' Intelligencer*, 11th Mo. 1, 1856, 51.

14. Elizabeth Margaret Chandler, *Essays, Philanthropic and Moral, Principally Relating to the Abolition of Slavery in America*, 2nd ed. (Philadelphia: T. E. Chapman, 1845), 116.

15. *Report of a Delegation of Friends, Appointed to Attend an Indian Council of Seneca Indians, at Cattaraugus in the 9th Month 1855* (New York: Baker & Duyckinck, 1856), 18–19.

16. Quoted in *NYYM Women's Minutes*, 1850, 9, Friends Collection and College Archives, Earlham College, Richmond, IN (FCCA).

17. [Samuel M. Janney], *The Yankees in Fairfax County, Virginia* (Baltimore: Snodgrass & Wehrly, 1845), 20–21.

18. Ann A. Townsend, *Brief Memoir of John Jackson* (Philadelphia: Merrihew & Thompson, 1855), 43, 53; Mary S. Bartram, "John Jackson," *Friends' Intelligencer*, 3rd Mo. 7, 1896, 155–56. For broader context, see Mary Kelley, *Learning to Stand and Speak: Women, Education, and Public Life in America's Republic* (Chapel Hill: University of North Carolina Press, 2006).

19. Eugenia Letter, *The Friend; or, Advocate of Truth* 3 (7th Mo. 17, 1830): 229–30.

20. "Genesee Yearly Meeting of Friends," *Friends' Intelligencer*, 7th Mo. 16, 1838, 98; "New York Yearly Meeting of Friends," *Friends' Intelligencer*, 6th Mo. 1, 1838, 64–65; "Exercises of the Yearly Meeting," *Friends' Intelligencer*, 6th Mo. 5, 1847, 77; *Ohio Yearly Meeting Minutes*, 1843, 11–12, FCCA.

21. Green Plain Monthly Meeting Men's Minutes, 8th Mo. 12, 1841, IYM Archives, Wilmington College, Wilmington, OH.

22. Green Street Monthly Meeting Women's Minutes, 12th Mo. 18, 1834, 2nd Mo. 19, 1835, PYM Archives, FHLSC; Western Quarterly Meeting Men's Minutes, 2nd Mo. 19, 1839, 1st Mo. 21, 1840, FHLSC; Benjamin Price to Jane Price, 4th Mo. 14, 1836, Price Manuscripts, FHLSC; *A Memoir of Hannah A. Price, Late of Fallston, Maryland* (Norristown, PA: Morgan R. Wills, 1889), 24; Margaret Hope Bacon, *Mothers of Feminism: The Story of Quaker Women in America* (San Francisco: Harper and Row, 1986), 179.

23. Quoted in Hannah B. Turner to Joseph and Rebecca Turner, 5th Mo. 16, 1843, box 2, Turner Family Papers, FHLSC.

24. Mary S. Lippincott to Benjamin Ferris, 2nd Mo. 25, 1851, box 3, Ferris Family Papers, FHLSC.

25. Thomas D. Hamm, "The Radical Hicksite Critique of the Emerging Capitalist Order: Cornelius C. Blatchly, Benjamin Webb, and Friends, 1827–1833," in *Quakers*,

Politics, and Economics, edited by David R. Ross and Michael T. Snarr (Philadelphia: Friends Association for Higher Education, 2018), 214–34.

26. See Faulkner, *Lucretia Mott's Heresy*. Mott's most significant letters are collected in Beverly Wilson Palmer, ed., *Selected Letters of Lucretia Coffin Mott* (Urbana: University of Illinois Press, 2002). For her public speaking, see Christopher Densmore, Carol Faulkner, Nancy Hewitt, and Beverly Wilson Palmer, eds., *Lucretia Mott Speaks: The Essential Speeches and Sermons* (Urbana: University of Illinois Press, 2017).

27. Thomas D. Hamm, "Hicksite Quakers and the Antebellum Nonresistance Movement," *Church History* 63, no. 4 (1994): 557–69; Thomas D. Hamm, "George F. White and Hicksite Opposition to the Abolitionist Movement," in *Quakers and Abolition*, edited by Brycchan Carey and Geoffrey Plank (Urbana: University of Illinois Press, 2014), 43–55.

28. Hamm, "George F. White," 49.

29. Sarah Hopper Emmons, ed., *Life of Abby Hopper Gibbons*, 2 vols. (New York: G. P. Putnam's Sons, 1897), 1:117.

30. Nancy A. Hewitt, *Radical Friend: Amy Kirby Post and Her Activist Worlds* (Chapel Hill: University of North Carolina Press, 2018), 65–117.

31. *Minutes of the Proceedings of the Annual Meeting of Friends [. . .] Who Have Adopted the Congregational Order* (Springfield, OH: Halsey & Emerson, 1848), 3–5, 7–8.

32. Allen C. Thomas, "Congregational or Progressive Friends: A Forgotten Episode in Quaker History," *Bulletin of Friends Historical Association* 10 (1920): 21–32.

33. *Proceedings of the Ohio Yearly Meeting of Progressive Friends [. . .] Including an Address to the Public* (Salem, OH: G. P. Smith, 1852), 6, 8, 19.

34. *Basis of Religious Association Adopted by the Conference Held at Farmington [. . .] 1848* (Waterloo, NY: n.p., 1848), 3–5, 7; A. Day Bradley, "Progressive Friends in Michigan and New York," *Quaker History* 52, no. 2 (1963): 97–101.

35. Elizabeth Cady Stanton, Susan B. Anthony, and Matilda Joslyn Gage, eds., *History of Woman Suffrage*, 4 vols. (Rochester: Susan B. Anthony, 1889–1902), 1:420; Faulkner, *Lucretia Mott's Heresy*, 127–47.

36. Sally G. McMillen, *Seneca Falls and the Origins of the Women's Rights Movement* (New York: Oxford University Press, 2008), 71–103, 237–41; Otelia Cromwell, *Lucretia Mott* (Cambridge: Harvard University Press, 1958), 149–50; Judith Wellman, *The Road to Seneca Falls: Elizabeth Cady Stanton and the First Woman's Rights Convention* (Urbana: University of Illinois Press, 2004), 206–7; Faulkner, *Lucretia Mott's Heresy*, 148–60.

37. "Ohio Women's Convention," *Salem (OH) Anti-Slavery Bugle*, April 27, 1850, 130.

38. "Woman's Rights Convention," *Indiana True Democrat*, October 23, 1851, 1.

39. *Green Plain Yearly Meeting Minutes, 1848*, 5, FCCA.

40. *Waterloo Yearly Meeting Minutes, 1850*, 8–9, FCCA.

41. *PYM Minutes, 1853*, 35, FCCA.

42. Wellman, *Road to Seneca Falls*, 215; Bacon, *Mothers of Feminism*, 116–19.

43. Cromwell, *Lucretia Mott*, 145–46.

44. *Waterloo Yearly Meeting Minutes, 1850*, 16, FCCA.

45. *PYM Minutes, 1853*, 34, FCCA.

46. Lucretia L. Blankenburg, "A Story of My Branch of Longshore Family," in *A Collection of Papers Read Before the Bucks County Historical Society* 6 (1932): 533–34.

47. Emma Lou Thornbrough, *Indiana in the Civil War Era* (Indianapolis: Indiana Historical Society, 1965), 37; "Dr. Mary F. Thomas," *Friends' Intelligencer*, 2nd Mo. 9, 1889, 90–91.

48. Pauline Poole Foster, "Ann Preston, M.D. (1813–1872): A Biography; The Struggle to Obtain Training and Acceptance for Women Physicians in Mid-Nineteenth Century America" (PhD diss., University of Pennsylvania, 1984), viii–ix, 152–87 (esp. 184), 343.
49. Joseph P. Plummer to Benjamin Ferris, 8th Mo. 1, 1850, box 3, Ferris Family Papers, FHLSC.
50. Joseph Foulke to Benjamin Ferris, 7th Mo. 15, 1852, box 2, Foulke Family Papers, FHLSC.
51. Annie Cooper to Mary Cooper, November 1856, in "1856 Presidential Election," box 1, Cooper-Richardson Family Papers, FHLSC.
52. Faulkner, *Lucretia Mott's Heresy*, 171–73.
53. Mary H. Child to Henry A. Wise, 12th Mo. 4, 1859, box 1, Ash-Schofield Papers, FHLSC.
54. Quoted in William Eyre diary, 4th Mo. 1, 1860, box 2, Eyre Family Papers, FHLSC.
55. A. Glenn Crothers, *Quakers Living in the Lion's Mouth: The Society of Friends in Northern Virginia, 1730–1865* (Gainesville: University Press of Florida, 2012), 237–71.
56. Palmer, *Selected Letters of Lucretia Coffin Mott*, 310.
57. *Memoir of Rachel Hicks*, 94–95.
58. Martha Schofield to Sadie Brower, May 10, 1861, box 1, Martha Schofield Papers, FHLSC.
59. Quoted in Margaret Hope Bacon, *Abby Hopper Gibbons: Prison Reformer and Social Activist* (Albany: SUNY Press, 2000), 86.
60. John E. Divine, Bronwen C. Souders, and John M. Souders, eds., *"To Talk Is Treason": Quakers of Waterford, Virginia on Life, Love, Death, and War in the Southern Confederacy* (Waterford, VA: Waterford Foundation, 1996), 24, 27, 34.
61. Quoted in Emily Foster, ed., *American Grit: A Woman's Letters from the Ohio Frontier* (Lexington: University Press of Kentucky, 2002), 291–92.
62. See, for example, E. J. Hibbard to A. M. Barnard, February 12, 1864, box 4, Kent-Barnard Papers, FHLSC.
63. Henrietta Stratton Jaquette, ed., *South After Gettysburg: Letters of Cornelia Hancock, 1863–1868* (New York: Thomas Y. Crowell, 1956), ix–x.
64. Lucretia Mott to Martha Lord, 2nd Mo. 5, 1864, box 3, Lucretia Mott Papers, FHLSC.
65. Henrietta Stratton Jaquette, "Friends' Association of Philadelphia for the Aid and Elevation of the Freedmen," *Bulletin of Friends Historical Association* 46 (Autumn 1957): 67–83.
66. Katherine Smedley, *Martha Schofield and the Re-Education of the South, 1839–1916* (Lewiston, NY: Edwin Mellen Press, 1987).
67. *Baltimore Yearly Meeting Minutes, 1870*, 6–7, FCCA; *Baltimore Yearly Meeting Minutes, 1869*, 31, FCCA.
68. *PYM Minutes, 1875*, 4; *PYM Minutes, 1876*, 25–28; *PYM Minutes, 1877*, 33–37, all in FCCA.
69. "The Administration of the Discipline," *Friends' Intelligencer*, 2nd Mo. 24, 1866, 805.
70. *Discipline of the Yearly Meeting of the Religious Society of Friends, Held in New York*, 92; *NYYM Minutes, 1872*, 12, FCCA; "Yearly Meeting," *Journal*, 6th Mo. 17, 1874, 153.
71. *Genesee Yearly Meeting Minutes, 1869*, 4, FCCA.
72. "A Proposed Change," *Journal*, 5th Mo. 12, 1875, 126.
73. S. N. Smith, "Women's Meetings," *Friends' Intelligencer*, 4th Mo. 17, 1875, 116.
74. Editorial, *Friends' Intelligencer*, 4th Mo. 4, 1874, 89.
75. "The Change in the Discipline," *Journal*, 6th Mo. 6, 1877, 156.

76. "Prairie Grove Quarterly Meeting, Iowa," *Journal*, 10th Mo. 8, 1873, 284; *NYYM Minutes, 1878*, 6, 10, FCCA.

77. Philip S. Benjamin, *The Philadelphia Quakers in the Industrial Age, 1865–1920* (Philadelphia: Temple University Press, 1976), 149–51.

78. Errol T. Elliott, *Quakers on the American Frontier* (Richmond, IN: Friends United Press, 1969), 380–99.

79. Christopher Densmore, "Swarthmore College," in *Founded by Friends: The Quaker Heritage of Fifteen American Colleges and Universities*, edited by John W. Oliver Jr., Charles L. Cherry, and Caroline L. Cherry (Lanham, MD: Scarecrow Press, 2007), 57–62.

80. *Seventh Annual Catalogue of Swarthmore College, Swarthmore, Pa., 1875–1876* (Philadelphia: Friends' Book Association, 1875), 48.

81. *Proceedings of Friends Union for Philanthropic Labor [...] 1890* (New York: Caulon Press, 1890), 3–4.

82. "Impressions of the Chappaqua Meetings," *Friends' Intelligencer*, 9th Mo. 1, 1894, 557.

83. Deborah L. Haines, "Friends General Conference: A Brief Historical Overview," *Quaker History* 89, no. 2 (2000): 7–8.

84. *Proceedings of Friends' General Conference [...] 1916* (Philadelphia: Friends' Intelligencer, 1916), 97.

85. *Friends' Presentation of Their Faith, Works, and Hopes [...] 1893* (Chicago: W. B. Conkey, 1893), 106.

86. See, for example, "A Brief Sketch of the Female Association of Philadelphia for the Relief of the Sick and Infirm Poor with Clothing," *Friends' Intelligencer*, 11th Mo. 17, 1880, 762.

87. *Baltimore Yearly Meeting Minutes, 1892*, 23–25, FCCA.

88. Benjamin, *Philadelphia Quakers in the Industrial Age*, 161–62, 183.

89. "Young Friends' Aid Association," *Young Friends' Review* 16 (9th Mo. 1901): 17–18.

90. Rebecca T. Osler, "The Christian Life," *Friends' Intelligencer*, 5th Mo. 27, 1916, 341.

91. Lucretia Mott to R. D. Webb, 1st Mo. 22, 1870, Anti-Slavery Collection, Boston Public Library, Boston.

92. Elizabeth H. Coale to Albert T. Mills, 3rd Mo. 14, 1900, box 1, Abel Mills Papers, Illinois Historical Survey, University of Illinois, Urbana.

93. "Philadelphia Quarterly Meeting," *Friends' Intelligencer*, 5th Mo. 17, 1879, 201; *Proceedings of Friends' Union for Philanthropic Labor [...]* (Philadelphia: Alfred J. Ferris, 1896), 225–26; *Proceedings of the Friends' General Conference [...] 1898* (Philadelphia: Friends' Intelligencer Association, 1898), 191–203; *NYYM Minutes, 1900*, 57–58, FCCA.

94. J. Hall, "In Support of the League of Nations," *Friends' Intelligencer*, 10th Mo. 25, 1919, 683; Anna L. Curtis, "Friends in New York," *Friends' Intelligencer*, 5th Mo. 6, 1916, 299–300.

95. Charles F. Howlett, "Quaker Conscience in the Classroom: The Mary S. McDowell Case," *Quaker History* 83, no. 2 (1994): 99–115.

96. Hugh Barbour and J. William Frost, *The Quakers* (Westport, CT: Greenwood Press, 1988), 335–36.

97. "Baltimore Epistle," in *Genesee Yearly Meeting Minutes, 1880*, 60, FCCA.

98. *NYYM Minutes, 1882*, 47, FCCA.

99. A. M. S., "An Appeal in the Cause of Temperance," *Friends' Intelligencer*, 4th Mo. 11, 1874, 101; "Friendly Items," *Journal*, 2nd Mo. 4, 1874, 4.

100. *Proceedings of the Friends' General Conference [...] 1898*, 139.

101. Bacon, *Mothers of Feminism*, 120–36.

102. "When the Women Vote," n.d., Robbins Family Papers, FHLSC.
103. *Proceedings of Friends' General Conference* [. . .] *1916*, 63.
104. See J. D. Zahniser and Amelia R. Fry, *Alice Paul: Claiming Power* (New York: Oxford University Press, 2014), esp. 3.
105. See, for example, Edward Farquhar, "Modern Literature and Quakerism," *Friends' Intelligencer*, 12th Mo. 28, 1901, 821.

CHAPTER 2

Elizabeth Robson, Transatlantic Women Ministers, and the Hicksite-Orthodox Schism

ROBYNNE ROGERS HEALEY

The Hicksite-Orthodox separation irreparably divided North American Quakers. The acrimony engendered by long-held disagreements did not end with the division of yearly meetings. In the aftermath of yearly meeting separations, disputes endured as Quakers clashed over control of local meetinghouses, burial grounds, and minute books.[1] More than a century would pass before North American Quakers were reunited.[2] The schism also ended the connection that had bound North American Friends to the London Yearly Meeting (LYM) for almost two centuries. In 1828, when the Philadelphia Yearly Meeting (Hicksite) forwarded its annual epistle to the LYM, following a 150-year-old practice, British Friends rejected the epistle and cut off correspondence with Hicksite Friends. The LYM minutes recorded the decision: "This Meeting thinks it right at this time to declare that it does not correspond with any body of individuals convened under the name of *Friends* on the Continent of America, which is not established in accordance with the regular and long settled order of our religious Society or which is not in fellowship with us as a Christian Community."[3] Despite Hicksite Quakers' subsequent efforts to reach out, to clarify their commitment to the testimonies of early Friends, and to restore fellowship with British Friends, the LYM severed its formal connection with American Hicksites until 1923.[4]

In the years leading to the separation, British Friends took an entirely different approach with the Hicksites. During the 1820s, British Quaker ministers—especially women—played an active role in trying to direct and correct theology in the turbulent transatlantic Quaker world of the early nineteenth century. The previous chapter, by Thomas Hamm, shows that the American Friends who played a prominent public role in the schism were largely men. This does not mean that American women were uninvolved in the divisive quarrels. Quaker records provide examples of American Quaker women, such as Priscilla Hunt Cadwalader (1786–1859), who contested strongly for their views on both sides.[5] British Quaker women did play a significant public role in the schism. Anna Braithwaite (1789–1859), Ann Jones (1774–1846), and Elizabeth Robson (1771–1843) were three prominent transatlantic women ministers who, along with men like William Forster (1784–1834), George Withy (1776–1837), Thomas Shillitoe (1754–1836), and Isaac Stephenson (1765–1830), crossed the Atlantic and crisscrossed the North American landscape, visiting individuals, families, and meetings in an attempt to eradicate what they saw as doctrine heretical to genuine Quakerism.[6]

This chapter examines the British Quaker minister Elizabeth Robson and her role in the Hicksite-Orthodox schism, relying heavily on the extensive Thomas and Elizabeth Robson manuscripts in the Library of the Society of Friends (LSF). Robson's experiences provide a lens through which to consider the impact of gender on transatlantic ministry and the Great Separation. Robson's experience points to the significant role that women played in this schism. They presented complicated models of nineteenth-century womanhood, advocating piety and domesticity while at the same time challenging one another and men in leadership. The instability of the doctrinal disputes in this moment opened space for women to claim a larger role for themselves in reform initiatives within and outside the Society after the separation.[7] This was a time when gender and Quakerism were in transition.[8] Helen Plant has shown that for English Quaker women ministers of this period, the relationship between gender and religious authority in the Society was incongruent. Through the late eighteenth century, women had emerged as the principal spiritual leaders among English Quakers, but they lacked the authority and "disciplinary jurisdiction" that one might expect to be associated with spiritual leadership. This led women to turn "to the authority of their own religious experience, and some even drew on Friends' gendered notions of spirituality in order to question male pretensions to govern."⁹ Similarly, Janet Moore Lindman's analysis of gender and language in the Hicksite-Orthodox schism contends that the "gendered conflicts that arose during the schism reflect larger divisions over women's proper place in American society." Occurring at a time of immense social change in American society, the separation "ignited a growing demand for equity" that could not be expressed in ministry alone but was fulfilled through active engagement in reform politics.¹⁰ This conclusion echoes Dale A. Johnson's assertion that the decline in the number of British women ministers over the nineteenth century coincided with the increased involvement of Quaker women in reform politics, higher education, and humanitarian work.¹¹ In the period during which Robson was active in ministry, British women ministers outnumbered their male counterparts, which Plant attributes to "temporal trends within contemporary Quakerism." As Quaker families became increasingly prosperous, business concerns demanded more of men's time; simultaneously, Quaker women were dedicating less of their time to family businesses, freeing them to commit more of their time to religious concerns.¹² Some men in the LYM were not pleased about this development. In his 1824 *Observations on the Religious Peculiarities of the Society of Friends*, Joseph John Gurney lamented the fact that women outnumbered men in public ministry, remarking, "such a circumstance can by no means be deemed a favourable sign."¹³ Whether their brethren in the LYM approved or not, these women ministers claimed their space as active public Friends.

Robson's actions, along with those of her counterparts, point to a form of British Quaker paternalism in the years between the end of the Napoleonic Wars and the separation. From its earliest days, the traveling ministry, together with epistolary correspondence, had been integral in maintaining the tightly woven network of transatlantic Quakerism. The Embargo Act of 1807, the War of 1812, and the Napoleonic Wars had all restricted travel across the Atlantic and had limited contact between British and North American Friends for almost a decade. Hugh Barbour and his colleagues suggest that during these years, the "kindest of the Public [British] Friends died and were replaced by harsher English visitors such as Anna Braithwaite, Elizabeth Robson and her brother Isaac Stephenson, and George and Ann Jones." These harsher Friends came "no longer like a 'nanny' eager to teach the colonials Quakerism but more like an uncle desperate to save his family from destruction by Deism."¹⁴ Whether nanny or uncle, the Hicksites viewed the transatlantic ministers as both interfering and paternalistic.

Viewed within the context of the family metaphor, the schism shed light on disagreements over familial relationships of power. Were the American meetings subordinate to the LYM as nineteenth-century wives were to be subordinate to their husbands? Or was the transatlantic Quaker family one of equals?

The outcome of these divergent outlooks, coupled with a considerable lack of charity on both sides in this dispute, fundamentally changed the nineteenth-century Religious Society of Friends. It set the precedent for using separation as the default mechanism for addressing significant disagreement. Further nineteenth-century schisms fractured the Society even more, laying the foundations for modern diverse Quakerism.[15] In the prelude to this first North American separation, the English ministers had a powerful impact on how the LYM viewed Hicks and his supporters. As Edwin Bronner says, "if there had been any tendency to overlook the statements of the [American] Orthodox Friends, to ascribe their statements to partisan feelings, such doubts were overshadowed by the vigorous corroboration from the English observers."[16] The English ministers' efforts to impose doctrinal uniformity on the North American meetings marked the end of the LYM's position, or authority, at the center of the Quaker world. American Orthodox meetings remained in relationship with the LYM, but the connection between British and North American Friends was significantly altered as a result of the LYM's severing the bond with Hicksite Quakers.

ELIZABETH STEPHENSON ROBSON AND HER RECORDS

Elizabeth Robson was a member of two relatively prominent English Quaker families. She was born June 25, 1771, at Bridlington Quay into the Yorkshire Stephenson family, the middle child of Isaac Stephenson, a master mariner, and his third wife, Elizabeth Mair(e) Stephenson. There was a substantial age difference between Elizabeth's parents. Her father was born in 1694, her mother in 1741. They married in 1762, when Isaac was sixty-eight and Elizabeth was twenty-one. When their daughter, Elizabeth, was born in 1771, Isaac was seventy-seven; when Elizabeth's younger brother, Samuel, was born in 1774, he was eighty.[17] After the death of her mother in 1795 (her father had died in 1783), she lived with her brother Isaac Stephenson (1765–1830), a miller, at Stockton-on Tees.[18]

In 1796, Elizabeth married Thomas Robson (1768–1852), a Darlington linen manufacturer, Quaker elder, and son of Thomas Robson and his wife, Margaret Pease Robson. Thomas was appointed elder the year he and Elizabeth married; he was only twenty-eight at the time. Over the course of their marriage, Elizabeth and Thomas Robson had seven children. Five were born between 1798 and 1805, and the last two were born, one year apart, in 1815 and 1816. Elizabeth first appeared in ministry in 1808 and became a recorded minister in 1810 when she began to travel in ministry, explaining, in part, the ten-year gap between her first five and last two pregnancies. From 1810 until her death in 1843, Robson traveled extensively in ministry, throughout Britain, to Europe (Germany, Switzerland, the Netherlands, France), and twice to North America.

In 1811, the Robsons moved to Sunderland in the northeast of England, and in 1821 they relocated to Liverpool and joined the Hardshaw West Monthly Meeting, to which Elizabeth belonged for the rest of her life. Robson was one of several British ministers who journeyed to North America in the years preceding the Hicksite-Orthodox separation. Her first transatlantic ministerial tour lasted almost four years (1824–28). During that time, she recorded that she had traveled more than eighteen thousand miles, attended 1,134 meetings, and recorded 3,592 family visits opposing the followers of Elias Hicks.[19] In 1838, her husband accompanied her on a second trip to America, an expedition that also lasted four years. When she returned to England in 1842, she continued regular visitation within her own meeting, traveled in ministry to Scotland, and attended the London Yearly Meeting, but generally lived a more retired life. On November 30, 1843, while attending her monthly meeting, she expressed her desire to visit Friends in the Quarterly Meeting of London and Middlesex. The following day she suffered a paralytic stroke that left her with almost no capacity for speech. She died twelve days later, on December 11, 1843, in Liverpool, where she is buried.

Despite leaving a significant collection of letters and diaries covering the years 1813–43 (the fonds at the LSF consists of twenty-six volumes, and the Joseph Joshua Green Papers include at least three boxes of Elizabeth and Thomas Robson material), remarkably little has been published about Robson. The organization of her records in the LSF indicates that the family may have intended to publish the journals of Robson's "American journeys." Undoubtedly, the collection had been curated carefully by the family before it was donated to the LSF. Her eldest son's small manuscript journal contains notes that allude to this.[20] It states, "Appendix, consisting of extracts from ER's Memorandum books Numbered I to XVII (to be hereafter embodied in the 'memoirs')," and "Interesting remarks in ER's letters not suitable (at least most of these) for insertion in 'Memoirs.'"[21] Both Elizabeth's husband, Thomas, and her eldest son, Henry, copied and recopied portions of Elizabeth's diaries and letters. Elizabeth herself appears to have recopied sections of her diaries. Henry's copies have segments of Robson's original pasted to the sides of the pages. Both Thomas's and Henry's hands are easier to read than Elizabeth's, but one wonders what might have been lost or expurgated in the transcription process. Henry did write a memoir of sorts that Joseph Joshua Green tells us "consisted of nine quarto volumes of several thousand pages."[22] The first three volumes were lost, and possibly became part of an estate sale when one of her granddaughters died.

In 1891, Green used the remaining volumes of his uncle Henry's memoir, along with Elizabeth Robson's papers, to produce the handwritten manuscript "Elizabeth Robson, 1770–1843."[23] The Robson letters and journals were deposited at the LSF in 1901 and 1908.[24] Despite efforts to preserve her records, Robson's grandson Joseph Joshua Green lamented, "it is a cause of much regret that no adequate Life of Elizabeth Robson has not [sic] yet been published, as few lives have been more fruitful or full of incidents, and few individuals have been enabled to accomplish so much for the well being of their fellow man, or have been more beloved by all who had the privilege of their acquaintance and friendship."[25] In 1914, Green wrote "Biographies in Verse—Thomas and Elizabeth Robson," extracted from a 113,000-word manuscript prepared by his mother, also named Elizabeth Robson.[26] These biographies were copied for the family. Of the sixty pages of verse, fifty are dedicated to Elizabeth and ten to Thomas. Green's dedication called Elizabeth "sainted." Clearly, the family thought Robson merited more formal attention. It may be that the 1905 publication of *Memoirs of Anna Braithwaite*, Robson's contemporary, served as a model for the type of work the Robsons hoped might be produced.[27]

Despite the volume of material written in her hand, Elizabeth Robson remains largely unstudied, if not unknown.[28] What we do know from her family's biographical efforts verges, at points, on the hagiographic. In forcing rhyme and extracting her experiences, Joseph Joshua Green's "biography in verse" is neither good poetry nor to be considered literally reliable. It does, however, provide a description of Robson's appearance and personality:

> She as a housewife ord'ly was and kind,
> In person neat, in aspect was refined;
> She was of medium height, of form robust,
> And bore the calm composure of the just.
> ....
> We have two silhouettes of Grandmamma,
> One in her prime, the other when she far
> Was in life advanced; the last indeed
> The former doth in beauty much exceed.
> It is a noble count'nance, calm, serene,
> Each feature good and of a striking mien.
> Though serious, as Isaac Sharp did say,
> To Social converse did attention pay,
> And could appreciate the <u>lively</u> side
> Of tales her many friends would her provide.[29]

What motivated her to spend so much time away from her family in such miserable circumstances? She was fifty-three years old when she set sail for North America in 1824. While her five older children were all adults, her younger daughters, Elizabeth and Mary Charlotte, were seven and eight years old, respectively, and she had no idea when she would see them again. She was not the only British woman who journeyed to North America to try to impose, or reimpose, doctrinal consistency. Anna Braithwaite visited American Friends three times, in 1823, 1825, and 1827. She was eighteen years Robson's junior, so travel may have been easier for her, although she left seven children ranging in age from five to fourteen when she first set out in 1823. Her husband, Isaac, accompanied her on her second and third journeys. Ann Jones, who traveled through North America from 1826 to 1830, was only slightly younger than Robson, but her husband, George, accompanied her for the duration. The Joneses were childless. Robson's husband, Thomas, did accompany her on her second four-year tour of the American meetings, but during her first journey, Thomas remained at home to care for the young Robson daughters.

One could argue that Elizabeth Robson was powerfully motivated by faith, as is evident from her letters, epistles, and recorded sermons. This is borne out in the family's biographical materials as well. What kind of person was she? One account paints her as "uncomfortably direct," as one American Friend recalled to her grandson: she was "a skilful woman of God who could throw a stone to a hairs breadth & never miss & never hurt or hit a friend but always hit a foe."[30] Was she controlling? The well-being of her youngest daughters, from whose lives she was absent for long periods, weighed heavily on her. At the same time, she worried that their behavior reflected on her parenting. Consider a letter to her youngest daughter, written in 1834. From Ireland, Robson reminded eighteen-year-old Elizabeth how much it cost her to leave her daughter, especially when she was at such "an important age." Robson then counseled Elizabeth to alter her wide sleeves, being "fully convinced it is one of the vain fashions of the world, and seeing the stations thy father & mother holds it weakens our hands in giving advice to others when our daughter indulges such things."[31] She appears to have been tenacious, if not stubborn. Her visiting every meeting and remaining in North America until both the Philadelphia Yearly Meeting (PYM) and the New York Yearly Meeting (NYYM) had separated, in 1827 and 1828, respectively, points to this. At this juncture, when nothing more could be done to stop the separation, she finally felt "released" to return home in July 1828. The lengthy diary entry on the day of her departure reflects the key themes of "deep awareness of personal insufficiency, cowering aversion to public exposure, followed by tranquility as human trepidation was overcome in obedience to the divine will" that characterized women's ministry in the early nineteenth century.[32]

> I have spent nearly 4 years of my Life in America—2 months and ten days short of completing the four years.... Looking at the service of visiting the Churches in America under our name it appeared too weighty for me, more especially as I had some knowledge of the comotions that had got into our society there owing to unsoundness in the faith—but as I endeavoured to keep quiet I was mercifully sustained in the prospect and enabled to give of my all into the Hands of my Great and merciful Creator—and in that I was strengthened to part from my tenderly beloved husband committing him and our dear chil[dre]n into the Hand of the Great Shepherd of Israel.... I have during my stay in a Foreign Land ... looked for a release, but the more I looked for it the faster I felt bound where I was, until my way without great anxiety on my part gradually spent and the prospect settled

for returning in the ship which I came in.... I feel that I have abundant cause of gratitude for the manifold mercies and favours vouchsafed to me while a sojourner on the American Continent—I have been mercifully sustained in many deep and painful conflicts and my head kept above the water—preservation has been witnessed in perils amongst false brethren—I have been priviledged with many dear bretheren and sisters in the truth which I account no small favour—the Unity of the bretheren is a very precious thing and I esteem it a great Blessing—kind agreeable companions have been provided for me without any contrivance of mine being such as have felt their minds drawn to the service—have happened very few accidents in the way of travelling [and] none that have proved injurious—and I believe my Great and Blessed Master has been pleased to grant me a release from the field of labour in which I have for some years been engaged and I have a humble hope that he will be pleased to bring me safe to my beloved husband and to my dear chil[dre]n.[33]

As much as Robson's story reflects common themes expressed by other Quaker women ministers at this time, her story is her own. As Hamm contends, "the religious history of the first half of the nineteenth century was not just one story. Rather, it was a constellation of individual stories, some more obscure and harder to pin down than others, but no less significant for their elusiveness."[34] This short chapter can hardly do justice to the complex character of Elizabeth Robson. There is space for much more work on Robson and the other English women who took it upon themselves to speak so volubly into this social and religious moment in Quaker history.

QUAKER WOMEN AND THE GREAT SEPARATION

Quaker women engaged actively in the theological disagreements of the early nineteenth century, whether they traveled in ministry or not. As the Society became more polarized, Friends were pressed to take sides. When transatlantic ministers traveled throughout North America, they often tried to visit every Quaker family in the communities to which they traveled.[35] Family visitation carried disagreements into the heart of Quaker households wherever ministers went. Additionally, traveling ministers advertised public meetings, drawing large crowds of Quakers and non-Quakers alike. To accommodate large mixed groups, they often used Methodist and Presbyterian churches and, on occasion, the local courthouse. These public meetings, featuring ministers like Robson, highlighted and exacerbated the mounting divisions among Friends. They also educated non-Quakers on the Society's disputes. Gatherings like these and traveling in ministry placed women at the center of swirling doctrinal debates. The work of the transatlantic ministers was carried out in local and regional contexts by Friends on both sides. As they defended their positions, women did not shy away from clashes with those whom they opposed. Robson's letters note her ongoing conflicts with women ministers like Martha Smith, Phoebe Johnson, Margaret Judge, and Priscilla Hunt Cadwalader, whom she encountered in all levels of meetings during her travels.

Robson did not confront these women and other supporters of Hicks alone. Her letters often refer to "fellow labourers," who, beyond her English counterparts, were an expansive group. She counted three women—Jane Bettle, Ruth Ely, and Philadelphia Pemberton—as her "dear friends," but letters to her family indicate that she relied heavily on a large network of Quaker women. Some traveled with her for varying periods of time. Many fed and lodged her and her companions. A number kept her company at night, a comfort during trying moments, and she commented often on the women who showed her "remarkable kindness." And, wherever she went, she met astonishing Quaker women whose stories reminded her that she was not alone in her ordeals, nor was she the only woman who had sacrificed much for the sake of ministry.

In one letter to her husband, Robson recounted lodging with Vermont minister Huldah Hoag and hearing Hoag's "extraordinary account of her family." Hoag and her husband, Joseph, had ten children. He too was a minister and was frequently away. Robson reveals that another Friend who had known the Hoags for twenty years "thought Joseph had been absent from home one half that time." Even with a supportive Quaker community, this had to have been a trial for Huldah, at home with several children on a frontier farm. Her circumstances did not stop Hoag from setting off herself across challenging terrain on ministerial journeys. According to Hoag's account, before one of her daughters was four months old, the infant had accompanied her mother "on horse-back and by water about three hundred and fifty miles." Another daughter, also an infant at the time, accompanied her mother and two other women across Lake Champlain to Peru, New York, where Hoag was the first Quaker minister to hold a meeting. The women and baby had to spend the night on a small island. Hoag's story was not only an endurance tale but was told in such a way as to evoke the rich spiritual reward that awaited mothers who gave up the comforts of home and closeness with their children for the sake of ministry. When Hoag recounted her story to Robson in the fall of 1826, and Robson in turn retold it, seven of the ten Hoag children and some grandchildren had already appeared in ministry, suggesting that Hoag and Robson interpreted this as a reward for Hoag's faithfulness.[36] Hoag's story was remarkable, especially considering the challenging frontier environment. Significantly, her story echoes those of other women ministers.

The nineteenth century is full of accounts of Quaker women who made significant personal sacrifices and experienced trials and tribulations for the sake of their faith and their own ministry. As Plant posits, "the language of suffering became, in a sense, the language of shared female experience."[37] Women like Robson who left their families and homes for years to travel in a "foreign land" under difficult circumstances felt that this sacrifice entitled them to inject themselves into local meetings and to offer their assessment of the spiritual health of meetings and their constituent members. They regularly couched their critiques in the language of sacrifices made and dangers endured. Robson invoked this refrain in letters to those with whom she disagreed. Writing from Queenston, Upper Canada, in February 1825, Robson began, "dear friend, I trust that in this thou wilt agree with me that it is right we should be honest with ourselves and with one another: this is what I desire to do: it was no small sacrifice for me to make, to leave my native country and tenderly beloved connexions in life and come to this Land to visit my bretheren and sisters in religious membership."[38] With this language, Robson tried to endow her religious critique with moral authority.

Robson also used this approach in oral communications, not only as a gendered justification for her right to speak but as a gendered defense of her ministry—evidence that she had placed "service to God before an attachment to home and family."[39] After the 1826 NYYM of Ministers and Elders, regarding a hostile disagreement about doctrine, Robson wrote in her journal, "I mentioned what I had passed through and [had given] up to leave my beloved husband and dear children to come to this land: that, being here, I only wished to do the Master's will not my own from day to day." This message was repeated twice at the same meeting. First, Anna Braithwaite invoked the same language to support Robson's ministry and to speak out against the unkind treatment of her, which included, at one point, the refusal of permission to perform a family visit. Henry Hull then endorsed Robson's ministry in the same way, "saying he could bear testimony to [her] faithfulness and dedication to [her] own land, having traveled with [her]." Notably, Hull mentioned that Robson "had been willing to leave [her] dear husband and family."[40]

The theme of personal sacrifice also runs through letters from various Quakers to Elizabeth's husband, Thomas Robson, as if he, too, needed to be reminded of the spiritual importance of his wife's ministry. Consider this passage in an 1826 letter from Esther French in Columbiana County, Ohio, to Thomas in Liverpool: "I am abundantly confirmed that nothing less than the unfailing arm of power has been her support, and borne her head above the conflicting billows that have raged around her. Though she may be buffeted by the blind zeal and unbelief of some amongst us, yet He whom *she has left all to follow*, will preserve her from harm; and I humbly hope and trust, restore her in safety to her native land, to the joy and rejoicing of her endeared and affectionate husband and children, and beloved friends."[41] Robson's journal tells us that she had been planning to return home in September 1826. After the 1826 NYYM, however, she decided to delay her return. She first broached the topic with Thomas shortly after the yearly meeting in a June letter: "I believe it is best for me to tell thee that I begin to be doubtful about being liberated to return in 9th month next, as I once hoped I might be permitted to do; and perhaps was too ready in communicating." She assured Thomas that her decision to remain in North America had caused her "very great conflict," and that she loved her "precious husband" and her "dear children." At the same time, she was resolved, and told her family "that thou wouldst not all desire me to return too soon."[42] Here, Robson appealed to "clinging emotional attachment to home and family," as Plant puts it, one of the "principal feminine traits against which women's ministry was understood."[43]

The decision to delay her return to England caused Robson anguish and disappointed her family. Robson's English Friends rushed to reassure her that her absence was not harming her family. Frances Thompson wrote a newsy letter from home to "console and cheer" her. Thompson assured

Robson that "it is really wonderful to observe how [your husband] is supported," and that "it is evident that he desires to give thee freely up." She ended her letter with a reminder that from sacrifice came reward:

> And now, my dearest E.R! I beg thee to believe that it is very evident to me, who sees much of thy dear family, that nothing is suffering at home through thy absence: indeed, I seem to have such a sense of the protecting arm of Divine Power being round about them for their preservation in and to the end of thy absence, that I think I have faith to believe that, comparatively speaking, not a piece of their heads shall be permitted to perish. Therefore I do desire that thou mayst be afreshed strengthened to resign them, and enabled to pursue the further work assigned thee, not only with a ready mind but with a cheerful heart. Besides, as thy dear little Mary Charlotte said to me lately, "I like as well—or I am willing that Mother should stay longer; because if she had come home this year she would, perhaps, have to go again!" Little sensible creature! do be cheered, my beloved friend! And strive to let the sacrifice be a perfect one; so shalt thou receive a full reward; which is what I sincerely desire for thee.[44]

The language of sacrifice suggests that Robson's lengthy absence from her family, her public ministry, and her clashes with Hicksite Friends were best understood through the lens of gendered expectations for nineteenth-century women. No woman of that era would *choose* to remain apart from her husband and children. No woman would *choose* to expose herself to ridicule or engage theologically, as Robson did. Despite the long history of powerful and intrepid Quaker women—and despite the existence of hardy, resilient women in their midst—nineteenth-century Quakers used the tropes of true womanhood and the weaker sex. At the end of her four-year journey, Robson herself adopted this language, referring to herself as "a poor weak creature" and concluding that "if any good has been done by any labour of mine to Him be all praise who is pleased to make use of poor weak instruments."[45] As women who operated outside the norms of true womanhood, even while they supported those norms in many ways, ministers like Robson could interpret the perils of their religious leadings only through the language of sacrifice and danger and the assurance that only obedience to God could help women overcome their inherent weakness.

Robson's apparent willingness to step into the fray does not mean that she found it easy. Her letters reveal how challenging she found the fractious circumstances, and the extent to which she relied on her faith to sustain her course. She wrote to Thomas, as she prepared to attend the PYM in 1826, "I have felt ready to shrink from going to Philadelphia to the Yearly Meeting; but, being a little quiet in myself, a degree of faith has sprung up, and I have felt thankful in being permitted to draw water where the arrows of the archers cannot come." While her detractors would disagree, Robson believed she exercised "very great care" in how she spoke, "lest anything should raise the wrong spirit." At times this kept her silent. More often, she spoke of overcoming great fear and heaviness before speaking out. This was the case at a session of the PYM held at Twelfth Street Meeting in which her "mind was enveloped in so much gloom for a while that [she] did not expect to have anything to express: but the cloud dispersed a little, and Light arose out of obscurity . . . and although it was hard work, and there evidently was much opposition in many minds to receive the doctrines of Christianity, [she] was strengthened to get through." At other times, Robson related a more forceful reaction to the fear, "exercise of mind," and burden of her ministry. On one occasion, she wrote, "the word became as a fire in my bones." On another, at a quarterly meeting, as she and several other women entered the men's session, Robson claimed, "I felt like a kettle that wanted vent." And in one session of the 1826 NYYM, her mind was racing "and like a bottle wanting vent," leading her to stand and speak "as soon as the meeting settled."[46]

While Robson supported, and was supported by, some men in her travels, her consistent focus on the support of other women points to its significance in the traveling ministry. When she and fellow English minister Anna Braithwaite attended the same meetings, their ministry was often collaborative, with one speaking and the other "supplicating."[47] Local women were another source of encouragement, helping her overcome self-doubt, as was evident during one session of the 1826 PYM: "I went to meeting under very great exercise about visiting the men; and, on laying it before the women, met with very great encouragement. My dear Jane Bettle and Bewlay Sansom accompanied me, wherein, I trust I was strengthened to deliver an honest testimony to the Truth.—no apparent opposition but from one man."[48]

Opposition from men was a particular challenge. Partly this was due to their authority in the Quaker meeting structure. Beyond that was the gendered nature of religious arguments in this period. Lindman contends that "the cultural scripts of white manhood and white womanhood were played out in the Hicksite schism."[49] This is evident in Robson's descriptions of events. For instance, following an afternoon session of the NYYM of Ministers and Elders attended by Elias Hicks, Thomas Wetherald, and Margaret Judge, Robson recorded, "we had not sat many minutes when Wetherald got up and pulled off his coat, before the meeting was settled, indeed it was extremely crowded with his people: I think he continued more than an hour, and delivered a strange and wild discourse, part of it quite cross, so that I even felt ashamed to be seen sitting there. His appearance was awful, without his coat—flinging his arms about as though he was either in the act of fighting or killing an ox: his countenance fierce and cruel: and his doctrines, dreadful." Equally troubling to Robson was how Hicks and Wetherald silenced Dorothy Ripley, who rose and "very notably declared against infidelity and setting aside the Scriptures." Hicks said something to Ripley "and a Friend went to her to get her to sit down," but Ripley refused to be suppressed. While Robson did not "in general, approve of her," she "wished they would have let her proceed," believing Ripley to be "a good expedient in case of extremety [sic]." Despite Ripley's "beg[ging] to be permitted to say a few more words," Hicks and Wetherald broke up the meeting.[50]

Authority to end a meeting belonged to men. Unable to silence their critic, they walked away from her. Hicksites were not alone in this practice. On more than one occasion, Robson lamented the absence of a man to break off a meeting in which principles with which she disagreed were being preached. On another occasion, in Ferrisburgh, Vermont, Robson spoke of a Hicksite "man who sat on a seat with his back to me," who, after she began speaking, "turned round, and looked right at me most of the time; and appeared restless: however it did in no way, move me, but helped to confirm me in my sense of the state of the meeting." While Robson did not record any verbal altercation with the man or any behavior beyond his staring, she was clearly unnerved by the experience, as is evident in her description: "that man—a violent man. How very lamentable it is that these things should have spread, even like a leprosy!"[51]

The tone of the correspondence between the transatlantic ministers and their families and meetings in England strongly influenced British opinion of the Hicksites. The British ministers may not have been entirely responsible for the schism, but their presence and persistence exacerbated conflicts at all levels. Hicksites viewed the interference as paternalistic and occasionally used meeting structures to try to stop it. This included refusing certificates of ministry or censuring a visit in the minutes. Both actions were serious and demonstrated significant disunity. Following Robson's visit to the Alexandria Monthly Meeting in Virginia, members of the meeting denounced her ministry. Robson's Orthodox supporters in the meeting were able to have the denunciation removed from the minutes, although not without some challenge. Robson wrote about the commotion after Andrew Scofield, a member of the meeting, informed her that the minute had been deleted. She declared, "they would not be able to wipe the disgrace of it from their minds:—stating in a feeling manner, what I had given up to visit them." Orthodox Friends extended their "pity and sympathy." Robson offered an interesting gendered assessment of her experience: "It is remarkable that the Virginians and Marylanders pride themselves on their good and gentlemanly behaviour; but this showed a total disregard even of common delicacy for men friends to bring forward a woman friend—a stranger to their meeting—without even acquainting the individual of their dissatisfaction, on account of the thing of which she was accused; letting the women know nothing of it." Women, too, spoke out against the meddling of the British ministers, again making use of meeting structures to register their discontent. This was the case when Martha Smith and Elizabeth Robson both attended the Byberry Monthly Meeting on the outskirts of Philadelphia. Smith "undertook to find fault with the clerk's minute respecting my services being comforting to many minds, saying that few expressed it."[52]

After the British Friends had returned home, American Hicksite Friends remained resentful of the transatlantic meddling. One cannot help but wonder whether the predominance of women's voices among the transatlantic ministers heightened the resentment of Hicksite men. New York Hicksite minister Sunderland P. Gardner classified the efforts of British ministers as "a palpable case of foreign interference" and equated the events leading to the separation to those that precipitated the American Revolution. At the time of the separation, at the 1828 NYYM, he reflected, "Being present, it seemed to me that London Yearly Meeting assumed authority as manifested by their numerous ministers here at that time, to endeavor to exercise a power over the Yearly Meetings in America in religious matters, similar to that exercised by the English Government politically toward the colonies, which they could not bear, and hence the revolution; the coincidence was clearly seen."[53] After the schism, the LYM formally severed its connection with Hicksite Friends. Informally, relationships continued with British ministers who unofficially visited Hicksites when they traveled in North America. Even though the connection between the LYM and Orthodox Friends continued, it was significantly weakened. While this was a small group of women (and men), its impact was substantial. With their own community torn apart and aware of their doctrinal similarities with other religious groups, Quakers created links with members of the larger society, and the activism of reshaping the Society of Friends was refocused into an activism that sought to reform the larger society.

NOTES

1. See esp. H. Larry Ingle, *Quakers in Conflict: The Hicksite Reformation* (Knoxville: University of Tennessee Press, 1986; reprint, Wallingford, PA: Pendle Hill Publications, 1998); Thomas D. Hamm, *The Transformation of American Quakerism: Orthodox Friends, 1800–1907* (Bloomington: Indiana University Press, 1988); Thomas D. Hamm, *Liberal Quakerism in America in the Long Nineteenth Century, 1790–1920* (Leiden: Brill, 2020).

2. Alson D. Van Wagner and Hugh Barbour, "Reunion," in *Quaker Crosscurrents: Three Hundred Years of Friends in the New York Yearly Meetings*, edited by Hugh Barbour, Christopher Densmore, Elizabeth H. Moger, Nancy C. Sorel, Alson D. Van Wagner, and Arthur J. Worrall (Syracuse: Syracuse University Press, 1995), 257–75.

3. LYM Minutes, May 27, 1828, quoted in Edwin B. Bronner, *"The Other Branch": London Yearly Meeting and the Hicksites, 1827–1912* (London: Friends Historical Society, 1975), 8.

4. Bronner, "Other Branch," 17–59. For theological shifts in the LYM in the early twentieth century, see Joanna Dales, *The Quaker Renaissance and Liberal Quakerism in Britain, 1895–1930: Seeking a Real Religion* (Leiden: Brill, 2020).

5. See, for instance, Janis Calvo, "Quaker Women Ministers in Nineteenth Century America," *Quaker History* 63, no. 2 (1974): 75–93; Nancy A. Hewitt, "The Fragmentation of Friends: The Consequences for Quaker Women in Antebellum America," in *Witnesses for Change: Quaker Women over Three Centuries*, edited by Elizabeth Potts Brown and Susan Mosher Stuard (New Brunswick: Rutgers University Press, 1989), 93–108; Robynne Rogers Healey, *From Quaker to Upper Canadian: Faith and Community Among Yonge Street Friends, 1800–1850* (Montreal: McGill-Queen's University Press, 2006), 133–68; Thomas D. Hamm, "Quakerism, Ministry, Marriage, and Divorce: The Ordeal of Priscilla Hunt Cadwalader," *Journal of the Early Republic* 28, no. 3 (2008): 407–31; Nancy A. Hewitt, *Radical Friend: Amy Kirby Post and Her Activist Worlds* (Chapel Hill: University of North Carolina Press, 2018), 15–45; Janet Moore Lindman, "'Deluded Women' and 'Violent Men': Women, Gender, and Language in the Hicksite Schism," *Quaker History* 109, no. 1 (2020): 1–26.

6. Bronner, "Other Branch," 5–6. See also Edward H. Milligan, "Robson [née Stephenson], Elizabeth, 1771–1843," in *Oxford Dictionary of National Biography* (Oxford: Oxford University Press, 2004), https://doi.org/10.1093/ref:odnb/47058.

7. Nancy A. Hewitt, Margaret Hope Bacon, Christopher Densmore, Thomas D. Hamm, Sabron Reynolds Newton, Katherine Sorel, and Alson D. Van Wagner, "Women's Rights and Roles," in Barbour et al., *Quaker Crosscurrents*, 169–70.

8. See Sandra Stanley Holton, *Quaker Women: Personal Life, Memory, and Radicalism in the Lives of Women Friends, 1780–1930* (London: Routledge, 2007).

9. Helen Plant, "'Subjective Testimonies': Women Quaker Ministers and Spiritual Authority in England, 1750–1825," *Gender and History* 15, no. 2 (2003): 298.

10. Lindman, "'Deluded Women' and 'Violent Men,'" 6, 19.

11. Dale A. Johnson, "From Pilgrimage to Discipleship: Quaker Women's Ministries in Nineteenth-Century England," *Quaker History* 91, no. 2 (2002): 20–26.

12. Helen Plant, "Patterns and Practices of Women's Leadership in the Yorkshire Quaker Community, 1760–1820," *Quaker Studies* 10, no. 2 (2006): 229.

13. Quoted in Johnson, "From Pilgrimage to Discipleship," 19–20.

14. Hugh Barbour, Thomas Bassett, Christopher Densmore, H. Larry Ingle, and Alson D. Van Wagner, "The Orthodox-Hicksite Separation," in Barbour et al., *Quaker Crosscurrents*, 116.

15. Thomas D. Hamm and Isaac Barnes May, "Conflict and Transformation, 1808–1920," in *The Cambridge Companion to Quakerism*, edited by Stephen W. Angell and Pink Dandelion (Cambridge: Cambridge University Press, 2018), 31–48.

16. Bronner, *"Other Branch,"* 7.

17. Joseph Joshua Green, "Notes for a Memoir of Elizabeth Robson," Joseph Joshua Green Papers, TEMP MSS 365/1/1, LSF.

18. Ibid.; "A Testimony from Hardshaw West Monthly Meeting Concerning Elizabeth Robson, Deceased," in *Testimonies Concerning Deceased Ministers* (London: Edward Marsh, 1844), 9–15.

19. Elizabeth Robson, "Diary of Elizabeth Robson, 1824–28," Thomas and Elizabeth Robson Manuscripts, MS vol. S 133, LSF.

20. Henry Robson's manuscript journal is in MS vol. S 129–54, LSF.

21. The first of Henry Robson's notes falls on a page numbered 352 (though the small notebook begins at p. 332), and the second at the end of the small volume on an unnumbered page. MS vol. S 147, LSF.

22. Green, "Notes for a Memoir of Elizabeth Robson."

23. Green's manuscript "Elizabeth Robson, 1770–1843" is in the Joseph Joshua Green Papers, TEMP MSS 365/17, LSF. Green got the year of her birth wrong; Robson was born in 1771.

24. Ibid., 3.

25. Green, "Notes for a Memoir of Elizabeth Robson."

26. Joseph Joshua Green, "Biographies in Verse—Thomas and Elizabeth Robson," Joseph Joshua Green Papers, MS box R1/10, LSF.

27. J. Bevan Braithwaite, *Memoirs of Anna Braithwaite, Being a Sketch of Her Early Life and Ministry, and Extracts from Her Private Memoranda, 1830–59* (London: Headley Brothers, 1905).

28. In a footnote in his 1975 work *"The Other Branch,"* Edwin Bronner comments, "Her journals for the four years of ministry and travel [in North America] are very illuminating and should be made available to a broader audience, perhaps through an extended article" (7n2).

29. Green, "Biographies in Verse," 36–37.

30. Quoted in Milligan, "Robson [née Stephenson], Elizabeth."

31. Elizabeth Robson to her daughter Elizabeth Robson, May 6, 1834, "Letters from Elizabeth Robson to Her Family, 1811–1843," Joseph Joshua Green Papers, MSS 365/1/8, LSF.

32. Plant, "Subjective Testimonies," 301.

33. "Diary of Elizabeth Robson, 1824–28," July 27, 1828, Thomas and Elizabeth Robson Manuscripts, MS vol. S 133, LSF. All spelling as in original.

34. Hamm, "Quakerism, Ministry, Marriage, and Divorce," 408.

35. See, for instance, "Diary of Elizabeth Robson," list of meetings visited 1824–25, MS vol. S 132; "Letters and Lists of Meetings, 1824–28," MS vol. S 134; and "List of Families Visited by Elizabeth Robson Belonging to Philadelphia Yearly Meeting," MS vol. S 136, Thomas and Elizabeth Robson Manuscripts, LSF.

36. "Elizabeth Robson's American Journeys," 4:139–41, MS vol. 32, LSF.

37. Plant, "Subjective Testimonies," 303.

38. Elizabeth Robson to unknown recipient, February 7, 1825, "Letters and Lists of Meetings," Thomas and Elizabeth Robson Manuscripts, MS vol. S 134, LSF. The recipient was probably Nicholas Brown or Peter Lossing, as the letter was written as Robson was at the end of her tour in Upper Canada.

39. Plant, "Subjective Testimonies," 306.

40. "Elizabeth Robson's American Journeys," 4:58.

41. Esther French to Thomas Robson, May 19, 1826, ibid., 4:47 (emphasis added).

42. Elizabeth Robson to Thomas Robson, June 17, 1826, ibid., 4:69.

43. Plant, "Subjective Testimonies," 299.

44. Frances Thompson to Elizabeth Robson, August 7 and 8, 1826, "Elizabeth Robson's American Journeys," 4:144.

45. "Diary of Elizabeth Robson, 1824–28," July 27, 1828.

46. "Elizabeth Robson's American Journeys," 4:16, 19, 24, 31, 33, 55.

47. See, for instance, ibid., 4:23, 31, 53, 57, 60, 63.

48. Ibid., 4:23.

49. Lindman, "'Deluded Women' and 'Violent Men,'" 19.

50. "Elizabeth Robson's American Journeys," 4:52.

51. Ibid., 4:29, 50, 138d.

52. Ibid., 4:20–21, 38.

53. Sunderland P. Gardner, *Memoirs of the Life and Religious Labors of Sunderland P. Gardner* (Philadelphia: Friends' Book Association, 1895), 283–85.

CHAPTER 3

Women in the World of George W. Taylor
The Public and Private Worlds of Orthodox Quaker Women

JULIE L. HOLCOMB

From 1845 to 1867, the Philadelphia merchant George W. Taylor was one of the most active Quakers in the transatlantic boycott of goods produced by slave labor, best known for his work with the Free Produce Association of Friends of Philadelphia Yearly Meeting (PYM), his long-running free-produce store at the corner of Fifth and Cherry Streets in Philadelphia, and his editorship of the *Non-Slaveholder*, an antislavery newspaper dedicated to the free-produce cause. In his free-produce work, Taylor relied on an extensive network of Quakers, friends, and family throughout the mid-Atlantic region and beyond. Of the nearly twelve hundred extant letters written by Taylor between 1825 and 1891, more than one thousand were written between 1847 and 1867, when Taylor's free-produce store was in operation. An additional four hundred extant letters were written to Taylor; of these, more than half were written between 1847 and 1867.[1] These letters are evidence of the active epistolary relationship Taylor maintained with the members of his personal and professional network. Although this network intensified in the 1840s, after Taylor opened his free-produce store, it still relied on established connections with family and Friends. Indeed, Taylor worked with many of his most important supporters in other endeavors long before he became involved in the free-produce movement.

This chapter explores the lives of the four most important women in Taylor's network. As it happens, all four women were named Elizabeth. To avoid confusion, I use their birth name and their married name: Elizabeth Magee Richards (maternal grandmother), Elizabeth Richards Taylor (mother), Elizabeth Taylor Whitson (sister), and Elizabeth Sykes Taylor (wife). An examination of their relationships with Taylor and other Quakers and non-Quakers, as well as with one another, sheds light on the permeable boundary between the public and private spheres and broadens our understanding of the relationship between Quaker women, especially Orthodox Quaker women, and the reform movements of the nineteenth century.

The four women profiled here are relatively unknown. Their interior lives are not preserved in journals. Of the four, only three—mother, sister, and wife—left behind a small body of letters. None of the four was recognized as a minister by the Society of Friends, and none held a leadership role in the benevolent or reform associations of the period. To put it simply, all four were ordinary Quaker women.

Only one of the four women, Elizabeth Taylor Whitson, participated in the antislavery societies of the antebellum period. Indeed, sister Elizabeth is an outlier among these four women. With her marriage to Moses Whitson in 1828, Elizabeth joined the Hicksites, the only member of her immediate family to do so. Four years later, in December 1832, Elizabeth and Moses, along with Moses's brother Thomas, helped form the Clarkson Anti-Slavery Society (CASS). The first local antislavery society in Chester County, Pennsylvania, the CASS was organized out of the Free Produce Society of Chester County. In 1838, the CASS organized the Requited Labor Convention, a national gathering in Philadelphia that resulted in the formation of the American Free Produce Association. Thomas Whitson also helped found the American Anti-Slavery Society in 1833. Moses and Thomas, and by implication Elizabeth, were also active in the Underground Railroad, aiding enslaved individuals who had fled north seeking freedom.[2] Despite their status as Hicksite Quakers, Elizabeth and her husband and children remained close and beloved members of the Taylor family, connections that remained strong even after Elizabeth's death in 1844.[3] It is for this reason that she is included in this chapter alongside her grandmother, mother, and sister-in-law.

The women in Taylor's world lived in a period of significant change in American society and in the Quaker community. In the early nineteenth century, a new economic order took hold, one based on large-scale manufacturing and trade, competition, consumption, and cash exchange. This so-called "market revolution" influenced the development of new ideas about gender, home, and work. Although more prescriptive than descriptive, these ideas were used to justify a distinction between the private world of the home, where women held sway, and the public world of business, where men held power and influence. Women were increasingly described as economic dependents who contributed nothing to the household economy.[4] For Quaker women, these economic changes and new gender ideals were also influenced by a series of divisions among American Quakers that reshaped their religious beliefs and social practices. Scholars such as Nancy Hewitt have explored the impact of the schisms on Quaker women and have found that among Hicksite Quaker women, division provided opportunities for female Friends "to reassert their rights and powers in the ministry and meetings of the Hicksite and Progressive Friends and, for some, to assume real prominence alongside men." Hicksite Quaker women like Lucretia Mott and Amy Kirby Post publicly advocated for the rights of women as well as the abolition of slavery. Orthodox Quaker women were noticeably absent from the reform movements of the period.[5] However, if we broaden our exploration of Orthodox Quaker women to focus more closely on their domestic labors, we find that the work of women like Elizabeth Richards Taylor and Elizabeth Sykes Taylor had a broader impact than first thought. Like the British Quaker women in Anna Vaughan Kett's chapter in this volume, the Taylor women routinely traversed the boundary between the private and public spheres. Taking these four women each in turn—uncovering their biographical details, their experience, and their relationships with Taylor and with one another—this chapter explores the lives of four Elizabeths in the world of George W. Taylor to better understand the experience of Quaker women in the first half of the nineteenth century and the ways they supported the reform movements of the period.

THREE GENERATIONS OF ELIZABETHS

Elizabeth Magee Richards (Maternal Grandmother)
Elizabeth Magee was born in Maryland in 1737, the daughter of Adam and Ann (Nichols) Magee.[6] Adam Magee was the son of wealthy Irish Protestants Thomas and Elizabeth "Betty" Magee. According to family history, the

Magees were so wealthy that their neighbors in Ireland "remarked they did not see what Betty Magee wanted more unless it should be a coach & six." Thomas and Betty had twenty-two children. Their eldest son, William, migrated to the North American colonies first. Settling in New Jersey, William sent home such glowing accounts of life in colonial America that his parents chose to migrate. Thomas and Betty Magee settled in Carlisle, Pennsylvania, where Adam and Ann joined them after the birth of their daughter Elizabeth. After Adam's death in 1750, Ann and her children moved to Chester County, Pennsylvania, where Elizabeth met David Richards, grandson of Penn land grantee John Richards, who had emigrated from Wales in the 1680s. In 1746, after their father died, David and two of his brothers received a portion of their grandfather's extensive landholdings in Radnor.[7]

Elizabeth and David married in Old Swedes' Church in Philadelphia in 1758. Marrying out of the Society of Friends placed David in conflict with his monthly meeting. In September 1759, one month after the birth of his son Abishai, David submitted a statement acknowledging his regret in marrying contrary to Quaker discipline. It was not David's first time to come before the meeting; two years earlier, Thomas Massey had brought a complaint against David for an unpaid debt. In 1760, David was restored to membership, but in 1763, he once again faced the elders of Radnor Monthly Meeting, this time for "drinking to excess and fighting." When David refused to admit and condemn his misbehavior, the meeting disowned him.[8] How Elizabeth felt about David's disownment is unknown.

David's ongoing conflict with the Society of Friends in the 1750s and 1760s was part of a broader change among Quakers in this period. Concerned that Quakers were drifting away from their core values, the Society of Friends began stepping up enforcement of the Quaker Discipline, including their rules pertaining to marriage. In the mid-eighteenth century, marriage delinquency—marrying a non-Quaker or having the marriage conducted by a priest—was the most common reason for disciplinary action. In the period when Elizabeth and David were married (1756–60), 53 percent of Friends who were disowned were cast out for exogamous marriage. By 1775, that number had increased to 75 percent. Drunkenness was the third most frequently reported Quaker delinquency. Disownment was not the same as excommunication, however. Within the Society of Friends, disownment meant that the individual could not participate in the business meeting or serve on committees. Those who had been disowned could still attend meeting for worship. Disownment also meant that the children of the disowned were not considered birthright Quakers.[9]

Elizabeth and David had nine children. The eldest, Abishai (1759), was permanently crippled at birth, a result of the "bad management of the women in attendance," according to one family document. Eight other children followed, at two-year intervals: John (1762), Anna (1764), Ann (1766), Davis (1768), Jonathan (1770), Hannah (1772), Jacob (1774), and Elizabeth (1776). In 1769, three-year-old Ann had an accident or illness that left her an invalid until her death in 1846. In a seventeen-year time span, Elizabeth gave birth to at least nine children, cared for two children who suffered debilitating injuries, and buried three children, including two in 1777. The events of this period had a lasting effect on Elizabeth. Her grandson George later recalled how she spoke often of her son John, who died in 1777 at the age of fifteen, and "of his good qualities," grieving so much that John sometimes appeared in her dreams.[10]

In 1777, as the Richardses dealt with the loss of two of their children, larger political events threatened the family. As the American Revolution shifted to the mid-Atlantic region, Pennsylvania Quakers faced increasing pressure to support the patriot cause. In September 1777, thirty men were arrested by the patriot government on suspicion of treason. Most were Quaker pacifists. Ten of the prisoners took an oath of "allegiance to the Commonwealth of Pennsylvania as a free and independent state" and secured their freedom. The other twenty, including nineteen Quakers, among them the wealthy Quaker merchant Henry Drinker, refused to take the oath and remained in prison. The men were exiled to Winchester, Virginia, for seven months.[11]

Living in Radnor, just outside Philadelphia, the Richards family would have been in the path of both armies as the British marched into Philadelphia. Their connection to the Quaker community would have made their loyalties suspect on both sides of the conflict. Given the significance of this period in the family's history, it is curious that the Richards family histories in the Taylor family papers make no mention of the war or its impact on Elizabeth, David, and their children. As historian Richard Godbeer notes in his history of the Drinker family, "That Henry and Elizabeth survived to tell their story was not a foregone conclusion, and their journey left deep scars."[12]

Elizabeth Richards Taylor (Mother)

Elizabeth Richards and Jacob Taylor were married in 1802 in Radnor. Taylor was one of ten children born to Francis and Eve Fisler Taylor, immigrants from England and Holland, respectively. The Taylors were not members of the Society of Friends. Elizabeth and Jacob had seven children: George (1803), Elizabeth (1805), Mary (1806), Thomas (1809), Joanna (1812), Ruthanna (1814), and Jacob (1819). The Taylor household also included Elizabeth's widowed mother and her invalid sister, Ann.[13]

In 1808, the Taylors moved from Radnor to East Caln, where Jacob had purchased a farm and store. Four years later, Jacob sold his property and purchased more than one hundred acres of land in New Garden, located several miles south of East Caln. Located along the new turnpike road, Jacob's purchase included a general store and a tavern. The move from East Caln to New Garden required several teams to haul the family's goods. Nine-year-old George helped drive the livestock while his sisters Elizabeth and Mary helped their younger brother and their mother, who had just given birth to Joanna. For Jacob, the New Garden purchase was a significant financial investment of nearly $7,000 (about $150,000 today). He hoped the purchase would provide his family with security and keep his sons close to home. Nearly all the children attended nearby Quaker day schools. George studied with Enoch Lewis in New Garden, while Elizabeth, Joanna, and Ruthanna attended Westtown Boarding School in rural Chester County.[14]

In New Garden, grandmother, mother, and daughter, along with the rest of the family, helped with the work of the farm and in the store. Jacob also served as postmaster during this period. In her study of mid-Atlantic farm women, historian Joan M. Jensen identifies three spheres of farm women's labor: the household, the domestic production sphere, and the public sphere of religious, educational, and reform activities. "Because these women worked in three spheres, their culture became rich, dense, and intricate," Jensen claims. "It bound them to husband, children, neighbor, market, and to other women. But the changing culture also loosened those bonds."[15] The letters of Elizabeth Richards Taylor capture her many and varied labors: caring for the aging members of the family; receiving and tending to visitors, both family and Friends; clothing her family; caring for those who came to help when it was time to harvest the wheat or butcher the hogs; supervising the hired help, whether in the home or in the store; and tending to the spiritual needs of her family, especially her children.[16]

Elizabeth Richards Taylor oversaw her children's religious education. In East Caln, she took her children to Methodist services at the home of Elizabeth and Thomas Batten, Jacob's sister and brother-in-law. Thomas Batten and his father were well-known Methodist ministers who conducted "zealous" services with a "great deal of loud weeping and telling of experiences, with much contrition," according to George. During one service, Elizabeth wept so much that she frightened her young son, who began to cry loudly. Elizabeth took him outside, calmed him down, and then returned to the service. Elizabeth may also have attended Quaker meetings in East Caln. In New Garden, she requested membership in the New Garden Monthly Meeting for herself and her children. Although Jacob and his mother-in-law did not make a similar request, both attended meeting for worship with Elizabeth and the children.[17]

George described his grandmother and his mother as "pious" women. "I well remember her tender care and solicitude for me and my brothers & sisters," he wrote of his grandmother. "We loved her almost as if she were our mother." Elizabeth Richards Taylor, George wrote, was "of gentle & lovely disposition, truly conscientious & pious. . . . She labored much for [her] children's spiritual and temporal welfare and earnestly guarded their morals and strove to improve their minds with love to their Creator and Saviour and their accountability for all their actions & thoughts."[18]

Elizabeth Taylor Whitson (Sister)
Like her siblings, Elizabeth Taylor, the eldest daughter of Jacob and Elizabeth, assisted with the work of the home and farm. The Taylor children grew up in a period of changing ideas about gender and sibling relationships. Brothers and sisters were encouraged to spend more time with one another and confide in one another. Gender differences were increasingly acknowledged, as was a clear ethic of gender difference. Although older brothers like George remained important and were expected to aid their younger siblings and help their parents raise and educate them, the prescriptive literature that began to appear in the 1830s emphasized the importance of the elder sister as sibling leader and parental advisor.[19] Born just two years apart, George and Elizabeth were especially close. Although their correspondence slowed after Elizabeth's marriage to Moses Whitson,

a surveyor and conveyancer from nearby Sadsbury, brother and sister remained close.

HICKSITE-ORTHODOX SCHISM

In 1826, George accepted a teaching position at the Quaker school for boys in Flushing, Long Island. The school was run by Lindley Murray Moore, who, before moving to Flushing, had taught at Nine Partners Boarding School and the Friends' Monthly Meeting School on the grounds of the meetinghouse on Pearl Street, both in New York City. Moore was married to Abigail Mott, niece of the well-known Quaker minister Richard Mott. Moore's daughter Ann M. Haines said of Moore, "He was a Friend by birth and conviction, a great lover of the Bible, and very familiar with it. He rarely failed to give chapter and verse to any one who asked where to find Scripture passages; he was, nevertheless, untinged by sectarianism, and always took a strong interest in everything that would advance the cause of Christ in every denomination."[20]

For George, the move to Flushing brought significant change and stress. He had never traveled so far from home; prior to his move to Flushing, Taylor had ventured only as far as Wilmington, Delaware, where he taught in the school operated by his teacher and mentor Enoch Lewis. Taylor was offered the position in Flushing as a result of a recommendation from Joshua Kimber, who operated the girls' school in Flushing. Unlike his experience in Wilmington, Taylor did not have a previous relationship with Moore. Taylor's move to Flushing also came at a time of great dissension among American Quakers, as outlined in this book's introduction. The Quaker community in New Garden was strongly Hicksite, while the community in Flushing was strongly Orthodox. Not surprisingly, George's transition to Flushing was difficult, and he relied upon the support of his family, especially his grandmother, mother, and sister.[21]

Letters from Elizabeth Richards Taylor and Elizabeth Taylor Whitson connected George to family, friends, and Quakers in New Garden, serving as stand-ins for the conversations they probably had when all were living together. Significantly, the women reinforced George's sense of self by reminding him where he came from and how much he mattered to those closest to him. Their letters often ended the same way, expressing greetings from other family members: "Our family all as if named send a great deal of love to thee, Mother particularly"; "Father & Mother, Grandmother and all the rest of the family as if individually named send their love to thee"; "Our family all send their love." In one letter, Elizabeth Taylor Whitson told George, "Mother is very frequently speaking of thee and often says as we're sitting alone, how comfortable it would be if George would unexpectedly step in, we would hardly place bounds in talking with him."[22]

During a visit home in 1827, George asked his grandmother to narrate the history of the Richards family. In her narrative, Elizabeth Magee Richards reminded George of his connection to the Quaker origins of Pennsylvania through his ancestor John Richards. She also emphasized the wealth and importance of the Magee family. In the summer of 1828, Elizabeth Magee Richards's health declined rapidly. George, unable to return home in time, received updates from his sister and mother. "Grandmother is yet with us," Elizabeth Taylor Whitson wrote on August 2. Her letter included a list of aunts, uncles, and cousins who had come to pay their respects. On August 7, Elizabeth Richards Taylor wrote George of the "death of my dear and aged mother." Her letter also listed the family members who had been in attendance. Elizabeth lamented that they had not received George's letter in time to read it to his grandmother before her death. Elizabeth concluded with a message from grandmother to grandson: "I asked if she had any thing she wisht me to tell thee. . . . She said give my dear and sincere love to him."[23]

In her letters, Elizabeth Taylor Whitson often included news of the neighborhood and of family and Friends. She described visits that she, her siblings, and her parents had made to other family members and the visits of family and Friends to the Taylor home: "Thomas is at Uncle [Thomas Batten] assisting him"; "Aunt E. Batten paid a visit here today"; "Father and Mother went to Wilmington . . . they intended going by Jasher's"; "Mary & Elizabeth Maule have been spending several weeks in New Garden." Elizabeth also shared news gleaned from the letters of others: "sister Mary is very ill"; "I received a letter from S. Williamson . . . they were all well." Elizabeth listed who had married or would be married soon.[24]

For a young man struggling with homesickness and spiritual questions, the connection to home helped ease the pain of separation. Letters also provided an opportunity for the family, especially brother and sister, to share news about various Quaker meetings in Pennsylvania and New York, to discuss the ministry of the British Quaker ministers who were traveling in the United States in this period, to weigh the accuracy of described events, and to consider which path each should take if division should occur. In late

1826, Elizabeth described for her brother Elias Hicks's meeting at Wilmington. Several neighbors had heard him speak and "returned very much in favour of his doctrine believing all that had been slightly spoken of him was false." In another letter, Elizabeth asked George about a rumor that the British minister Anna Braithwaite was moving to Philadelphia. As George began to drift away from Hicks and toward the Orthodox views espoused by Moore and others in Flushing, Elizabeth warned her brother to be more circumspect in sharing his anti-Hicksite views outside the family: "I would be careful in expressing many sentiments that I did not wish exposed ... to any of thy correspondents in New Garden.... [Jeremiah Starr] was telling me ... that thee was an <u>Orthodox</u> stating what thee had mentioned.... Thee [must] be aware of who thee places confidence in." Elizabeth and George disagreed about a sermon that the British minister Ann Jones had delivered at Rose Street Meeting in New York. Elizabeth described it as "dreadful," "wicked," and "of great hurt to the cause she says she supports," while George defended Jones, explaining that he "did not consider it so very pointed as some would have it."[25] Ultimately, George chose the Orthodox path, while Elizabeth went Hicksite. But their differing Quaker views seemed to have little impact on their relationship.

Elizabeth Sykes Taylor (Wife)
In 1823, Elizabeth Sykes, a Quaker from Burlington, New Jersey, accepted a position at Westtown Boarding School. Born in 1790 in Springfield, New Jersey, Sykes was the youngest of three daughters born to Benjamin and Hannah Leeds Sykes. Benjamin's father, John Sykes, traveled with Quaker minister and reformer John Woolman to Maryland in 1748. Years later, the two men were appointed to a committee of five ministers charged with visiting slaveholding families in the Delaware Valley after the PYM renounced Quaker slaveholding. After the deaths of her sister Rebecca in 1799, her father in 1802, and her mother in 1814, Elizabeth and her surviving sister, Hannah, took up residence with Peter and Abigail Barker.[26]

Benjamin Hallowell, who taught at Westtown from 1821 through 1824, had hired Elizabeth as the boys' parlor keeper. "There was no woman on the boys' side of the house to exert a favorable influence upon them," Hallowell recalled. "I had felt a concern for some time that the boys should have a parlor on their end, with a suitable matron to whom the little boys could go and get a cut finger wrapped up, and who could fix their collars, smooth their hair, and produce a humanizing, civilizing, and motherly influence upon them generally." The parlor, which was comfortably furnished, was strategically located so "all boys had to pass its door to go either upstairs to bed or downstairs to meals." For her part, Elizabeth enjoyed the "little world" that was Westtown, although she dearly missed her friends in Burlington. "Tis not an easy thing to get wean'd from Burlington," Elizabeth wrote her close friend Sybil Allinson. "Indeed I never expect to be.... My friends here ask me if I do not intend to bring my certificate [to transfer her membership from Burlington Monthly Meeting] but it seems as if I could not bring my mind to it yet."[27]

Founded in 1799 by the members of the PYM, Westtown was not from the beginning an Orthodox school. However, in the 1820s, the pro-Hicksite behavior of some of the students at Westtown may have frightened some teachers into supporting Orthodox ideas, while other, Hicksite-leaning instructors and committee members left the institution altogether. Benjamin Hallowell resigned in 1824. His sister, Mary, left in 1826 because of "her uneasiness at remaining in a place where her opinions were not those of the majority." John Buntin, an elder of Darby Monthly Meeting, resigned from the Westtown Boarding School Committee, which included prominent Orthodox Quakers Samuel Bettle, Jonathan Evans, and Evans's son William.[28]

Elizabeth worried about the state of things at Westtown. "It is a very low time with me," she told her friend Sybil, and with "discouragements from within and without, I mourn over myself. I mourn over our poor desolate society." Elizabeth had "serious thoughts of leaving" after an incident in April 1827 involving several boys who refused to comply with the school's rules for reading scripture. British Quaker minister Stephen Gould described the event as an "insurrection." The teachers used every means "by argument & persuasion to convince [the boys] of the impropriety of the course they were pursuing," Gould wrote, "but they persisted urging their right to freedom of opinion, calling the New Testament the 'Popes Book,' till they began to cut up their Bibles & burn the New Testament." The teachers called a meeting of the Westtown Boarding School Committee, "who also used persuasion & argument," Gould noted, "but all proving unavailing." According to Gould, on a recent visit to the school, Hicks had told the students "there was but one New Testament in the world for some Hundreds of years after the Christian era & that was in the Hands of the Pope." The committee's minutes of the incident noted "the prevalency of a spirit of insubordination and resistance of the salutary regulations in the school." The board condemned "the lamentable situation of the boys, and their conduct in rejecting and destroying the Bible, and in attempts made by some amongst them to bring the Holy Scriptures into contempt & ridicule." After the incident, a satisfactory visit from the school committee encouraged Elizabeth to "stay a while longer."[29]

In 1830, at the prompting of his former teacher Enoch Lewis, who was a member of the Westtown Boarding School Committee, George accepted a position at Westtown teaching grammar, history, mathematics, and philosophy. He appears to have been a popular teacher among the students.[30] "We had a lecture last evening and we were all charmed and smitten with our lecturer," wrote Westtown student Hannah Richard in 1830. "He is the most elegant man I have seen lately. His name is George Taylor and he made out extremely well considering it was the first time he had ever made such an exhibition."[31] George also made out "extremely well" with the boys' parlor keeper; the two were married the following year. Unfortunately, the extant correspondence gives no clue as to what drew Elizabeth to George. Elizabeth was thirteen years older than he—forty to his twenty-seven. A birthright Quaker, Elizabeth had close relationships with many important Quaker families, including the Allinsons and the Gummeres. In 1831, Elizabeth and George visited the Burlington Quaker druggist William J. Allinson, nephew of Elizabeth's close friend Sybil: "Eliz[abet]h Sykes and her beloved Geo. Taylor took tea with us—he is a very interesting man."[32]

Elizabeth and George were married at the Friends meetinghouse in Burlington in September 1831. They stood before the meeting and vowed to be "loving and faithful." Elizabeth did not pledge obedience because the Quaker marriage ceremony did not include such a promise. Elizabeth and George shared a close emotional connection throughout their marriage. Their union was framed by the egalitarianism of Quaker marriage and the patriarchal relationship established by American common law that made George Elizabeth's legal, financial, and political protector. For Elizabeth and George, however, marriage was a partnership of man and woman, "joined together, not by lust or economic coercion, but as comrades seeking humanity's greater good." Although Elizabeth did not assume as public a role as George did, she was nonetheless a partner with him in his various reform and business enterprises.[33]

For Elizabeth, marriage brought a welcome return to her beloved Burlington, where she introduced George to the inner circle of the Burlington Quaker community. In October 1831, George assumed responsibility for the

Friends' Preparative Meeting School, which was located on the original site of the school run by Samuel Gummere, the son-in-law of Peter and Abigail Barker. George and Elizabeth operated the school for two years. George's brothers Thomas and Jacob joined George and Elizabeth in 1832; Thomas helped with teaching responsibilities while Jacob was a student at the school.[34]

By late 1832, exhausted by his duties in running the school, George began to consider other options. He and his brother Thomas discussed the possibility of opening a temperance grocery. A temperance grocery distinguished itself as a family grocery, which might sell liquor but, unlike more nefarious grocers, did not serve it to customers. Black abolitionists William Whipper and David Ruggles operated temperance groceries in Philadelphia and New York, respectively, in this period. Elizabeth Richards Taylor weighed in on her sons' deliberations, suggesting several options, including sites in Philadelphia and West Chester. Elizabeth Sykes Taylor dismissed an opportunity in Mount Joy, Pennsylvania, because it was too far from "any settlement of Friends." Elizabeth told her husband, "It would never do to give up the Society of Friends as we undoubtedly would have to do if we should go to M.J."[35] After several months of searching without success, the brothers gave up the idea. George and Elizabeth moved to Philadelphia, where George had accepted a position as agent for the Bible Association of Friends, and Thomas returned to Chester County, where he opened a store near Coatesville.

In Philadelphia, as in Burlington, Elizabeth supervised the household and assisted George with his work. Her responsibilities were as varied as George's many enterprises. She prepared invoices and presented Bibles to young Quakers, assisted George in his work with the Friends' Reading Room Association, and advised him on hiring employees. For example, in 1846, a new employee whom George had hired led both his mother and his wife to raise concerns. "Thee knows thy father & I have had a long experience in the business," Elizabeth Richards Taylor wrote; "we both say we never would have been willing to put him in the Store to manage the business." Elizabeth Sykes Taylor added her own objections: "I find the principal objection to Cyrus is his want of qualification for business. . . . He is a very poor accountant. . . . It is very important for thee to have a well qualified person." For emphasis, Elizabeth added, "The prospect of thy having him is very unpleasant to Mother; and judging from the past I think it would be well to have regard to her judgment."[36]

Elizabeth also aided George's publishing duties for the *Friend*, the Orthodox weekly that began in 1827; the *Farmer's Cabinet*, a popular agricultural monthly; and the *Non-Slaveholder*, an antislavery newspaper, commenting on content in the papers he published. For example, in 1846, Elizabeth criticized George's decision to include an obituary of Daniel Neall, a Hicksite and abolitionist who had twice been the target of angry anti-abolitionist mobs. "The obituary of D Neal[l] may perhaps increase the prejudice against your paper on account of his principles—I would rather not have seen it there, but in a common newspaper."[37]

Elizabeth also assisted in more traditional ways by caring for members of George's family, including his parents and his siblings and their spouses and children. Unburdened by childbirth and child-rearing and financially able to secure domestic help to run her own home, Elizabeth could travel Chester County and elsewhere to assist. In 1835, Thomas married Margaretta Hughes. By early 1836, Margaretta was struggling with poor health and pregnancy. Elizabeth offered to bring her to Philadelphia, where she could care for her. As Margaretta's health continued to decline, Elizabeth offered to travel to Chester County to care for her. At the same time, Elizabeth Richards Taylor also fell ill, straining the family's resources. Elizabeth Sykes Taylor relieved her sisters-in-law Elizabeth and Ruthanna. For Elizabeth Taylor Whitson, her sister-in-law's assistance allowed her to return home to care for her own three children. In September 1836, Elizabeth, George, and the rest of the family rallied around Thomas as he struggled with the loss of his wife and child, the failure of his business, and his increasingly acrimonious relationship with his former in-laws. Once again, Elizabeth opened her home, encouraging Thomas to spend time in Philadelphia, where he could escape the tensions in Chester County and grieve the loss of his wife and child. In Philadelphia, Thomas went to work for the Second Bank of the United States. He remarried in 1841, wedding Mary Ann Phillips, a close friend of his sister Ruthanna's.[38]

Elizabeth and George's home often expanded and shrank as George's siblings, their spouses, and their children moved in and out of the Taylor home. For four years, George's brothers Jacob and Thomas, Thomas's wife, Mary Ann, and Thomas and Mary Ann's children shared a large home. Located at the corner of Broad and Spruce Streets in Philadelphia, the house was remodeled to meet the needs of the extended family and to provide space for Jacob's pharmaceutical business. Shared responsibilities extended beyond business and housekeeping, however. Thomas traveled frequently for work, which left Mary Ann to care for the children alone. Elizabeth and George helped with the parenting, so much so that Thomas and Mary Ann's daughters, Phebe and Elizabeth, who were born during this period, developed a close bond with their "Auntie E" and "Uncle G," as did Mary Ann. Mary Ann had six children between 1842 and 1852. Two of them, both named George W. Taylor, died in infancy. Mary Ann's mother had died in 1839, so it was Elizabeth who stepped in to help Mary Ann. Elizabeth often traveled with the girls to New Garden to visit their grandparents, providing Mary Ann a much-needed respite or time to travel to Wilmington to tend to her own aging father.[39]

Elizabeth traveled frequently to Burlington, New Garden, and beyond, visiting family and Friends. Female Quaker ministers often traveled away from home for extended periods. Although Elizabeth was not a recognized minister in the Society of Friends, her travel would not have been unusual. Elizabeth's travels created and sustained informal networks of family and Friends and promoted George's many business ventures. In 1846, for example, Elizabeth took an extended trip to Cincinnati. Her letters home to George are filled with lists of those she visited. "We are to take tea this evening at Achilles Pew's; don't thee remember he & his wife calling at our house perhaps two years ago—he thinks favourable of the Non Slaveholder," Elizabeth wrote George. "He has only seen the first number given him by S. N. Pearce. I will take him the two no's that I have." In another letter, Elizabeth commented on an account that had been published in the *Friend*. "The account . . . I suppose is correct respecting Dublin Y. M. at least as far as it goes," Elizabeth told George. "There is a friend living here, W[illia]m Bott's wife whose Father lives in Ireland, and he gave her a similar account how he or she stands I do not know." In 1847, Levi Coffin established a free-produce store in Cincinnati, purchasing goods from Taylor and other suppliers. Elizabeth's travels to the area the previous year may have nurtured the networks necessary for that venture.[40]

For George W. Taylor, family was his first and most important network. Elizabeth Magee Richards, Elizabeth Richards Taylor, Elizabeth Taylor Whitson, and Elizabeth Sykes Taylor influenced the ways in which he lived his life and conducted his business. George's grandmother and mother recounted the family's history, helping him to better understand where he came from and what his future might hold. This sense of self sustained George through the difficult years of operating his free-produce store. George in turn shared that family history and sense of identity with his nephews and nieces, who were in many ways the children he never had. From these four women, George gained an appreciation for women's private and public labors. He recognized the ways in which they maintained the informal networks that were important to his work. Even when the women who were closest to him were critical of his work, George recognized the spirit behind their comments. From these close relationships, George gained an appreciation of the varieties of religious experience. George remained an Orthodox Quaker his entire life; still, he worked comfortably across Quaker and denominational lines, probably as a result of his early experiences with grandmother, mother, and sister. Although only one of these four women, Taylor's sister, was involved in the organized reform movements of the antebellum period, all four contributed to the movement through their influence and their labor on behalf of one of the era's most active reformers.

NOTES

1. The Quaker Collection at Haverford College has the largest collection of materials related to George W. Taylor and his family, including letterpress books, account books, and hundreds of letters written by and to Taylor.
2. "Constitution of the Free Produce Society of Chester County, Pa.," *Genius of Universal Emancipation* 13 (July 1833); Julie L. Holcomb, *Moral Commerce: Quakers and the Transatlantic Boycott of the Slave Labor Economy* (Ithaca: Cornell University Press, 2016), 132, 141–46; Christopher Densmore, "'Be Ye Therefore Perfect': Anti-Slavery and the Origins of the Yearly Meeting of Progressive Friends in Chester County, Pennsylvania," *Quaker History* 93, no. 2 (2004): 30–31; George W. Taylor, *Autobiography and Writings of George W. Taylor*, edited by John Collins (Philadelphia: n.p., 1891), 30.
3. Moses Whitson Jr. to George W. Taylor, November 10, 1855, Taylor Family Papers (TFP), HC.MC-1233 (TFP 1233), HCLQSC. On family divisions, see Emma J. Lapsansky-Werner and Margaret Hope Bacon, "Benjamin Coates and the Colonization Movement in America," in *Back to Africa: Benjamin Coates and the Colonization Movement in America, 1848–1880*, edited by Emma J. Lapsansky-Werner and Margaret Hope Bacon (University Park: Penn State University Press, 2005), 11–12.
4. Jeanne Boydston, *Home and Work: Housework, Wages, and the Ideology of Labor in the Early Republic* (New York: Oxford University Press, 1990); Nancy Isenberg, *Sex and Citizenship in Antebellum America* (Chapel Hill: University of North Carolina Press, 1998); Charles Sellers, *The Market Revolution: Jacksonian America, 1815–1846* (New York: Oxford University Press, 1991).
5. Nancy A. Hewitt, "The Fragmentation of Friends: The Consequences for Quaker Women in Antebellum America," in *Witnesses for Change: Quaker Women over Three Centuries*, edited by Elizabeth Potts Brown and Susan Mosher Stuard (New Brunswick: Rutgers University Press, 1989), 103; Carol Faulkner, *Lucretia Mott's Heresy: Abolition and*

Women's Rights in Nineteenth-Century America (Philadelphia: University of Pennsylvania Press, 2011).

6. There are several variant spellings of Magee, even in the family papers. The most frequent are Megee and Meegee.

7. Elizabeth Magee Richards and George W. Taylor, "Some Account of the Richards Family as Narrated to George W. Taylor in 1827 by His Grandmother Elizabeth Richards," October 25, 1888, TFP, HC.MC-950 (TFP 950). This account is a longer version of an earlier account dated March 31, 1827, located in TFP 1233. See also Katharine Cummin, *A Rare and Pleasing Thing: Radnor Demography (1798) and Development* (Philadelphia: Owlswick Press, 1977), 152–53, 158.

8. Minutes, Radnor Monthly Meeting, March 10, 1757, September 13, 1759, October 9, 1759, February 13, 1761, March 12, 1761, April 10, 1761, May 8, 1761, June 11, 1761, July 14, 1761, August 14, 1761, September 10, 1761, October 13, 1761, May 13, 1763, June 9, 1763, July 12, 1763, August 12, 1763, December 8, 1763, and January 10, 1764, all in FHLSC.

9. Jack D. Marietta, *The Reformation of American Quakerism, 1748–1783* (Philadelphia: University of Pennsylvania Press, 1984), 5–7, 63. See also J. William Frost, *The Quaker Family in Colonial America: A Portrait of the Society of Friends* (New York: St. Martin's Press, 1973).

10. Richards and Taylor, "Some Account of the Richards Family," annotated by George W. Taylor; Elizabeth Magee Richards, "Some Account of the Richards & Megee Families, Given to Geo. W. Taylor in 1827 by His Grandmother Elizabeth Richards at His Request," March 31, 1827, TFP 1233, unpaginated; Taylor, *Autobiography and Writings*, 7–8.

11. Richard Godbeer, *World of Trouble: A Philadelphia Quaker Family's Journey Through the American Revolution* (New Haven: Yale University Press, 2019).

12. Ibid., 5.

13. Taylor, *Autobiography and Writings*, 7, 9, 11; Elizabeth Richards Taylor, "A Brief Account of the Richards Family Dictated by Elizabeth Taylor, 5 mo. 18th 1868, to Her Son Geo. W. Taylor," TFP 1233.

14. Taylor, *Autobiography and Writings*, 11; indenture made May 9, 1812, from Enoch Chandler to Jacob Taylor, New Garden Township, Deed Book G-3, 400; indenture made May 9, 1812, from John Chandler to Jacob Taylor, New Garden Township, Deed Book G-3, 401, both in Chester County Archives, West Chester, PA.

15. Joan M. Jensen, *Loosening the Bonds: Mid-Atlantic Farm Women, 1750–1850* (New Haven: Yale University Press, 1986), xiv–xv.

16. See, for example, Elizabeth Richards Taylor to George W. Taylor, August 7, 1828, TFP 1233; Elizabeth Richards Taylor to Thomas B. Taylor, November 20, 1832, TFP, HC.MC-818 (TFP 818); Elizabeth Richards Taylor to Thomas B. Taylor, March 22, 1832, TFP 818; Elizabeth Richards Taylor to George W. Taylor, March 5, 1837, TFP 1233; Elizabeth Richards Taylor to Thomas B. Taylor, January 11, 1838, TFP 1233. See also Taylor, *Autobiography and Writings*, 12.

17. George W. Taylor, "Recollections of My Life and What I Have Learned of My Ancestors," manuscript, TFP HC.MC-975 (TFP 975); New Garden Monthly Meeting Minutes, September 4, October 9, and December 1, 1817, all in FHLSC.

18. Taylor, "Recollections of My Life," unpaginated.

19. C. Dallett Hemphill, *Siblings: Brothers and Sisters in American History* (New York: Oxford University Press, 2011).

20. Quoted in Committee of the Alumni Association, *A History of Haverford College for the First Sixty Years of Its Existence* (Philadelphia: Porter and Coates, 1892), 186.

21. Holcomb, *Moral Commerce*, 81–88. See also H. Larry Ingle, *Quakers in Conflict: The Hicksite Reformation* (Knoxville: University of Tennessee Press, 1986; reprint, Wallingford, PA: Pendle Hill Publications, 1998).

22. Elizabeth Taylor Whitson to George W. Taylor, July 5, 1827, September 18, 1827, and August 2, 1828, TFP 1233.

23. Elizabeth Taylor Whitson to George W. Taylor, August 2, 1828, TFP 1233; Elizabeth Richards Taylor to George W. Taylor, August 7, 1828, TFP 1233.

24. Elizabeth Taylor Whitson to George W. Taylor, November 30, 1826, March 15, 1827, September 18, 1827, November 15, 1827, and February 2, 1828, TFP 1233.

25. Elizabeth Taylor Whitson to George W. Taylor, November 30, 1826, December 8, 1826, January 3, 1828, January 27, 1828; George W. Taylor to Jacob Taylor, January 10, 1828, TFP 1233.

26. Geoffrey Plank, *John Woolman's Path to the Peaceable Kingdom: A Quaker in the British Empire* (Philadelphia: University of Pennsylvania Press, 2012), 117; John Woolman, *The Journal and Major Essays of John Woolman*, edited by Phillips P. Moulton (Richmond, IN: Friends United Press, 1971), 95–96; Minutes, Burlington Monthly Meeting, August 6, 1798, May 2, 1799, April 27, 1802, April 3, 1814, all in FHLSC. Abigail Drinker Barker was the niece of Henry Drinker of Philadelphia.

27. Benjamin Hallowell, *Autobiography of Benjamin Hallowell*, 2nd ed. (Philadelphia: Friends' Book Association, 1884), 86; *Susanna Smedley and Anna Hartshorne Brown, comps., Catalog of Westtown Through the Years, Officers, Students, and Others, Fifth Month 1799 to Fifth Month 1945* (Westttown, PA: Westtown Alumni Association, 1945), 378; Helen G. Hole, *Westtown Through the Years, 1799–1942* (Westtown, PA: Westtown Alumni Association, 1942), 130; Elizabeth Sykes to Sybil Allinson, October 8, 1824, Westtown Boarding School Archives, West Chester, PA.

28. Margaret A. Hogan, "The Schoolhouse and the Schism: The Influence of the Hicksite Schism on Friends' Central School, Friends Select School, and Westtown Boarding School, 1827–1845" (BA thesis, Swarthmore College, 1992), 70–96.

29. Elizabeth Sykes to Sybil Allinson, May 9, 1827; Stephen Gould to Thomas Thompson, April 16, 1827; Minutes, Westtown Boarding School, April 4, 1827, all in Westtown Boarding School Archives, West Chester, PA.

30. Westtown School Committee Minutes, 1794–1840, 322, ibid.

31. Hannah Richard to Beulah Coates, November 9, [1830], Families of Philadelphia Papers, 1700–1942, HC-MC 1184, HCLQSC.

32. William J. Allinson to Bernice Allinson, ca. 1831, Allinson Family Papers, HC-MC 968, HCLQSC.

33. Taylor, *Autobiography and Writings*, 31, 36–38; marriage certificate, George Taylor and Elizabeth Sykes, TFP 1233; Faulkner, *Lucretia Mott's Heresy*, 37–38; Lewis Perry, *Childhood, Marriage, and Reform: Henry Clarke Wright, 1797–1870* (Chicago: University of Chicago Press, 1980), 255.

34. Taylor, *Autobiography and Writings*, 38–39; Ruth Ketring Nuermberger, *The Free Produce Movement: A Quaker Protest Against Slavery* (New York: AMS Press, 1942), 84; George W. Taylor, "Select Boarding School for Boys," September 1831, TFP 1233; George W. Taylor to Thomas B. Taylor, November 1 and December 24, 1831, TFP 1233; George W. Taylor to Jacob and Elizabeth Taylor, November 4, 1832, TFP 818; "Select Boarding

School for Boys, Members of the Society of Friends, at Burlington, New Jersey," *Friend*, May 5, 1832.

35. Elizabeth Richards Taylor to Thomas B. Taylor, January 5, 1833, September 13, 1833, and February 18, 1832; Elizabeth Richards Taylor to Thomas B. Taylor and George W. Taylor, November 20, 1833; Jacob and Elizabeth Taylor to Thomas B. Taylor and Jacob Taylor, January 25, 1833, all in TFP 818. See also Cindy R. Lobel, *Urban Appetites: Food and Culture in Nineteenth-Century New York* (Chicago: University of Chicago Press, 2014), 76; James Oliver Horton and Lois E. Horton, *In Hope of Liberty: Culture, Community, and Protest Among Northern Free Blacks, 1700–1860* (New York: Oxford University Press, 1997), 207, 222–23.

36. Elizabeth Richards Taylor to George W. Taylor, October 31, 1846; Elizabeth Sykes Taylor to George W. Taylor, November 7, 1846, both in TFP 818.

37. George W. Taylor to Thomas B. Taylor, February 6, 1835, TFP 1233; Elizabeth Sykes Taylor to George W. Taylor, June 13 and June 22, 1846, TFP 818; *Non-Slaveholder*, June 1846, 94; Celia Caust-Ellenbogen, "Daniel Neall, Sr.," *Quakers and Slavery*, https://web.tricolib.brynmawr.edu/speccoll/quakersandslavery/commentary/people/neall_sr.php.

38. George W. Taylor to Thomas B. Taylor, February 22, September 20, and September 23, 1836, TFP 818; George W. Taylor to Thomas B. Taylor, September 12, 1836, TFP 1233.

39. Elizabeth Sykes Taylor to George W. Taylor, July 7, 1847, December 13, 1848, and July 31, 1850, TFP 818.

40. Elizabeth Sykes Taylor to George W. Taylor, May 14, June 10, June 13, June 16, June 20, June 22, and June 27, 1846, all in TFP 818.

PART 2

Engaging Diversity

CHAPTER 4

Vocation, Religious Identity, and the Abolitionist Networks of Sarah Mapps Douglass and Sojourner Truth

STEPHEN W. ANGELL

This chapter looks at several core aspects of the lives and witness of Sarah Mapps Douglass (1806–1882) and Sojourner Truth (1797–1883), two African American women who had a long association with various types of Quakers. It begins with a consideration of their early lives and proceeds to examine intersections between their race, gender, social class, religious identities, vocations, appropriations of literacy, engagement with abolitionist networks, and, finally, involvement with Quakers. During their lifetimes, Quakers endured numerous separations, and this chapter takes account of those when considering reasons for Douglass's and Truth's different forms of engagement with Quakerism. For both women, engagement with the immediatist abolitionist networks associated with William Lloyd Garrison, Lucretia Mott, and others was a central aspect of their vocational and religious development.

EARLY LIVES OF SARAH MAPPS DOUGLASS AND ISABELLA

Isabella (later known as Sojourner Truth) and Sarah Mapps Douglass were born about nine years apart. Isabella was born in Ulster County, New York, in 1797, to James Bomefree, of half-Mohawk and half-Coromanti ancestry, and Elizabeth, whose ancestors were from Kongo. She was the eleventh of Elizabeth's twelve children. Both of her parents were enslaved, as was Isabella.[1] At her birth, her enslavers were deeply religious Dutch Americans, the Hardenbergs. When Isabella was two, in 1799, the New York legislature enacted a gradual emancipation statute. For African Americans born after that date, all females would be held in slavery until age twenty-five and all males until age twenty-eight. This had no immediate effect on Isabella's condition. When Isabella's master, Charles Hardenberg, died in 1808, her mother and father were given their freedom, but Isabella was sold, along with cattle and horses, in an estate sale, causing both Isabella and her mother heartbreak.[2]

After 1808, Isabella was sold three times within three years, leading to a life of endless and difficult labor. The last of these sales was to the prosperous John Dumont, and she lived in the Dumont household for the next sixteen years. Her African American lover, Robert, also enslaved, was driven away from Isabella by her enslaver Dumont. John's wife, Elizabeth, disliked Isabella intensely, while John treated her favorably. Isabella would give birth to five children; at least one, Diana, was light-skinned, suggesting Dumont as the probable father. Historians give different assessments of the degrees of love and coercion involved in this extramarital relationship; Sojourner Truth's own scribe, Olive Gilbert, writing in 1850, says of this time only that Truth experienced "a long series of trials . . . which we must pass over in silence."[3]

Isabella's knowledge of Quakers was evident during a series of upheavals that she endured in the mid-1820s. New York law required the emancipation of all remaining slaves on July 4, 1827. Dumont promised her that he would emancipate her one year early, but he reneged on his promise, claiming that Isabella had lost too much time recovering from an injury. In 1826, he sold her five-year-old son to a neighbor. One day in the fall of 1826, she decided on self-emancipation and, carrying her youngest daughter, walked twelve miles to the home of the Quaker Levi Roe. Roe was on his deathbed, but he gave her directions to an antislavery Dutch family, that of Isaac van Wagenen. Dumont followed her there, but he could not persuade Isabella to return to his home. Van Wagenen purchased her for twenty-five dollars, with the promise that she could work off this debt. Meanwhile, in violation of New York law, Dumont's neighbor had sold her son, Peter, out of state, but with the support of Quakers and antislavery Dutch folk, Isabella initiated a lawsuit and was successful in having Peter returned to her.⁴ At multiple levels, this was concrete enactment of a kind of liberation theology. Tenacious resistance and the vigorous use of all available legal means were lessons that she never forgot.

Sarah Mapps Douglass was born free in Philadelphia on September 9, 1806, to Robert Douglass and Grace Bustill Douglass. Her father was a hairdresser and her mother a milliner, selling the modest dresses and bonnets preferred by Quaker women. Both were religious and civic-minded. In 1807, Robert Douglass helped found the First African Presbyterian Church in Philadelphia. On her mother's side, the family was closely related to Quakers. Sarah's maternal grandfather, Cyrus Bustill, who died the year she was born, had been a baker, educator, and pillar of Philadelphia's Black community, and in 1787 he helped found the Free African Society, the first institution in Philadelphia solely for people of African descent.⁵ Many venerable institutions were founded by members of the Free African Society, including the Mother Bethel Church of the African Methodist Episcopal (AME) Church, which, under the guidance of Richard Allen, built its first edifice in 1794 and achieved independence from the predominantly White Methodist Episcopal Church in 1816, and the African Episcopal Church of St. Thomas, also founded in 1794 and pastored by Absalom Jones.⁶ Pennsylvania had enacted a gradual emancipation statute in 1780, but it would take until the 1840s before all slaves in Pennsylvania were freed.⁷

Thanks to her parents, Sarah Mapps Douglass got a good education. By the 1810s, Philadelphia had a long tradition of educating certain African American children, which had begun in 1750 with the foundation of a school for African Americans by Anthony Benezet and other Quakers. Sarah and her brother Robert attended Quaker Arthur Donaldson's school from 1809 to 1813. When Sarah was not able to attend school, her parents hired tutors to teach her. Later, she took courses at a school for African Americans sponsored by the Augustine Society, a joint project of Philadelphia's Black community leaders largely funded by James Forten (1766–1842), one of Philadelphia's wealthiest African American businessmen. Douglass undoubtedly was an outstanding student at this and the other schools she attended; in 1825, at the age of nineteen, she was hired as a teacher at Forten's school.⁸

During her youth, education for African American children was under sharp attack from the White Philadelphian community. Between 1800 and 1804, White antislavery reformers withdrew financial support from Black schools. They claimed that Black teachers were "too lenient" with their pupils and wanted Black children to be taught only by White teachers. Black community leaders attempted to make up the financial shortfall, but the number of Black pupils in Philadelphia dropped from 556 in 1805, the year before Douglass's birth, to 414 in 1813. When Philadelphia started a public school system in 1812, Black children were at first excluded and later admitted only to separate and unequal schools.[9]

THE RELIGIOUS AND SPIRITUAL BACKGROUNDS OF DOUGLASS AND TRUTH

Sarah Mapps Douglass grew up with parents from different religious affiliations. Her father served as an elder in the First African Presbyterian Church, which grew rapidly under the charismatic pastoral leadership of John Gloucester, a formerly enslaved man from Tennessee. Sarah's mother, Grace Bustill Douglass, attended Quaker meetings in Philadelphia. Her father's church had an all-Black membership, whereas the Quaker meetings were predominantly White, with African Americans relegated to seating in the rear of the meetinghouse, a situation similar to that of other White congregations in Philadelphia. The Black Presbyterians had found it "inconvenient and unpleasant . . . to attend the houses of worship frequented by white people," but also felt that "there was no cause of ill-treatment upon the part of existing organizations or Churches to drive the colored membership to seek a separation."[10]

While Grace Bustill Douglass loved the liturgy of quiet in the Quaker meeting, it would be a mistake to think that African Americans encountered less racial prejudice in the Quaker meetings of Philadelphia than they did in the Presbyterian churches there. Sometimes, however, Quaker meetings were held specifically for them in Philadelphia and adjacent regions. One such meeting, established in Haddonfield, New Jersey, in 1799, was said to have attracted nearly two hundred African Americans to Quaker worship. But such separate meetings for African Americans do not seem to have been held regularly in Philadelphia in the early nineteenth century.[11] When Philadelphia Quakers suffered a major schism in 1827, the meetings that Sarah and Grace attended (Northern District and Arch Street) became affiliated with the more theologically conservative Orthodox branch of Quakerism.[12]

Eventually, White Quakers' treatment of African American Quakers like the Douglasses would become a major theme of Sarah's writing. An early series of letters, written by the twenty-five-year-old Sarah in 1832, under the pseudonym "Zillah," to William Lloyd Garrison's *Liberator* in Boston, explored many religious themes. She compared the oppression of African Americans, targeted by legislation that aimed to prohibit the migration of Black folk into Pennsylvania, with the oppression of seventeenth-century English Quakers such as Barbara Blaugdone, who was moved by the Spirit to sing while her state-sanctioned tormentor whipped her. Looking to the future, Zillah saw "black and white mingle together without a shadow of disgust appearing on the countenance of either; no wailing is heard, no clanking of chains; but the voice of peace and love and joy is wafted to my ears on every breeze. And what has wrought this mighty change? Religion, my sister; the religion of the meek and lowly Jesus."[13] She remarked on the kindness of one of her students, an orphan, who gifted his teacher with a bouquet of violets. She hoped that her readers "would learn that gratitude is not confined to a fair complexion. I hope none of my little readers are so wicked as to despise children whose complexions God has caused to differ from theirs."[14] Reflecting upon a hotly contested subject within the African American community in Philadelphia, she expressed her opposition to African American emigration to the Black-run Republic of Haiti: "There is no spot in the known world where people are happier than America. . . . If we should bend our steps to Hayti, there is no security for life and property; too many of the people are desperately wicked."[15] She recounted the story of an enslaved woman being beaten by a White female enslaver because the enslaved woman paused to hold her baby when the enslaver thought that she should be working. "American Mothers! Can you doubt that the slave feels as tenderly for her offspring as you do for yours?"[16]

Douglass loved the Bible. Although her letters were written in the third person, surely she was the prototype for the obedient, gentle, and patient girl for whom "the holy Bible was her delight; she knew many of the longest Psalms and chapters in Proverbs by heart; and it was her practice to repeat them daily."[17] Douglass was acquainted with the newest trends in revivalist Christianity, and she had attended a "protracted meeting" of the kind that Charles Finney and other evangelists were prolifically promoting in order to gain Christian converts. But she still preferred the quiet of the Quaker meeting: "Sweet voices sang a sweeter hymn; but while the notes of the glorious music were ringing in my ear, my heart acknowledged the superior eloquence of silence—the beauty of sitting down in humility and heartbrokenness to wait the operation of the holy spirit—and then to feel its gentle influence distilling like dew upon the soul, and subduing every unholy and wandering thought."[18]

Isabella's religious outlook drew on diverse influences. Since her grandparents were from Kongo, her spirituality had strong African elements. The name Isabella suggests strong Catholic roots in Kongo and the popularity there of the pious fifteenth-century Spanish queen; the sister of a leading Kongolese king, Pedro IV, was named after her.[19] Isabella's considerable powers of memory and storytelling and her insights into the realms of the Spirit also connected her strongly with African religious traditions. Religious doctrine, by contrast, was not important to Isabella; she reportedly did not know that Christians believed that Jesus was the son of God.[20] After she moved to New York City in 1829, her spirituality was deepened and widened during the evangelical revivals of the period, first in the predominantly White Methodist Episcopal Church, and then in the African Methodist Episcopal Zion Church, a strongly antislavery African American church centered in New York City, which she joined in 1831.[21] She participated in the reform efforts of the Second Great Awakening, preaching on the subject of moral reform to sex workers in New York, and in 1833 she even joined for a short time the millennialist cult of a prophet named Matthias.[22] Isabella was never a doctrinaire Christian—far from it. When others asked whether she was baptized, she responded that she had been baptized by the Holy Ghost.[23] That answer comported well with Quakerism, but with few other Christian sects.

VOCATION

As a traveling orator and preacher, Sojourner Truth, the name Isabella adopted in 1843, followed a path blazed by numerous African American preachers before her. When she was introduced to the Congregational minister Henry Ward Beecher, she professed love for preachers, adding, "I'm kind of a preacher myself."[24] Black female Methodist preachers like Jarena Lee informally conducted evangelistic campaigns, sometimes even with the approval of Black clerics such as Bishop Allen of the AME Church.[25] In 1832, in the quasi-religious radical abolitionist movement, Maria Stewart may well have been the first Black woman known to address a mixed-gender audience. Stewart could have spoken for many of the African American women who followed in her footsteps when she asked, "What if I am a woman; is not the God of ancient times the God of these modern days? Did he not raise up Deborah, to be a mother, and a judge in Israel? Did not queen Esther save the lives of the Jews? And Mary Magdalene first declare the resurrection of Christ from the dead?" The very public nature of such speaking roles provided many occasions for obloquy and condemnation from male opponents. Stewart's speech was met with a fusillade of rotten tomatoes.[26] Jarena Lee reported that the "oppositions I met with . . . were numerous," and that sometimes she "was pressed down like a cart beneath its shafts," yet she persevered.[27] Truth handled her opponents with great wit and dramatic authority. For example, when on a speaking tour in northern Indiana, a physician named T. W. Strain challenged even her gender, saying that her voice was that "of a man." Truth refused to feel shame, saying that her breasts "had suckled many a white babe," and proceeded to show her breasts to the entire congregation, stating that "it was not to her shame, but to their shame" that she was undressing in this fashion.[28]

Seeking to exercise fully their respective callings, Quaker women, mostly White, and African American women of several denominations seemed to converge in working to establish a central role for "Spiritual Mothers."[29] In regard to Quakers, Michele Lise Tarter has emphasized the leadership role played by spiritual mothers.[30] Many African American women, Sojourner Truth among them, derived strength from traditions that saw motherhood and nursing as a powerful dimension of genuine ministry. The positive features of such a ministry could overcome the violent and dehumanizing intentions of leering and obscene detractors. Jarena Lee was wont to call the Sabbath the "seventh-day," explaining that after her conversion, she "preferred the plain language of the quakers."[31] Lee, like Truth, also preferred plain dress. Pamela Klassen explains that Lee's early experiences with Quakers probably exerted a major influence on her, leading to her (and Truth's) choosing to wear plain dress. Klassen attributes such preferences to appreciation for Quaker antislavery work, including Friends' participation in the free-produce movement,[32] but one might equally surmise that Truth's and Lee's appreciation for the well-established tradition of women's preaching among the Quakers would extend to Quaker women's style of plain and modest dress.

Sarah Mapps Douglass was an educator for more than half a century, until 1877. Except for the year 1833–34, when she worked in New York, she taught that entire time in Philadelphia. She was an excellent teacher and her students loved her. By 1825, at the age of nineteen, she was already employed as a teacher.[33] But education provided no refuge from the torrents of racist abuse. In a later article, Douglass admonished White children that if they had known "the bitterness of having the finger of scorn pointed at you wherever you appear, at school, in the streets, and even in the Lord's house; could you feel for one moment the anguish of being despised merely for your complexion, surely you would throw this unholy prejudice from you with disdain.... Children, love one another."[34]

Douglass wrote and published poetry, taught watercolor painting, and, after attending the Female Medical College of Pennsylvania in Philadelphia in 1852–53, lectured on anatomy.[35] In short, she was a skillful, dedicated, and versatile teacher with a deep and insatiable curiosity. A report by the Black journalist Samuel Cornish on his 1837 visit to her classroom, published in his newspaper the *Colored American*, attests to her gifts as a teacher:

> Wednesday last, we passed two of the most gratifying, satisfactory hours of our life, with Miss Douglass and her interest in improving scholars. The school numbers over 40, selected from our best families, where their morals and manners are equally subjects of care, and of deep interest. All the branches of a good and solid female education are taught in Miss Douglass' school.... Miss Douglass has a well-selected and valuable cabinet of shells and minerals, well-arranged and labelled. She has also a mind richly furnished with a knowledge of these sciences, and she does not fail, through them, to lead up the minds of her pupils, through Nature, to Nature's God.[36]

LITERACY AND ABOLITIONIST NETWORKS

Individually, Sojourner Truth and Sarah Mapps Douglass differed greatly in their literacy. Truth could not read or write, while Douglass was exceptionally learned and literate. But simply to point out this difference would be to misrepresent their situations profoundly. Truth and Douglass both excelled, in distinct ways, in mobilizing the literacy skills and talents needed for their demanding work through their abolitionist networks.

Truth needed both readers and scribes. Since she preached with extensive allusions to scripture, she needed to hear the Bible read in order to fix it in her mind. She would compare what was read to her with what her inner witness was telling her, and she concluded that the spirit of truth was speaking through scripture, but also that the authors of the Bible had combined these sacred matters of truth with "ideas and suppositions of their own."[37] She received what she needed this way, and the inward witness was able to supply the rest. "I don't read such small stuff as letters, I read men and nations" is a dictum plausibly attributed to Truth.[38]

When she wished to compose her autobiography, she needed scribes. For the first edition of her *Narrative*, dictated in the late 1840s, she found an amanuensis in Olive Gilbert, while both were living in the Northampton community in Massachusetts. The second edition of the *Narrative* was compiled by her neighbor Frances Titus in Battle Creek, Michigan, in 1878. This book may be considered a mediated autobiography. Truth self-published her *Narrative* and made a living by selling her autobiographies and pictures of herself. Thus her photographic likeness and life story became well known to the American public in large part through her successful business plan for self-promotion. Abolitionist publishers such as William Lloyd Garrison advertised her work, and American abolitionists tended to be avid readers and purchased it readily.[39] On at least some occasions, when the proceeds from sales of her book and portraits were insufficient to support her, she apparently sought work as a domestic servant, and was assisted by fellow abolitionists in doing so.[40]

Douglass was renowned as one of the most highly educated African American women in the United States. One correspondent to the *Friends' Weekly Intelligencer* in 1846, responding to a Missouri slaveholder who had deprecated the intellectual abilities of African Americans, named Sarah Mapps Douglass and three African American men as evidence of the very high intellectual potential and achievements that the named persons had attained and that other African Americans were capable of.[41] Douglass entered public life around 1830 with her active participation in Philadelphia's Female Literary Association, which combined strong literary pursuits with support for the antislavery cause. As historian Julie Winch notes, participation in such women's literary societies served as a means of "apprenticeship" for many of the leaders of abolitionist organizations later in the decade.[42]

Unlike Truth, who published under her own name, Douglass and her friends in the association published their work mostly under pseudonyms. This has provided satisfying labor for a legion of historians attempting to sort out who wrote what. This pseudonymous writing provided a kind of limited and carefully controlled visibility that Truth never sought.

In 1838, when her pseudonymous challenges to White supremacists, published by White abolitionist allies, were challenged by hostile White readers who refused to believe in the truth and accuracy of her charges, Douglass was willing to drop her anonymity and support her claims, which drew her further into the public arena.[43]

Douglass's involvement in the Female Literary Association was a precursor to her participation in the Philadelphia Female Anti-Slavery Society (PFASS) almost from its founding in 1833. She and her mother, Grace Mapps Douglass, formed a tight partnership in this regard. Of the eighty-four women members of the PFASS whose religious affiliations were known, seventy-five, or 89 percent, were Quakers; and of these, fifty-four were Hicksite Quakers and twenty-one were Orthodox. Five others were members of the St. Thomas African Episcopal Church, so at least six of the eighty-four women (Douglass and the Black Episcopalians) were African American.[44] Douglass would have been among the Orthodox Quakers. She was appointed treasurer of the PFASS in 1838.[45] Later, she also served as recording secretary, librarian, and manager. The PFASS financially supported Douglass's school for eleven years, and it had a history of attempting to micromanage her efforts—for example, disapproving of her attendance policy as too lenient. The PFASS withdrew its support in 1849. That year, the PFASS took in much more income than in previous years, but it "cited lack of funds as its excuse to abandon its commitment to the education of African American children."[46]

SOJOURNER TRUTH'S QUAKER INVOLVEMENT

Sojourner Truth (as Isabella) knew about Quakers from her childhood and youth in Ulster County, New York. At least one Friend (Levi Roe) assisted her in her 1826 escape from bondage, and she received extensive help from several Quakers in her successful legal action to recover her son, Peter, when he was illegally sold outside the state of New York. In their humanitarian outreach to her, Truth felt, the Quakers had shown themselves to be especially dedicated to living "out the principles of the gospel of Christ."[47] According to Margaret Washington, her youthful "association with the

Quakers would blossom into a lifelong connection with this white sect in the vanguard of the black liberation struggle."[48]

Truth was also profoundly influenced by the Methodists and other Christian denominations, including the Adventists. The Methodists nurtured her during and after an intense conversion experience on a campground in 1827, during which she came to the conclusion that Christ dwelled within her. In the 1830s, she was often closely associated with New York City's John Street African Methodist Episcopal Zion Church.[49] Later in life, she explained her choice to join the Methodists (at least during her young adulthood) as hinging on which sect would let her sing. The Methodists permitted worshipful singing, while Quakers, with their silent worship, did not encourage singing, although at times during her long life she would be moved by the Holy Spirit to sing in Quaker worship anyway.[50]

Truth never sought membership in any Friends' meeting, nor did she claim an exclusive connection with the Religious Society of Friends, but she did affirm, "I have always loved the Quakers."[51] Truth had a very irenic, undogmatic, ecumenical witness, during a period in American religious history when there were great pressures to draw stricter denominational boundaries. While she liked to associate with Abolitionist "come-outer" groups, she never spoke harshly of other Christian groups, and in turn she was well liked by a wide variety of Christians, including Congregationalists, Presbyterians, and Adventists. It was possible for believers as different as Methodists, "conservative Adventists, and progressive Quakers, to feel that she was one of them," according to her biographers Carleton Mabee and Susan Mabee Newhouse. To one abolitionist, Progressive Friend Henry C. Wright, who urged Friends to attack conservative Christian churches for cooperating with slavery, Truth countered, "We ought to be like Christ, who said, 'Father, forgive them, for they know not what they do.' If we want to lead them, we should not get out of their sight."[52]

Nevertheless, Truth came to associate ever more closely with Quakers during her long life, especially with the Progressive Friends, the offshoot of Hicksite Quakers formed during the 1840s and 1850s, who were especially vigorous in the abolitionist cause and a multitude of other reform causes, including temperance, women's rights, and spiritualism. Many of her closest friendships from the 1850s onward were with Progressive Friends such as Isaac and Amy Post and Joseph and Ruth Dugdale. Beginning in the 1850s, her settled residence was in Battle Creek, Michigan, among a variety of mostly White radicals with varied allegiances to spiritualism and Quakerism. Some of the Quakers in Battle Creek came from her old home of Ulster County, New York, so there was some overlap between the two Quaker communities that befriended her.

The spiritualists, who believed that it was possible to converse with the spirits of the dead through the appropriate religious ceremony, also attracted Truth's great interest, as she sought to converse with relatives and friends who had entered the afterlife. But Progressive Friends had blended so thoroughly with spiritualists that there was no choice being forced upon her with this dual attraction. In 1878, when Truth was asked if she had ever joined the spiritualists, her reply was, "Why, there's nothing to join." She could have made the same reply had she been asked whether she had joined Progressive Friends, as the latter prioritized general meetings to which all were welcome, including non-Quakers, and they never set up the kind of church structure in which formal membership would be necessary.[53]

Truth's later-in-life attraction to Quakers (and to Progressive Friends in particular) was the result of a convergence of ideals and convictions. Margaret Washington details a long list of Truth's beliefs that resembled nineteenth-century Quaker faith more closely than any other sectarian appropriation of Christianity: the emphasis on listening to the Holy Spirit, rather than insisting on the unvarying divine inspiration of all scripture; emphasis on the mystical and ethical import of scripture rather than giving it a rationalist interpretation; a sense that physical sacraments were relatively unimportant; and the importance of Christ's moral example. As a traveling minister, Truth could not fail to note these long-standing Quaker traditions, including equality between the genders in ministry. All of this was in addition to Quakers' strong support for temperance and abolition.[54] When Truth turned her attention to the Progressive variant of Quakerism, she found even more to regard highly, including Progressive Friends' heavy emphasis on eradicating all kinds of social injustice, their ready inclusion of non-Quakers, and their openness to spiritualism. According to Washington, "Sojourner's relationship with these unorthodox Progressive Friends was as close as she came to a religious affiliation."[55] Other biographers concur, arguing that she "may informally be called a Progressive Friend."[56]

During Truth's last decade of life, she devoted many of her waning energies to assisting the "Exodusters," freed people fleeing to Kansas from the massive violence that White supremacists unleashed against African Americans in the former Confederacy. She hoped that Quakers would provide large-scale support to the Exodusters, similar to the assistance that they were giving to Native Americans on the Great Plains as part of the Grant administration's "Peace Policy."[57] While Quakers did not respond as readily as she had hoped, two energetic Quaker women, Elizabeth Comstock and Laura Haviland, did work alongside Truth in aiding the Exodusters.[58]

SARAH MAPPS DOUGLASS'S QUAKER INVOLVEMENT

In 1913, Douglass's longtime associate and supervisor at Philadelphia's Institute for Colored Youth (ICY), Fanny M. Jackson-Coppin, wrote the following tribute in her memoirs: "Sarah M. Douglass was one of the most unique figures in the field of education. A native of this city, and born over one hundred years ago, she was educated by tutors, and began teaching directly after and continued that work for more than sixty years. She began at the ICY in 1853. . . . She adhered to the tenets of Friends and always attended their meetings. Her whole course was as teacher in the Girls' Preparatory Department. She was a contributor to the early antislavery publications, and a lecturer of note."[59]

Jackson-Coppin, an eminent African American educator in her own right, managed to foreground the extraordinary significance of Douglass's career as an educator and public intellectual, and she coupled that description with a careful statement of Douglass's religious identification: "she adhered to the tenets of Friends and always attended their meetings." What she avoided saying (she made no claim that Douglass was ever a member of a Quaker meeting, for instance) was as significant as what she did say. She stressed Douglass's utter faithfulness and regularity in her Quaker presence and practice. Whether Quakers valued Douglass as much as she valued Quakerism, however, was left an open question in Jackson-Coppin's account. Unlike the small, nonconformist Quaker meetings in New York and Michigan, through which Truth found liberationist support and assistance, a greater culture of conformity[60] pervaded the Quaker meetings in Sarah Douglass's Philadelphia, at the epicenter of North American Quakerism. Given that much of the US culture was deeply affected by racial prejudice, this was not promising for the development of a kind of Quakerism in Philadelphia that would welcome and affirm African Americans as part of Friends' religious communities in the early to mid-nineteenth century.

African Methodist Episcopal Church bishop William Paul Quinn observed to an AME audience in 1852 that "nine times out of ten, when we look into the face of a white man, we see our enemy."[61] Philadelphia Quakers all too often shared the racial prejudices of their White neighbors. English Friend Joseph Sturge wrote, after an 1840 visit, that Philadelphia was a "metropolis of prejudice against color, of Anti-Abolition feeling among Friends, as well as others."[62] In 1851, the eminent African American clergyman Samuel Ringgold Ward criticized White Quakers' opposition to educating African Americans alongside their own children, describing many Friends in the Philadelphia area as "bitter and relentless Negro despisers."[63]

African Americans were required to sit at the back of Friends' meetinghouses on a separate "Negro bench." Whites guarded this bench to ensure that no non-Black persons sat on it. This was common practice at the time among almost all American churches; Philadelphia Quakers were deeply conformist in this respect.[64] Sarah's mother, Grace Bustill Douglass, took her children, including Sarah, to Quaker meeting and was instructed to sit on the "Negro bench." When she became an adult, Sarah Douglass remained subject to the same requirement. "Even when a child," she later wrote, "my soul was made sad by hearing five or six times, during the course of our meeting, this language of remonstrance addressed to those who were willing to sit with us. 'This bench is for the black people,' 'This bench is for the people of color'—and often times I wept, at other times I felt indignant & queried in my own mind, are these people Christians? Now it seems clear to me, that had not that bench been set apart for oppressed Americans, there would have been no necessity for the often repeated and galling remonstrances, galling indeed *because I believe they despise us for our color*."[65] Like Bishop Quinn, Douglass used the word "enemies" to describe her White supremacist neighbors and co-religionists: "The hardest lesson my Heavenly Father ever set me to learn, was to love Friends; and in anguish of spirit I have often queried; why the Lord should require me to go among a people who despise me on account of my complexion; but I have seen that it is designed to humble me and to teach me the lesson, 'Love your enemies, and pray for them who despitefully use you.'"[66]

The relationship of the Douglasses to the Philadelphia meetings was made even more vexing by the question whether they could become members. The eighteenth-century applications of two light-skinned Black women, Abigail Franks and Cynthia Miers, resulted in a reluctant but seemingly clear affirmation by the Philadelphia Yearly Meeting that membership in the Society of Friends "is not limited with respect to Nation or Color." This language was retained in the books of Discipline by both the Hicksite and the Orthodox Philadelphia Yearly Meetings after the separation. Both Franks and Miers were received as members, Franks after a three-year delay, Miers after a shorter wait. But that declaration in the Discipline was often disregarded. African American applicants, such as James Alford in 1810, were often discouraged from applying for membership.[67] The Douglasses' experience in this respect mirrored that of Alford. Sarah wrote of her mother:

> While her children were in their infancy she had a great concern to become a member of Friends Society not only because she was fully convinced of the excellence of the principles professed by that society, but because she earnestly desired that her children should receive the guarded education Friends give to theirs. She mentioned her concern to a Friend who said, do not apply, you will only have your feelings wounded. Friends will not receive you. Thus admonished, and feeling that prejudice had closed the doors against her, she did not make her concern known to the Society. There was nothing but my Mother's complexion in the way to prevent her from being a member, she was highly intelligent & pious; her whole life was blameless.[68]

Some African American women, such as Hannah Burrows, who aspired to teach and preach among Quakers, especially in Douglass's Philadelphia neighborhood, encountered staunch resistance, mostly from entrenched White Quaker male elites, who often were inhospitable to African American women seeking to exercise their spiritual leadership within the context of Quaker meetings. More scholarly exploration of the lives of women like Burrows, Franks, and Miers is needed, if the sparse data on their lives can be augmented.[69]

Why did White Quakers want to hold at arm's length aspiring Black Quakers like Douglass? There was one allegedly well-meaning reason, but others—barely (if ever) acknowledged—were more racist and more real. The well-meaning reason was that African Americans simply preferred more emotional and louder religious formats, and it would be inappropriate to confine them to a form of worship that was not fitting for them. In 1843, writing for the conservative journal the *Friend*, a contributor writing under the initials P. R. put the point this way: "The fact is, that very few of them incline to attend our meetings. Friends' mode of worship does not suit their dispositions; they are fond of music and excitement, and hence they prefer their own meetings, where they regularly hear singing and preaching."[70] The view that exciting singing and preaching was a natural worship format for African Americans did not lack African American advocates. Here, for example, is how Richard Allen, the founding bishop of the AME Church, argued for enthusiastic preaching: "I feel thankful that ever I heard a Methodist preach. We are beholden to the Methodists, under God, for the light of the Gospel we enjoy; for all other denominations preached so high-flown that we were not able to comprehend their doctrine. Sure am I that reading sermons will never prove so beneficial to the colored people as spiritual or extempore preaching."[71] Allen's reference to "reading sermons" shows that his argument was pitched more toward African American Episcopalians than African American Quakers, but his confidence that people of color would gravitate toward exciting preaching is clear nonetheless. Sarah Douglass would have no part of either man's argument: "I have frequently heard my mother say that very many of our people inclined to Friends' mode of worship; she lamented the unchristian conduct that kept them out. I myself know some, whose hearts yearn for the quiet of your worshiping places, and who love the 'still small voice' better than harp or viol. Some have gone out from 'Friends,' not because they prefer their own meetings, where they regularly hear 'singing and preaching,' but because they could not bear the cross of sitting on the 'black bench.'"[72]

As for the more overtly racist reasons why most White Quakers did not want Black Quakers attending their children's schools or integrated into their meetinghouses, it was because they were afraid that interracial marriages would result. In the first half of the nineteenth century, Quakers still insisted on endogamous marriage, so admitting only a few Black members would create an insoluble dilemma as to where their spouses would come from. Black Quakers were also convinced that White Quakers did not want to admit to membership young Black couples whose children would automatically become meeting members through Philadelphia Yearly Meeting's "birthright" membership. The few African Americans who were admitted to membership tended to be past childbearing age. White Pennsylvanians were consumed with worry that even small numbers of Black citizens might shape governmental decision-making processes in a way that the majority of White voters might disapprove of, so in 1838 the state constitution was amended to prohibit free African American men from voting, something that had been their right since the establishment of Pennsylvania as a state.[73] It is not hard to imagine that most White Quakers at that time, holding tightly, if quietly, to views of White supremacy, harbored similar worries about Black Quaker participation in Quaker consensus decision-making processes. So the Delaware Valley Quaker principle that membership was not limited by "Nation or Color" tended to be observed inconsistently at best.

In 1831, Sarah Douglass, as a twenty-five-year-old schoolteacher, was one of the first Pennsylvanians to join William Lloyd Garrison's new abolitionist movement. From the outset, Garrison proved to be a staunch ally, forthrightly condemning separate seating for people of color in American churches. Writing as "Ella," Douglass sent the following comment to Garrison:

> I was much pleased with your remarks on the absurd practice of placing the people of color behind all others, in our houses of worship. I, Sir, would have gladly sat among the humblest of my despised race; but have been obliged, for conscience' sake, to sit with white Christians; and often as I have met the look of scorn, and heard the whispered remark of "This bench is for the black people," — "This bench is for the people of color," has the tear gathered in my eye, and the prayer ascended from my heart to God, that he would in his own time take away our reproach; and oh! most firmly do I believe he will.[74]

In the abolitionist movement, Douglass found close White Quaker friends. She carried on an extensive correspondence with South-Carolina-slaveholders-turned-Philadelphia-Quaker-abolitionists Angelina and Sarah Grimke. Much of this correspondence survives. Some of her White Quaker women friends tried to sit with her on the separate "Negro bench." Mira Okrum, a young White woman, attempted to sit with Sarah Douglass and her mother during Quaker worship but was prevented by other Whites. In the spring of 1837, the Grimke sisters succeeded in sitting beside Sarah and Grace during worship at Philadelphia's Arch Street Meeting, and for that act, faithful to God's leading (as they saw it), they earned themselves a visit from the meeting's overseers, who rebuked the Grimkes for having "no occasion to sit so near" the Douglasses.[75]

In her letters to the Grimkes and other Quaker abolitionists, Sarah Douglass was candid about the discrimination she experienced at Quaker meetings. Excerpts of these letters, stripped of her name, eventually appeared in print, most notably in a short pamphlet, published in England by Elizabeth Pease in 1840, titled *Society of Friends in the United States: Their Views of the Anti-Slavery Question, and Treatment of the People of Colour, Compiled from Original Correspondence*. Douglass's heartrending description of the "Negro bench," and the discouragement or rejection of African Americans' applications for membership in certain American Quaker meetings, were features of such pamphlets that garnered much attention from their abolitionist readers. In 1843, for example, Rhode Island Quaker Arnold Buffum denounced the denial of membership to a Black woman in Philadelphia on the floor of the Anti-Slavery Convention in London.[76] P. R. launched an attack against Buffum in the pages of the *Friend* and accused him of making "statements derogatory to the reputation of the religious Society of Friends in America, in reference to the subject of slavery." P. R. thought that American meetings might be absolved of responsibility if the Black Quakers in question could be demonstrated never to have actually applied for membership. He also drew on the humanitarian reputation of Quakers from the life witness of John Woolman and Anthony Benezet onward as showing the manifest good intentions and good works of that religious sect.[77]

P.R.'s screed drew Sarah Douglass back into the public arena. Writing, as mentioned above, about many African Americans who would be attracted to Quaker worship if they were met with a warm Christian welcome, Douglass concluded her letter: "Ah, there are many poor stray starving sheep, wandering in this world's wilderness, who would gladly come into your green pastures, and repose them by your still waters; did not prejudice bar the entrance! I am persuaded the Lord has a controversy with 'Friends' on this account. Let them see to it. S.M.D."[78]

At this point (the mid-1840s), the abolitionist come-outer movement was gathering steam. We have already seen how Sojourner Truth benefited from one branch of the come-outer churches, namely, the Progressive Friends, for whom she showed a preference of association, if not affiliation. But Progressive Friends broke off from the Hicksite wing of the Quaker movement, and the come-outer movement had a much more limited effect on the Orthodox wing. While Progressive Friends formed yearly meetings in New York, Ohio, Michigan, and Pennsylvania, there was only one small come-outer movement among Orthodox Friends, in Indiana, far away from Douglass's Philadelphia home.[79] In terms of livelihood, Douglass was very much tied into the existing abolitionist societies and the Orthodox Friends'

Yearly Meeting in Philadelphia. We know less about her Quaker meeting involvement after 1845 than before. Extensive correspondence with Orthodox Friends Rebecca White and Hannah White Richardson shows that she continued to attend Quaker worship. Some of the Quaker worship she attended in the 1850s had segregated seating by race, but others probably did not.[80] The tribute by Jackson-Coppin, quoted above, written about thirty years after Douglass's death in 1882, contains the strong suggestion that while Douglass continued to attend Quaker worship regularly, she never gained actual membership in a meeting.

CONCLUSION

These two Quaker women, Sarah Mapps Douglass and Sojourner Truth, accomplished an extraordinary amount in their lifetimes, Truth as an orator and political organizer, Douglass as an educator and public intellectual. In each case, the immediatist abolitionist movement provided networks through which they could accomplish their valuable public witness. The forms of Quakerism that each of these women engaged, however, were highly disparate. The Great Separation between Hicksites and Orthodox affected their lives; Truth associated mostly with Hicksites and Douglass mostly with Orthodox Friends. But the comeouterism associated with abolitionism, and the degree to which Quakers could be true to their nonconformist roots when faced with widespread White American condemnation of abolition in the antebellum United States, affected their lives far more strongly. We have seen that the relatively nonconformist Progressive Friends in Michigan were able to provide a physical and spiritual home for Truth that empowered her, or at least did not detract from her important work for a variety of worthy causes. By contrast, the conformity shown by most Orthodox Quakers in Philadelphia meant that Douglass's work as a writer and truth teller was directed largely against the callous disregard and outright opposition of that community toward her fuller participation and the prospect of her (and her family's) membership in the meeting community. This helped galvanize a portion of the abolitionist community to demonstrate why a critique of even Quaker churches that were committed to the broader antislavery cause was needed, whether or not that led to a comeouterist response. Beyond this sharp controversy, however,

Douglass carefully maintained her persistent educational labors, yielding excellent results with her students, an enduring facet of her career for which she also deserves to be remembered.

NOTES

1. Margaret Washington, *Sojourner Truth's America* (Urbana: University of Illinois Press, 2009), 9–12; Carleton Mabee and Susan Mabee Newhouse, *Sojourner Truth: Slave, Prophet, Legend* (New York: New York University Press, 1995), 3.

2. Washington, *Sojourner Truth's America*, 13–32.

3. Sojourner Truth, *Narrative of Sojourner Truth*, edited by Olive Gilbert and Frances Titus (Battle Creek, MI: published for the author, 1878), 30.

4. Washington, *Sojourner Truth's America*, 55–68.

5. Kenneth Ives, *Black Quakers: Brief Biographies* (Chicago: Progresiv Publishr, 1991), 43–49; Margaret Hope Bacon, *Sarah Mapps Douglass, Faithful Attender of Quaker Meeting: View from the Back Bench* (Philadelphia: Quaker Press of FGC, 2003), 2–3.

6. C. Eric Lincoln, *The Black Church in the African American Experience* (Durham: Duke University Press, 1990), 51–52; Richard S. Newman, *Freedom's Prophet: Bishop Richard Allen, the AME Church, and the Black Founding Fathers* (New York: New York University Press, 2008), 70–73.

7. Gary B. Nash and Jean R. Soderlund, *Freedom by Degrees: Emancipation in Pennsylvania and Its Aftermath* (New York: Oxford University Press, 1991).

8. Scott Miltenberger, "James Forten," in *Encyclopedia of African American History* (Santa Barbara: ABC-CLIO, 2010); Bacon, *Sarah Mapps Douglass*, 6; Gary B. Nash, *Forging Freedom: The Formation of Philadelphia's Black Community, 1720–1840* (Cambridge: Harvard University Press, 1988), 269–70; Fanny Jackson-Coppin, *Reminiscences of School Life and Hints on Teaching* (Philadelphia: AME Book Concern, 1913), 148.

9. Nash, *Forging Freedom*, 204–8.

10. William T. Catto, "A Semi-Centenary Discourse, Delivered in the First African Presbyterian Church, Philadelphia, on the Fourth Sabbath of May, 1857: With a History of the Church from Its First Organization; Including a Brief Notice of Rev. John Gloucester, Its First Pastor, 1857," 19, 52, quoted in Donald Scott, "John Gloucester," in *African American National Biography*, edited by Henry Louis Gates Jr. and Evelyn Brooks Higginbotham (New York: Oxford University Press, 2013); Bacon, *Sarah Mapps Douglass*, 5–6; Newman, *Freedom's Prophet*, 227–28.

11. Donna McDaniel and Vanessa Julye, *Fit for Freedom, Not for Friendship: Quakers, African Americans, and the Myth of Racial Justice* (Philadelphia: Quaker Press of FGC, 2009), 182.

12. H. Larry Ingle, *Quakers in Conflict: The Hicksite Reformation* (Knoxville: University of Tennessee Press, 1986; reprint, Wallingford, PA: Pendle Hill Publications, 1998), 220.

13. Zillah, "Ladies Department: To a Friend," *Liberator*, June 30, 1832, 2, 29, quoting William Sewel, *History of the Rise [. . .] of Quakers* (Burlington, NJ: Isaac Collins, 1774), 107.

14. Zillah, "Juvenile Department: A True Tale for Children," *Liberator*, July 7, 1832, 2, 27.

15. Zillah, "Excerpt from a Letter Written to a Friend," *Liberator*, July 21, 1832, 2, 29.

16. Zillah, "A Mother's Love," *Liberator*, July 28, 1832, 2, 29.

17. Zillah, "Juvenile Department: For the Children Who Read the Liberator," *Liberator*, August 18, 1832, 2, 33.

18. Zillah, "A Leaf from My Scrapbook," *Liberator*, December 15, 1832, 2, 50.

19. Washington, *Sojourner Truth's America*, 11.

20. Erlene Stetson and Linda David, *Glorying in Tribulation: The Lifework of Sojourner Truth* (East Lansing: Michigan State University Press, 1994), 68.

21. Washington, *Sojourner Truth's America*, 130.

22. Stetson and David, *Glorying in Tribulation*, 67–74; *Narrative of Sojourner Truth*, 87–96; Washington, *Sojourner Truth's America*, 91–92.

23. Stetson and David, *Glorying in Tribulation*, 67.

24. *Narrative of Sojourner Truth*, 154.

25. William L. Andrews, *Sisters of the Spirit: Three Black Women's Autobiographies of the Nineteenth Century* (Bloomington: Indiana University Press, 1986), 45; Washington, *Sojourner Truth's America*, 260.

26. Maria Stewart, "Mrs. Stewart's Farewell Address to Her Friends in the City of Boston (1835)," in *African American Religious History: A Documentary Witness*, edited by Milton C. Sernett (Durham: Duke University Press, 1999), 204, 202.

27. Jarena Lee, *Religious Experience and Journal of Mrs. Jarena Lee* (Philadelphia: published for the author, 1849), 24.

28. Washington, *Sojourner Truth's America*, 285–86.

29. For Quakers, see Rebecca Larson, *Daughters of Light: Quaker Women Preaching and Prophesying in the Colonies and Abroad, 1700–1775* (Chapel Hill: University of North Carolina Press, 1999); Michele Lise Tarter, "Written from the Body of Sisterhood: Quaker Women's Prophesying and the Creation of a New Word," in *New Critical Studies on Early Quaker Women, 1650–1800*, edited by Michele Lise Tarter and Catie Gill (Oxford: Oxford University Press, 2018), 81–82. For African American women, see Cheryl Townsend Gilkes, "'The Politics of Silence': Dual-Sex Political Systems and Women's Traditions of Conflict in African-American Religion," in *African-American Christianity: Essays in History*, edited by Paul E. Johnson (Berkeley: University of California Press, 1994), 80–110; Anthea D. Butler, *Women in the Church of God in Christ: Making a Sanctified World* (Chapel Hill: University of North Carolina Press, 2007), chap. 1; and Stephen W. Angell and Anthony B. Pinn, eds., *Social Protest Thought in the African Methodist Episcopal Church* (Knoxville: University of Tennessee Press, 2000), 267.

30. Tarter, "Written from the Body of Sisterhood," 74.

31. Andrews, *Sisters of the Spirit*, 47.

32. Pamela Klassen, "The Robes of Womanhood: Dress and Authenticity Among African American Methodist Women in the Nineteenth Century," *Religion and American Culture* 14, no. 1 (2004): 45–47.

33. Bacon, *Sarah Mapps Douglass*, 32–33.

34. Zillah, "Juvenile Department: For the Children Who Read the Liberator," 2, 33.

35. Ibid., 7–8, 12, 24; Emma Jones Lapsansky, "'Discipline to the Mind': Philadelphia's Banneker Institute, 1854–1872," *Pennsylvania Magazine of History and Biography* 117, nos. 1–2 (1993): 83–102.

36. Quoted in Bacon, *Sarah Mapps Douglass*, 12.

37. *Narrative of Sojourner Truth*, 108–9.

38. Stetson and David, *Glorying in Tribulation*, 3.

39. Nell Irvin Painter, "Representing Truth: Sojourner Truth's Knowing and Becoming Known," in *This Far by Faith: Readings in African-American Women's Religious Biography*, edited by Judith Weisenfeld and Richard Newman (New York: Routledge, 1996), 269–80.

40. Mabee and Newhouse, *Sojourner Truth*, 98.

41. M., untitled essay, *Friends' Weekly Intelligencer*, October 31, 1846, 3, 31.

42. Julie Winch, "'You Have Talents—Only Cultivate Them': Philadelphia's Black Female Literary Societies and the Abolitionist Crusade," in *The Abolitionist Sisterhood: Women's Political Culture in Antebellum America*, edited by Jean Fagan Yellin and John C. Van Horne (Ithaca: Cornell University Press, 1994), 103; Bacon, *Sarah Mapps Douglass*, 8.

43. Bacon, *Sarah Mapps Douglass*, 21; Martha S. Jones, *All Bound Up Together: The Woman Question in African American Public Culture, 1830–1900* (Chapel Hill: University of North Carolina Press, 2007), 38–39.

44. Jean R. Soderlund, "Priorities and Power: The Philadelphia Female Anti-Slavery Society," in Yellin and Van Horne, *Abolitionist Sisterhood*, 73.

45. Winch, "'You Have Talents,'" 117.

46. Soderlund, "Priorities and Power," 76, 77.

47. *Narrative of Sojourner Truth*, 46.

48. Washington, *Sojourner Truth's America*, 63.

49. Ibid., 71, 73–75, 89–90, 130–31, 244.

50. Mabee and Newhouse, *Sojourner Truth*, 119–20, 141; Stephen W. Angell, "The Early Period," in *Black Fire: African American Quakers on Spirituality and Human Rights*, edited by Harold D. Weaver Jr., Paul Kriese, and Stephen W. Angell (Philadelphia: Quaker Press of FGC, 2011), 24–26.

51. Quoted in Washington, *Sojourner Truth's America*, 151.

52. Mabee and Newhouse, *Sojourner Truth*, 246, 209.

53. Ibid., 96–100, 240–42; Washington, *Sojourner Truth's America*, 216–17, 251, 274–78; Nancy A. Hewitt, *Radical Friend: Amy Kirby Post and Her Activist Worlds* (Chapel Hill: University of North Carolina Press, 2018), 177–78.

54. Washington, *Sojourner Truth's America*, 151.

55. Ibid., 251.

56. Mabee and Newhouse, *Sojourner Truth*, 241.

57. Jennifer Graber, *The Gods of Indian Country: Religion and the Struggle for the American West* (New York: Oxford University Press, 2018), 80–81, 89–90.

58. Mabee and Newhouse, *Sojourner Truth*, 161–65.

59. Jackson-Coppin, *Reminiscences of School Life*, 148–49.

60. Pink Dandelion, *The Cultivation of Conformity: Towards a General Theory of Internal Secularisation* (London: Routledge, 2019), 148–49.

61. Quoted in Stephen W. Angell, "'The Shadows of the Evening Stretched Out': Richard Robinson and the Shaping of African Methodist Identity, 1823–1862," *Journal of Africana Religions* 3, no. 3 (2015): 237.

62. Quoted in Henry J. Cadbury, "Negro Membership in the Society of Friends," *Journal of Negro History* 21, no. 2 (1936): 180.

63. Quoted in Ryan P. Jordan, *Slavery and the Meetinghouse: The Quakers and the Abolitionist Dilemma, 1820–1865* (Bloomington: Indiana University Press, 2007), 78.

64. Carleton Mabee, *Black Freedom: The Nonviolent Abolitionists from 1830 Through the Civil War* (New York: Macmillan, 1970), 127–38; Jordan, *Slavery and the Meetinghouse*, 67–80.

65. Quoted in Elizabeth Pease, *Society of Friends in the United States: Their Views of the Anti-Slavery Question, and Treatment of the People of Colour: Compiled from Original Correspondence* (Darlington, UK: John Wilson, 1840), 22; Bacon, *Sarah Mapps Douglass*, 7; Angell, "Early Period," 27–30.

66. Quoted in Bacon, *Sarah Mapps Douglass*, 5.

67. Cadbury, "Negro Membership," 170–73, 181–82, 209.

68. Quoted in Dorothy Sterling, *We Are Your Sisters: Black Women in the Nineteenth Century* (New York: W. W. Norton, 1984), 130.

69. Nash, *Forging Freedom*, 180.

70. P. R., "The Society of Friends and Abolition," *Friend*, August 19, 1843, 47.

71. Richard Allen, "The Life Experience and Gospel Labors of the Rt. Rev. Richard Allen (1833)," in Sernett, *African American Religious History*, 149.

72. Quoted in Bacon, *Sarah Mapps Douglass*, 21.

73. Cadbury, "Negro Membership," 179, 212; Jordan, *Slavery and the Meetinghouse*, 71, 74; Angell, "'Shadows of the Evening,'" 229, 245.

74. Ella, "A Question," *Liberator*, June 4, 1831, 23.

75. Bacon, *Sarah Mapps Douglass*, 31, 17.

76. Jordan, *Slavery and the Meetinghouse*, 49.

77. P. R., "Society of Friends and Abolition."

78. Bacon, *Sarah Mapps Douglass*, 21.

79. Chuck Fager, *Remaking Friends: How Progressive Friends Changed Quakerism and Helped Save America* (Durham, NC: Kimo Press, 2014); Walter Edgerton, *A History of the Separation in Indiana Yearly Meeting of Friends* (Cincinnati: Achilles Pugh, 1856).

80. Margaret Hope Bacon, "New Light on Sarah Mapps Douglass and Her Reconciliation with Friends," *Quaker History* 90, no. 1 (2001): 33.

CHAPTER 5

"She Hath Done What She Could"
The Charitable Antislavery Work of Eleanor Clark of Street

ANNA VAUGHAN KETT

This chapter examines the wide-ranging charitable work of the Quaker Eleanor Stephens Clark (1812–1879), with a focus on her antislavery activity. Eleanor was the wife of James Clark, the British industrial shoemaking pioneer, who in 1825 (with his older brother Cyrus) formed the company C. & J. Clark in Street, Somerset, in the West Country of England.[1] Much has been written about this successful global brand and its founders, but with the exception of works by Sandra Holton, far less has been written on the lives of the female members of the Clark family.[2] These lives are extremely interesting; alongside domestic and caring duties, Eleanor, her sisters, and her daughters and nieces were busy in roles that took them from the domestic, private sphere into both the public world of commerce and the charitable sphere, a space defined by Clare Midgley as a semipublic or "third sphere."[3] Julie Holcomb's chapter in this volume discusses patterns of female activity and the permeable boundaries between private and public spaces. In the context of abolitionism, Midgley and Julie Roy Jeffrey have unpacked women's roles in their landmark books on Britain and America.[4] Jeffrey, Jean Fagin Yellin, and John C. Van Horne declare these eighteenth- and nineteenth-century women a "sisterhood" of antislavery activists on both sides of the Atlantic that transgressed boundaries of class and race.[5]

This chapter adds to the reclamation of less-researched Quaker women's lives and it focuses on active, passionate, influential women who have been less visible in historical accounts of activism.[6] The chapter examines the rapidly changing environment of the 1840s to 1870s, the period when Clark was married, raising her family, and living in Street. Owing to the success of the burgeoning shoe company, this small agricultural village, despite its rural location, was being transformed into a thriving and well-appointed small industrial town.[7] I discuss Clark's empathy with the poor and the enslaved and I draw primarily upon archival materials in the Library of the Society of Friends in London (LSF) and the Alfred Gillett Trust at C. & J. Clark in Street (AGT). Sources include Clark's letters and writings for the Village Album, a family-run literary society that she founded in 1857. The society also produced the *Village Album*, a handwritten, illustrated periodical of members' contributions.[8] It was customary to use a pen name, and Eleanor chose "Eva" in reference to Evangeline in *Uncle Tom's Cabin*. This emphasized her identification with Harriet Beecher Stowe's enormously popular novel and positioned her within the wave of abolitionism sparked by its publication in 1852.[9]

Clark was a passionate, practical, busy woman. Her fourteen children were born in quick succession: Amy (1836), Amy-Jane (1837), William (1839), Frances (1840), Mary (1842), Thomas Bryant (1843), Ann (1844), Eleanor (1846), Florence (1847), Sophia Sturge (1849), James (1850), Edith (1852), Francis (1853), and Mabel Bryant (1857). Despite suffering from tuberculosis, she remained as active as possible until her death from the disease in 1879. When she was dying, her sisters Ann and Eliza and her daughters Sophia and Ann took on her charitable work, reinforcing the thread that joined women and their female kin.

The first study of British abolition made clear that Quakers were integral to its organization, implementation, and eventual success.[10] Writing in 1806, Thomas Clarkson observed that Friends were compelled primarily by Christian belief to help others and that this coincided with the evangelical movement, with which many British Quakers, including the Clarks, were aligned.[11] Clarkson noted with delight that Quaker women worked closely with one another and that their "public character" signaled "a new era in female history."[12] Historians have subsequently established that Quakers had extremely effective business networks.[13] The Quaker family was also closely networked, and endogamy had established close kinship ties between families in Britain and America. Women Friends were adept at maintaining these ties through letter writing, personal recommendations, their membership in charitable organizations, and frequent visits to help one another with family trials. It is evident that strong and affectionate ties were forged between the Clark women and their kinswomen in other families: the Sturge family in Birmingham, the Reynolds family in Bridport, the Gurney family in Norwich, the Bancroft family in Manchester, and the Thompson family in Bristol.

Another layer of connectivity was created through transatlantic abolitionism, which linked Clark to networks that included non-Quakers. Women were excluded from public positions of power in the British and Foreign Anti-Slavery Society (BFASS), but women formed their own system of all-female societies beginning in the 1820s.[14] While James was listed at the BFASS, there is no record that Eleanor was a member of any female equivalents, despite the nearby location of some in Bristol and Bath, though poor rural roads may have made these unappealing. Perhaps Clark preferred to be independent, for it is evident that she ran her own informal "society," ordering in bulk from suppliers and distributing free-produce foods such as sugar and tapioca from her home.[15]

Clark was, however, closely associated with the Birmingham Ladies' Negro's Friend Society, an important connection with the area's leading metropolitan ladies' society.[16] She was a friend of Hannah Dickinson Sturge (1816–1896), the leader of the society and the second wife of Joseph Sturge (1793–1859), the foremost antislavery activist in Britain, the leader of the BFASS, and the editor of its newspaper, the *Anti-Slavery Reporter*. Sturge was also James Clark's first cousin, making the women close relatives as well as friends who shared the same views. To cement their connection, the Clarks' daughter Sophia Sturge was named after her cousins. Significantly, both Hannah and Eleanor ran "slave-free" households, purchasing only goods made using free labor. As Holcomb explains, the free-produce movement was both radical and transformative; it advocated a primarily female consumer-based approach to abolition enacted through the boycott of slave-made goods and their replacement with free-labor alternatives.[17] We may conclude that women's networks and friendships played a part in spreading abolitionist messages. For example, while staying with the Sturge family in Birmingham, Harriet Beecher Stowe was so impressed by Sturge's excellent housekeeping and the plentiful luxury of food she was served that she converted to free produce.[18]

Clark's most notable contribution to the antislavery cause undoubtedly came through her role in the free-produce community. Until recently, free produce has received little historical attention, but Holcomb's work reopens and reinforces this instance of the power of harnessing consumers.[19] Significantly, free produce connected consumer activity with the capitalist marketplace and with the practice of slavery in producing goods, a theme discussed in Bronwen Everill's book.[20] Thus free produce resonates with the modern experience of consumers who seek ethically made or responsibly farmed products, even if these goods may cost a little more, are difficult to verify, and may be harder to find. In 1853, ever practical and entrepreneurial, Clark set up the Street Free Labour Cotton Depot, run from a stall in the village temperance hall, to make articles made from free-labor cotton available in the village. The little shop ran for five years, selling goods at cost and with no profit motive. It supplied a carefully selected range of goods to suit Clark's cohort of female shoppers, procuring a variety of cloths made in Britain, using raw cotton from several global sources. It was endorsed by Joseph Sturge at the BFASS, who held it up as a template of good practice. Undoubtedly, Clark's good standing in the community and the respect that she commanded inspired confidence among her shoppers; indeed, the free-produce movement ran substantially on trust, for labels and stamps indicating the ethical credentials of goods were rare. As Manchester cotton warehouseman Josias Browne explained, free-produce consumers needed to exert "extreme caution" and to buy only from those of "unquestionable integrity, upon whose word we can rely."[21]

Clark's antislavery work was part of the couple's wider charitable commitments, for it was customary that Quaker women participated in the same philanthropic milieu as their male kin.[22] At the same time, James and Cyrus Clark were implementing philanthropic initiatives in the shoemaking company, such as a reading room and subsidized housing for the workforce.[23] The couple's household accounts in the 1830s show their joint involvement with a variety of organizations: the Temperance Society, the Bible Society, the Missionary Society, the Penny Clothing Society, the Irish Evangelical Society, and the British and Foreign School. In addition, the couple collected donations "for anti-slavery" from seven family members over a number of years.[24] Such extensive involvement was normal in Quaker circles, and, while Roger Clark suggests that Street was an especially "fertile ground," similar philanthropic patterns of giving were replicated across the country, especially in cities such as Bristol, Norwich, and Birmingham.[25]

Of course, the wealth of some Quaker families enabled generous donations to charities.[26] Success presented a moral paradox; given their historical identification with the poor and compounded by evangelical beliefs, some wealthy Friends felt conflicted. The solution was charitable giving, or what became known in Quaker circles as "doing good whilst doing well." In 1768 charity was enshrined in *Quaker Advices*: "Let us impress it especially upon Friends in affluent circumstances to ... relieve the wants of the needy of all denominations with a *liberal* hand."[27] Joseph Sturge wrote of the "strong pangs of conscience" that compelled him to direct his fortune to charity.[28] In the opinion of banker Samuel Gurney, there was a direct correlation between spiritual reward and charity, a "supernatural insurance" to ensure "a good market above," as he put it.[29] William Wilberforce's words on duty rang true, that love of one's fellow man was "the indispensable and indeed charitable duty of Christians."[30]

As for the question of whether Quaker women's participation in philanthropy conflicted with domestic demands, Quakers had always encouraged women's independence through protracted sojourns in ministry, and the schooling of girls was considered as important as that of boys. However, essentialist views on women's nature and gendered spaces exerted a powerful pressure on women, especially middle-class women, to stay at home. While this may look restrictive to our modern eyes, many women took great pride in their domestic, homemaking, and child-rearing identities. There was great permeability between spheres of interest, and it was perfectly acceptable for women to elide the boundaries via what Midgley explains was "an intermediate social sphere of organized philanthropic work." This "charitable sphere" had far-reaching implications, opening the door for women and girls to participate in campaigns for social and political justice. Furthermore, Midgley explains that evangelicalism, rather than suppressing it, may have actually promoted women's ingenuity in "finding practical ways of working around" gender restrictions, notably by using the home and "motherly" capabilities to further campaigns.[31] Eileen Yeo explores how women's self-representation as mothers was compatible with their political work, calling it a form of "social motherhood" that echoed the nurturing and practicalities of raising children.[32] This rings true for Clark, for as her obituary stated, for many years "her motherly interest in the concerns and welfare of the village was well known and appreciated."[33] The justification for charitable work was also found in scriptures—for example, Proverbs 31:20: "She stretcheth out her hand to the poor ... she reacheth forth her hands to the needy." The popular Quaker abolitionist poet Elizabeth Margaret Chandler summarized the Christian argument: "It is on all sides acknowledged, that the domestic circle is the proper sphere of woman. We do not say that her talents and influence should be confined within these boundaries. . . . If homebred usefulness forms no part of her character ... she fails of one half of her perfection."[34] Thus women's actions in "reaching forth" beyond the home were both validated and sacralized.[35] This was the case for the pious Clark, whose poem "Alleluia! Alleluia! Jesus Died for Thee and Me" (1862) shows that she felt comforted by "Christ's love" after the death of her beloved cousin Hannah Impey.[36] Indeed, as Clark was dying, she wrote that she was happy to be "in a loving father's hands ... [for] he will do all things well."[37] While women were not (in Chandler's words) "confined in these boundaries," the majority of their charitable work did emanate from home; thus it is logical that Clark's cotton shop was located a five-minute walk from her house, for this was the only way it could have functioned for this busy woman.

Clark's upbringing equipped her for a charitable life. She was born into a family of birthright Quakers in the market town of Bridport in Dorset. Her parents, Amy Metford and William Stephens, ran a prosperous drapery shop and both were weighty Friends in the meeting and public-minded in the town.[38] In addition to the shop and a home crowded with sixteen children, the family supported a range of charitable societies and welcomed many guests to their home. The diaries kept by William and by Eleanor's sister Rebecca listed one hundred such visitors, including abolitionists such as Amelia Opie and Thomas Clarkson.[39] Amy was a powerful influence on her children, and her horror of slavery was well known.[40] Using Quaker child-rearing guides, she instilled the "habits of industry" in each of her children. A song she sang to them shows her approach to keeping busy:

> The truest enjoyment consists in employment
> In having something to do
> I pity the child who is forced to run wild
> Without any object in view.[41]

Eleanor and James began courting in 1827 and planned to marry in 1831, though the marriage was postponed until 1835 after Eleanor became ill with tuberculosis. Their home, Netherleigh, was a large stone-faced villa that James had built for his new wife in the center of Street, adjoining the shoe-making factory and companionably close to Eleanor's sisters Eliza and Ann and to James's brother Cyrus and his wife, Sarah, and their family. Significantly, Netherleigh's kitchen became a nucleus for charitable activity. For example, in 1845 Cyrus and James formed the Street Teetotal Society at the kitchen table. This was not unusual, as the kitchen was the preferred meeting place for Quakers, in contrast to non-Quakers, who preferred to entertain visitors in the parlor, dining room, or drawing room. The kitchen was a woman's terrain, symbolic of women's authority in the household.[42] In *Uncle Tom's Cabin*, Stowe describes the kitchen of Quaker Rachel Halliday as a multifunctional space, a paragon of domestic order and family cooperation, and a social space for frequent visitors. It was also a political space, for the house was a station on the Underground Railroad.[43]

Evidence suggests that Clark was happily absorbed in running the home, managing the kitchen, superintending the kitchen garden, buying cloth and provisions, and caring for her children. She was an affectionate mother who worried that she "loved them too much" and who took the responsibilities of parenting very seriously indeed.[44] While employing both residential and daily staff (three servants were recorded on the UK 1851 Census), she was often the single parent when James was away visiting clients. Clark's letters to James suggest that the home was noisy and crowded and that her personal space was minimal. Her domestic duties were relentless, especially when the children were ill, and at times she wrote to him with a sick child sitting on her knee. Out of necessity, Clark spent much time sewing, a task so ubiquitous that it was known simply as "woman's work."[45] Sewing was essential to a woman's identity and the responsibility to sew everything that the household needed fell entirely upon women's shoulders.[46] In addition to "plain" everyday sewing and mending, Clark enjoyed recreational projects such as "fancy" embroidery and decorative sewing. There was not as much time for this as she would have liked, as she observed in one letter to James: "As to my needlework, it comes to nothing, ... by the evening I am too tired ... it is indeed very trying."[47]

By the 1840s, Clark's charity work had gone from strength to strength, and she was now part of a close-knit cohort of roughly twenty kinswomen, some of whom were Friends who attended the local Quaker women's monthly meeting.[48] Clark and her cohort were evidently interested in both current affairs and politics, and this undoubtedly provided a platform for subsequent generations. Daughters from some of these families would go on to become famous in national campaigns for health, education, suffrage, antiracism, and temperance. Especially notable were Catherine Impey (1847–1923), the Black rights activist and niece of the Clarks, and Helen Priestman Bright Clark (1840–1927), the suffrage campaigner and daughter of John Bright, who married the Clarks' son William in 1866.[49] That same year, Helen wrote to Eleanor asking her to support the inclusion of women's voting rights in the forthcoming parliamentary reform bill tabled by her father. Clark supplied Bright's petition with eighteen or nineteen signatures from what Helen called her "independent lady friends."[50] In the 1840s, Eleanor and James's antislavery work also gained momentum, and they forged links with the antislavery movement in America. Eleanor wrote to James in 1843 that the "distinguished American visitor" James Canning Fuller from New York State had arrived to stay at the house, on a mission to garner support for the Underground Railroad.[51]

By the 1840s, sewing had become very important in Clark's life, and in addition to supplying her household with textile items, she was an early member of the Street Sewing Circle, a thriving group of approximately twenty local women who sewed for public causes.[52] Women's sewing circles were extremely popular and existed in many forms, including the church-based Dorcas Societies, which made clothing for the parish poor and for missionaries overseas.[53] Sewing circles were especially popular among Quakers, as sewing was a hallmark of female identity and self-sufficiency, and many circles were attached to women's meetings. Sewing circles generally bought plain-quality cloth and generated quantities of clothing for domestic or overseas distribution or for sale at charity fairs and bazaars. Some circles functioned specifically to stock antislavery fairs, as was the case in Newcastle, Norwich, Birmingham, Bath, Bangor, and Bristol. Many (such as Clark's own circle) also sent goods to sell at American antislavery fundraising fairs, linking the women to a sisterhood of activist producers on both sides of the Atlantic.[54] Roger Clark, Eleanor's grandson, recalled that the Street Sewing Circle was very productive with Clark's aunt Keturah Clothier at the helm.[55] Not only were the circles industrious, and central to the many organizations that relied upon them; they were also pivotal to women's lives across social classes. They offered sociability, companionship, and mentoring, and they taught women the market value of their labor.[56] Sewing circles also promoted literacy, for it was common practice to take turns reading aloud while sewing. The Street Circle enjoyed literature when the

Village Album committee joined the seamstresses at tea to read and discuss contributions. It is probable that they also read and discussed antislavery literature, as William Lloyd Garrison acknowledged when he dubbed them "festive reading or conversation parties."[57] This is borne out by the fact that in 1859, on behalf of the sewing circle, Clark wrote to the BFASS, enclosing money for copies of antislavery tracts to distribute among her friends.[58] It is likely that *Uncle Tom's Cabin* was read aloud in this setting, since it is well known that women's groups contributed to its rapid dissemination across society.[59] Significantly, group reading fostered empathy with the characters, allowing readers, as Douglas Lorimer observes, to "enter the world of the plantation" and feel the pain of the enslaved.[60]

In 1843, Clark had commenced corresponding with Martha Ball of the Massachusetts Female Emancipation Society (MFES), which drew support from evangelical women on both sides of the Atlantic. Hannah Sturge introduced Clark and Ball to each other and two surviving letters from Ball demonstrate their affectionate connection and shared opinions on temperance, the usefulness of women's sewing, and the importance of fostering antislavery sentiment in children. Ball appreciated Clark's donations to an upcoming antislavery fair, and she was particularly pleased with the shoes she had received. It is probable that these came from C. & J. Clark, were not yet marketed in the United States, and were therefore valued for their rarity. The letters these two women exchanged provide fascinating insights into the world of the ladies' fair, including the judgment women workers exercised and the shrewd knowledge of markets and customer tastes required of organizers. While the larger fairs issued strict guidelines and could afford to be choosy, Ball adopted a more inclusive approach to the goods, writing, "indeed nothing ever comes out of place ... the more variety the better." She added that she would "take pleasure in showing them with the labels attached."[61] This may be interpreted in two ways; that the goods were labeled as British or that they carried abolitionist slogans.[62] Catchy, humorous phrases captured the sentiments of the movement and were very popular at fairs; for example, the *Liberator* reported that a ladies' fair in Philadelphia in 1837 sold bundles of quill pens labeled "Twenty-five Weapons for Abolitionists."[63]

As part of the transatlantic sisterhood, Clark's contributions should be seen within a wider network of sending goods for sale in America to defray the costs of running American antislavery societies. Beginning in the 1840s, the Massachusetts Anti-Slavery Society became increasingly reliant on the income from its famous annual Boston Fair, which in turn relied on British women for almost half of the goods it sold.[64] Although the MFES fair was a more modest event, Clark's goods contributed to the organizers' income stream, taking Clark's cohort to the heart of the public or commercial sphere. Julie Roy Jeffrey concludes that such fairs were deeply radical, for they relied completely on female agency, propelled women into the commercial arena, transcended class and racial divides (especially in America), and gave political meaning to women's work, proving them to be able propagandists.[65] Becoming galvanized was evidently part of women's experience, as Maria Weston Chapman, organizer of the Boston Fair, heard from one woman who felt positively "abolitionized" by her involvement in making goods for sale.[66] Despite being pleasurable and exciting, fairs were something of a minefield in terms of the tastes and styles offered by producers, and the sensible prices charged by the organizers. Choosing which antislavery fair to support also caused some anguish. Supporters were influenced by controversies within antislavery and Quaker cultures, especially the rivalry between William Lloyd Garrison and Frederick Douglass and their respective fairs in Boston and Rochester. A practical solution—which Clark adopted—was to donate to the less controversial fairs, such as the one run by the MFES.

In 1852, the village of Street became somewhat "abolitionized" itself by the publication of *Uncle Tom's Cabin*. Following the book's American success, it sold one million copies in Britain within a year and was declared the "book of the day" by the *Times* of London, surpassing in sales any other nineteenth-century publication except the Bible.[67] Perhaps the book resonated so deeply with British readers because the British economy relied so heavily on American slave-grown cotton.[68] Moreover, through vivid characterization and moving depictions of plantation slavery, the book humanized the struggle against the vicious and dehumanizing practice. Lynn Hunt has discussed the connection between literature and the formation of empathy, and ultimately the notion of human rights. Hunt writes that identification with literary characters "enabled readers to empathize across class, sex and national lines."[69] Since it was written by a woman, *Uncle Tom's Cabin* spoke especially to other women, sparking in them a passionate identification, and above all prompting them to "do what they could" to end slavery. This was both transformative and highly motivational, and Eleanor Clark's personal response was to open the free-cotton shop. "At the present time," she wrote in the flyer advertising its opening, "when the subject of Slavery is exciting so much attention in the public mind, through the reading of 'Uncle Tom's Cabin,' it is thought very desirable that increased facilities should be afforded for the sale of FREE LABOUR COTTON ARTICLES."[70] Feelings also ran high when it became known that Stowe was not paid royalties for the novel. In late 1852, Hannah Sturge organized a national collection of a penny from each reader to be presented to Stowe when she visited Britain the following year. The "Penny Offering" raised an impressive £1,800 which exceeded the annual income of the BFASS.[71] Clark was the collection agent for the village of Street, raising a total of 18s. 1d. from seventy male and female contributors.[72] Although the names on the surviving subscription card are not all decipherable, many are. They include Eleanor's daughters Frances, Mary, and Ann, her sister-in-law Sarah (Cyrus's wife), her sisters Ann, Rebecca, and Eliza Stephens, and her kinswomen Catherine and Mary Hannah Impey, Mary Reynolds, and Catherine, Priscilla, Julia, and Keturah Clothier. This confirms the interconnected nature of the female networks to which Clark belonged, and it reveals the core of women activists in Street.

In the 1850s, the family became acquainted with the work of Henry Highland Garnet (1815–1882), the radical African American abolitionist who advocated resistance to enslavement.[73] Garnet was also a powerful advocate of free produce as the safest method of attacking the "root of the evil." Anna and Henry Richardson of Newcastle mobilized the Quaker network to support Garnet and his campaign to free the enslaved Weims family. In 1851, they brought Garnet, his wife Julia, and their daughter Stella (whom they had adopted from the Weims family) to Britain for an extensive lecture tour—a pivotal moment for British abolitionism. While we do not know whether Clark attended Garnet's lectures, she may have read reports in the press about the electrifying atmosphere, the use of horrifying props, and "monster" audiences that included many women across the country who signed on the spot to form free-produce associations. In 1852, the "Weims campaign" snowballed, and £300 was raised between September and December of that year.[74] In November, James placed notices in the local and Quaker press, directing contributions to be sent to the Clark home. Letters from donors that have survived provide us with insights into the formidable efficiency and reach of the Quaker network, for not all the correspondents were Friends. It is striking that Friends such as the Clarks had the ability to reassure those contemplating donating that this was a legitimate collection and not a scam.[75]

In the 1840s and '50s, the Clarks also became deeply involved with Elihu Burritt (1810–1879), a charismatic Calvinist preacher and prolific pamphleteer from Connecticut who came to Britain to generate support for his various campaigns.[76] In 1846, Burritt founded the League of Brotherhood, which promoted world peace, and looked to Britain for funding. Joseph Sturge introduced him to James Clark and firm friendships were forged between Burritt and the whole family, most notably with Eleanor, her sisters, and her mother.[77] Burritt needed considerable funds, and his clever solution was to create an extensive network of fundraising auxiliaries or "Olive Leaf Societies or Circles" that were entirely female domains. This was a sizeable undertaking. By 1852 there were 150 branches, comprising more than two thousand women, or "League Sisters," as the women fondly called one another. The societies raised funds through a monthly subscription of one shilling and a highly productive system of bazaars, where the costs of making goods, especially sewn ones, were met by League Sisters and all profits were donated directly to the League.[78]

In January 1851, Burritt invited Eleanor Clark to join the Olive Leaf family. She accepted and opened a branch in Street.[79] Two subscription cards have survived; the first lists eighteen names, and the second, twenty-four. Some illegible names notwithstanding, most are familiar: S[arah], F[anny], and E[leanor] Clark; A[nn] Stephens; K[eturah] and Catherine Clothier; Elizabeth Palmer; H[annah] Impey; and E[liza] Palmer. Rose Luggling, a housemaid at the Clark home, and Mrs. Coole, the wife of Street draper John Coole, were also listed.[80] Burritt was acutely aware of the importance of appealing to families, and he seems to have been popular with women and children. It is notable that he produced a series of small books for Sabbath reading, and that even the notepaper he used was printed with intriguing illustrations of foreign lands and oceangoing ships, which would have been of interest to children. Evidently, Burritt made a good impression on Clark, for he was a guest in the Clarks' home on several occasions. League Sisters were also supportive; in 1851 they collected money to refurbish his London office in order to make it more like "a real home," and Clark sent money for a writing table.[81] League Sisters also wrote a poem extolling the virtues of home-based women's work:

> And as, despite of all that's said
> Of woman's rank and right,
> We feel our happiest work is found

> Within the dear home-circle bound,
> Where glows the hearth fire's light.[82]

This verse epitomizes the sanctity and centrality of home in the lives of activists like Eleanor Clark.

Clark's charitable work in the 1860s is less well documented. Tuberculosis may have begun to limit her activity, and letters show that she was periodically confined to her room and was carried into the village in a chair. Her charitable work reappears at the end of the decade, when she is associated with a significant postslavery campaign known as the freedmen's aid movement. Formed in 1861, the British Freedmen's Aid Society was led by the Sturges, with the full support of the Clarks. As Carol Faulkner explains, "women were especially active" in filling the practical roles of making, collecting, and distributing clothing, shoes, bedding, and food to the newly emancipated, formerly enslaved people experiencing poverty.[83] The range of goods that British philanthropists shipped to America was impressive, as seen in the donations from British companies, many of which were Quaker.[84] Beyond providing emergency relief, the donations were also intended to be sold, contributing to financial independence for freed people.[85]

Freedmen's aid was in full swing during the 1870s and 1880s, a time of exceptional violence in the American South.[86] With the loss of hope for the equitable allocation of land to Black farmers, and with Black Americans facing innumerable acts of persecution and appalling violence, church communities, especially from the African Episcopal Church, organized the removal of emancipated people to safety in the North. As this church-led migration resembled the movement of the Israelites out of Egypt, it became known as the "Black Exodus."[87] A sort of "Kansas Fever" took hold, fueled by the belief that the North could be the promised land. The exodus from the South reached a peak between 1879 and 1881, when an estimated twenty thousand refugees, or Exodusters, traveled north. After a hazardous journey, their situation in Kansas was desperate, and it was clear that relief organizations needed to mobilize. In 1879, Sojourner Truth, William Lloyd Garrison, and Henry Highland Garnet called for action and the Clark family became involved; James's December 1879 letter to the *British Friend* solicited donations and other aid.[88] This was seven months after Eleanor's death, and despite their grief, James and their daughter Sophia Sturge continued Eleanor's work collecting clothing and textiles that were shipped to Kansas by friends in Bristol.

These shipments were more than parcels of donations; they signaled an awakening in Britain of the campaign for Black rights. Notably, Catherine Impey became active in collecting goods for freed people, beginning her long-standing campaign for social justice.[89] It seems that the village was indeed a fertile ground for philanthropy, and Impey's scrapbook recorded the political milieu at Askew, the family home. Impey went on to become a national figure, raising awareness of the racial segregation, endemic prejudice, and lynching in America. In March 1888, Impey founded *Anti-Caste*, Britain's first antiracist periodical, which she wrote at the kitchen table in Askew between 1888 and 1895.[90] Not long thereafter, Frederick Douglass would be seen walking down Street's High Street, brought as the guest of Impey and Helen Clark. Impey also arranged for Ida B. Wells to tour Britain in 1893, lecturing about lynching. This tour led to the formation of two organizations, the Anti-Lynching Committee, founded in London, and the Society for the Recognition of the Brotherhood of Man.[91] As Caroline Bressey writes, "a small town in Somerset far from spaces of cosmopolitan exchange in London may seem an unlikely place to have hosted the publication of a radical paper [*Anti-Caste*] that challenged racial prejudice in the British Empire and the United States."[92]

Finally, it is useful to discuss the empathy that Clark felt toward the enslaved and the poor, which guided her antislavery work. In her handwritten essay "Cotton" (1861), Clark catalogued the injustices meted out to the enslaved, the "terrible work" they were forced to do, "urged until they are ready to drop, weary and exhausted by hunger, the heat and cruel driving."[93] It is evident that Clark felt passionately about this brutality, for the writing becomes difficult to read; words are frequently crossed out and scratches made by the pen nib are very deep, indicating her anguish and her anger. To inform her writing, Clark drew from *Uncle Tom's Cabin* and from accounts published in the *Slave; His Wrongs and Their Remedy*, the antislavery free-produce newspaper edited first by Anna and Henry Richardson and then by Elihu Burritt. This monthly newspaper was both a vital source of information and a means of fostering a sense of community, with its passionate declarations of "solidarity with brothers and sisters in bonds."[94] As noted above, empathy was also stirred by the poetry of Elizabeth Margaret Chandler, whose death was published widely in the Quaker and antislavery press, notably in the *Anti-Slavery Reporter*. In her poem "Slave Produce," Chandler wrote that everyone should be wary of slave-made products, for they were irrevocably polluted or "stained" with the sweat, blood, and tears of the enslaved.⁹⁵ It was deeply troubling that slavery could be manifested through its products, and the notion that the "shriek and groan of the slave" were embedded in clothing and foods was deeply repellent. No wonder abolitionists like Clark wanted to distance themselves from slave-made items and to maintain "clean hands."⁹⁶

While revulsion at the products of slavery motivated her work, Clark also felt strong allegiance with the disadvantaged, as shown by her interest in shoddy cloth, a deeply unpopular form of coarse recycled wool used for making the very poorest clothing. Items made from shoddy included cheap, ready-made garments, including military uniforms and the blankets and clothing used by the enslaved on plantations.⁹⁷ Clark wrote of her delight in this humble cloth, made from shredded and reconstituted rags, in an essay with the ironic title "On Pride in Dress."⁹⁸ Her attitude toward personal possessions certainly challenged convention; although Quakers respected plainness and simplicity in dress, one might have expected the wife of one of the most successful industrialists in the west of England to own more than a handful of clothes at the time of her death. Clark actually had few possessions that could be distributed among her daughters; as Ann informed her sister Florence, "There is not much to divide."⁹⁹ We may infer that Clark's interest in "poor," shoddy clothing and her lack of possessions stemmed from her moral values rather than from constrained finances.

This chapter has examined how the upbringing, family, domestic life, and cultural and religious milieux affected the charitable and antislavery work of Eleanor Clark from the 1840s to the 1870s. From her arrival in Street in 1835, Clark threw herself into charitable work, which led to her involvement in various networks of Quaker families, close friends, sisters, aunts, daughters, and cousins in the United Kingdom and the United States. Street may have lived in the middle of rural Somerset, but it proved to be a most "fertile ground" for philanthropy. The strong cohort of "independent lady friends" who came chiefly from Clark's extended family participated in an interconnected range of social and public activities extending from the 1840s into the twentieth century. Catherine Impey's work is a perfect example of how campaigns were continued by successive generations of women activists in the extended Clark family, who built upon the foundations established by their aunts, mothers, and grandmothers.

While Eleanor Clark's activism was run from home, she was also active outside the home, as exemplified in the Street Free Labour Cotton Depot and as encouraged by leading activists Hannah and Joseph Sturge and Elihu

Burritt. Clark's identity as a "motherly" woman who loved sewing underwrote many of her public activities, and sewing emerged as an appropriate activity through which a wealthy middle-class woman might express her commitment to public culture. Put simply, it was through cloth and stitches that Clark made direct, practical contributions to the antislavery cause. Finally, we may conclude that Clark was both emotionally and spiritually motivated to rectify injustices. Her deep empathy with her "brothers and sisters in bonds" led her to apply herself, and to do what she could to bring down slavery.

NOTES

1. Mark Palmer, *Clarks Made to Last: A History of Britain's Best-Known Shoe Firm* (London: Profile, 2013).
2. Sandra Stanley Holton, *Quaker Women: Personal Life, Memory, and Radicalism in the Lives of Women Friends, 1780–1930* (London: Routledge, 2007); and Sandra Stanley Holton, "Kinship and Friendship: Quaker Women's Networks and the Women's Movement," *Women's History Review* 14, nos. 3–4 (2005): 365–84.
3. Clare Midgley, *Women Against Slavery: The British Campaigns, 1780–1870* (New York: Routledge, 1992); Clare Midgley, *Feminism and Empire: Women Activists in Imperial Britain, 1790–1865* (London: Routledge, 2007).
4. Midgley, *Women Against Slavery*; Julie Roy Jeffrey, *The Great Silent Army of Abolitionism: Ordinary Women in the Antislavery Movement* (Chapel Hill: University of North Carolina Press, 1998); and Julie Roy Jeffrey, "Permeable Boundaries: Abolitionist Women and Separate Spheres," *Journal of the Early Republic* 21, no. 1 (2001): 79–93.
5. Jeffrey, *Great Silent Army of Abolitionism*, 111; Jean Fagin Yellin and John C. Van Horne, eds., *The Abolitionist Sisterhood: Women's Political Culture in Antebellum America* (Ithaca: Cornell University Press, 1994).
6. Leonore Davidoff and Catherine Hall, *Family Fortunes: Men and Women of the English Middle Class, 1780–1850* (London: Routledge, 1992); Catherine Hall, *White, Male, and Middle Class: Explorations in Feminism and History* (Cambridge: Polity Press, 1992); Eileen Janes Yeo, ed., *Radical Femininity: Women's Self-Representation in the Public Sphere* (Manchester: Manchester University Press, 1998); and Simon Morgan, *A Victorian Woman's Place: Public Culture in the Nineteenth Century* (London: I. B. Tauris, 2007).
7. Michael McGarvie, *The Book of Street: A History from Earliest Times to 1925* (Buckingham, UK: Barracuda, 1987).
8. Roger Clark, *Somerset Anthology* (York, UK: Sessions Books, 1975); Alison Horgan and Anna Vaughan Kett, "Village Albums: A Collage of Quaker Life," *Collage Research Network* (November 11, 2019), https://collageresearchnetwork.wordpress.com/blog/.
9. Sarah Meer, *Uncle Tom Mania: Slavery, Minstrelsy, and Transatlantic Antislavery in the 1850s* (Athens: University of Georgia Press, 2005).
10. Thomas Clarkson, *The History of the Rise, Progress, and Accomplishment of the Abolition of the African Slave-Trade by the British Parliament*, 2 vols. (London: Longman, Hurst, Rees, and Orme, 1808).

11. Thomas Clarkson, *A Portraiture of Quakerism* [...] *in Three Volumes*. (London: Longman, 1806), 3:289–95; Ian Bradley, *The Call to Seriousness: The Evangelical Impact on the Victorians* (London: Cape, 1976).

12. Clarkson, *Portraiture of Quakerism*, 3:289.

13. James Walvin, *The Quakers: Money and Morals* (London: John Murray, 1997); J. William Frost, ed., *The Quaker Origins of Antislavery* (Norwood, PA: Norwood Editions, 1980); Howard Temperley, *British Antislavery, 1833–1870* (London: Longman, 1972); Brycchan Carey and Geoffrey Plank, eds. *Quakers and Abolition* (Urbana: University of Illinois Press, 2014).

14. Midgley, *Women Against Slavery*, 206–7.

15. Receipts for her large purchases of tapioca, lump, and golden sugar are in MS box 8, folder 3, LSF; MSS Brit. Emp., 818 C1549, Bodleian Library, University of Oxford.

16. Clark's papers are archived under "BLNFS" in MS box 8, LSF.

17. Julie Holcomb, *Moral Commerce: Quakers and the Transatlantic Boycott of the Slave Labor Economy* (Ithaca: Cornell University Press, 2016), esp. chaps. 5 and 7.

18. Harriet Beecher Stowe, *Sunny Memories of Foreign Lands* (London: Sampson and Low, 1854), 184–86.

19. See, for instance, Holcomb, *Moral Commerce*; see also Carol Faulkner, "'The Root of the Evil': Free Produce and Radical Antislavery, 1820–1850," *Journal of the Early Republic* 27, no. 3 (2007): 378–405; Temperley, *British Antislavery*.

20. Bronwen Everill, *"Not Made by Slaves": Ethical Capitalism and the Age of Abolition* (Cambridge: Harvard University Press, 2020).

21. Josias Browne, *To the Members of Anti-Slavery Societies and All Friends of the Slave* (n.p., n.d. [1853]), MS box 8, folder 3, LSF.

22. Davidoff and Hall, *Family Fortunes*, 107–49.

23. George Barry Sutton, *C. & J. Clark: A History of Shoemaking in Street* (York, UK: Sessions Books, 1979); McGarvie, *Book of Street*.

24. "The Household Accounts of Eleanor and James Clark" (October 1835–December 1838), Papers of Helen Sophia Heath Clark (HSHC), folder 52, Alfred Gillett Trust at C. & J. Clark in Street (AGT).

25. Clark, *Somerset Anthology*, xix.

26. Elizabeth Isichei, *Victorian Quakers* (Oxford: Oxford University Press, 1970); Walvin, *Quakers: Money and Morals*; Edward Milligan, *Biographical Dictionary of British Quakers in Commerce and Industry, 1775–1920* (York, UK: Sessions Books, 2007).

27. *Quaker Advices*, quoted in Walvin, *Quakers: Money and Morals*, 57.

28. Quoted in Stephen Hobhouse, *Joseph Sturge: His Life and Work* (London: n.p., 1919), 16.

29. Quoted in Isichei, *Victorian Quakers*, 214.

30. Quoted in Frank K. Prochaska, *Women and Philanthropy in Nineteenth-Century England* (Oxford: Clarendon Press, 1980), 9.

31. Midgley, *Feminism and Empire*, 8, 43.

32. Eileen Yeo, *The Contest for Social Science: Relations and Representations of Gender and Class* (London: Rivers Oram Press, 1996), 122.

33. Obituary for Eleanor Clark, *Central Somerset Gazette*, March 23, 1879.

34. Elizabeth Margaret Chandler, "Influence of Slavery on the Female Character," in *Essays, Philanthropic and Moral, by Elizabeth Margaret Chandler, Principally Relating to the Abolition of Slavery in America* (Philadelphia: Lemuel Howell, 1836), 116.

35. Carol Lasser, "Immediatism, Dissent, and Gender: Women and the Sentimentalization of Transatlantic Anti-Slavery Appeals," in *Women, Dissent, and Anti-Slavery in Britain and America, 1790–1865*, edited by Elizabeth Clapp and Julie Roy Jeffrey (Oxford: Oxford University Press, 2011), 111–31; Elizabeth A. O'Donnell, "'Woman's Rights and Woman's Duties': Quaker Women in the Nineteenth Century, with Special Reference to Newcastle Monthly Meeting of Women Friends" (PhD diss., University of Sunderland, 2000), 143.

36. Eva, "Alleluia! Alleluia! Jesus Died for Thee and Me" (1862), HSHC, folder 55, AGT.

37. Eleanor Clark to her sister Rebecca Thompson, March 16, 1879, ibid.

38. Biographical information on William Stephens can be found in the "Dictionary of Quaker Biography," manuscript, LSF.

39. William Stephens, diary (1788–1836), LSF; Rebecca Stephens Thompson, *journal* and *diary*, quoted in Morwenna Stephens, "The Stephens Family," 1999, manuscript, 114, LSF.

40. It is tempting to suggest that she may have been a sugar boycotter, but there is no evidence for this.

41. James Mott, *Observations on the Education of Children: And Hints to Young People on the Duties of Civil Life* (York, UK: n.p., 1819), 26–27; Rebecca Stephens Thompson, *journal*, quoted in Stephens, "Stephens Family," 114.

42. Lynne Walker and Vron Ware, "Political Pincushions: Decorating the Abolitionist Interior, 1787–1865," in *Domestic Space: Reading the Nineteenth-Century Interior*, edited by Inga Bryden and Janet Floyd (Manchester: Manchester University Press, 1999), 66.

43. Harriet Beecher Stowe, "The Quaker Settlement," chap. 13 in *Uncle Tom's Cabin; or, Life Among the Lowly* (1852; reprint, New York: Penguin Classics, 1981).

44. Eleanor Clark to James Clark, July 31, 1846, HSHC, folder 55, AGT.

45. Clare Rose, preface to *Clothing, Society, and Culture in the Nineteenth Century*, edited by Clare Rose, 3 vols. (London: Pickering and Chatto, 2011), 3:xiv.

46. Rozsika Parker, *The Subversive Stitch: Embroidery and the Making of the Feminine* (London: Women's Press, 1984), 173.

47. Eleanor Clark to James Clark, n.d. (ca. 1843), HSHC, folder 53, AGT.

48. "Minute Book: Women's Monthly Meeting Book, Middle Division, Somerset, 1845–1874," Taunton DD/SFR.m26, Somerset Record Office, Taunton, UK.

49. Holton, *Quaker Women*, 131–47, 163–222.

50. Helen Priestman Bright Clark to William Clark, May 17, 1866, quoted in ibid., 144.

51. Eleanor Clark to James Clark, July 28, 1843, HSHC, folder 53, AGT.

52. Clark, *Somerset Anthology*, 1–8.

53. Parker, *Subversive Stitch*, 162–64.

54. Jeffrey, *Great Silent Army of Abolitionism*, 111; Yellin and Van Horne, *Abolitionist Sisterhood*.

55. Clark, *Somerset Anthology*, 4–5.

56. O'Donnell, "'Woman's Rights and Woman's Duties,'" 256–57; Jeffrey, *Great Silent Army of Abolitionism*, 108–10; Midgley, *Women Against Slavery*, 188–90.

57. William Lloyd Garrison, editor's note, *Liberator*, December 4, 1842.

58. Eleanor Clark to Louis Chamerovzow, secretary of the BFASS, December 4, 1859, MSS Brit. Emp. 818 29/06, Bodleian Library, University of Oxford.

59. Meer, *Uncle Tom Mania*, 1.

60. Douglas Lorimer, *Colour, Class, and the Victorians* (Leicester: Leicester University Press, 1978), 84.

61. Mary Ball to Eleanor Clark, September 15, 1843, MS box 8, folder 4, LSF.

62. "Request for Goods," *British Friend*, May 1846; Deborah van Broekhoven, "'Better Than a Clay Club': The Organization of Antislavery Fairs, 1835–1860," *Slavery and Abolition* 19, no. 1 (1998): 24–45; Jeffrey, *Great Silent Army of Abolitionism*, 116–17.

63. *Liberator*, January 2, 1837, quoted in Jeffrey, *Great Silent Army of Abolitionism*, 117.

64. Van Broekhoven, "'Better Than a Clay Club,'" 31.

65. Jeffrey, *Great Silent Army of Abolitionism*, 109–24.

66. Hannah S [illegible] to Maria Chapman, October 17, 1839, quoted in ibid., 119.

67. "Uncle Tom Slavery Movement," *Times (London)*, March 21, 1853.

68. Sven Beckert, *Empire of Cotton: A New History of Global Capitalism* (London: Penguin Random House, 2014); Richard Huzzey, *Freedom Burning: Anti-Slavery and Empire in Victorian Britain* (Ithaca: Cornell University Press, 2012).

69. Lynn Hunt, *Inventing Human Rights: A History* (New York: W. W. Norton, 2007), 38.

70. "Free Labour Cotton Depot," flyer, May 1853, MS box 8, folder 4, LSF.

71. Midgley, *Women Against Slavery*, 126–27.

72. "Birmingham Ladies Negro's Friend Society Tribute to Mrs. Stowe," subscription card, MS box 8, folder 4, LSF.

73. Benjamin Quarles, *Black Abolitionists* (New York: Oxford University Press, 1969; reprint, New York: Da Capo Press, 1991), 226; Richard Blackett, *Building an Anti-Slavery Wall: Black Americans in the Atlantic Abolitionist Movement, 1830–1860* (Baton Rouge: Louisiana State University Press, 1983).

74. Letter to the editor, *London Daily News*, December 6, 1852.

75. Letters to Eleanor and James Clark from various correspondents, 1852–53, MS box 8, folder 1, LSF.

76. On Burritt, see Merle Curti, *The Learned Blacksmith* (New York: Erikson, 1937); Peter Tolis, *Elihu Burritt: Crusader for Brotherhood* (Hamden, CT: Archon Books, 1968); Wendy Chmielewski, "Women's Work Against War in 1846: The Transatlantic Peace Movement in Exeter and Philadelphia," paper delivered at the British International Studies Association Conference, University of Exeter, Exeter, UK, December 15–17, 2008.

77. Joseph Sturge to James Clark, August 18, 1846, MS box 8, folder 5, LSF; Elihu Burritt to James Clark, February 6, 1847, ibid., 7.

78. "Olive Leaf Society Ipswich Branch," flyer, ca. 1851, 2, MS box 8, folder 5, LSF.

79. Elihu Burritt to Eleanor Clark, January 27, 1851, no. ONE, 36/13, AGT; Caroline Fry to Eleanor Clark, January 27, 1851, MS box 8, folder 5, LSF.

80. "Olive Leaf Subscribers," subscription card, MS box 8, folder 5, LSF.

81. Ellen Colgate to Eleanor Clark, November 1851, HSHC, folder 55, AGT; Elihu Burritt to League Sisters, December 31, 1851, MS box 8, folder 5, LSF.

82. E. B. P., "The Sisters' Offering," December 8, 1851, MS box 8, folder 5, LSF.

83. Carol Faulkner, *Women's Radical Reconstruction: The Freedmen's Aid Movement* (Philadelphia: University of Pennsylvania Press, 2004), 9.

84. Birmingham City Libraries, Iron Room, "Birmingham Freed Men's Association," https://theironroom.wordpress.com/2016/09/26/birmingham-freed-mens-aid-association.

85. See Faulkner's introduction in *Women's Radical Reconstruction*.

86. See, for example, Nell Irvin Painter, *Standing at Armageddon: The United States, 1877–1919* (New York: W. W. Norton, 1987), 87.

87. Nell Irvin Painter, *Exodusters: Black Migration to Kansas After Reconstruction* (New York: W. W. Norton, 1979), 113–17.

88. James Clark, letter to the editor, *British Friend*, December 1, 1879, 304.

89. Caroline Bressey, *Empire, Race, and the Politics of Anti-Caste* (London: Bloomsbury, 2013), 1.

90. See *Anti-Caste* 1, no. 1 (March 1888): 1.

91. *Quaker Strongrooms*, "Catherine Impey of Street, Somerset, and Her Radical Anti-Racist Newspaper," a blog from the LSF, September 18, 2012, https://quakerstrongrooms.org/2012/09/18/catherine-impey-of-street-somerset-and-her-radical-anti-racist-newspaper/.

92. Bressey, *Empire, Race, and the Politics*, 7.

93. Eva, "Cotton," *Village Album* 14 (1861), AGT.

94. Anna and Henry Richardson, "The Free Labour Movement," *The Slave; His Wrongs and Their Remedy*, August 1851, 30.

95. Elizabeth Margaret Chandler, *Slave Produce*, in *The Philanthropic and Moral Essays by Elizabeth Margaret Chandler, Principally Relating to the Abolition of Slavery in America*, edited by Benjamin Lundy (Philadelphia: Lemuel Howell, 1836), 111.

96. Eva, "Cotton."

97. Hanna Rose Shell, *Shoddy: From Devil's Dust to the Renaissance of Rags* (Chicago: University of Chicago Press, 2020). See also Anna Vaughan Kett, "Dressing Abolitionists and the Enslaved: Free-Labour and Slave-Labour Gingham Cloth in Carlisle in the 1850s," in *Clothing the Enslaved in the Eighteenth-Century Atlantic World*, edited by Chris Evans and Naomi Preston, Pasold Research Studies in Textile, Dress and Fashion History (forthcoming).

98. Eva, "On Pride in Dress," *Village Album* 14 (1861), AGT.

99. Ann Clark to Florence Impey, March 28, 1879, HSHC, folder 55, AGT.

CHAPTER 6

Ruth Esther Smith (1870–1947)
Foremother to Friends in Central America

JENNIFER M. BUCK

Quaker mission work has a rich history of women (known among early Quakers as Mothers of Israel) who shepherded the Friends' churches worldwide from their genesis to their flourishing. Quaker female missionaries typically outnumbered their male counterparts, and often served in key leadership roles, founding Bible training schools, churches, orphanages, hospitals, and the like. Ruth Esther Smith exemplifies the powerful leadership and historic legacy of this type of Quaker female missionary. This chapter examines Smith and her work in the non-Western Quaker movement, especially her efforts empowering Central American Friends, which came to shape Spanish-speaking Quakerism worldwide.

"Miss Ruth," as she was known, served as the one of the original Quaker missionaries in Central America. Raised in Ohio and Kansas, Smith and her family relocated to Long Beach, California, in 1895. She attended Huntington Park Training School for Christian Workers, later known as Azusa Pacific University, graduating in 1900 and becoming a recorded minister in the Society of Friends in 1904.[1] Female teachers at the school influenced Smith. The culture there encouraged a focus on ameliorating issues related to poverty and urban concerns. This focus reflected an ethic that viewed service as an expression of God's love for the world.[2]

The training school and its style of education served as a model for Smith's later work in building schools in Central America. It produced the majority of pastors and missionaries serving the California Yearly Meeting (CYM) during the first half of the twentieth century.[3]

Service became a hallmark of Ruth Esther Smith's life. She ministered at the Sunshine Mission in San Francisco, working with recent immigrants and those displaced by the 1906 earthquake. She then became a pastor at First Friends Church in Long Beach and worked at the training school. During a missionary conference at the school, Smith forged boundary-transgressing friendships that would later be pivotal in the growth of the Quaker mission movement. She was also a member of the seven-person "Guatemala Band," the first group of Quaker missionaries to go to Central America. The group included Thomas J. Kelly, a Quaker from Whittier who persuaded the board of the training school to allow the group to go to Guatemala to try to establish a mission. Other members were Clark J. Buckley, the Bodwell family, Alice C. Zimmer, Esther Ada Bond, and Ada Mina.[4] The members of the group arrived in Guatemala not all at the same time but separately, between 1901 and 1906. After completing her studies at the training school, Smith became a longtime contributor to the CYM's *Christian Workman* (ironically named, given the predominance of women missionaries), writing a column on missions. This launched her career in mission mobilization and participation, which she viewed as a religious calling.

Smith described a life-changing mystical experience that occurred while she was walking the streets in Oakland during her service at the Sunshine Mission. She claimed to have heard a distinct call from God to evangelize in Guatemala.[5] She was eager to join the mission and the training school friends who had preceded her. When she arrived in Chiquimula in 1906, there were only eight converts. As a result of her missionary vision and zealous efforts, Friends' yearly meetings grew in Guatemala and Honduras. Smith quickly learned the Spanish language and within a year was fluent enough to preach and teach in Spanish.

Smith described her early missionary work as a period of building relationships. Through conversations with families and couples, she cultivated friendships with the local people and learned the culture. For instance, she attended a child's funeral, provided meals to a sick person, attended graduations and parades, and invited friends to her home. At one point, she hosted an evening party with cake and coffee for thirty-five people. She also began teaching a Bible class at the missionaries' home and applied to start a school. All of these relationships can be seen as an expression of how Smith interpreted her evangelistic ethic. This included a deep desire to connect with the community and treat the people with dignity and respect. Quaker historian and former missionary Ron Stansell writes that Smith's evangelism "was indeed an extension of the Sunshine Mission of San Francisco, with poor and ill-kept children flocking around her for love and attention."[6] Her commitment to children did not prevent her from simultaneously building relationships with parents and grandparents. She consistently aimed to serve as a "faithful presence" in the community. When she opened a girls' school in 1908, it was thought to be the only such school in Central America; in addition to basic education and manual skills, the students received theological training. Smith considered this school a holistic ministry to children and critical to her work in Guatemala, "a form of evangelism and more faithful in its results than passing through a town and shouting out John 3:16."[7] Schools provided a consistent, systematic program of spiritual growth for young Guatemalans and contributed significantly to the development of Smith's ministry in the early years.

Smith's early years in Guatemala presented numerous challenges. The Guatemalan government accused Quaker missionaries of kidnapping children, deceiving Catholic Christians, and spying for the US government.[8] Smith ran understaffed, underfunded, and undersupplied schools. Nevertheless, alongside her commitment to the growth of Friends' churches, her work indicates that she believed in and lived out the Quaker testimony of equality for all people. She worked with both Ladino and Indigenous Guatemalans, describing the Indigenous people as "neglected and shunned by their Spanish neighbors . . . perhaps as much to be pitied as any class of persons in the world."[9] She navigated complicated situations during this time. Social gatherings and parties near the mission took place in the shadow of rumors of war near Chiquimula. During her years there, Smith considered the strongest opposition to her missionary work to be the control that priests exerted over the people through the Roman Catholic Church. Writing from an evangelical perspective, Stansell describes this opposition as a form of "Christo-paganism . . . built around ritual form and little Bible knowledge."[10] Smith's spiritual formation at the training school, along with her holiness convictions (an emphasis on the doctrine of a second work of grace, often called entire sanctification or Christian perfection), stood in opposition to what Smith considered the hierarchical expression of religion. She deemed Catholicism a controlling religion that had failed to serve or improve the lives of Guatemalans. Her spirit-led convictions and concern for the oppressed became a distinguishing feature of her missionary work in Central America and went on to influence Quaker mission work in South America.

Smith's convictions moved her to preach and teach a clear evangelical message of salvation. In her words, the truth of the Christian message lay not in "the nailing of a dead Christ to a cross, but the hope of new life."[11] She taught a sanctifying grace, a deep adherence to scripture, and a strong contrast between the "life of faith" and the "life of the world." In Smith's words, "civilization is not Christianity, and neither is reformation regeneration."[12] This statement gets to the heart of Smith's interpretation of the Christian faith, which stood in strong contrast to the way she viewed Catholicism. She preached against the Catholic model of faith and works, and instead was deeply influenced by her Protestant-holiness roots of *sola fide* (justification by faith alone). Her Quaker understanding of holiness was not that of sinless Christian perfection, but she opposed any form of penance and did teach against works' righteousness. She taught from the New Testament and the sermons of John Wesley, generally following the model she was taught at Huntington Park Training School.

Missionary movements around the turn of the century, beginning in the 1880s, built upon a kind of American moral reform that was based on the development of communication networks and technological advances. As the nation itself became more interdependent, expansionist missionary aims harnessed both social reform and cultural expansion alongside a broader global communications revolution. The increased ease of travel, coupled with the fetishism of tourism and foreign cultures, paralleled and helped fuel the growing missionary movement. Missionaries' ideologies and religious belief systems invigorated the rapid growth of Protestant missionary work. This work simultaneously brought technological advancements but also damaged Indigenous cultures. Western missionaries now became builders of transnational networks of leadership, creating church and business alliances. As Ian Tyrrell observes in *Reforming the World*, "moral reform organizations subtly contributed to the broader sociopolitical context of American power abroad and aimed at the creation of a Christian state to effect this goal."[13] American exceptionalism and crusades against alleged vices emerged with the support of Christian convictions shaped by missionaries and reformers. Missionaries thus aided in building a Christian empire in America that would expand to include as many nations as possible around the globe.[14]

Quaker missions in non-Western countries and the global South, particularly during the late 1800s and early 1900s, emerged primarily from programmed pastoral branches of evangelical Friends. Though not exclusive to Latin America, this kind of mission work was heavily influenced by the Second Great Awakening and the American holiness movement. As a result, Smith's missionary approach was grounded in a theological Arminianism that emphasized doctrine, the high authority of scripture, and total sanctification as the result of a conversion experience. The preparation Smith received at Huntington Park Training School was rooted in the school's goals to inspire "missionary enthusiasm; and to cultivate a passion for winning souls."[15] Smith was a product of this type of spiritual formation, which was typical of holiness training schools. This kind of missionary training resulted in Latin American Quaker churches in the evangelical tradition of pastoral and programmed gatherings, in which communities shared a commitment to an evangelical Gospel message. This included an encouragement to share and spread that same Gospel message to their neighbors through worship, music, prayer, and scripture.

Quaker missions can be distinguished from Protestant forms of mission primarily through their emphasis on social activism and reform in the Quaker tradition. Quaker principles such as peacemaking and equality characterized the first Quaker missionaries—sometimes called the "Valiant Sixty"—who experienced harassment and persecution. Their "holy experiment" in Pennsylvania focused not only on preaching and evangelism but on creating a more democratic alternative community. This allowed for less hostile relationship building among British North American Quakers and Indigenous peoples, as Jacalynn Welling suggests: "The concept of 'divine universal light' would resonate with Amerindians... from which flourished a lasting good will between Friends and indigenous peoples." This original philosophy of Quaker missions, shaped by the principle that the light of God dwelt in everyone, created a sensitivity to the issues of society's marginalized, leading scholars to suggest that the Indigenous peoples of North America were more willing to cooperate with Quakers than with other religious groups.[16] In 1756, for example, Philadelphia Friends founded the Friendly Association for Regaining and Preserving Peace with the Indians by Pacific Measures, which advocated for Indigenous peoples and was the first formal European-American Quaker organization to defend Indigenous rights.[17] Such efforts continued with Quaker mission compounds established to aid American Indians. In partnership with federal agencies across the United States, Quaker missionaries introduced plough architecture and domestic arts.[18] While this was a form of cultural privileging, Indigenous Americans used these skills in partnership alongside neighbors who built upon the Quaker philosophy of the equality of all peoples.

Twentieth-century Quaker mission work was rooted in previous Quaker mission work but developed to address twentieth-century concerns. East Africa had served as the largest-scale Quaker overseas mission, but Quakers also became interested in other regions of the world. In Central America, and Guatemala in particular, work began when the Huntington Park Training School for Christian Workers sent Quaker students Thomas Kelly and Clark Buckley to Guatemala in 1901. The CYM took over the support of the work when Guatemalan Friends reached out, requesting assistance in starting meetings in Honduras and El Salvador. Distinctive Quaker principles were reflected in the Friends' missions and churches that developed in Latin America. Pacifist teachings, and the subsequent refusal to participate in civil wars, emerged as a result of the Friends' peace testimony. Church governance was often nonhierarchical, as in Quaker meetings and churches. Decision making reflected the Quaker practice of consensus through listening to the Spirit. Friends' perspectives on the sacraments, particularly on not practicing baptism by water or communion with bread and wine, were part of Quaker church development during this period. Finally, and most evident in Smith's work in Chiquimula, the combination of fervent evangelism and compassionate service, often in the areas of education and health care, became a key attribute of Quaker missions worldwide.

Even so, there is room for skepticism about Protestant missionary projects of the time, including Quaker efforts in such endeavors, even if Quakers believed that their missions were more humane and culturally intelligent than those of other denominations. Scholars like Peggy Pascoe have reminded us of the dynamic between female reformers and the marginalized populations they served. In the context of incomplete cultural literacy, both groups encountered social control alongside varying cultural understandings of feminism and moral authority.[19] Emily Conroy-Krutz's book *Christian Imperialism* identifies the ways in which early nineteenth-century Protestants, not unlike Ruth Esther Smith, may have been motivated by multiple factors. Some of these factors originated in a view of international relations that saw Christians and Christian nations as having a duty to use their power and influence to spread Christianity and Western culture.

Conroy-Krutz explores the paradox that this power could result in community development that both benefited receiving communities and delivered commercial gain to the sending nation. Though economics was less of a motivating factor in Quaker missions in Honduras and Guatemala, Anglo-American models of development rooted in Western power structures still informed evangelization efforts. Language, agriculture, arts, trade, and domestic work were all considered from a Western perspective. Conroy-Krutz calls this attitude "evangelical Christian imperialist ideology" that emerged from a sense of Christian-motivated benevolent activity that would be for the benefit of the world.[20]

Some women of the period adopted a racist ideology that defended patriarchy and White privilege in their imperialist mission work. Ironically, at the same time that these women labored to ameliorate the impact of racism and patriarchy in the American context, they actively engaged in conversion and "civilizing" in their overseas missions.[21] Was this less the case among Quakers, including Ruth Esther Smith herself? It is difficult to answer this question definitively. Certainly, it is tempting to believe that it was less true of those who built their theological convictions on the equality of all persons, regardless of race or gender. But did their racialized work as missionaries help women like Smith "create white identities for themselves to compensate for their exclusion from economic, political, and social forms of power," as Louise Michelle Newman suggests?[22] Though Smith, who never married, was well educated for the time, she lacked many other forms of social power, especially where gender relations were concerned. As a single White woman in the early twentieth century, she was able to gain status on the mission field that she could never have achieved at home.

Smith was a successful missionary. In 1910, there were eighty-nine church members across six areas in the Chiquimula region; by 1912, membership had increased to three hundred, and a boys' school had been founded. Church districts expanded to include multiple congregations, and in 1914 the Guatemala mission sent missionaries to the Tegucigalpa region of Honduras. Throughout this period, Smith was committed to supporting local leaders and empowering them—women as well as men—whenever possible. Stansell describes her gifts in this work as Smith's greatest strength, an impressive achievement in that context.[23] Chiquimula served as a central point in the mission and ministry of Friends in Central America. Under Smith's leadership, the city became a hub for establishing both churches and regular meetings. Her faithful commitment to this calling bore fruit in the steady, incremental growth of converts in the region and in meeting the needs of the people.

In September 1918, a revival broke out in Central America that led to dramatic numerical growth in the Quaker mission in Guatemala. Smith believed that the revival was a fulfillment of Isaiah 60:1: "Arise, shine; for thy light is come, and the glory of the Lord is risen upon thee." Students from the school saw visions, experienced holy laughter, worshipped, and prayed for many days. Phrases such as *gloria a Dios* were recorded as being repeated again and again over the course of three months.[24] Surprisingly, Smith's conservative Quaker missionary colleagues did not question this charismatic movement, and though the accounts are limited, these "days of revival" are considered the starting point of a decade-long season of growth for the Friends in Honduras, Bolivia, and Guatemala. By the end of this revival season, the number of converts had grown to nearly two thousand.

After this revival, Smith felt convinced of the need for ongoing balance between discipleship and the spread and growth of the Quaker church in Guatemala, and she believed that a training school would help establish that balance. This conviction was no doubt influenced by her holiness roots in the Huntington Park Training School for Christian Workers. "God was speaking to His servants in Central America," she recalled in an essay, "telling them on the 3rd of May 1920, that He would have them organize for Him a Bible Training School. At once, they said, 'This is born of the Spirit.' On the 10th of May the letter ... written at La Paz, Bolivia arrived at Chiquimula and the missionaries said, 'This is a seal to the indications of the Spirit.'"[25] Smith understood this seal as a sign from God; she saw great hope in her vision of the opportunity to work for "God's kingdom" in Central America. Smith's commitment to education was unwavering, and her work extended beyond elementary education to include formalized seminary training. Her efforts helped establish training schools, one of which later became Berea Bible Seminary. This vision of evangelization joined to education helped sustain the growth of the Quaker church in Central America. Berea Seminary, in its plan of study and its practical work, was in large part modeled after other Quaker holiness training schools—the Cleveland Bible Institute (later Malone University), Pacific College (later George Fox University), and the Training School for Christian Workers (later Azusa Pacific University).

From 1920 until her death in 1947, Smith served as superintendent of the Guatemala Yearly Meeting, a powerful example of early Quaker women's leadership. In this role she oversaw the various ministries, supervised the missionaries and recruited new ones, and raised funds. She helped build a loyal constituency of supporters back in the United States as well. She also served as the editor of the *Harvester*, the missionary magazine of the CYM. Undoubtedly, her writings contributed to the development of that constituency. She often related conversion stories and recalled dramatic conversions in detail, never wavering in her belief in the Gospel's power to transform lives.

Smith's relationships across racial and community lines broke boundaries in her day. Quaker missionary Nancy Thomas's recent book, *A Long Walk, a Gradual Ascent: The Story of Bolivian Friends Church in Its Context of Conflict*, includes a description of the relationship between Smith and the origin of Quaker missions in Bolivia. Smith developed good friendships with Juan Ayllón (a Bolivian who studied in Guatemala) and William Abel (a Navajo from North America). These friendships began when Abel and Smith attended the Training School for Christian Workers in 1900–1901. As two of the school's first students, Abel and Smith noted the school's missionary zeal and "immediate preparation of students for entering upon the important and interesting work of spreading the Gospel and winning souls to Christ."[26] Through Smith's encouragement, Abel joined the missionary work in Bolivia under her oversight, and he was influential in Ayllón's conversion to Christianity. These relationships emerged from Smith and Abel's initial friendship at the training school. The Southwest Yearly Meeting (formerly the CYM) archives contain extensive primary sources detailing their ministry partnership and legacy. Nancy Thomas's work highlights the seminal connection between Smith and the growth of the Friends' church in both Honduras and Bolivia, which was in large part due to partnerships between the Indigenous population and American women.

Smith advocated that Central America start sending its own missionaries to South America in 1923. She wrote to the CYM and requested that Juan Ayllón be its first missionary to Bolivia. "We never chose Bolivia," she wrote, "but God has chosen for us service in Bolivia. We feel that it is no man-made plan. We dare not falter on the threshold of the open door. . . . North America has given to Central America, and Central America will in turn give to South America."[27] After visiting the mission in Bolivia herself in 1928, she wrote to the Oregon Yearly Meeting, asking its members to sponsor the work, as the Central American mission and national church faced severe financial constraints. She appealed to the Oregon meeting "in the soundness of the Quaker faith and the doctrine of Holiness," viewing its members as partners and co-laborers in foreign mission work, while continuing to expand her own influence as a Quaker leader.[28] Oregon Yearly Meeting agreed to support the mission in 1930 as a direct result of Smith's influence.

Smith remained in leadership in Guatemala until her death in 1947; she is buried there. "She died with no will and left no property," her successor in the mission noted on her death certificate.[29] But material possessions were never the legacy she sought to leave. Retirement or returning to the United States were not options for her, because Guatemala had truly become her home. "Miss Ruth" was surrounded by her "spiritual children" in Guatemala, who grieved her passing. Though she never married, she considered the mission's converts to be her children in the faith. They were her spiritual heirs.

Much had changed since Smith first moved to Guatemala in 1906. As a result of her vision and labors, the original eight converts in Chiquimula grew to forty-five hundred Quakers in fifty organized congregations. Her pioneering work is largely responsible for the more than twenty thousand Quakers in Guatemala and the more than two thousand in Honduras today. Toward the end of her life, it became apparent that the job of superintendent of the Central American Yearly Meeting had outgrown the capacity of one individual. No single person could effectively do all the work Smith was attempting to do. Furthermore, much work needed to be done to ensure the transfer of leadership, including creating a "faith and practice" document. Smith's efforts in the last years of her life facilitated this process.

Smith served as an ecumenical bridge builder outside the boundaries of Quakerism. She made acquaintances and interacted with the Wesleyan holiness movement, and her training at the Huntington Park Training School points to that. Speakers at the school from the National Holiness Missionary Society were prominent and influential in her life. She established close connections with friends outside Quakerism, including holiness Methodists from the United States who visited her in Guatemala, and Church of the Nazarene missionaries in Guatemala, with whom she lived while recovering from a major illness.[30]

Smith's own commitment to education was due in no small part to the education she received at the training school, and it served as the model for the primary and seminary schools she helped to found.[31] Her model of evangelism, deeply grounded in theological training and service, extended beyond the revival movements of the day, with their focus on conversion, to discipleship directed at the development of "faithful Christian living." The fruition of the 1918 revival in Chiquimula can be attributed in large part to the decades of Smith's committed Christian service in the community, where she established trust and deep faith with the locals.[32]

Smith's legacy continues to shape Quaker missions. This is evident in missions that integrate service with evangelism. Rather than adopt a posture of hegemonic Western cultural imperialism, Smith and her colleagues at the Chiquimula mission resourced the local community, learning from their neighbors in an attitude of mutual benefit and exchange. Despite the colonizing overtones of her mission work, Smith never viewed herself as bringing the Holy Spirit to Central Americans. Rather, she claimed that the populations she ministered alongside were image bearers of God already fully formed, with wisdom and insight that helped her better understand her own Christian faith.[33]

Latin American Quakers, and Central American Quakers in particular, have developed a liturgical style that is a hybrid of evangelical Quaker theology and Latin American culture. Smith's missional philosophy stipulated that local cultural practices should be accepted rather than devalued. Though they do not observe traditional Quaker silence or quiet worship, Friends in Central America practice enthusiastic, exuberant worship. The role of celebration, including music with traditional instruments, informed a Latin American Friends' expression of spirituality.[34] Such an expression, full of the range of human emotion given voice in worship, shaped a holistic and culturally honoring worship style in Guatemala and Honduras. Worship extends beyond church services to large family gatherings and meals. The ethic of investment and care in the broader neighborhood community came to be characteristic of Friends' churches under Smith's leadership.[35]

Smith deserves to be remembered as a pioneer of service, education, and local empowerment in Quaker mission work. She was considered a woman of great faith and vision, gifted with organizational and administrative skills as well as deep compassion. Smith's life and ministry in Central America helped shape the twentieth-century evangelical Quaker mission movement. The growth of yearly meetings in the global South, which included the development of Quaker schools, was influenced by her work and that of those whom she empowered. Stansell claims that her example and her empowerment of other women helped establish the egalitarian leadership in the Friends Yearly Meeting in Central America that persists to this day.[36] Her vision of ministry was advanced for her time, not only in her position on gender equality but also in her efforts to weave education and social improvement into evangelism. From schools to hospitals, Smith saw all of this work as part of the "upward climb" of the goal of the mission.[37]

Finally, Smith's practice of empowering local leaders, both in Central America and in Bolivia through the Ayllón family, led to the self-run yearly meetings of Friends' churches today in much of Central and South America. In the words of Quaker missionary Ray Canfield, "[Smith's] prolonged, scripturally-based leadership and her seeking the guidance of the Holy Spirit through godly women and men firmly cast a vision for a growing church."[38] Her fervency and commitment to her vocation was demonstrated throughout her entire life. Her legacy continues to shape the Quaker mission movement today.

NOTES

1. Ken Otto, *Azusa Pacific University* (Mount Pleasant, SC: Arcadia, 2008), Kindle loc. 1902 of 2013.
2. David L. Johns, ed., *Hope and a Future* (Richmond, IN: Friends United Press, 1993).
3. Sheldon Jackson, *Azusa Pacific University: One Hundred Years of Christian Service and Scholarship, 1899–1999* (Azusa, CA: Azusa Pacific University, 1999), 27.
4. Otto, *Azusa Pacific University*, loc. 1907 of 2013.
5. Ron Stansell, *Missions by the Spirit: Learning from Quaker Examples* (Newberg, OR: Barclay Press, 2009), 88.
6. Ibid., 92, 93 (quotation).
7. Paul Enyart, *Friends in Central America: A History of Church Growth* (Pasadena: William Carey Library, 1970), 109.
8. Jacalynn Stuckey Welling, "Mission," in *The Oxford Handbook of Quaker Studies*, edited by Stephen W. Angell and Pink Dandelion (Oxford: Oxford University Press, 2013), 317.
9. "Spanish Speaking Countries," *TSCW Bulletin* (January 1902): 4, Azusa Pacific University Archives, Azusa, CA.
10. Stansell, *Missions by the Spirit*, 85.
11. Ruth Esther Smith, "Diary of the Friends Mission, Chiquimula, Guatemala," 1907–8, April 17, 1908, Azusa Pacific University Archives.
12. R. Esther Smith, untitled essay, *Harvester* (June 1910), Evangelical Friends Church Southwest Archives, East Whittier, CA.
13. Ian Tyrrell, *Reforming the World: The Creation of America's Moral Empire* (Princeton: Princeton University Press, 2010), 9.
14. A small minority of transnational reformers opposed American imperialism—Ida B. Wells, for example, spoke out against racism and empire—but such radical agitation was the exception to the rule.

15. Ramon Gonzalez Longoria and Nancy Thomas, "Latin American Quakerism," in *The Cambridge Companion to Quakerism*, edited by Stephen W. Angell and Pink Dandelion (Cambridge: Cambridge University Press, 2018), 184.

16. Welling, "Mission," 308 (quotation), 309.

17. Kari Elizabeth Rose Thompson, "Inconsistent Friends: Philadelphia Quakers and the Development of Native American Missions in the Long Eighteenth Century" (PhD diss., University of Iowa, 2013), 4.

18. Paula Palmer, "Quaker Indian Boarding Schools," *Friends Journal*, October 1, 2016, https://www.friendsjournal.org/quaker-indian-boarding-schools/.

19. Peggy Pascoe, *Relations of Rescue: The Search for Female Moral Authority in the American West, 1874–1939* (Oxford: Oxford University Press, 1993).

20. Emily Conroy-Krutz, *Christian Imperialism: Converting the World in the Early American Republic* (Ithaca: Cornell University Press, 2015).

21. For more on this irony, see Louise Michelle Newman, *White Women's Rights: The Radical Origins of Feminism in the United States* (Oxford: Oxford University Press, 1999).

22. Ibid., 19.

23. Stansell, *Missions by the Spirit*, 107.

24. Ibid., 102. Stansell quotes Helen Kersey's impressions of the revival as recounted to Josephine Still, since few detailed accounts of the revival exist.

25. R. Esther Smith, "Beautiful Story," *Harvester* 17, no. 1 (1923): 2–3, Evangelical Friends Church Southwest Archives.

26. *TSCW Bulletin* 1, no. 8 (1912): 4, Azusa Pacific University Archives.

27. R. Esther Smith, "Bolivia Beckons," *Harvester* 17, no. 7 (1924): 5, Evangelical Friends Church Southwest Archives.

28. Oregon Yearly Meeting Minutes, 1930, 29, Northwest Yearly Meeting, George Fox University Archives, Newberg, OR.

29. American Friends Board of Foreign Missions, *Foreign Mission Work of American Friends: A Brief History of Their Work from the Beginning to the Year 1912* (n.p.: American Friends Board of Foreign Missions, 1912), 236–38, https://archive.org/details/foreignmissionwoooameriala.

30. Stephen Carter Dove, "Local Believers, Foreign Missionaries, and the Creation of Guatemalan Protestantism, 1882–1944" (PhD diss., University of Texas at Austin, 2012), 115.

31. Nancy Thomas, *A Long Walk, a Gradual Ascent: The Story of Bolivian Friends Church in Its Context of Conflict* (Eugene, OR: Wipf & Stock, 2019), 15.

32. Dove, "Local Believers," 206.

33. Stansell, *Missions by the Spirit*, 108.

34. Longoria and Thomas, "Latin American Quakerism," 192.

35. Stansell, *Missions by the Spirit*, 132.

36. Ibid., 133.

37. *Minutes of California Yearly Meeting, 1933* (Whittier, CA: California Yearly Meeting Press, 1933), 19.

38. Quoted in Virginia Miller, *His Story, 1902–2002: Friends Church in Central America* (Whittier, CA: Evangelical Friends Church Southwest, 2002), 7.

PART 3

Engaging Sacred and Secular Literature

CHAPTER 7

An Unforeseen Consequence of the Orthodox-Hicksite Schism (1827–1828)
The Fiction Writing of Amelia Opie, Helen Hunt Jackson, Mary Howitt, and Mary Hallock Foote

ISABELLE COSGRAVE

> Neither novels nor their readers benefit from attempts to divine whether any facts hide inside a story. Such efforts attack the very idea that made-up stories can matter, which is sort of the foundational assumption of our species.
> —John Green, *The Fault in Our Stars*

John Green's assertion seems utterly logical to the twenty-first-century Anglo-American literary sphere: making up stories for our own and others' entertainment is part of what makes us human. But the rise of the novel in the nineteenth century emphasized the degree to which fiction was a distrusted medium, and Quakers had particular objections to its use. Where many groups were suspicious of fictional works and the dubious morality they contained, Quaker mistrust was fundamental to the very conceptional theology of the Society of Friends, ideas of Truth, and the inadequacies of mere representation and reliance on human creative imagination.

Recent research has considered the reading of fiction, with the logical extension that what should not be read certainly should not be written.[1] But there has been very little research into the problematic nineteenth century with specific regard to the writing of fiction, or not in the level of detail required to advance scholarship in this area. This chapter shifts the approach, not seeking strict chronological progress but instead looking at four individuals and tracing an unlikely consequence of the Orthodox-Hicksite schism for their writing careers. Elias Hicks (1748–1830) did not argue for relaxed attitudes toward the arts; Hicks was particularly concerned that the Bible was becoming more highly valued than the Holy Spirit.[2] But his insistence that "salvation is entirely within man and cannot be achieved by external acts" seemed to allow a space for fiction and the arts to develop, although Hicks himself would never have endorsed such an interpretation.[3]

The analysis here focuses on four female writers—two English and two American, two birthright Quakers and two who joined the faith much later in life—to explore how trends in the writing of fiction developed differently on either side of the Atlantic over the nineteenth century. It was a century that would see many subsequent Quaker schisms, as Robynne Rogers Healey and Carole Dale Spencer outline in the introduction to this volume. But I argue here that the Orthodox-Hicksite schism unintentionally created a space for quite a different attitude toward fiction among North American Quakers, and, in turn, a reiteration of Orthodox Quaker values among British Friends in reaction to Hicksite Quakerism.

AMELIA OPIE (1769–1853) AND HELEN JACKSON (1830–1885)

If Amelia Opie and Helen Jackson are remembered at all, it may be for their influence as writers of fiction, but probably more for their involvement in social reform.[4] For Opie, this reform interest was most obvious in her antislavery work; for Jackson, it was her considerable involvement in defending the rights of Indigenous Americans in the expanding West. Both women came to the Quakers later in life. But the versions of Quakerism with which they came into contact had vastly different effects on their careers. If it was merely the passage of time that caused this difference, scholarly research would reflect this shift. But the ease with which Jackson pursued a career in fiction writing indicates strongly that the strict censure Opie faced had long ceased to be a facet of the Quakerism Jackson encountered.

Alongside Maria Edgeworth and Jane Austen, Amelia Opie was one of the most famous female writers of novels and moral tales in the first decades of the nineteenth century. Growing up in Norwich, a hub of radical thought, Amelia Alderson mixed with fashionable and dissenting society from an early age. Her wide social group included prominent radicals like William Godwin and Mary Wollstonecraft; through them, she met the famous painter John Opie, and they married in 1798. But Amelia Opie was also close with the Norwich branch of the prominent Quaker Gurney family, especially Elizabeth (Gurney) Fry (1780–1845) and Joseph John Gurney (1788–1847). Opie's awareness of, and respect for, Quakers found literary representation in her most studied novel, *Adeline Mowbray* (1805), and in one of her *New Tales*, "The Quaker and the Young Man of the World" (1818). When, after a very long period of discernment (1814–25), Opie decided to join the Quakers by convincement, it was Joseph John Gurney in particular who guided her path.

Out of concern for Opie's worldly lifestyle, Gurney initiated their correspondence in 1814, while Opie was enjoying the London summer season. She had lost her husband in 1807 to a short illness, when John Opie was at the height of his career as a portrait artist; the widowed "Mrs. Opie" received attention owing to this connection, while her works also attracted fame. By 1814, Opie had published four novels, two collections of tales, a play, and numerous poems and short tales for journals and periodicals. But there was a marked difference in Opie's literary output once she started corresponding with Gurney. Her acknowledged novels, *Valentine's Eve* (1816) and *Madeline* (1822), were much more religious than any before. She also published two novels anonymously, *The Only Child; or, Portia Bellenden* (1821) and *Much to Blame* (1824), that signal a much more frivolous attitude than Opie was willing to own, and which demonstrate her inner struggles at this time. Her short prose works included many more nonfiction items, and her poems generally became more religious in tone. She also produced some nonfiction material that was clearly designed to please her Quaker acquaintance: *Illustrations of Lying in All Its Branches* (1825), which coincided with her joining the Quakers officially, and *Detraction Displayed* (1828).

Opie's letters to Gurney and to William Hayley—her spiritual and literary mentors—clearly demonstrate her struggles between these two worlds at this point. *Valentine's Eve* (1816) follows the most devoutly Christian character Opie ever created; her decision to kill off this innocent heroine indicates her own difficulty in asserting herself as a truly religious woman of letters. Gurney had approved early drafts of the work, and Opie wrote of him to Hayley that, "as he has imagination himself, works of imagination, if he allowed himself to read them, would take great hold of him, but he forbids himself the gratification."[5] Gurney ultimately was clear: if Opie were to join the Quakers officially, her various vanities, including "her novel writing, in which her reputation was high, must be laid at the foot of the cross of Christ."[6] Opie's final acknowledged novel, *Madeline* (1822), shows her attempt to write a novel that could be acceptable to Quakers. Not only does Opie choose the format of a journal, a much-loved and much-used medium for Quakers, but she also stresses repeatedly the veracity of her account. The work "came into my hands," she writes, and readers are assured that "I lay before them a story which is, in many respects, literally true," with characters who are "not entirely the creatures of the imagination."[7] Opie's insistence on having written the "Truth" should be compared and contrasted with the attitudes of both Helen Jackson and Mary Hallock Foote, who would later place much less importance on the truthfulness of their writings.

This fixation of Opie's on writing the "Truth" should also be considered alongside Joseph John Gurney's Quakerism. Gurney placed strong emphasis on the benefit of biblical knowledge, which was not necessarily a standard Orthodox Quaker focus. The Bible was important, of course, but less important than the Inward Light and an individual connection thereby with the Spirit. Gurney's approach was too evangelical for many Orthodox English Friends, like Sarah Grubb, "one of the recognized leaders of the conservatives."[8] In his emphasis on scripture, it is unsurprising that Gurney became stricter about other types of writing, especially fiction. In her chapter in this volume, Julie Holcomb discusses, by contrast, certain Hicksites' disrespect and distrust of the New Testament as the "Popes book." Holcomb refers to Hicks's alleged comment that "there was but one New Testament in the world for some Hundreds of years after the Christian era & that was in the Hands of the Pope." Although Hicks did not approve of fiction, there is evidence here of how interpretations of his theology might have contributed to gradual attitudinal shifts regarding various forms of the written word, including fiction.

Illustrations of Lying in All Its Branches (1825) further emphasized Opie's commitment to the truth, and in any circumstance. But reviewers who had enjoyed Opie's earlier fiction were not complimentary; one commented that "it has pleased Mrs. Opie, since she had turned Quakeress, to read a lecture to the world.... [She] tells mankind pretty roundly that they are a generation of liars."[9] Explaining to Mrs. S. C. Hall her inability to contribute further to literary annuals, Opie wrote, "since I became a Friend I am not free to what is called 'make a story.' ... I must not write pure fiction; I must not *lye*, and say, 'so and so occurred,' or 'such and such a thing took place,' when it did not."[10] For Opie, and with Gurney's guidance, there was no possible compromise between Orthodox Quakerism and fiction.

In the case of the American Helen Hunt, the Quaker influence that came into her life in the form of William Sharpless Jackson was quite different. Both Opie and Hunt were celebrated authors of a similar age; both were widowed. Unlike Opie, who had always been inclined and encouraged to write in all literary forms, Helen Fiske's childhood had not fostered literary experimentation. Her father was a college professor and a Congregational minister, and her mother was also a devout Calvinist. So Fiske was raised in a "strict religious household stressing Christian morality" from traditions that, like Orthodox Quakers, disapproved of fiction.[11] Following the death of her first husband, Edward Bissell Hunt, and then that of their nine-year-old son, Rennie, Helen Hunt started writing poetry in her grief-stricken state. Her literary mentor in this new stage of her life, Thomas Wentworth Higginson, encouraged her also to try other literary forms.[12] She published anonymously, as part of the "No Name Series" of novels, or as "H. H.," and later as "Saxe Holm." Hunt moved to Colorado Springs to cure her tuberculosis (1873–74), and there she met William S. Jackson, who not only accepted but encouraged Hunt's thriving literary career before and after they married. Like many nineteenth-century women writers, Jackson felt the need to justify her position, but not owing to her husband's opinions of her writing: she was "particularly burdened by the memory of her father's moral opposition to purely imaginative, nondidactic literature," as one of her biographers observes.[13]

Indeed, it was William S. Jackson who actively encouraged a turn to fiction, after Jackson's nonfiction work failed to excite the desired reaction. Following her attendance at a lecture by the Ponca chief Standing Bear in Boston (October 29, 1879), Jackson found the concrete moral purpose in her writing for which she had been searching.[14] She was disgusted by evidence of White settlers' treatment of the Indigenous populations, and she very speedily wrote *A Century of Dishonor: A Sketch of the United States Government's Dealings with Some of the Indian Tribes* (1881). Jackson remarked that she had become "the most odious thing in the world, 'a woman with a hobby,'" but she could not help it.[15] One of her driving impulses was to expose the nation's deceptive handling of the "Indian

Question." Borne of her father's distrust in pure fiction, Jackson's literary interest in the "ethics of sincerity and deception" found representation in *Mercy Philbrick's Choice* (1876), in all of her subsequent novels, and in *A Century of Dishonor*.[16]

This last work was not a success, but "somehow it stirred things—for you see books, pamphlets, & mag[azine] articles are steadily pouring out on the subject.... The world moves."[17] William S. Jackson's suggestion that a fictional story might be more effective indicates that his Hicksite upbringing in Pennsylvania might have presented little distrust of fiction, or that scholarly criticism has not yet considered a possible inconsistency. Helen agreed, writing to friends that "people will read a novel when they will not read serious books."[18] But she went even further, and her comments are definitely not in the Orthodox Quaker vein of commitment to Truth. She wrote to Thomas Bailey Aldrich, editor of the *Atlantic Monthly*, that she wanted to "draw a picture so winning and alluring in the beginning of the story, that the reader would become thoroughly interested in the characters before he dreamed of what was before him:—and would have swallowed a big dose of information on the Indian question, without knowing it."[19]

In her attempt to deliver this "big dose," Jackson based her novel *Ramona* (1884) on real places and real people, using the meticulous research she had collected to compose *A Century of Dishonor* three years earlier. Months after finishing *Ramona*, Jackson wrote that "every episode of the 'Indian history' in her book was true," but the reasons for this authenticity were different from Opie's attempts to justify her last acknowledged novel (*Madeline*, 1822) as a real history.[20] Instead, Jackson wanted people's interest to be sparked by some of the identifiable southern Californian locations.

In line with her feeling of "spontaneous inspiration" to write *A Century of Dishonor*, Jackson felt driven to write *Ramona*, describing the force and certainty with which the whole process took hold, and the considerable speed with which she composed the novel.[21] Although the *Christian Union* published *Ramona*, initially in installments, for less money than Jackson wished, she favored the publisher on two counts: for the speed with which the work would appear, and for its ability "to hit the religious element." The *Christian Union* was publishing *Ramona* "to push the paper—not to help the Indian!—but each will react on the other," reasoned Jackson.[22] She "did not write for money, but published for it," saying that "'Cash is a vile article'—but there is one thing viler; and that is a purse without any cash in it."[23] Her motives were clearly twofold.

Ramona was not the success Jackson had hoped; her book "failed completely as a social problem novel," as one critic later put it.[24] But it still had an impact that was apparent in Jackson's final years. In one of her (now) most famous statements, Jackson reflected, "If I could write a story that would do for the Indian a thousandth part what Uncle Tom's Cabin did for the Negro, I would be thankful the rest of my life."[25] Her final years also indicate a personal turn toward the Quakers: the entry on her life in the "Dictionary of Quaker Biography" suggests that both Jackson herself and others considered her a Quaker in later life.[26] Jackson had worked with various Quakers in her "Indian Reform" work, both Orthodox and Hicksite. But whereas many of those Quakers concluded that assimilation, including embracing Christianity, was the best solution to the "Indian Question," Jackson could not agree.[27] Her interest in Indigenous Americans lay rather "in defending them" as individuals with their own cultures and beliefs.[28] It seems more likely, therefore, that Jackson's attraction to the Quakers came from her husband's tradition. As Jackson was dying, she told Thomas Wentworth Higginson, her very first literary mentor, that he had "never fully realized how for the last four years my whole heart has been full of the Indian cause—how I have felt, as the Quakers say, 'a concern' to work for it."[29] Owing to an accident in her Colorado home, in which she broke her left leg in three places, Jackson had to relinquish many literary projects in her last year, including a novel about Quaker life. She sent all the materials she had gathered to a friend, Sarah Woolsey, so that the novel might one day be written.[30]

Where Opie made a very clear choice to adapt her writing to accommodate Orthodox Quaker views, Jackson's writing went in the opposite direction. Opie's novel-writing career essentially came to an end because she tried, in *Madeline*, to write a novel in journal form based on a true story. The novel might have met strict Quaker demands regarding its closeness to the truth, but it was a literary disaster. Jackson, by contrast, tried to increase awareness of the plight of Indigenous Americans in the nonfiction *Century of Dishonor*, but she failed to get the desired result. She therefore turned to fiction, having (accurately) surmised that people would be more readily stirred if their emotional sympathies were aroused. The effects of the versions of Quakerism that Opie and Jackson encountered seem quite different and led them in very different directions. A consideration of Mary Howitt and Mary Hallock Foote reveals a comparable difference.

MARY HOWITT (1799–1888) AND MARY HALLOCK FOOTE (1847–1938)

Mary Howitt and Mary Hallock Foote were two birthright Quakers who negotiated the writing of fiction within their different Quaker traditions. Both Foote's *Reminiscences* (published in 1972 but written during the 1920s) and Howitt's *Autobiography* (published 1889) detail their respective upbringings in the Quaker faith. Scholars have not yet examined Howitt's struggle between literary ambition and religious commitment, nor have they actively attempted to address Foote's Quakerism alongside her career. But I would suggest that Foote was a fiction writer who happened to be a Quaker, whereas Howitt's literary career was obviously negatively affected by her affiliation with the Religious Society of Friends.

Mary (Botham) Howitt grew up in a strict Quaker household. Her father, Samuel Botham, was an Orthodox Quaker with a very long Quaker lineage; her mother, Ann Wood, had become a Quaker by conviction, for which she was stigmatized in their insular Quaker community in the English Midlands.[31] Mary and Anna Botham had a varied education, with nannies, a Church of England school, and then a Friends' school. Early in her autobiography, Mary writes that she understood the "constant exhortation to take up the cross" as a reference to Quaker plain speech and dress. But "our peculiar garb, many degrees more ungainly than that of most strict Friends, was already a perfect crucifixion to Anna and me," and "there was no religion to me in that cross."[32] With only religious books at home, Mary and Anna became insatiable readers of what they could find at school, and then through a neighbor. Anna had a great talent for art, as did their father, Samuel, and a love of music too. But "all artistic sense was ruthlessly suppressed in himself and later in those around him" for fear of its power and possible idolatry.[33] Mary identified her desire to be a famous writer as early as seventeen, so the potential obstacles she faced are clear.

An immediate contrast can be seen in the upbringing of Mary Hallock. She also had a somewhat isolated Quaker upbringing, but that did not mean the same thing in her Quaker tradition. Mary's uncle, Nicholas Hallock, had preached too strong an antislavery position before abolition became a widespread Quaker cause, and the consequence was "exclusion of the 'Hicksite' Hallocks" from the New York meeting.[34] Mary Hallock's family was very rich in Quaker heritage; five generations of Quaker Hallocks had farmed in Milton (in the Hudson Valley), and Mary's father joked that she was related to the other half of the New York Yearly Meeting on her mother's side.³⁵ An education "in a private Quaker school on the family property" in Milton might give the impression of a limited, restricted, insular education. But this background in an "Old World Quaker family ... put her in the orbit of the reigning values of the eastern establishment," and stood Hallock in very good stead.³⁶ Mixing with non-Quaker cousins taught Mary and her sister Bessie all they knew about dancing and singing, activities with which they otherwise had no contact in their house "of Quaker traditions." Mary's aunt, Sarah Hallock, was very outspoken: a member of the New York Anti-Slavery Society and a champion of women's rights, she not only ensured that the Hallock family had a stream of exciting visitors but was also "the family purveyor of literature," as Mary later recalled.³⁷

In her early teenage years, Mary Hallock was already known as the artist of the family. She pursued her education in Poughkeepsie, New York, and then went to the Cooper Union Institute of Design in New York City at age seventeen. She stayed with her sister-in-law's family, the Walters; these "gay Friends" were from "the rich Quaker set of Brooklyn Heights," and "they danced, they went to the theatre, they dressed as the World did." They also allowed Mary unlimited use of their extensive library.³⁸ Hallock consequently read widely, keeping up with the classic nineteenth-century texts of both Britain and North America, "often through serializations of novels in the *Atlantic Monthly*, *Harper's*, and *Century*."³⁹ Hallock's family encouraged her artistic ability, which led her to a liberal arts college. The combination of "liberal arts" and "Quaker" in England, however, would have been anathema for most English Quakers well into the 1870s, and the stark contrast with Mary Howitt's need to suppress such talents must be kept in mind.

Mary Hallock's time at Cooper Union introduced her to Helena de Kay, with whom she enjoyed a very close friendship and a correspondence that lasted more than forty years, and to many of the Boston literati, through whom she met the "makers of American Literature."⁴⁰ Hallock was soon making decent money as an illustrator, and she even joked about being commissioned to do the artwork for "not a very Quakerish tale!"—"The Skeleton in Armor," by Henry Wadsworth Longfellow, which was clearly a very fanciful poem.⁴¹ Hallock also illustrated editions of John Whittier Greenleaf's poetry, a "collaboration of the young Quaker from New York with New England's famous Quaker poet," when she met Arthur De Wint Foote at one of her many social engagements in New York City. Foote was a civil engineer and not a Quaker. But they married in the Hallock family home in a Quaker ceremony that Mary describes in some detail in her *Reminiscences*, before they moved out to California with his work.[42] It is clear from the whole first section of Foote's *Reminiscences*, titled "Quaker Beginnings" (1–117), that her Quaker upbringing was very important to her. But how different was her experience of Quakers and Quakerism from that of Mary Botham (Howitt) as the latter approached marriage.

By the time she met William Howitt, Mary Botham's upbringing had been so limited that, to her mind, Quakers "were so stupid; read nothing; knew nothing—most Friends were so dull."[43] William also had a relatively strict Quaker upbringing. But his Quaker acquaintances, including Mary's cousins, were more accustomed to discussing their faith, which immediately made it seem less strict, more approachable, and more attractively scholarly to both Botham sisters. William Howitt traced his love for literature back to his grandfather (a Quaker), but his Quaker schooling prohibited fiction. Mary Botham and William Howitt shared a love for poetry, both reading and writing it, and nature. After their marriage in 1821, they lived in Hanley and Nottingham, both in the English Midlands.

The Howitts found in Nottingham a hotbed of dissent and radical politics in the years preceding the Reform Bill of 1832; the Friends' meetinghouse there was not particularly strict in dress or behavior. But when the Howitts' first literary venture appeared, a collection of poetry called *The Forest Minstrel* (1823), Friends did not welcome it. Quaker poets at the time wrote religious verse, if Quakers wrote poetry at all. The Howitts hoped that "the latitude of phrase and sentiment which as members of the Society of Friends we have allowed ourselves" would not offend. They were disappointed.[44]

The following years established a pattern of publications, either joint or individual, often with some attempt to appease Quaker attitudes but consistently falling short in that endeavor. Joseph John Gurney, on a visit to Nottingham in 1824—where his charismatic persona charmed everyone—confessed that William Howitt's "A Poet's Thought at the Internment of Lord Byron" was "a beautiful, very beautiful thing." But the Quaker minister and theologian said at the same time that he could not quite approve of "the almost *unqualified* praises bestowed on Byron," which was more consistent with the reaction of most Friends, who had "looked rather askance at the subject."[45] In a very similar vein to his deft treatment of Amelia Opie's manuscript for *Valentine's Eve* (1816), Gurney managed to gauge the need to encourage literary endeavor while meting out censure. In 1824, when Quaker disputes that would culminate in the Orthodox/Hicksite schism were already acute, such diplomacy was essential in an Orthodox English Quaker who feared the threat of an imminent breach.

From 1827, the Howitts' literary endeavors and their reputations increased, and both felt the Orthodox English Quaker backlash. Poems in the joint *Desolation of Eyam* (1827) were considered "anti-Quakerish," even "licentious" and "atheistical."[46] Mary was becoming resigned to such reviews, commenting to her sister in 1830 that she looked out for criticism from annual-reading Friends "on account of my writings ... for I have a set of the most un-Friendly ballads in them."[47] In the same year, Mary wrote again to Anna about Quaker habits; her reference to the "disadvantage and absurdity of Friends' peculiarities" further indicates her dissatisfaction.[48]

Even when they tried, the Howitts' works failed to meet with approbation from Friends. William's 1833 *History of Priestcraft* was an attack on clerical religion; despite professing principles with which Quakers might agree, "Friends were cautioned not to read" this "libellous work" and denounced it in yearly meeting. Dramatic poems that Mary intended to be of the highest moral teaching were labeled "licentious" and "irreligious."[49] Where Quaker criticism had been leveled at the content of her works, mostly poems at this juncture, Howitt's decision to write a novel (*Wood Leighton*, 1836) indicated that she was no longer interested in seeking Quaker approval. Opie had been so eager, in attempting to combine novel writing with her nascent Quaker faith, to assert that everything she wrote about was true. Howitt instead emphasized in the preface to *Wood Leighton* that she was writing the characters from her imagination, not her acquaintance.[50]

After the couple moved from Nottingham down to Surrey in 1836, the stricter Friends in southern England gave Howitt an "unpleasant confirmation of my opinion of Friends' contracted and sectarian feeling," which promoted only "warning and prohibition." The effects of the Orthodox-Hicksite schism were clearly in evidence, as Orthodox English Quakers became even stricter in reaction to the perceived Hicksite threat. Mary Howitt's impressions of London Yearly Meeting in 1837 reinforced the differences between her own faith and that of Orthodox Quakers. She wrote that Sarah Grubb, an ultraconservative Quaker minister, preached a sermon that was so "full of denunciation, and in a spirit of animosity and division" that Howitt considered it "unchristian"; it was "such a sermon as Christ could not have preached."[51] Howitt expressed much more sympathy with the "Seceders'" position, even if she herself was uninterested in becoming a Hicksite.

The Howitts' discontent with Orthodox Quakerism came to a head in June 1840, when female delegates from the United States, attendees at the Anti-Slavery Convention in London, were denied a dignified reception. Both Howitts were disgusted that London Quakers refused to let Lucretia Mott speak at public meetings, "alleging that as a woman she was stepping out of her sphere in publicly representing her country." Since Quaker women, equal with men in the Spirit, constantly spoke in public, preaching both at home and abroad, the ban on Mott's public speaking was clearly not a sex prejudice but hypocritical religious bigotry—Mott was known to be a Hicksite. Howitt wrote to Mott to express "the sense I have of your unworthy reception in this country," and the Howitts dined with James and Lucretia Mott before moving (temporarily) to Germany.[52] Back in England, Mary told her sister in August 1847 that she and William had resigned their membership in the Society, adding that "the majority of Friends are narrow-minded, living as much in the crippling spirit of sectarianism as any denomination whatever." She also found "a want of real spirituality" in all religious bodies at this point, and she could not yet settle anywhere else.[53]

In 1853, Harriet Beecher Stowe visited Britain. While some recent scholarly criticism considers *Uncle Tom's Cabin* (1852) a pivotal work in changing Quaker attitudes toward fiction in Britain, Mary Howitt referred only to Stowe's interest in spiritualism when writing about her visit.[54] By this point, both Howitts had shown their disdain for Quaker literary constraints through their publication decisions. They had many prominent literary contacts, including Tennyson and Dickens, and helped Elizabeth Gaskell launch her career. So much of Howitt's life was related to her literary investment, and to that of her husband, but there came a point when both writers had simply had enough of Quaker constraints on or criticism of their work.

Mary Hallock Foote seemingly had no such difficulties with a vocation that was incompatible with her faith tradition. "Armed with book commissions, wooden engraving blocks, and pen and ink," Foote moved to the western United States with her husband; a critical comment mentions the lack of compromise in her "gentility or femininity" through drawing and writing for profit, but there is no sense of any Quaker need for compromise.[55] Helena de Kay and her husband, Richard Watson Gilder, asked Foote to provide magazine articles, and, along with published travel sketches, Foote turned from illustration to fiction.[56] Like the Howitts early in their marriage, the Footes found themselves living too far from a Quaker meeting for Mary to be able to practice. Nevertheless, "the gentle demeanor yet firm resolve which characterized her ancestors" was something Foote retained for her whole life. An early series of children's tales was set in the familiar Hudson Valley of her youth, rather than her new home in coastal California, and Foote's writings often expressed her internal conflict about moving west.[57]

On a long visit with her family in Milton, New York, Foote wrote "Friend Barton's Concern," a short story that drew on various details of her family's experiences. Numerous relatives took her to task for "the exploitation in print of the faith of our common ancestors"; the objections were, however, to the content of the story rather than the form. Mary's father argued that certain theological points in the story were not accurate, and that the Quakers in the tale would not have acted in the ways depicted. Foote reflected in her *Reminiscences*, "I could not dispute the point, but if I had acted on it there would have been no story! I sent it as a thing of mere barter and sale to the editors who took it, and I took my cheque."[58] Despite the businesslike attitude, Foote did indeed consider and value what the Quaker faith meant for her personally. On the very next page of the *Reminiscences*, she reflected on the position of prayer in her growing family and quotes the very celebrated Quaker Robert Barclay on the subject, the same Robert Barclay who had condemned fiction so thoroughly in his *Apology for the True Christian Divinity* (1676).[59] But Foote clearly saw no contradiction.

Financial security was also a constant concern for the Foote family. Foote's first novel, *The Led-Horse Claim* (1883), was inspired by a dispute about two mines that left Arthur De Wint Foote without employment. Mary wanted a realistic ending to the novel, "but my publisher wouldn't hear of that! I had to make a happy ending."[60] There is little sense of frustration here, though; it was often Mary's income that kept the family afloat, and she knew that compromise regarding her art would be necessary to support her struggling family.[61] Foote also asserted that the novel, "with the exception of one incident, which is very much changed, is *entirely a story*."[62] This assertion is quite different from Opie's need to assert that her final novel was based on fact and indicates in turn the quite different Quaker traditions with which they were affiliated.

Subtitling this first novel *A Romance*, and developing her style from romance to realism, naturalism, and historical fiction, Foote followed the prevailing literary trends of the time.[63] In contrast to Jackson, Howitt, and Opie, Foote demonstrated no philanthropic interest in improving women's societal status; she wrote sentimental tales and family sagas, with conventional, and "frequently predictable," plots and characters, and she emphasized class.[64] Foote received a visit from Helen Jackson when living in Leadville, Colorado, and while she wrote respectfully of Jackson in her autobiography, Foote articulated elsewhere her objections to Jackson's improper and insistently realistic writing about the "Indian Question."[65] Writing to Richard Gilder, she expressed a lack of desire to address unpleasant, unladylike subjects, saying that she had a wonderful idea for a story, but "it is too strong for me. I shouldn't succeed, and if I did all my lady friends would wish I hadn't. Can't I write it anonymously?"[66]

Although Foote continued into the twentieth century to portray female characters who were less autonomous than their male counterparts, her final novel, *The Ground Swell* (1919), proved an exception; the main character was based on her own daughter, Agnes, who had died in 1904 (at age seventeen) after surgery for appendicitis. The focus on the mother-child relationship in *The Ground Swell* allowed Foote to present her "tribute to the independent spirit of the daughter she had lost."[67] Foote's works often dealt with the demands on women of the isolating experiences of frontier life, "emphasizing female anguish at being transplanted from the settled social world of the East to the barren cultural soil of the West."[68] But Foote generally kept her female characters solidly within their conventional social roles, keeping her own role suitably feminine at the same time.

In addition to the lengthy treatment of Foote's "Quaker Beginnings," there are little hints throughout Foote's *Reminiscences* of her sense of Quaker identity. One small reflection considers what Foote acknowledged as her "Quaker Negative." Having declined an invitation to visit her dear friend Helena de Kay Gilder, Foote commented that it was "the Quaker Negative acting automatically from generations of habit. It may be; there was something in me which knew as a rule when it was time to stop."[69] But Foote's literary career demonstrates just how little her Quaker tradition affected decisions about her fiction writing. In addition to the fiction she wrote, and in line with the contemporary literary currents, Foote felt a real sense of freedom even to publish quite a supernatural tale in her grief following Agnes's death, making no attempt to "explain the inexplicable." Foote's granddaughter remembered fondly that Foote in her dotage "wore skirts to her ankles and white caps in the Quaker tradition over hair," and "she also followed the Quaker custom of using 'thee' instead of 'you' when talking to members of the family."[70] Her Quaker customs were clearly important to her throughout her life; restraints on fiction writing were apparently not part of those customs.

CONCLUSION

For the most part, Quakers in the twenty-first century are much more relaxed about the reading and writing of fiction, in both the United Kingdom and North America, although some groups in the United States still actively discourage (or even prohibit) the consumption of fiction.[71] Some of the differences between the United Kingdom and North America are logical: the greater number of Quakers in North America over the centuries has allowed for the maintenance of Quaker communities and Quaker education in a way that has not been possible in the United Kingdom. North America has therefore been able to keep certain doctrinal particularities in some Quaker groups, while other Quakers in wider North American society can hold much less strict views, according to their individual beliefs.

The aim of this chapter is not to suggest that Hicksite Quakerism was more lenient toward fiction. Indeed, Lucretia Mott is only one example of many Hicksites who maintained a "rather narrow-minded prejudice against fiction and drama," and Hamm's reference to "licentious literature" in his chapter on Hicksite women indicates a widespread concern.[72] But the breaking away of this faction, and its legitimization with the name "Hicksite," demonstrated that serious Quakers in North America no longer had to be Orthodox. Hicks's shifted focus resulted in an "embrace of theological diversity" that became "integral to Hicksite Quakerism."[73] It follows that strict "doctrinal" charges that fiction was untruth or mere representation might have become eclipsed by personal experiences of how fiction related to an individual's connection with the Inner Light, with the Spirit, and with inspiration.

When Amelia Opie came to join the Quakers officially in 1825, her Quaker mentor Joseph John Gurney was witnessing the rise of the Hicksites in North America with disgust.[74] He continued to push Opie toward Orthodox Quakerism, or to the strain of evangelical Quakerism that would eventually bear his name, mostly in North America. In one of her last extant letters to Gurney (February 1844), Opie asserted her abiding belief in fiction as a great didactic tool. But she also acknowledged that, in joining the

Quakers, she had had to relinquish its use.⁷⁵ The perceived threat of Hicksite Quakerism similarly pushed Mary Howitt's Quaker contemporaries away from fiction and toward increasingly conservative Orthodox Quaker ideas. This shift led Howitt to choose her career over the Society of Friends. In contrast, the mere presence of a legitimate Quaker group (in the Hicksites) that was opposed to the Orthodox Yearly Meetings in North America contributed over time to a relative freedom regarding the arts that Helen Jackson and Mary Hallock Foote found in their Quaker traditions.

In the last quarter of the nineteenth century in England, Quaker periodicals concerning the arts and non-Quaker literature started to appear, something that would have been unthinkable fifty years earlier.⁷⁶ In North America, by contrast, the examples of Helen Jackson and Mary Hallock Foote demonstrate how much more acceptable fiction already was in many quarters of the Quaker population. What this chapter illustrates is that the general path from Quaker distrust to tolerance of fiction over the nineteenth century is one that inevitably differs between the United Kingdom and North America, and the Orthodox-Hicksite schism offers one unforeseen reason for this difference.

NOTES

1. James W. Hood, ed., *Quakers and Literature* (Philadelphia: Friends Association for Higher Education, 2016); Nancy Jiwon Cho, "Literature," in *The Cambridge Companion to Quakerism*, edited by Stephen W. Angell and Pink Dandelion (Cambridge: Cambridge University Press, 2018), 69–87; James W. Hood, "'Novel Reading and Insanity': Nineteenth-Century Quaker Fiction Reading Practices," *Quaker Studies* 23, no. 1 (2019): 3–24.

2. Thomas D. Hamm, "Hicksite, Orthodox, and Evangelical Quakerism, 1805–1887," in *The Oxford Handbook of Quaker Studies*, edited by Stephen W. Angell and Pink Dandelion (Oxford: Oxford University Press, 2013), 3.

3. Mary H. Foote, *A Victorian Gentlewoman in the Far West: The Reminiscences of Mary Hallock Foote*, edited by Rodman W. Paul (San Marino: Huntington Library Press, 1972), 70.

4. Jackson never called herself "Helen Hunt Jackson" and detested this amalgamated name. See Kate Phillips, *Helen Hunt Jackson: A Literary Life* (Berkeley: University of California Press, 2003), 4, 275. I refer to her in this chapter as Fiske, Hunt, or Jackson.

5. Amelia Opie to William Hayley, February 28, 1816, William Hayley Papers, XXVII 16, Fitzwilliam Museum, Cambridge University.

6. Joseph J. Gurney, *Memoirs of Joseph John Gurney; with Selections from His Journal and Correspondence*, edited by Joseph B. Braithwaite, 2 vols. (Norwich, UK: Fletcher and Alexander, 1854), 1:235.

7. Amelia Opie, *The Works of Mrs. Amelia Opie; Complete in Three Volumes* (Philadelphia: James Crissy, 1843), 1:9.

8. Edward H. Milligan, "Grubb [née Lynes], Sarah [Sally] (1773–1842)," in *Oxford Dictionary of National Biography* (Oxford: Oxford University Press, 2004), https://doi.org/10.1093/ref:odnb/47052.

9. "Newspaper Chat," *Examiner* (London), March 13, 1825.

10. Quoted in Samuel C. Hall, *A Book of Memories of Great Men and Women of the Age, from Personal Acquaintance* (London: Virtue, 1871), 169n.

11. Helen Hunt Jackson, *A Call for Reform: The Southern California Indian Writings of Helen Hunt Jackson*, edited by Valerie S. Mathes and Phil Brigandi (Norman: University of Oklahoma Press, 2015), 3.

12. Steven L. Piott, *Americans in Dissent: Thirteen Influential Social Critics of the Nineteenth Century* (Lanham, MD: Lexington Books, 2014), 142.

13. Phillips, *Helen Hunt Jackson*, 202, 207.

14. Ibid., 221–22, 224.

15. Helen Hunt Jackson to Thomas Wentworth Higginson, January 17, 1880, quoted in Siobhan Senier, *Voices of American Indian Assimilation and Resistance: Helen Hunt Jackson, Sarah Winnemucca, and Victoria Howard* (Norman: University of Oklahoma Press, 2001), 30.

16. Carol E. Schmudde, "Sincerity, Secrecy, and Lies: Helen Hunt Jackson's No Name Novels," *Studies in American Fiction* 21, no. 1 (1993): 62; Phillips, *Helen Hunt Jackson*, 206, 207.

17. Quoted in Piott, *Americans in Dissent*, 145.

18. Helen Hunt Jackson to the Coronels, November 8, 1883, in Jackson, *Call for Reform*, 70.

19. Helen Hunt Jackson to Thomas Bailey Aldrich, December 1, 1884, quoted in Valerie S. Mathes, "Helen Hunt Jackson and Southern California's Mission Indians," *California History* 78, no. 4 (2000): 271.

20. Jackson, *Call for Reform*, 70.

21. Phillips, *Helen Hunt Jackson*, 229, 253.

22. Helen Hunt Jackson to Mrs. Quinton, April 2, 1884, quoted in Mathes, "Southern California's Mission Indians," 271.

23. Helen Hunt Jackson, *Ramona*, edited by Siobhan Senier (Peterborough, ON: Broadview Press, 2008), 19.

24. Errol W. Stevens, "Helen Hunt Jackson's *Ramona*: Social Problem Novel as Tourist Guide," *California History* 77, no. 3 (1998): 167.

25. Helen Hunt Jackson to Thomas Bailey Aldrich, May 4, 1883, quoted in Phillips, *Helen Hunt Jackson*, 252.

26. "Helen Maria (Fiske) Hunt Jackson, 1830–1885," in "*Dictionary of Quaker Biography*," manuscript, FHLSC. My thanks to Jordan Landes (curator) and Pat O'Donnell (retired archivist) at FHLSC for their help in researching the Quaker affiliations and backgrounds of Helen Jackson, William Sharpless Jackson, and Mary Hallock Foote.

27. Clyde A. Milner II, "Albert K. Smiley: Friend to Friends of the Indians," in *Churchmen and the Western Indians, 1820–1920*, edited by Clyde A. Milner II and Floyd A. O'Neil (Norman: University of Oklahoma Press, 1985), 160–61.

28. Valerie S. Mathes, *Divinely Guided: The California Work of the Women's National Indian Association* (Lubbock: Texas Tech University Press, 2012), 154; Senier, *Voices of American Indian Assimilation*, 32.

29. Helen Hunt Jackson to Thomas Wentworth Higginson, July 27, 1885, quoted in Phillips, *Helen Hunt Jackson*, 265.
30. Phillips, *Helen Hunt Jackson*, 266, 271.
31. Amice Lee, *Laurels and Rosemary: The Life of William and Mary Howitt* (Oxford: Oxford University Press, 1955), 1, 4, 18, 21.
32. Mary Howitt, *Mary Howitt: An Autobiography*, edited by Margaret Howitt (London: Isbister and Co., 1889), 26, 52.
33. Lee, *Laurels and Rosemary*, 4, 39.
34. Lee A. Johnson, *Mary Hallock Foote* (Boston: Twayne, 1980), 16.
35. James H. Maguire, *Mary Hallock Foote* (Boise: Boise State College, 1972), 5.
36. Christine H. Smith, *Social Class in the Writings of Mary Hallock Foote* (Reno: University of Nevada Press, 2009), 1, 5.
37. Foote, *Reminiscences*, 48, 52, 54, 57.
38. Ibid., 66–67.
39. Smith, *Social Class*, 2.
40. Maguire, *Mary Hallock Foote*, 7.
41. Foote, *Reminiscences*, 102, 104.
42. Johnson, *Mary Hallock Foote*, 22, 105–7, 121.
43. Quoted in Lee, *Laurels and Rosemary*, 43.
44. Ibid., 73.
45. Howitt, *Autobiography*, 104; Lee, *Laurels and Rosemary*, 76.
46. Lee, *Laurels and Rosemary*, 79.
47. Quoted in Joy Dunicliff, *Mary Howitt: Another Lost Victorian Writer* (London: Excalibur Press, 1992), 114.
48. Howitt, *Autobiography*, 119.
49. Lee, *Laurels and Rosemary*, 90, 92.
50. Dunicliff, *Mary Howitt*, 126.
51. Howitt, *Autobiography*, 139, 141.
52. Lee, *Laurels and Rosemary*, 121–22.
53. Howitt, *Autobiography*, 190–91.
54. Anna P. Vaughan Kett, "'Without the Consumers of Slave Produce There Would Be No Slaves': Quaker Women, Antislavery Activism, and Free-Labor Cotton Dress in the 1850s," in *Quakers and Abolition*, edited by Brycchan Carey and Geoffrey Plank (Urbana: University of Illinois Press, 2014), 61, 63; Howitt, *Autobiography*, 221–23.
55. Smith, *Social Class*, 2, 3.
56. Maguire, *Mary Hallock Foote*, 8.
57. Johnson, *Mary Hallock Foote*, 16, 32, 34.
58. Foote, *Reminiscences*, 189–89.
59. Ibid., 190; Robert Barclay, *Barclay's Apology in Modern English*, edited by Dean Freiday (Manasquan, NJ: Dean Freiday, 1967), 389.
60. Quoted in Johnson, *Mary Hallock Foote*, 44, 50.
61. Smith, *Social Class*, 4; Foote, *Reminiscences*, 32–33.
62. Foote, *Reminiscences*, 19.
63. Maguire, *Mary Hallock Foote*, 26, 33.
64. Smith, *Social Class*, 7–8.
65. Noriko Suzuki, *The Re-Invention of the American West: Women's Periodicals and Gendered Geography in the Late Nineteenth-Century United States* (Lewiston, NY: Edwin Mellen Press, 2009), 115.

66. Quoted in Smith, *Social Class*, 15.
67. Johnson, *Mary Hallock Foote*, 149.
68. Maguire, *Mary Hallock Foote*, 44.
69. Foote, *Reminiscences*, 261.
70. Johnson, *Mary Hallock Foote*, 127, 154.
71. Cho, "Literature," 85.
72. Margaret Hope Bacon, *Valiant Friend: The Life of Lucretia Mott* (New York: Walker and Co., 1980), 22.
73. Hamm, "Hicksite, Orthodox, and Evangelical Quakerism," 4.
74. Gurney's disparaging comments about Hicksites in letters to Opie from his missionary activity in North America are too numerous to list here. See Joseph J. Gurney, *A Journey in North America, Described in Familiar Letters to Amelia Opie* (Norwich: printed for private circulation by Josiah Fletcher, 1841).
75. Amelia Opie to Joseph John Gurney, February 23, 1844, Gurney MSS, Temp MSS 434/1/380, LSF.
76. Jennifer Milligan, "British Quakerism, 1837–1914, as Seen Through Ten Periodicals," paper presented at the Quaker History Meeting, Friends House, London, April 24, 2012.

CHAPTER 8

A Friendly Daughter
Lucy Barton's (Ex-)Quaker Identity, Cultural Negotiations, and Authorial Inheritance

NANCY JIWON CHO

Lucy Barton (1808–1889) is footnoted in literary history as the daughter of the Romantic-era Quaker poet Bernard Barton (1784–1849) and as the ill-matched wife of Edward Fitzgerald (1809–1883), the translator of *The Rubaiyat of Omar Khayyam*.[1] In fact, she was a productive author in her own right, as Joseph Smith's inclusion of seven of her books in *A Descriptive Catalogue of Friends' Books* (1867) indicates.[2] In addition to poetry published in *The Reliquary* (1836), a volume coauthored with her father, and a scriptural and poetic commentary on prayer titled *The Oratory* (1841), she wrote books of religious instruction for children that were circulated transatlantically.[3] These included *Bible Letters for Children* (1831), an epistolary work introducing the stories of the Hebrew Bible; *The Gospel History of Our Lord and Saviour Jesus Christ* (1837), a New Testament counterpart to *Bible Letters* written in the same form; *The Life of Christ: A Gospel History for the Use of Children* (1857); and *Natural History of the Holy Land and Other Places Mentioned in the Bible* (1856). In the present century, Barton's scriptural writings have started to be recognized as female biblical exegesis; for instance, discussions of and representative extracts from her work are included in Marion Ann Taylor and Heather Weir's *Let Her Speak for Herself: Nineteenth-Century Women Writing on Women in Genesis* (2006) and their *Women in the Story of Jesus: The Gospels Through the Eyes of Nineteenth-Century Female Biblical Interpreters* (2016). These studies consistently identify Barton as a Friend. Yet the influence of Quakerism on her writings—for instance, the impact of her Quaker family connections; theology, such as peace testimony and gender egalitarianism; literary strategies, such as using the epistolary mode for sincerity and plainness; and religio-cultural practices, such as interest in natural science as a means of understanding creation—has not yet been considered.

In fact, Barton was an Anglican, and not a member of the Society of Friends, by the time she published. Like many Quakers in the early nineteenth century, she turned to evangelical religion from the quietism of her father's faith. Yet analysis of the form and content of her writings, along with the influence of her literary family connections, suggests that Quaker culture was formative in shaping her authorial development. This chapter clarifies the impact of Quaker networks, theology, and culture on Barton's writings. In this process, it broadens our understanding of Quaker identity in transition during the nineteenth century, it contributes to the recovery of Barton as an (ex-)Quaker woman writer and female interpreter of the Bible, and it deepens our understanding of nineteenth-century Quaker literary networks.

QUAKER IDENTITY IN TRANSITION

Scholars, including Joseph Smith, may have assumed that Lucy Barton was a Quaker on the basis of her renowned father's religion. The exact nature of her religious affiliation growing up is difficult to ascertain. Doris Alexander states that Barton's grandmother (probably Martha Jesup, her maternal grandmother, who lived in Barton's hometown of Woodbridge) raised her as a member of the Church of England after her mother's death in childbirth.[4] However, Bernard Barton wrote in a letter, "My Lucy was, comparatively, a chit when she apostatized"; in other words, she was not raised in another church tradition but left the Society as an adult.[5] Indeed, an album poem for Lucy written by Charles Lamb, a "correspondent and confidant" of Bernard's, in 1824, when she was sixteen years old, designates her in the final line a "quiet Quakeress," suggesting that she had not yet embraced the Anglican Church at this age.[6]

In adulthood, Lucy became an evangelical Anglican. Indeed, her preoccupation with writing about the Bible signals her evangelicalism; biblicism, which stressed the primacy of the scriptures as the inspired word of God, was a cornerstone of British evangelicalism, as D. W. Bebbington has established.[7] Moreover, *The Oratory* (1841) is dedicated to "My Valued Pastor" (an evangelical term for priest, as opposed to "Father" in the high church tradition, for instance), and profits from its sale are offered to support "THE BUILDING OF THE NEW CHURCH AT WOODBRIDGE."[8] This church is likely to have been St John's, Woodbridge, the foundations of which were laid in 1842 and which was built in response to a revival instigated by the preaching of the Reverend Henry Hardinge, the rector of St Mary's, Woodbridge.[9]

Lucy's shift from the previous generation's quietism to evangelical religion reflects a common trend among Friends during the early nineteenth century. By the 1820s, as Thomas Hamm explains, "Many Friends . . . had enthusiastically joined non-Quaker evangelicals in humanitarian, religious, and reform activities, which they saw as forwarding Quaker commitments." At this time, Quakers' traditional stance regarding "the Light within" as the guiding spiritual principle was also under challenge from those, like Isaac Crewdson and Joseph John Gurney, who privileged the teachings of the Bible on Christ's atonement.[10] Evangelicalism became a dominant force within the Society during the nineteenth century; yet this shift in Quaker history remains underresearched. Examination of the Bartons' relationship widens our understanding of the religious and cultural negotiations that took place in nineteenth-century households when evangelical converts and Quakers who maintained quietist beliefs had to learn to live together. Bernard Barton's writings in particular illuminate the veracity of Robynne Rogers Healey's statement that "Quietist Quakers were deeply suspicious of this enthusiastic religious movement, but they were not untouched by it."[11]

Surviving poems and letters record Bernard Barton's conscientious attempts to be sensitive to and accommodate his daughter's divergent faith. His religious liberalism is evidenced by his poetic identity. Owing to their commitment to truth and simplicity, Friends had historically rejected imaginative, crafted writing; within this context, when verse was used, it was often for prophetic ends, to convey the idea of God's power pouring through the human, rather than for artistic expression.[12] Unusually, against this background, Bernard published eight volumes of poetry during the period of British Romanticism and became eponymously identified as "the Quaker poet." His broad-mindedness is also evidenced in his extensive friendship network outside the Society at a time when Quakers still perceived themselves as a peculiar people. As Christopher Stokes observes, "his epistolary connections included Southey, Lamb, Wordsworth, Hogg, Landon, Hemans, Scott—even Byron."[13] A memoir written by Edward Fitzgerald suggests that Barton was exceptional in his flexibility regarding Quaker discipline practices: "While duly conforming to the usages of his Society on all proper occasions, he could forget *thee* and *thou* while mixing in social intercourse with people of another vocabulary, and smile at the Reviewer who reproved him for using the heathen name *November* in his poems."[14] His tolerant nature is further demonstrated in the ways in which he accommodated and encouraged his daughter's non-Quaker faith.

Bernard Barton's conscientious effort to nurture his daughter's faith, despite her different religious practices, is evident in "Written in a Prayer-Book Given to My Daughter," which conveys Bernard's recognition of and respect for his daughter's unquakerly application of liturgy:

1. My creed requires no form of prayer;
Yet would I not condemn
Those who adopt with pious care
Their use as aids to them.

2. One God hath fashion'd them and me
One Spirit is our guide;
For each, alike, upon the tree
One common Saviour died!

3. Each the same trumpet-call shall wake.
To face one judgment-seat;
God give us grace, for Jesus' sake,
In the same heaven to meet.[15]

Barton's sympathy for his daughter's faith, which uses "aids" to enable devotion, is apparent in content and form. His explanation that the spirit in which such external forms of faith are used is crucial—"Those who adopt *with pious care*" (emphasis added)—reveals his belief that true piety can exist outside his sect and thus expresses his tolerance. The poem's metrical form also suggests Barton's sensitivity to his daughter's religion, because it is written in hymnic common meter, as used in John Newton's "Amazing Grace" and Phillips Brooks's "O Little Town of Bethlehem." Indeed, the poem could be sung as a prayerful hymn to these tunes. As Kirstie Blair has pointed out, "Victorian religious practitioners—a category that includes religious poets—knew what was at stake in formal choices and were highly self-conscious about them.... To choose Gregorian chant over a contemporary hymn, for instance, signified a great deal in mid-Victorian England."[16] By using a hymnic form, Bernard chose a poetic mode that reflected his daughter's evangelical culture and religious identity. The work's message that both father and daughter worship the same God is both peaceable and comforting. Here, the popular contemporary belief that heaven was a place where family members would be reunited after death takes a poignant ecumenical turn.[17] This idea goes against the grain of earlier Quakerism, which viewed Friends as a chosen people set apart from the established Church of England.

In contrast to the idealized resolution offered above, Bernard's letters, published in Lucy's posthumous *Selections from the Poems and Letters of Bernard Barton*, record the tensions, frustrations, and pain of familial sectarian differentiation. For instance, a poignant letter records Barton's grief at seeing his family members leave the Society. In September 1837, he reflected in a letter to a friend on the deep sense of personal loss he felt at the conversion of nearly his entire family to the Church of England:

> My only remaining near Quaker relative, my sister Lizzy ... has gone over to your church, having received the ordinances of Baptism and the Supper from my nephew, a clergyman, who married my sister Hack's eldest daughter. My sister H. herself had been previously baptized, three of her children had long before done the same; my brother and his family are all Church-folk, Lucy the same, and I am now almost the sole representative of my father's house, quite the only one of his children, left as an adherent to the creed he adopted from a conscientious conviction of its truth. I am left all alone, like Goldsmith's old widow in the Deserted Village, looking for water-cresses in the brook of Auburn. Lucy tells me I must turn too, but unfortunately, all the results of my reading, reasoning, reflection, observation, and feeling, make me more and more attached to my old faith. It seems only rendered dearer to me by the desertion of those whom I most love. Yet I love them not a whit the less for abandoning it; believing, as I do, that they have done so on principle.[18]

Bernard describes both the grief and the loneliness of desertion and provides a glimpse of the conflict that must have ensued within the home ("Lucy tells me I must turn too"). At the same time, he takes pains to assert that he does not resent his family members for making a conscientious decision. Other letters offer Bernard's reflections on his daughter's departure from the Society: "I sometimes think that if Lucy, as well as a few others who have left us, I believe from sincere but mistaken apprehension of duty, could have been content, when they first doubted, to have looked more inward and less outward; they might have found the object of their search without any separation from their early friends."[19] That Lucy, as editor, included such letters in *Selections* suggests that she came to recognize the pain that her conversion caused her father, and to value his continued efforts to support her religious life.

This correspondence is significant in throwing light on the shifting landscape of nineteenth-century Quakerism, in particular the rise of evangelicalism during its early decades. The leading figure in Quaker evangelicalism was Joseph John Gurney. Rejecting the previous century's quietist position of social retreat, Gurney urged that "Friends join 'vital Christians among all the Orthodox denominations'" and "re-oriented Quaker understandings of vital points of doctrine: the role of the Bible, the place of the early Friends, the guidance of the Light Within, and the nature of justification and sanctification."[20] As leading Quaker cultural figures, Bernard and Gurney were acquainted with each other; for instance, Gurney was instrumental in raising £1,200 for Barton in 1824.[21] Gurney envisioned "a Quakerism harmonious with non-Quaker evangelicalism," and the literary relationship between Quaker father and evangelical Anglican daughter indicates that this aspiration resonated within the Barton household.[22]

The Bartons' ongoing exertions to accommodate each other's faiths are recorded in their writings, which provide insights into the day-to-day negotiations of their religiously pluralist household. For instance, in a letter to Mrs. Sutton dated "9 mo' [September] 1846," Barton accounts for his reputation for wearing an unquakerly swansdown waistcoat. He explains that, a couple of years earlier, Lucy embroidered him a waistcoat "in worsted work" as a birthday present, "the pattern of which, being rather larger than I should have chosen, had choice been allowed me, gave it some semblance of the striped or flowered waistcoats which for aught I know may be designated as swansdown." He goes on to say, however, that "the colours, drab and chocolate, were so very sober, that I put it on as I found it, thinking no evil and wore it first and week-days, all last winter" without apparent disapproval from Friends: "I had not heard before a word of scandal, or even censure on its unfriendliness."²³ Although the size of Lucy's embroidered patterns exceeded the conventions of Quaker plain dress, her choice of colors indicates that she was sensitive to Quaker testimony. Plain dress was still enforced during the first half of the nineteenth century, and surviving garments from the period show that Friends favored a "muted and plain colour palette."²⁴ At the same time, Bernard's decision to wear his daughter's labor of love, despite the potential for judgment, demonstrates his support for her work despite her divergent religious observances. In fact, Bernard's endorsement of Lucy's creative work and the family's striving for spiritual harmony is further attested by the Bartons' multiple literary collaborations.

Bernard's prefatory materials were crucial in endorsing Lucy as a legitimate Christian woman teacher to the public. For instance, her *Bible Letters for Children* includes a preface and two preliminary poems by Bernard. The second poem, "A Postscript on Ruth," about the Bible's exemplar of female filial piety, clearly also speaks of Lucy's Christian character and devotion:

> 1. How could I pass in silence by,
> On Scripture's sacred page,
> One, unto childhood's partial eye,
> The heroine of her age?
> Still peerless shines her gentle fame
> For tenderness and truth;
> Who can forget the honour'd name
> Of warm, devoted RUTH?²⁵

Read without contextual knowledge, Bernard's multiple prefatory materials could insinuate a controlling paternalism. In fact, however, he expressed egalitarian gender views in keeping with his Quakerism. In a letter to an unspecified "Friend" written in January 1843, he explains that he does not view the "real spirit" of St. Paul's oft-quoted strictures against women's teaching or speaking in church as "opposed to the lawfulness (under the gospel dispensation) of a female ministry."²⁶ Stating that the "new priesthood ... is limited to no sex, or rank, or station," he asserts that "in the earlier age of the church, and in the primitive purity of its apostolic government, women did exercise their gift in the ministry."²⁷ Indeed, "A Postscript on

Ruth" may be interpreted as a reminder to readers of the significance of female faith, as its final lines highlight Ruth's twofold significance as an exemplar for the faithful—"A picture of a Christian life!"—and as a female "ancestress" (line 53) of "THE SAVIOUR OF MANKIND!" (line 56).[28] In fact, another letter, to a Mrs. Shawe, records Bernard's view that his prefatory support of Lucy's *Bible Letters* was an attempt to find common ground with his Anglican daughter:

> In one respect the work itself,* [*Bible Letters*] and my office of Preface writer, have afforded me some soothing and gratifying reflections. Differing as Lucy and I do on certain points, it is to me a comforting thought, that we can forget and forego all such differences in a cordial though humble and feeble effort to uphold the life and character of our common Lord and Master as a pattern for the imitation of his followers of whatever sect or name; and can freely join in the effort to turn the attention of the young to its beauty and excellence. It would say little, indeed, for Lucy's Churchanity [*sic*] or my Quakerism, could we have thought, felt, or done otherwise.[29]

Bernard promoted Lucy's female ministry doubly, as her father in a patriarchal society and as a published Christian author.

The Bartons also pursued religious harmony through ecumenism in their literary collaborations. Their conciliatory poetics is illustrated in their coauthored volume *The Reliquary* (1836), which does not attribute specific authorship to individual poems. The OED defines a reliquary as "a receptacle, often made of precious metal and richly decorated, in which a religious relic or relics are kept, as a small box, casket, or shrine." The title thus suggests that the book contains devotional poetry, though, in fact, the table of contents reveals a combination of Romantic lyric musings on natural scenes—including "The Sea Shell," "To a Skylark," "To a Robin in Autumn," and even a prospect sonnet titled "On a View Near Woodbridge"—and didactic narratives teaching Bible stories such as "Elijah on Mount Horeb," "King Herod," "The Prodigal Son," and "A Christian Heroine," a poem about Dorcas from the Acts of the Apostles. It would be convenient to ascribe all nature-inspired poems to the Romantic poet Bernard and all scriptural verse to the evangelical writer Lucy, but it is difficult to ascertain individual authorship. For instance, as scholars have shown that a common trait of women's biblical exegesis is interest in female scriptural characters,[30] it could be inferred that Lucy wrote "A Christian Heroine." In fact, it is similar in lyric voice, and in the intention to celebrate women of faith, to Bernard Barton's "Postscript on Ruth," quoted above, which also presents a biblical "heroine of her age" as an exemplar for the present day:

1. Thou didst not soar to deathless fame
By deeds of high emprize;
Yet not the less thy honour'd name
With dark oblivion vies.

2. Far more the Christian's heart reveres,
By Christian precepts tried,
Thy works of love, those widows' tears,
Than many a heroine's pride.[31]

Neither does the form help identify its author, as the alternating tetrameter and pentameter lines could be understood as both Romantic ballad meter, which Bernard used in works like "The Convict's Appeal" and "An Invitation," and as common meter, a ubiquitous form of English hymnody and devotional poetry, which Lucy would have encountered often in Anglican worship.

Similarly, when we consider that Bernard's verse more often used the lyric first-person voice than it did the third person, "Elijah on Mount Horeb" may seem attributable to Lucy: "The prophet stood in Horeb's cave, and saw with tranquil eye, / The whirlwind in its awful might and majesty sweep by."[32] Indeed, didactic biblical exposition would seem more in keeping with Lucy's evangelicalism than with Bernard's orthodox Quakerism. Yet the poem's conclusion of internal faith corresponds with the ideals of Quaker quietism:

3. . . . .
Though howling beasts affrighted fled before its lurid glare,
Calm and unmov'd the prophet stood, and felt God was not there.

4. But when he heard the STILL, SMALL VOICE;—upon his spirit fell:—
Its whispered accents with a power that bound him by its spell;
He in his mantle veil'd his face, and breath'd a voiceless prayer;
While every thought and feeling own'd that God himself was there![33]

Such difficulty in differentiating authorship in *The Reliquary* testifies to the Bartons' mingled authorial practice and striving for religious accord through ecumenism.

This aspect of the Bartons' relationship was admired by contemporaries, as evidenced by Robert Southey's letter thanking Bernard for gifting him Lucy's *Gospel History of Our Lord* (1837):

> I am much obliged to you for your daughter's very elegant little volume,* and heartily wish it may prove both as successful as she can wish, and as useful as she intends it to be.
>
> The worst of all errors in religion, because in its consequences the most heart-hardening to individuals, and the most dangerous to society, is the belief that salvation is exclusively confined to a particular church or sect. Wherever that opinion prevails there is an end of Christian charity. I rejoice therefore that you and your daughter are both catholic Christians, and are agreed that though one goes to church and the other to meeting, both may go to heaven, and both are on the road thither.[34]

Southey perceived in Bernard's promotion of his daughter's writings about the Bible (which, like the prayer book, historically did not hold as privileged a place in Quakerism as it did in the Church of England) a moving example of conciliatory Christianity, which would effect heavenly reunion. The Bartons' collaborative works, written not long after American Friends divided in the Great Separation over the primacy of the spiritual versus the scriptural, show that the Bartons, who would have wrestled with the same dispute, managed to cooperate without estrangement. As Hamm explains, "British Friends were more unified" during this period, and the Bartons offer an illuminating example of comparatively successful conflict resolution, adding nuance to our understanding of Quaker divisions in the nineteenth century.[35]

THE INFLUENCE OF QUAKER PEACE TESTIMONY

In fact, the content of Lucy Barton's writings reveals her privileging of reconciliation and peace in line with Quaker testimony. Barton repeatedly takes a peaceable stance throughout her teachings. For instance, "Letter II" of *Bible Letters for Children*, about the story of Adam and Eve, teaches that the original sinners should not be blamed:

> Now, perhaps, some of my young friends may think, how silly it was of Eve to take this fruit, and of Adam to be tempted by his wife; and it *was* very wrong in them to disobey the commands of the Great Master of the garden. But I would have you think a moment, and you will find this idea proceeds from *pride*. You think you would have done better: that had you been Eve, you would not have taken the fruit.
>
> But are there not many things in which you have not been equally to blame?[36]

A critical discussion of *Bible Letters for Children* by biblical scholars identifies the distinctiveness of Barton's commentary in its egalitarian teaching with respect to gender; it does "not distinguish between the results of the fall for man and woman" and contains the conciliatory request "to empathize with Adam and Eve rather than blaming them or thinking them foolish for their sin."[37] Amanda W. Benckhuysen, who also views this commentary as exceptional, states that Barton "invites her readers not to judge Eve for her failing but to sympathize with her and recognize ourselves in her, that we might become more aware of our inclination to sin and our need for salvation in Jesus Christ."[38] While this interpretation is apt in terms of Barton's evangelical reverence for atonement, the content also reveals a privileging of quakerly conflict resolution when Barton seeks to reconcile her readers with the first offenders.

Significantly, when Barton provides an appendix of "explanatory notes" for difficult terms in *Bible Letters*, the first term to be explicated is "Reconciled":

> to reconcile, means to make friends those who were not so before. When the Almighty created the first man and woman, He made them *good*, and their hearts were right in His sight; but when they had done wrong, by eating the fruit of that tree of which God had told them they were not to taste, they were no longer His friends, and from that time the heart of man has not been good in His sight, and is not pleasing to a holy God. But it was promised to our first parents, that mankind should again be reconciled to the Almighty, by means of His

Son Christ Jesus, who came down from heaven, and brought into the world peace from God to sinful man.[39]

Here, teaching about Christ's atonement ends not with evangelical focus on the Crucifixion but with the explanation that it accomplishes God's peace with humanity. Barton took a similar stance, privileging peace and reconciliation, in *Gospel History of Our Lord*, her New Testament counterpart to the *Bible Letters*. In "Letter XXV," her teaching of the Gospel story of the adulterous woman from John 8, she asks: "Dear children, when you hear of people who have been very wicked, . . . do you not feel in your hearts that you are a great deal better than they are? And, instead of feeling pity and sorrow for them, do you not despise, and almost hate them?" Teaching of Christ's compassion, she educates children to avoid aggressive responses: "instead of thinking harshly of others who may seem to be more wicked than we are willing to think ourselves, search our own hearts; and we shall soon feel that it is of God's mercy that we have been kept from falling."[40] As Taylor and Weir note, "She contrasted the usual human response of despising or even hating the wicked with Jesus' response of pity and sorrow. She encouraged her readers to emulate Jesus rather than the scribes and Pharisees."[41] Barton's lesson here may also be understood as supplementary evidence of her commitment to conflict resolution, in keeping with her Quaker upbringing.

Although Barton was officially an Anglican, her teaching promotes a Quaker understanding of peace as a process that "requires addressing the damage done during conflict."[42] Strikingly, her commentary on the Sermon on the Mount in "Letter XIII" allocates almost the same amount of discussion to "peacemakers" as it does to "the meek," "the merciful," and "the pure in heart" put together:

> It is a blessed thing to be peace-makers; for remember, dear children, they shall be the children of God. It is the command of Christ in this very sermon, that we love our enemies, do good to them that hate us, and pray for those who despitefully use us; that we may be the children of our Father which is in heaven; for he maketh his sun to shine on all alike, the evil as well as the good, and sendeth rain on the just and on the unjust. If therefore our heavenly Father, who is so holy, wise, and good, sends this blessing on us all, should not we, who have

done much that is wrong, shew kindness to our fellow-sinners? And again, he says, "If ye forgive men their trespasses, your heavenly Father will also forgive you; but if ye forgive not men their trespasses, neither will your Father forgive your trespasses."[43]

Here, peace is again tied to reconciliation—forgiving "men who trespass [against us]" and restoring harmony by overcoming division. Lucy's privileging of this beatitude over others may well have been shaped by her formative immersion in Quaker culture and the peace testimony of her father and friends. In fact, although *Bible Letters* has been used to exemplify nineteenth-century authors' tendency to paint God as wrathful, Barton is consistently careful to counterweigh violence with love. Russell Dalton asserts, "To prevent the possibility that children might miss the message of God's wrathful judgement, authors often made God's wrath quite explicit as can be seen in Lucy Barton's *Bible Letters*. . . . Barton concludes her story of the flood by warning children, 'Oh! how very dreadful it is to disobey such a powerful God, who can destroy us in a moment, if he please.'"[44] But Dalton leaves off the end of her sentence, which continues: "but this mighty God is also called, in the Bible, the God of love; and the same Being who commanded the waters to destroy the earth, condescends to love little children, if they do but wish to please *Him*."[45] The Bartons' mutual commitment to the ideal of reconciliation is likely to have been significant in enabling their literary collaborations and enduring cohabitation despite their religious differences.

A FEMALE QUAKER INHERITANCE: EDUCATIONAL WRITING FOR CHILDREN

Lucy Barton's Quaker family networks, which connected her with Quaker women who wrote for children from previous generations, were also formative to her authorship. As Elizabeth Bouldin states, "Education and the socialization of youth were important to the Society of Friends from its earliest days," and several early Friends wrote instructional works for children.[46] In fact, although creative writing was eschewed in Quaker circles, Friends' belief in the seriousness of religious and moral education meant that this task enabled women to enter into print culture and earn money: "Educating children offered a way for women to support themselves financially, but it also gave them their main alternative for public service apart from the structure of the meetinghouse."⁴⁷ In the decades before Lucy Barton started publishing, Romantic-era Quaker women writers, including Priscilla Wakefield (1750–1832), Sarah Hoare (1767–1855), and Maria Hack (1777–1844), had pioneered educational writing for children. Often publishing on natural history and scientific topics rather than purely fictional stories, in keeping with Quaker commitment to truth, these women experimented with various literary forms, including epistles and dialogues, for pedagogical ends. As Ann B. Shteir notes, they were enabled by "the Quaker call for members to study nature as a salutary amusement and as a source of spiritual knowledge."⁴⁸ Significantly, the form and content of Barton's texts indicate the formative influence of these earlier Quaker women's writings; for instance, she used the epistolary mode and wrote on scriptural natural history. As such, although she was not officially a Friend, Barton should be understood as an inheritor and successor of Romantic-era Quaker women writers, who expands our knowledge of this still underresearched literary network.

Barton's connection to this network was direct and personal. In particular, Maria Hack—one of the best-selling authors of the Quaker firm Harvey and Darton, a leading publisher of children's books by the early nineteenth century—was her aunt (Bernard's eldest sibling). Furthermore, the Bartons lodged for a period with Anne Knight (1792–1860), who also published children's literature with Harvey and Darton, including *Mary Gray: A Tale for Little Girls* (1831), a quakerly narrative, which, as the preface explains, disapproving "of fictitious tales, or those which have no truth in their composition," is "interspersed with anecdotes of various animals, and other subjects that have already afforded much pleasure to other children."⁴⁹ Although a personal relationship with Wakefield has not been established, she was a local personality, as she resided in Ipswich, just nine miles away from the Bartons in Woodbridge, from 1812 until her death in 1832. Wakefield was also an aunt to Joseph John Gurney, who knew Bernard Barton, as stated above, and to Gurney's sister, Elizabeth Fry, who stayed with Maria Hack in 1830.⁵⁰ Given the close connections of Quaker society in this period, it seems probable that Lucy would have known of Wakefield and her works, some of which were printed by Harvey and Darton, a company that also published her aunt, father, and, later, herself.⁵¹ Reading Lucy Barton's oeuvre within this history, she may now be understood as a third-generation writer in this female literary lineage.

The formal influence of earlier Quaker women writers for children can be seen in Barton's *Bible Letters*. Although epistolary narratives were popular during the eighteenth century and were not a Quaker invention, Wakefield in particular had used this mode from the 1790s as a "formal instructional method" for educating children.[52] For instance, in *An Introduction to Botany, in a Series of Letters* (1796), she sought to make scientific instruction, hitherto "principally written in Latin," accessible by introducing the subject "in an easy, familiar form."[53] Following this pattern, Barton used the epistolary form not as a means of producing "affective sensibility, [self-]contemplation or personal exposure,"[54] but to make scriptural content accessible for children. Indeed, the letter's relative conciseness makes it digestible for the young, the idea of receiving a letter is exciting, and the straightforward language of the familiar letter is appropriate for children. As Mary A. Favret notes, "popular letter-writing promoted a flowing, 'natural' style,"[55] and Barton's letters feign a familiar and personal relationship with their child readers. For instance, the introductory letter's salutation, "MY DEAR CHILDREN," invokes the voice of the mother-teacher.[56] The sentence that follows maintains this intimate tone:

> So much do I feel interested about you, that while I am well aware you may all have dear parents or kind friends, who make it their duty and pleasure to instruct you in that path which leads to happiness, still there is much time in which you are left to yourselves; and I have thought that if you had a few letters written by one who loves you very dearly, that now and then, in your play hours, you would take them up and read them; and might chance to find therein something to interest and instruct your young hearts; something that would lead you early to think upon that great and good Being who made you, and me, and all this beautiful earth, and not these things only, but also a glorious and happy heaven.[57]

While Barton's plain and straightforward language is evidence of her effort to write appropriately for her young readers, it is also in keeping with Quaker testimony. Indeed, Bernard Barton articulated this point in his preface to the volume: "The epistolary form of narrating the incidents selected, seemed to invite and warrant a *simplicity and plainness of style* [emphasis added], which without descending to homely familiarity, might render the events related more intelligible and attractive to children than they were likely, perhaps, to be in their original historical form, blended as they are, in the Old Testament, with numerous details less adapted to interest a child."⁵⁸ Certainly, the letter's predisposition to plainness, sincerity, and truth must have made the form seem appropriate for religious instruction.

The content of Barton's writings also points to the influence of Romantic-era Quaker women's writing for children. Specifically, a later work, *Natural History of the Holy Land, and Other Places Mentioned in the Bible* (1856), suggests her engagement with earlier writings on natural science by Friends. The volume contains eighty short entries, mainly on Middle Eastern fauna and flora, each accompanied by a plate containing an illustration and a verse quotation written or selected by Bernard Barton. Education is provided on zoology, ornithology, etymology, and botany (for instance, entries are included on the lion, hippopotamus, ostrich, dove, flea, spider, ant, fly, sycamore tree, olive, and cedar). Although natural histories of the Bible were not a Quaker innovation, Barton's text echoes the topics of earlier Quaker women's natural history writing for children.⁵⁹ Barton is likely to have been familiar with this tradition, given that Wakefield and Hack were pioneers in this field and published their works during Lucy's childhood. Wakefield's works include *Instinct Displayed in a Collection of Well-Authenticated Facts: Exemplifying the Extraordinary Sagacity of Various Species of the Animal Creation* (1811) and *An Introduction to the Natural History and Classification of Insects* [. . .] (1816), and Hack's include *Stories of Animals, Intended for Children Between Five and Seven Years Old* (1820) and *Harry Beaufoy: Or the Pupil of Nature* (1821). Indeed, it is possible that Barton was introduced to this genre through her aunt's works.

Early immersion in Quaker culture is likely to have made natural history writing accessible to Barton. As Geoffrey Cantor explains, "By the early eighteenth century, they [Quakers] rarely turned to the Bible in order to understand the creation, but instead sought to comprehend through the senses the observable world that God had created."⁶⁰ Moreover, Camilla Leach has argued that Quaker hermeneutics meant that Friends were less challenged by new scientific ideas than biblicist Christians were during the nineteenth century: "In contrast to the established Church of England, the Quakers rejected all formal worship, had no liturgy and believed that the Bible should always be read while under the leading and guidance of the Holy Spirit. Unlike the many evangelical Christians of this period who believed that God's word as revealed in the Bible was fixed, the Quakers' approach created a space whereby God's word could be reinterpreted and revealed anew to each generation. This had important consequences for their study and assimilation of scientific ideas into their religious belief system."[61] The Society's gender egalitarianism, which had actuated a long tradition of female teaching and scientific instruction for girls as well as boys, may have further enabled Barton to write on natural history.[62] For instance, her scholarly proficiency is suggested in her frequent inclusion of observations by experts such as Georges Cuvier, the French zoologist and naturalist; the British zoologist Reginald Innes Pocock; and Karl Christian Gmelin, the German botanist, which demonstrate her wide scientific reading.

Like Barton's earlier publications, which were heavily influenced by Quaker thinking and practice, her *Natural History* may be deemed a religiously hybrid work. Specifically, it brings together Quaker observations of creation and the evangelical impulse to increase Bible literacy and may thus be understood as blending Quaker natural history writing with evangelical biblical interpretation. At first glance, this text may seem atypical compared with the rest of Barton's biblicist oeuvre, because most entries impart information about the natural world rather than religious instruction, scriptural knowledge, or moral edification.[63] For instance, "The Wolf" contains no scriptural reference or explication, and although "The Bear" discusses David's victory over the animal in 1 Samuel 17:34–36, this story is covered in only one of the entry's eight paragraphs.[64] However, Barton's work should be understood as aiming to bolster Bible literacy. As Heather Weir has asserted of Esther Hewlett Copley's earlier *Scripture Natural History for Youth* (1828), "While this kind of discussion may not seem to be biblical interpretation, it is important to realize that readers are left with the firm impression that the creatures, plants, and minerals of the biblical world are a part of the real world of sense experience," and Barton's *Natural History* similarly "anchors the Bible in the reality of the world around young readers and dispels any notion that the biblical world might be a fantasy realm."[65] In fact, this strategy was shared by contemporary Quakers, who were also drawn to evangelicalism during the nineteenth century. For instance, Hack, who left the Society in 1837, writes in *Oriental Fragments* (1828) that teaching about "the customs and peculiarities" of scriptural cultures attempts "to illustrate the accuracy of Scripture."[66] That Barton had a similar objective in *Natural History* is intimated in her inclusion of several entries about the customs of the Holy Land rather than its natural history, including "The Camel's Furniture," "The Threshing-Floor," and "Eastern Waggon." Extending this understanding, Barton's *Natural History* can be deemed, as

Amy King puts it, a "*reverent*" work; "observing nature and describing it was a reverential practice, and supportive of (though not a definitive proof of) the generally held belief that nature was God's creation."[67] As such, Lucy Barton's *Natural History*, published seven years after Bernard's death and the end of the Bartons' ecumenical collaborations, may be understood as another work of religious and cultural hybridity, which unites earlier Quaker and contemporary evangelical literary traditions.[68]

CONCLUSION: THE SIGNIFICANCE OF LUCY BARTON'S (EX-)QUAKERISM

Lucy Barton has consistently been identified as a member of the Society of Friends. In fact, her association with Quakerism was complex. Although she left the Society in her youth, the publications of her maturity reflect the abiding influence of her formative Quaker upbringing and literary connections. It is now possible to locate Barton more accurately in Quaker culture. As Dalton has stated, "Children's Bibles ... lend insight into the minds of the authors, illustrators, and the cultures that created them," and Barton's works reveal that Quaker theology and literary practices continued to inform her art long after she left the Society.[69] As Verna M. Cavey has stated, "Quakers shared a cultural identity, a unique culture with its own history, language, system of meetings, religious testimonies, rules and sanctions."[70] Barton's writings, which retain many of these communitarian features, show that Quaker beliefs and practices could live on and influence the dominant culture through its ex-members. Indeed, they attest that Quaker theological ideas had afterlives, even when individuals left the Society and membership declined. In particular, Friends' religious beliefs and cultural practices lived on in the orientations of their former members, and presumably those of their children, even after they had officially left the tradition.

The recovery of Barton's intricate and persistent ties with Quaker social networks, literary practices, and theology after her Anglican conversion means that we can now recognize her as a fluid figure—an (ex-)Quaker—who throws much light on Quakerism in transition and the ministry of female Friends during the nineteenth century. Reconstituting the details of Barton's life, including her departure from the Society, the ecumenical support that she gained from her father, and her peaceable collaboration with him, deepens our understanding on the impact of the rise of evangelicalism on the Society, especially in relation to family life. Recent major studies on Quakerism have discussed how religious conflict in the early nineteenth century brought about the divisions that led to Quaker diversity today.[71] But the case study of Lucy's conversion and her subsequent decades of household life with Bernard Barton demonstrates that other narratives exist. The Bartons' history is significant in providing a broader understanding of the diversity of responses during the transitional period of the nineteenth century. It offers an example of tolerant accommodation and collaboration in the face of religious difference, which lends nuance to our understanding of Quakerism in transition in the nineteenth century and also points to the development of liberal Quakerism in Britain at the end of the century. Uncovering the enduring influence of Romantic-era Quaker women's writing for children on Lucy Barton's work also reveals that, although she formally left the Society, she should be understood as a third-generation member of a distinctly female lineage of educational writers who emerged from Quaker culture. Barton's lack of membership in the Society of Friends did not stop her from being witness to Quaker values, forms, and ideas in her art.

NOTES

1. I would like to thank the Centre for Research in Quaker Studies at the Woodbrooke Quaker Study Centre for the Visiting Fellowship during which I undertook research for this chapter.

2. Joseph Smith, *A Descriptive Catalogue of Friends' Books; or, Books Written by Members of the Society of Friends, Commonly Called Quakers* [...] (London: n.p., 1867), 201.

3. Russell Dalton, "The American Children's Bible," in *The Oxford Handbook of the Bible in America*, edited by Paul J. Gutjahr (Oxford: Oxford University Press, 2017), 25.

4. Doris Alexander, *Creating Literature Out of Life: The Making of Four Masterpieces* (University Park: Penn State University Press, 2010), 57.

5. Bernard Barton, *Selections from the Poems and Letters of Bernard Barton*, edited by his daughter [Lucy Barton] (London: Hall, Virtue, and Co., 1849), 13. He adds of "apostatized," "(I don't use the word in its malignant sense)."

6. Edward Verrell Lucas, "The Late Mrs. Edward FitzGerald," *Academy* 55 (1898): 380–81; Charles Lamb, "In the Album of Lucy Barton," in *The Poetical Works of Charles Lamb* (London: Edward Moxon, 1836), 175.

7. D. W. Bebbington, *Evangelicalism in Modern Britain: A History from the 1730s to the 1980s* (London: Routledge, 1989), 12–14.

8. Lucy Barton, *The Oratory; or, The Testimony of Scripture on the Subject of Prayer* (London: Harvey and Darton, 1841), v.

9. See the website of St. John's, Woodbridge, at https://stjohnswoodbridge.org.uk/Groups/272882/Our_History.aspx.

10. Thomas D. Hamm, "Hicksite, Orthodox, and Evangelical Quakerism, 1805–1887," in *The Oxford Handbook of Quaker Studies*, edited by Stephen W. Angell and Pink Dandelion (Oxford: Oxford University Press, 2013), 64, 70.

11. Robynne Rogers Healey, "Quietist Quakerism, 1692–c. 1805," ibid., 51–52.

12. Nancy Jiwon Cho, "Literature," in *The Cambridge Companion to Quakerism*, edited by Stephen W. Angell and Pink Dandelion (Cambridge: Cambridge University Press, 2018), 69, 71.

13. Christopher Stokes, "Poetics at the Religious Margin: Bernard Barton and Quaker Romanticism," *Review of English Studies* 70 (June 2019): 512.

14. Edward Fitzgerald, "Memoir of Bernard Barton," in Barton, *Poems and Letters of Bernard Barton*, xxxi.

15. Barton, *Poems and Letters of Bernard Barton*, 297.

16. Kirstie Blair, *Form and Faith in Victorian Poetry and Religion* (Oxford: Oxford University Press, 2012), 10.

17. For more on the idea of familial reunion in heaven, see chap. 6, "Death," in David Cressy, *Birth, Marriage, and Death: Ritual, Religion, and the Life-Cycle in Tudor and Stuart England* (Oxford: Oxford University Press, 1999).

18. Barton to Mrs. Shawe, 9 mo. 1, 1837, in *Poems and Letters of Bernard Barton*, 11. Hack's life also illuminates shifts in nineteenth-century Quakerism. She was a sympathizer with Isaac Crewdson. After she was baptized by Crewdson in 1837, she left the Society and converted to the Church of England.

19. Barton to Mrs. Shawe, 12 mo. 16, 1834, ibid., 14.

20. Hamm, "Hicksite, Orthodox, and Evangelical Quakerism," 70.

21. A. H. Bullen, revised by James Edgar Barcus Jr., "Barton, Bernard (1784–1849)," in *Oxford Dictionary of National Biography* (Oxford: Oxford University Press, 2004), https://www.oxforddnb.com/view/10.1093/ref:odnb/9780198614128.001.0001/odnb-9780198614128-e-1595.

22. Hamm, "Hicksite, Orthodox, and Evangelical Quakerism," 70.

23. Barton to Mrs. Sutton, 9 mo. 1846, in *Poems and Letters of Bernard Barton*, 41.

24. Hannah Frances Rumball, "The Relinquishment of Plain Dress: British Quaker Women's Abandonment of Plain Quaker Attire, 1860–1914" (PhD diss., University of Brighton, 2016), 118.

25. Bernard Barton, "A Postscript on Ruth," in Lucy Barton, *Bible Letters for Children* (London: John Souter, 1831), xviii, lines 1–8.

26. Barton, *Poems and Letters of Bernard Barton*, 22.

27. Ibid., 22, 23.

28. Barton, "Postscript on Ruth," xx.

29. Barton to Mrs. Shawe, 12 mo. 5, 1837, in Barton, *Poems and Letters of Bernard Barton*, 14–15. The asterisk is in the text and points to a footnote explaining the work being discussed in *Bible Letters for Children*.

30. See Marion Ann Taylor's introduction to *Handbook of Women Biblical Interpreters: A Historical and Biographical Guide*, edited by Marion Ann Taylor, with Agnes Choi (Grand Rapids: Baker Academic, 2012), 15–17.

31. "A Christian Heroine," in Bernard Barton and Lucy Barton, *The Reliquary* (London: John W. Parker, 1836), 91, lines 1–8.

32. "Elijah on Mount Horeb," ibid., 29, lines 1–2.

33. Ibid., 30, lines 11–16.

34. Robert Southey to Bernard Barton, December 29, 1837, in Barton, *Poems and Letters of Bernard Barton*, 124–25.

35. Hamm, "Hicksite, Orthodox, and Evangelical Quakerism," 63.

36. Barton, *Bible Letters for Children*, 3–4.

37. Marion Ann Taylor and Heather Weir, introduction to "Lucy Barton (1808–1898)," in *Let Her Speak for Herself: Nineteenth-Century Women Writing on Women in Genesis*, edited by Marion Ann Taylor and Heather Weir (Waco: Baylor University Press, 2006), 30.

38. Amanda W. Benckhuysen, *The Gospel According to Eve: A History of Women's Interpretation* (Downers Grove, IL: InterVarsity Press, 2019), 151.

39. Barton, *Bible Letters for Children*, 153.

40. Ibid., 137.

41. Marion Ann Taylor and Heather E. Weir, eds., *Women in the Story of Jesus: The Gospels Through the Eyes of Nineteenth-Century Female Biblical Interpreters* (Grand Rapids: Eerdmans, 2016), 197.

42. Elaine Bishop and Jiseok Jung, "Seeking Peace: Quakers Respond to War," in Angell and Dandelion, *Cambridge Companion to Quakerism*, 118.

43. Lucy Barton, *The Gospel History of Our Lord and Saviour Jesus Christ* (London: W. Tweedie, 1838), 67.

44. Dalton, "American Children's Bible," 25.

45. Barton, *Bible Letters for Children*, 12.

46. Elizabeth Bouldin, "'The Days of Thy Youth': Eighteenth-Century Quaker Women and the Socialization of Children," in *New Critical Studies on Early Quaker Women, 1650–1800*, edited by Michele Lise Tarter and Catie Gill (Oxford: Oxford University Press, 2018), 202. For earlier examples of Quaker writings for children, see George Fox, *Catechism for Children* (1660), and John Perrot, *A Primer for Children* (1660).

47. Bouldin, "'Days of Thy Youth,'" 203. For more on Quakers and imaginative writing, see James W. Hood's introduction to *Quakers and Literature* (Philadelphia: Friends Association for Higher Education, 2016), 1–8; and Cho, "Literature."

48. Ann B. Shteir, *Cultivating Women, Cultivating Science: Flora's Daughters and Botany in England, 1760 to 1860* (Baltimore: Johns Hopkins University Press, 1996), 74.

49. Anne Knight, *Mary Gray: A Tale for Little Girls* (London: Harvey and Darton, 1831), xi.

50. Fry's diary records that she "slept the night at Maria Hack's." *Memoir of the Life of Elizabeth Fry, With Extracts from Her Letters and Journal*, edited by two of her daughters, vol. 2 (London: Charles Gilpin, 1847), 117.

51. For instance, Bernard's *Poems* (1820) and Lucy's *Oratory* (1841).

52. Bouldin, "'Days of Thy Youth,'" 203.

53. Priscilla Wakefield, preface to *An Introduction to Botany, in a Series of Letters* (London: Harvey and Darton, 1807), v.

54. Mary A. Favret, *Romantic Correspondence: Women, Politics, and the Fiction of Letters* (Cambridge: Cambridge University Press, 1993), 133.

55. Ibid., 24.

56. In this manner, it re-creates the kind of concerned and caring mother-teacher established by earlier dissenting woman writer Anna Laetitia Barbauld in *Lessons for Children* (1778–79).

57. Barton, *Bible Letters for Children*, 1.

58. Bernard Barton, "Preface," ibid., v.

59. Botanical writing was undertaken widely by women during the Romantic and Victorian periods, and natural history writing emerged as a distinct genre during the Victorian era, but Quaker women wrote more broadly on natural science.

60. Geoffrey N. Cantor, *Quakers, Jews, and Science: Religious Responses to Modernity and the Sciences in Britain, 1650–1900* (Oxford: Oxford University Press, 2005), quoted in Bouldin, "'Days of Thy Youth,'" 232.

61. Camilla Leach, "Religion and Rationality: Quaker Women and Science Education, 1790–1850," *History of Education* 35, no. 1 (2006): 71–72.

62. Bouldin, "'Days of Thy Youth,'" 215.

63. An exception is "The Cow and Bull," in *Bible Letters for Children*, 55–56.

64. Lucy Barton, *Natural History of the Holy Land and Other Places Mentioned in the Bible* (London: Thomas Allman and Son, 1856), 7–8, 9–12.

65. Heather Weir, "Copley, Esther Beuzeville Hewlett," in Taylor and Choi, *Handbook of Women Biblical Interpreters*, 139.

66. Maria Hack, *Oriental Fragments* (London: Harvey and Darton, 1828), iii.

67. Amy M. King, *The Divine in the Commonplace: Reverent Natural History and the Novel in Britain* (Cambridge: Cambridge University Press, 2019), 4.

68. In fact, as the frontispiece clarifies, the volume, interwoven with "Poetical Illustrations, Original and Selected, by Bernard Barton," must have commenced during Bernard's lifetime and been envisioned as another collaboration between Quaker father and evangelical Anglican daughter.

69. Dalton, "American Children's Bible," 19.

70. Verna M. Cavey, "Fighting Among Friends: The Quaker Separation of 1827," in *Social Conflicts and Collective Identities*, edited by Patrick G. Coy and Lynne M. Woehrle (Lanham, MD: Rowman and Littlefield, 2000), 135.

71. See, for instance, Hamm, "Hicksite, Orthodox, and Evangelical Quakerism," 63–77; and Thomas D. Hamm and Isaac Barnes May, "Conflict and Transformation, 1808–1920," in Angell and Dandelion, *Cambridge Companion to Quakerism*, 31–48.

CHAPTER 9

The "Mystic Sense" of Scripture as Taught by Holiness Quaker Hannah Whitall Smith

CAROLE DALE SPENCER

Hannah Whitall Smith is a prime example of one of many nineteenth-century Quaker women who maintained multiple and often paradoxical identities. She was a deeply family-oriented wife and mother, yet she chafed against women's domestic sphere, challenged patriarchal traditions, and abhorred male domination. She was a highly public figure who spoke at churches, popular religious conferences, and holiness camp meetings, lecturing on women's suffrage and writing best-selling devotional books. A birthright Quaker, she wove in and out of Friends' circles as she strove to find agency and identity in an age of radical change in the Society of Friends. She valued much about the Quaker tradition, such as the greater freedom it allowed women to be a "public Friend," but she also found many aspects of traditional quietism and separatism culturally and spiritually confining. Although Hannah would often lament that she did not fit comfortably in any of the religious communities of her time, she also celebrated the freedom she found living on the edges of those communities. One of the freedoms that pushed across the boundaries of tradition is that of female biblical interpreter.

In 1903, at the age of seventy-one, Smith published her memoir, *The Unselfishness of God*, in which she proudly admitted, "I have always rather enjoyed being considered a heretic, and have never wanted to be endorsed by any one. I have felt that to be endorsed was to be bound, and that it was better, for me at least, to be a free lance, with no hindrances to my absolute mental and spiritual freedom."[1]

As she challenged gender constructs and explored the emerging spiritualities of her time and place, she was able to forge her own unique middle way through popular religious movements and to reaffirm her Quaker faith with renewed insight. She maintained an evangelical piety throughout her life, but, contrary to mainstream Christianity, she experienced the nature of God as maternal and feminine, and as so infinitely loving and merciful that she was certain salvation was universal.

While many aspects of Hannah's unique life and writings have been explored in family biographies[2] and more recent feminist and holiness studies,[3] an area in which she was highly celebrated in her time, as a teacher and popular interpreter of the Bible, has been generally overlooked.[4] Yet four of Hannah's published works are studies of scripture.[5] Surprisingly for a self-taught Quaker woman, Hannah crossed vocational boundaries into the male domain of biblical interpretation and became a prominent Bible teacher in holiness circles, where her meetings were widely attended by both men and women. However, since women biblical interpreters in the nineteenth century were not trained academically, their publications were only read as popular devotional books, and their works have been forgotten.

This chapter examines Hannah Whitall Smith's Quaker witness to the inward, Spirit-directed approach of continuing revelation that prompted her divergence from mainstream Christian doctrine and shaped her reading of the Bible as a mystical text with many layers of meaning. Recent research has uncovered some of the forgotten women of the nineteenth century who wrote studies and expositions of scripture. Although Hannah was a widely read female Bible teacher in her time, her work as a biblical interpreter has been largely unexplored.[6]

HANNAH WHITALL SMITH'S RELIGIOUS CONTEXT

Hannah Whitall Smith was born in Philadelphia to an Orthodox Quaker family on February 7, 1832, and died May 1, 1911, in Oxford, England, at age seventy-nine. Her mother was Mary Tatum Whitall, descended from a notable Quaker family, and her father, John Mickle Whitall, was a partner in a profitable glass company. She was raised in a guarded Quaker community of devout Friends, but she also came from a family of privilege and wealth.

She is best known today as the author of *The Christian's Secret of a Happy Life*, first published in 1875, a Victorian self-help book of practical holiness and positive psychology.[7] It is perhaps the most enduring book to emerge from the literature of the nineteenth-century holiness movement, an evangelical renewal movement that swept across the American continent and into Europe, affecting almost all denominations, but none to the degree that it transformed a large portion of the Society of Friends. Hannah became an important voice in the movement, both in the United States and in England. She continues to be identified historically with the holiness tradition today.

A biography of her son,[8] who died suddenly at age eighteen, launched her successful writing career, but *The Christian's Secret of a Happy Life* became her signature book. It was published in numerous editions and translated into many languages. Still in print today, it coheres well with many aspects of mainstream evangelicalism. But the bulk of her readers (then and now) remain unaware of her universalism, outspoken radical politics, lifelong feminism, unique interpretation of scripture, and strong Quaker identity, as none of these things is obvious in this publication.

Hannah's early journals reveal a loving but strictly plain Quaker childhood. Plain meant strictly following peculiar Quaker customs of dress and speech. Her parents were influenced by the more culturally open views of the British Quaker minister (but still plain Friend) Joseph John Gurney, whose travels in America set the stage for the Gurneyite schism among the Orthodox. Though her parents had been influenced by Gurney, who encouraged Bible study and cooperation with other denominations in social reform, most Philadelphia Orthodox, including Hannah's parents, remained traditional quietists, maintaining a separatist Quaker culture.

After graduating from a Quaker day school (the extent of her formal education), Hannah took her first step outside the Quaker fold by joining a reading club, a group of young women (many of whom were non-Quaker) who met for education and entertainment. She also began a process of self-education by reading voraciously—history, philosophy, natural science, theology, mysticism, and forbidden fiction—and began to expand her world beyond her strict Quaker horizons.

At age eighteen she wrote in her journal of a desire to reform the Society of Friends (a goal shared by many of her peers at that age). While some of her friends chose to "take up the cross" and become plain Quakers, adopting a separatist stance, Hannah found that path of reform unappealing. She wrote in her journal at age nineteen, "I love the friends, and value their doctrine, and their beautiful spiritual belief far beyond all price, but I am afraid to be one."[9] She began to question the necessity of suffering, plainness, and peculiarity as normative spirituality.

Her marriage at age nineteen to Robert Pearsall Smith brought her first real-life struggles and intensified her spiritual searching. (He was also from a prominent Philadelphia Quaker family descended from a line of colonial Quakers.) In her early twenties, she experienced a crisis of faith she called her "years of skepticism." By 1856, at age twenty-four, she publicly supported women's rights and joined the "Bloomerites," a movement to reform women's dress introduced by the feminist Amelia Bloomer. (I have found no evidence that Hannah ever wore bloomers; she maintained a modified traditional Quaker form of dress all her life.) In 1859 she and her husband, Robert, resigned from the Society of Friends to explore the wider religious world, finding Philadelphia Orthodoxy too sectarian and parochial.

In a period of grief and spiritual seeking after the death of her first child, Nellie, at the age of five, Hannah happened upon a "noon-day prayer meeting" in downtown Philadelphia. Such meetings were part of a popular renewal movement among urban businessmen and workers, which she considered at the time "only another effort of a dying-out superstition to bolster up its cause." But out of curiosity she joined in, and had a life-changing mystical experience: "Then suddenly something happened to me. What it was or how it came I had no idea, but somehow an *inner eye* seemed to be opened in my soul.... I do not remember anything that was said. I do not even know that I heard anything. A tremendous revolution was going on within me that was of far profounder interest than anything the most eloquent preacher could have uttered. God was making Himself manifest as an actual existence, and my soul leaped up in an irresistible cry to know Him." She wrote of this experience many years later in her autobiography, "It was not that I felt myself to be a sinner needing salvation, or that I was troubled about my future destiny. It was not a personal question at all. It was simply and only that I had become aware of God, and that I felt I could not rest until I should know him.... All I wanted was to become acquainted with the God of whom I had suddenly become aware." She had a clear awakening to the God within, but she didn't call it her "conversion" until a Plymouth Brethren friend told her that this experience meant she had become a Christian and was "born of God." But, she added, "I had only touched the surface of the spiritual realities *hidden* under the doctrines I had so eagerly embraced."[10]

In 1864, her husband became manager of her father's Tatum-Whitall Glass Company and the family moved from Philadelphia to Millville, New Jersey, a rustic factory town where Hannah was to discover a very different religious and social culture. The mill workers were all Methodists, and when she joined them in their meetings she was introduced to their teaching on sanctification, which they called "the Second Blessing," a crisis experience of a deeper conversion and empowerment for change. She equated it with what early Quakers called "the baptism of the Spirit." Reflecting on this teaching in light of her Quaker upbringing, she wrote, "The Quaker examples and influences around me seemed to say there must be a deliverance somewhere, for they declared that they had experienced it; although they never seemed able to explain the 'what' or the 'how' in such a manner as I could understand it."[11] With great zeal she convinced most of her family and friends, one by one, of "the what and the how" of Methodist holiness, which she felt corresponded with Quaker experience.

Even though she had officially resigned from the Society of Friends, she was nevertheless active, speaking at Friends' gatherings, and her Quaker heritage, with its theology and values and distinctive dress and speech, continued to be her primary religious identity. In 1866 she started a Friends meeting in Millville that met until the 1890s, but it was never granted official status. Revivalism did not appeal to the Philadelphia Orthodox. She wrote an article for a Friends' journal and in 1869 published a small book, *The Early Friends: Their Message and the Secret of Their Power*, with long extracts from early Friends. Their message, she declared, was the indwelling Christ; the secret of their power was the baptism of the Spirit.

By the 1870s, Hannah had become one of the leading female voices in what became known as the holiness revival, and she and her husband, Robert Pearsall Smith, who also became a charismatic lay preacher, brought the American revival to England in 1873. In England and Europe this movement became known as the "Higher Life movement" and later the Keswick Convention. It was sparked in its earliest iteration by Hannah and Robert. Their teaching on holiness became known as the "Keswick theology," at least in its beginnings. With the Smiths as leaders, preaching to audiences of thousands of Oxford and Cambridge students, Anglican and Free Church ministers, poets, writers, and English aristocrats, it became a kind of evangelical Transcendentalism. Earnest striving after holiness became the religious version of the Romantic impulse in Britain. Progressive (for the time), inclusive, and ecumenical, it was heavily flavored with Quaker spirituality, at least in its first three years (1873–75), when Robert and Hannah were celebrity leaders. But after the departure of the Smiths (precipitated by rumors of Robert's inappropriate relationship with a woman disciple—the truth of which will probably never be fully known),[12] Keswick spirituality gradually became less open and more conservative, as it was increasingly shaped by the forces of fundamentalism.

Returning to the United States from England after speaking at the Higher Life conferences, she admitted to a friend that "my orthodoxy has fled to the winds. I am Broad, Broader, Broadest."[13] Despite the scandal that caused her husband to lose his faith and withdraw from public life, Hannah proved to be resilient, and her career blossomed. She turned her attention to the Woman's Christian Temperance Union, which she viewed as a powerful women's liberation movement. She became an early leader and longtime friend of its president, the suffragist Frances Willard.[14] Hannah's ministry gradually shifted from evangelism to political action for temperance and suffrage. She described her spiritual evolution in these words:

> I feel myself to have gotten out into a limitless ocean of the love of God that overflows all things. My theology is complete, if you but grant me an omnipotent and just creator I need nothing more. 'God is love,' comprises my whole system of ethics. There is certainly a very grave defect in any doctrine that universally makes its holders narrow and uncharitable, and this is always the case with strict so-called orthodoxy. I find that every soul that has traveled on this highway of holiness for any length of time, has invariably cut loose from its old moorings.[15]

As the holiness revival became more polemical and doctrinally rigid within Quakerism, Smith distanced herself from those who were interpreting holiness in a narrow, dogmatic paradigm. She maintained an open, all-embracing, mystical vision of holiness as the pure love of God, which explains, at least in part, why she came to embrace restitution, a type of universalism. While her "heresy" did not prevent her from being invited to speak at holiness conferences (including Indiana Yearly Meeting in 1877) it did prevent her from being accepted back into the Society of Friends when she applied for membership in Whitewater Monthly Meeting in Indiana in 1881 (in spite of the support of her weighty friends Charles and Rhoda Coffin, who were leaders in the meeting). It took five more years of trying to rejoin the Quakers before she was finally granted membership, in 1886, in Baltimore Yearly Meeting (where her sister, Mary Thomas, was an influential Quaker minister). Not long after rejoining Friends, she was offered the opportunity to become "recorded as a Friends Minister," but she chose to remain a freelancer. "I am much freer now," she wrote to a friend. "It would be I fear a dreadful hamper to me."[16]

In 1888, she and her husband returned to England to be close to her elder daughter, Mary, who had married an Irish barrister. She lived there for the remainder of her life. She continued her successful writing career, essentially raised her two granddaughters, Ray and Karin (after their mother, Mary, left her husband and ran off to Italy with Bernard Berenson). Hannah became a well-known activist for temperance and women's rights in England as well as America. At the age of seventy, confined to a wheelchair for the final years of her life, she gave up public speaking, though not protesting. In 1902, in her wheelchair, she joined her granddaughter Ray in demonstrating with women textile workers for women's suffrage at Westminster. In 1928, Ray, who became a feminist politician and a writer, edited and published posthumously Hannah's last book, *Religious Fanaticism*, based on her grandmother's research and personal experience of the many sects, cults, and new religious movements that flourished in the Victorian era.[17]

HANNAH WHITALL SMITH AS A QUAKER BIBLE INTERPRETER

In the chapter "Quakers and Scripture" in *The Oxford Handbook of Quaker Studies*, Howard R. Macy calls the early Quaker engagement with scripture a "paradoxical approach." Quakers "developed a distinctive approach to the Bible that witnessed to their experience with scripture and to their experience of God."[18] The remainder of this chapter examines how Hannah Whitall Smith, as a holiness Quaker in the nineteenth century, continued to apply this both/and approach of direct experience and scripture, despite the tensions inherent within it. This approach led her to diverge from mainstream Christian orthodox doctrine. While the Quaker interweaving of the authority of spiritual experience and scripture declined among most holiness Quakers, who inclined toward strict biblicism, the Quaker witness to the inward, Spirit-directed path continued to inform Smith's study of the Bible in a decidedly nonliteral style.

Hannah's love of scripture hearkens back to Quaker women in the seventeenth century who were among the earliest female biblical interpreters in the emerging modern period. Hannah would find a strong precedent in Margaret Fell, often considered a feminist pioneer in biblical interpretation, though nowhere in Smith's writings did she refer to Fell's 1667 *Women's Speaking Justified*, an early influential Christian defense of women's preaching based entirely on scripture, and it is unlikely that Hannah was aware of this early work.[19] Early Quaker women's pamphlets, though well preserved in Quaker archives, were largely eclipsed by male writings well into the twentieth century. They were "hidden in plain sight" until the 1970s, when feminist historians began to uncover them and reprint them in modern editions.[20] However, Hannah never doubted that women's preaching was supported and defended in her Quaker tradition, and she expressed her desire to be a "famous Quaker minister" in her early journals.

In her preface to *The Christian's Secret of a Happy Life*, she offered the usual female disclaimer that she was not a "theologian," a self-presentation strategy that Christian women have used in writing since the Middle Ages. "This is not a Theological book," she wrote, and asked the reader to "forgive the blundering way" in which her ideas were expressed. "Say, if you choose, 'Well, she is only a woman, and cannot be expected, therefore, to understand Theology:'—but remember that God sometimes reveals, even to babes, secrets that He has hidden from the wise and prudent."[21] (In her revised 1885 edition, this sentence is deleted.) One feminist historian, commenting on Hannah's tactic, noted, "Having pre-empted potential criticism, she paved the way to speak exactly as she pleased."[22]

Her right to teach the Bible seemed completely ingrained in her, and she rarely felt the need to defend it. Though an outspoken feminist, she did not generally engage specific biblical texts to argue for women's equality. But in a letter to her daughter Mary, about her first official public speech for women's suffrage in 1882, she related how she came to this conviction:

In my speech I said I had come to the advocacy of this reform by the way of the gospel, that Christ came to break every yoke and set free all that were bound, and that I wanted to follow in his steps and share in his work. I said the gospel did not arbitrarily upset the existing order of things, but it put a mine under all wrong and oppression that finally blew it up. And that therefore women were made free by the working out of the principles of Christ who had declared there is neither male nor female in Him.[23]

For Hannah, the matter was settled through her reading of the Gospels. Her Quaker "inner reading" of scripture confirmed not only her belief in women's equality but also the revelation of God's universal and unlimited love, a love that would redeem and restore all persons.

In her 1903 autobiography, she described how the Bible was approached in her quietist Quaker community:

> When the Bible was read to us, which was frequently done, ... very little explanation was ever attempted, but instead a few moments of profound silence were always observed at the close of the reading, in order that the "Inward Light" might, if it should be the Divine Will, reveal to us the meaning of what had been read. I am afraid however that personally I was still too unawakened for much ever to be revealed to me. But so strong was this feeling among the Quakers in my day, that direct religious teaching from the lips of human beings, except in inspired preaching, always seemed to me to be of the world, worldly, and I felt it was good only for the "world's people," who, because of their ignorance regarding the inward light, were necessarily obliged to look outward for their teaching. In fact all Bible expositions, except such as might be directly inspired, were felt to be worldly; and Bible classes and Sunday-schools were considered to be places of worldly amusement, which no true Quaker ought to attend. Our teaching was to come to us, not from the lips of human teachers, but from the inward voice of the Divine Teacher Himself.[24]

Interestingly, Smith quoted Augustine to support this Quaker approach to scripture: "In this the early Friends only believed what Saint Augustine taught when he said: 'It is the inward Master that teacheth, it is the inspiration that teacheth; where the inspiration and unction are wanting, it is vain that words from without are beaten in.'" She asserted that one of the great religious principles of Friends was "the spiritual interpretation of the Bible instead of the literal."[25] Moreover, it was this principle, which she attributed to her Quaker forebears, that underlay her approach to scripture.

As she became drawn into the religious world beyond the boundaries of Friends, she was attracted first to the Plymouth Brethren, who were a kind of "emerging church" in Philadelphia at the time, the avant-garde of Victorian evangelicalism. Smith had no formal religious training beyond growing up in her strict, quietist Quaker family. She claimed that the foundation for her Bible teaching came at the feet of the Plymouth Brethren, a church she attended for a few years after resigning from the Society of Friends in 1859. Through her sojourn with the Plymouth Brethren, she discovered her lifelong passion for Bible study. However, within a few years of meeting with them, she began to struggle with their "extreme Calvinism" (as she termed it). She agonized over the question of how a loving and just God could damn the greater part of humankind to eternal torment, a struggle that first emerged in her adolescence and led to her "eclipse of faith" as a young adult.

Resolution of her struggles occurred sometime in the 1860s (she never gave the exact year). She had a powerful revelation of the infinite love of God, which would somehow save everyone. In her autobiography, she described in detail how this inner conviction came about.[26] She revealed that after having a "definite conversion" experience, the struggle with the idea of eternal torment intensified. Feeling selfish, in that she was now among the privileged few, she received an illumination from God that finally revealed "the real nature of things": "I felt hopeless of reconciling the love and justice of the Creator with the fate of His creatures, and I knew not which way to turn.... I began to feel that the salvation in which I had been rejoicing was, after all, a very limited and a very selfish salvation. But one day a revelation came to me that vindicated Him, and that settled the whole question forever.... I did not think it, or imagine it, or suppose it. I *saw* it. It was a revelation of the real nature of things."[27] After describing how an inward voice spoke to her, she exclaimed, "And with this a veil seemed to be withdrawn from before the plans of the universe, and I saw that it was true, as the Bible says that 'as in Adam all die—even so in Christ should all be made alive.'[28] As was the first, even so was the second. The 'all' in one case could not in fairness mean less than the 'all' in the other. I saw therefore that the remedy must necessarily be equal to the disease, the salvation must be as universal as the fall." Convinced of the essential fact of a final "restitution of all things," she concluded that "somewhere and somehow God was going to make everything right for all the creatures He had created. My heart was at rest about it forever."[29]

Although Hannah attributed this insight to a direct revelation from God, her reading of Robert Barclay's *Apology for the True Christian Divinity* also pointed to this conclusion. Her revelation that "the remedy must necessarily be equal to the disease, the salvation must be as universal as the fall," echoes Barclay, who writes, "this Light enlighteneth the hearts of all . . . and would work out the salvation of all, if not resisted: nor is it less universal than the seed of sin."[30] Hannah would agree that the Inward Light could be resisted, but not forever. Most Orthodox Quakers in her time, like holiness advocates, would have accepted the traditional doctrine of eternal damnation and judged her belief in a restoration of all things a heresy.

Immediately after this revelation, she rushed home to see if what God had revealed through her direct experience would also be consistent with scripture. She wondered if "the magnificent fact I had discovered could possibly have been all this time in the Bible, and I not have seen it." As she began her search, she exclaimed, "Immediately the whole book seemed to be illuminated. On every page the truth concerning the 'times of restitution of all things,' of which the Apostle Peter says 'God hath spoken by the mouth of all His holy prophets since the world began,' shone forth, and no room was left for questioning."[31]

When Hannah searched her Bible for the explicit doctrine of eternal damnation, she was surprised to find it absent. It was nowhere in Paul's writings or the other epistles; instead, there was the promise of final salvation and the restitution of all things. And where Jesus might have seemed to refer to it, she realized, it could be understood as figurative or rhetorical hyperbole. To her surprise, she found universalist statements surprisingly numerous. She discovered with delight that the teaching of endless torment for the reprobate and eternal bliss for the saved, as she had been led to believe through Christian tradition, was not really to be found in scripture. Continuing in this state of wonder, she exclaimed, "I turned greedily from page to page fairly laughing aloud for joy at the blaze of light that illuminated it all. It became a new book. Another skin seemed to have been peeled off every text, and my Bible fairly shone with a new meaning, I do not say with a different meaning, for in no sense did the new meaning contradict the old, but a deeper meaning, the true meaning, hidden behind the outward form of words."[32] Her esteem of scripture and the joy of her newfound meaning finds echoes in Isaac Penington (1616–1679), her most beloved teacher among the early Quaker leaders:[33] "thou must read in the Spirit, if ever thou come rightly to understand the letter. And the end of words is to bring men to the knowledge of things beyond what words can utter. So learn of the Lord to make a right use of the Scriptures: which is by esteeming them in their right place, and prizing *that above them which is above them.*"[34]

Hannah's witness to the historic Quaker approach of the primacy of the Spirit in leading to the inward meaning of the words of scripture confirmed to her the truth of the restitution of all things. She did not explicitly reveal this belief in her published writings until later in life when she announced to her friends in 1901:

> Not to be outdone by the younger generation, I too am preparing something for publication. It is a part of my autobiography, and I call it "How I discovered God" [the original title of her autobiography]. It is the story of my soul life from my early Quaker days, on through all the progressive steps of my experience until I reach that peace which cannot fail to come to the soul who has "discovered God"!—I am putting all my heresies into my story, and am trying to show the steps that have led to them; and I flatter myself that it is going to be very convincing! So if you feel afraid of becoming heretics, I advise you not to read it.[35]

In 1878, established as a spiritual writer and celebrated Bible teacher, Hannah published her third book, titled *Bible Readings on the Progressive Development of Truth and Experience in the Books of the Old Testament*. Among her many publications (fifteen in all) are three subsequent books on interpreting the Bible.[36] Like most Quakers and all evangelicals of her time, she believed that the Bible was divinely inspired and authoritative. She taught that one must approach the Bible in faith with a will to believe. She described her approach as a kind of leap of faith. "It may seem like stepping off a precipice into an apparently bottomless abyss," she warned her readers, "but it is safe to step, because God is there, and will receive us."[37] For Hannah, the authority of the Bible lay not in its infallibility but in its power to reveal the love of God, which she called "the unselfishness of God" or "the mother-heart of God."[38]

She explained her interpretive method in detail in *Bible Readings* as a way to understand "the deep inner sense of the Books of the Old Testament in their progressive development of truth and experience." She called her method "an experimental approach," neither critical nor exhaustive. While her view of scripture was essentially orthodox, she endorsed a style similar to the ancient spiritual (or allegorical) interpretation of scripture, which looked beyond a literal or historical interpretation to the "mystical meaning"—to discover the deeper, inner reading of the biblical text following the Quaker approach, "beyond the outward form of words." She called this kind of interpretation a "spiritual sense" and noted that this "symbolical interpretation" was common in the inspired writers of the New Testament. She gave some examples of the New Testament writers' use of allegorical interpretation, adding, "I feel, therefore that we are justified in seeking for this mystic sense in that which might otherwise be of but little value to us spiritually." And she sent forth these readings to "those who can receive them" (meaning those who were essentially awakened and reading from the heart).[39]

The idea of reading the Bible for its "spiritual sense" came from Hannah's Quaker childhood and the profoundly devout environment of her upbringing. But she also acknowledged that "these views have been opened to me principally through the writings and teachings of a few of the Lord's see-ers" (or seers—those she would call mystics). She mentioned the Reverend Andrew Jukes as one such seer, though we can assume that she also had her beloved Isaac Penington in mind, and perhaps others. Letters between Hannah and Jukes preserved in the Smith archives confirm that she and Jukes were dialogue partners in scriptural exposition.

Though Andrew Jukes (1815–1901) is an obscure name today, in Victorian England he was a well-known, though controversial, biblical scholar and clergyman who became a theological mentor to Smith. A graduate of Cambridge and ordained an Anglican, he became a dissenter, leaving the established church. Like Hannah, he had an early association with the Plymouth Brethren. In 1865 he founded an independent chapel in Hull, England, which flourished until he published *The Second Death and the Restitution of All Things* in 1867. That Hannah was attracted to this eclectic Bible scholar is hardly surprising, since he advocated a form of universalism that corroborated hers and made a similar dissenting pilgrimage through various churches. Not surprisingly, his book caused such a storm of controversy that he resigned from the ministry and his once-thriving church died.

Hannah read his book in 1873, at least ten years after her own discovery of the restitution of all things, and found in him a kindred spirit. Her interpretation of scripture, as we have seen, was rooted in the distinctive Quaker approach that required the inward experience of the Spirit as essential to understanding the meaning behind the words. But she also found the Quaker idea of a deeper, truer meaning that lies hidden behind the outward form of words in Jukes's approach to divine revelation, which he saw as a necessary paradox of scripture. "The letter of scripture is a veil quite as much as a revelation," he wrote, "hiding while it reveals, and yet revealing while it hides."[40] Smith believed from the very beginning of her Christian life that the "Bible revealed itself only to the need and faith of those who came to it. Just as science never reveals its secrets except to its students, so neither does the Bible." Thus she called her Bible lessons a "sort of experimental study."[41]

For Hannah, the meaning of a biblical text or story could both reveal and hide, and could exceed the single, literal sense to include a meaning known only from a higher viewpoint far beyond the meaning of the original human author of the text. This perspective became a well-developed theory in the hands of the Catholic biblical scholar Raymond Brown in the mid-twentieth century; he called it the *sensus plenior*, or "fuller sense," though it has its roots in the ancient patristic tradition.[42] Smith's exegesis used a *sensus plenior* method to interpret entire books as symbolic and metaphorical. The Bible, she contended, showed "a progressive development of truth all through from beginning to end." Moreover, "each book takes us forward a definite step from the one before it." So a deeper or higher perspective gives fuller revelation. She likened reading the Bible to climbing a mountain, and the higher up spiritually we are, the more we can see, "our view limited only by our power of vision."[43]

On the one hand, her approach to scripture was mainstream evangelical in her view of the Bible as the authoritative revelation of God. On the other, she departed from strict biblicism in her mystical reading, which had more in common with early Quaker reading of scripture and with the Roman Catholic Church's notion of *sensus plenior*, or multiple senses of scripture. Her allegorical/symbolic reading did have its proponents among some Victorian evangelicals, such as Jukes, especially the Keswick holiness branch, where Jukes was a popular speaker, and where Hannah was the most admired Bible teacher.

It is difficult to discern how Hannah's book on Bible interpretation was received within the holiness movement, which was still celebrating her *Christian's Secret of a Happy Life*. One indication is a brief review in the *Advocate of Christian Holiness*, a principal organ of the holiness movement, which offered this somewhat ambiguous and cautious evaluation of what the reviewer called "a unique book": "Mrs. Smith yields a vigorous pen, and never writes without saying something both interesting and instructive. Whatever may be thought of her method of explaining the Bible, or some of her religious views, the Readings will do any reader good." The review notes her interesting connections between Genesis and Revelation as "strange likenesses" and "striking contrasts." Knowingly or unknowingly, the reviewer highlights how she subtly conveys her belief that the Bible teaches a final restoration. For example, "In Genesis the curse was pronounced; in Revelation, there will be no more curse. In Genesis, man was driven from 'the tree of Life'; in Revelation 'the tree' is in full fruitage. In Genesis, Satan, 'that old serpent,' made his first appearance, in Revelation he meets with his final doom."[44] In another holiness periodical, an annual journal called the *Primitive Methodist Magazine*, Smith's book is recommended as "on the whole . . . sound and trustworthy in its spiritual teachings, and will be read with advantage by such as hunger for the inner sense of God's word," but with the caveat that this method of reading "has its dangers" and should be read "with due care."[45]

Smith's Quaker hermeneutics was experiential and subjective, attributing meaning in the text to spiritual experience and divine guidance that could not have been known by the human author but was intended by the divine author as fuller revelation. The mystical meaning is additional value that comes through the faith of readers for the good of their spiritual growth. Thus, for Hannah, the belief in restitution furthered her spiritual development, as she considered it the essential "third epoch" in her spiritual understanding.

She did not dismiss the literal sense of the Bible but saw the mystical sense as growing organically out of it. The mystical meaning was the more profound meaning, available through experience and faith. Hannah was not a biblical fundamentalist who saw the words of the Bible as having one plain, literal, single meaning, but she viewed scripture as part of a living, dynamic, and progressive process of revelation. For example, following the ancient patristic allegorical interpretation, she showed how the books of wisdom were symbolic of the stages of the spiritual journey—purifying, illuminating, and uniting, adopting the model of Origen's threefold path:[46] "Self must die as in Job, and the hidden resurrection life must be known, as in Psalms. Divine wisdom must be submitted to as in Proverbs, and the world must be tried by this wisdom, and found to be utter vanity, as in Ecclesiastes, before the heart is prepared for the experience set forth in this mystic song." Song of Songs was the mystic song, the metaphor of the soul's realized union with God, which could be understood only by "those who have passed through all the preceding stages.... Through emptying to fullness is always the Divine way."[47]

Hannah's engagement with scripture wove together historical Quaker approaches and a mystical interpretation similar to the allegorical method of the early patristic tradition. In *Bible Readings on the Progressive Development of Truth and Experience*, she was able to take the dense scholarly biblical interpretation of her mentor, Jukes, and simplify it into a popular work of imaginative biblical interpretation for a lay audience. Her mystical and paradoxical approach of direct revelation from God, which gave the faithful deeper insight and opened their eyes to the hidden meanings behind the letter, enabled her reading of the Bible to confirm her insight that God would save everyone, even though this view was at odds with more than a millennium of Orthodox theology. She was certain that the Bible contained God's divine revelation to humanity, and just as certain that universalism did not contradict the teaching of scripture.

Despite her "heresies," Hannah continued writing popular devotional books for almost thirty more years after the publication of *Bible Readings*. Her final two books were published in 1906, and they reflect her radical optimism in their titles: *The God of All Comfort* and *Living in the Sunshine*.[48] By the end of her life, her trust in the "mother-heart of God" without wrath was so unshakable that she had no fear of death. She concluded her autobiography by declaring, "I await the moment with joy."[49]

NOTES

1. Hannah Whitall Smith, *My Spiritual Autobiography, or How I Discovered the Unselfishness of God* (New York: Fleming H. Revell, 1903), 220.
2. See, for example, Ray Strachey, *A Quaker Grandmother* (New York: Fleming H. Revell, 1914).
3. See Meg Ann Meneghel-McDonald, "Becoming a 'Heretic': Hannah Whitall Smith, Quakerism, and the Nineteenth-Century Holiness Movement" (PhD diss., Indiana

University, 2000); Carole Dale Spencer, "Hannah Whitall Smith and the Evolution of Quakerism: An Orthodox Heretic in an Age of Controversy," *Quaker Studies* 18, no. 1 (2013): 7–22; Kerri Allen, "Representation and Self-Representation: Hannah Whitall Smith as Family Woman and Religious Guide," *Women's History Review* 7, no. 2 (1998): 227–39; Debra Campbell, "Hannah Whitall Smith (1832–1911): Theology of the Mother-Hearted God," *Signs: Journal of Women in Culture and Society* 15, no. 1 (1989): 79–101.

4. See Carole Spencer, "Hannah Whitall Smith's Highway of Holiness," in *Quakers and Mysticism: Comparative and Syncretic Approaches to Spirituality*, edited by Jon R. Kershner (London: Palgrave, 2019), 154, for a brief initial discussion of Smith's mystical approach to scripture.

5. These four works are *Bible Readings: On the Progressive Development of Truth and Experience in the Books of the Old Testament* (Boston: Willard Tract Repository, 1878); *The Open Secret; or, The Bible Explaining Itself* (New York: Fleming H. Revell, 1885); *Every-Day Religion; or, The Common-Sense Teaching of the Bible* (New York: Fleming H. Revell, 1893); and *The Veil Uplifted: The Bible Its Own Interpreter* (London: F. E. Longley, n.d. [1890s?]).

6. Christiana de Groot and Marion Ann Taylor, *Recovering Nineteenth-Century Women Interpreters of the Bible* (Leiden: Brill, 2007) examines a number of forgotten works written by women on the Bible, but Smith is not among them.

7. Hannah Whitall Smith, *The Christian's Secret of a Happy Life* (London: Willard Tract Repository, 1875); a revised and enlarged edition was published in New York by the Fleming H. Revell Company in 1883.

8. Hannah Whitall Smith, *The Record of a Happy Life: Memorials of Franklin Whitall Smith* (Boston: Willard Tract Repository, 1873).

9. Hannah Whitall Smith, diary, vol. 5, April 27, 1851, Lilly Library, Indiana University, Bloomington.

10. Smith, *Unselfishness of God*, 172–73, 182.

11. Ibid., 232.

12. For a recent investigation and analysis of this event and its aftermath, see M. J. D. Roberts, "Evangelism and Scandal in Victorian England: The Case of the Pearsall Smiths," *History* 95, no. 4 (2010): 237–57; see also Spencer, "Hannah Whitall Smith's Highway of Holiness."

13. Hannah Whitall Smith to Mary [Beck], August 8, 1876, box 9, Lilly Library, Indiana University.

14. Hannah's granddaughter Ray wrote a biography of Willard. See Ray Strachey, *Frances Willard: Her Life and Work* (New York: Fleming H. Revell, 1913).

15. Smith, *Unselfishness of God*, 120.

16. Hannah Whitall Smith to Priscilla Mounsey, November 20, 1887, box 9, Lilly Library, Indiana University.

17. Ray Strachey, ed., *Religious Fanaticism: Extracts from the Papers of Hannah Whitall Smith* (London: Faber and Gwyer, 1928), reprinted as *Group Movements of the Past* (1934).

18. Howard R. Macy, "Quakers and Scripture," in *The Oxford Handbook of Quaker Studies*, edited by Stephen W. Angell and Pink Dandelion (Oxford: Oxford University Press, 2013), 187.

19. Margaret Fell, *Womens Speaking Justified, Proved, and Allowed by the Scriptures, etc.* (1667), edited by David J. Latt, Augustan reprint no. 194 (Los Angeles: William Andrews Clarke Memorial Library, UCLA, 1979).

20. See Mary Garman, Judith Applegate, Margaret Benefiel, and Dortha Meredith, eds., *Hidden in Plain Sight: Quaker Women's Writings, 1650–1700* (Wallingford, PA: Pendle Hill Publications, 1996).
21. Smith, *Christian's Secret of a Happy Life*, 6.
22. Allen, "Representation and Self-Representation," 235.
23. Hannah Whitall Smith to her daughter Mary, November 11, 1882, Asbury Seminary Library Special Collections, Wilmore, KY.
24. Smith, *Unselfishness of God*, 38–39.
25. Ibid., 39, 56.
26. Chaps. 21–23 of the original 1903 edition of her autobiography, which comprise this essential and critical "third epoch" of her spiritual journey, were removed from all subsequent editions.
27. Smith, *Unselfishness of God*, 199–203.
28. She is quoting 1 Corinthians 15:22: "For just as in Adam all die, so also in the Christ all will be given life."
29. Smith, *Unselfishness of God*, 204–6.
30. Robert Barclay, *An Apology for the True Christian Divinity [. . .]* (London: n.p., 1678), 12.
31. Smith, *Unselfishness of God*, 206, quoting Peter's preaching in Acts 3:21.
32. Ibid., 207.
33. Hannah Whitall Smith, *The Early Friends: Their Message and the Secret of Their Power* (Philadelphia: King & Baird, 1869). In a letter to her parents from Millville, she wrote, "reading Isaac Pennington [sic] with the greatest delight—it is almost equal to Madame Guyon." Smith to her parents, November 1, 1867, Asbury Seminary Library Special Collections. See also Isaac Penington, "A Brief Account Concerning the People Called Quakers [. . .]," in *Works of Isaac Penington*, vol. 3 (Farmington, ME: Quaker Heritage Press, 1997), 355, http://www.qhpress.org/texts/penington/flesh.html#page355.
34. *Letters of Isaac Penington*, "Letter XVI: Advice on Reading the Scriptures," in *Friends Family Library*, 2nd ed., vol. 7 (Philadelphia: Joseph and William Kite, Printers, 1842), 58.
35. Quoted in Logan Pearsall Smith, *Philadelphia Quaker: The Letters of Hannah Whitall Smith* (New York: Harcourt, Brace, 1950), 141.
36. These are *The Open Secret*; *Every-Day Religion*; and *The Veil Uplifted*.
37. Hannah Whitall Smith, *Bible Readings on the Progressive Development of Truth and Experience in the Books of the Old Testament* (Boston: Willard Tract Depository, 1878) (also published in London by Eliot Stock), 8.
38. Smith, *Unselfishness of God*, 215–16.
39. Smith, *Bible Readings*, iii–iv.
40. Andrew Jukes, *The Second Death and the Restitution of All Things* (London: Longmans, Green, 1867), 9.
41. Smith, *Bible Readings*, 5–6.
42. Raymond Brown, *The "Sensus Plenior" of Sacred Scripture* (Baltimore: St. Mary's University, 1955), 92.
43. Smith, *Bible Readings*, 14, 16, 12.
44. *Advocate of Christian Holiness*, December 1878, 287, https://www.google.com/books/edition/The_Advocate_of_Christian_Holiness/N9k6AQAAMAAJ?hl.
45. *Primitive Methodist Magazine* 60 (1879): 249, https://babel.hathitrust.org/cgi/pt?id=coo.31924057453700&view=1up&seq=273&q1=Bible%20readings.

46. Smith, *Bible Readings*, 24.
47. Ibid., 345–46.
48. Hannah Whitall Smith, *The God of All Comfort and the Secret of His Comforting* (London: J. Nisbet, 1906), and *Living in the Sunshine* (New York: Fleming H. Revell, 1906).
49. Smith, *Unselfishness of God*, 214–16, 311.

PART 4

Engaging the Wider Social and Cultural World

CHAPTER 10

"Radicalism Within Boundaries"
Excavating the Contribution of Women Quakers to Radical Reform in Britain and Their Transnational Networks in the Nineteenth Century

JOAN ALLEN AND RICHARD C. ALLEN

The nineteenth century was a period of profound change, which not only transformed the economy but also heralded a major shift in social and cultural norms. As people struggled to navigate new ways of working and living, British radicals increasingly embraced a progressive reform agenda. Their campaigns for electoral, social, and cultural change, which Patricia Hollis calls "pressure from without," encompassed both male and female activism.[1] Researchers have extended our appreciation of female activism, especially in the last few decades, but many aspects of the role of women remain relatively underresearched and imperfectly understood. To some extent, scholars have been hindered by the limitations of the primary sources. Those that have survived tend to document the work of elite, wealthy women and have not adequately captured the range of reform activities in which other women engaged. The comparable invisibility of female reformers in the historical record is compounded by the patchy and selective attention paid to Quaker women. In throwing the spotlight on a few "weighty" Quaker women, such as the prison reformer Elizabeth Fry and the suffrage and abolitionist Anne Knight,[2] the service of countless women who acted in a supportive capacity has not been fully appreciated.

Significantly, Quaker women who engaged in social and political radicalism often did so against the prevailing conditioning of their religious community. As Sandra Holton notes, Quaker women "differed among themselves as to how to enact the 'public' character." For example, Elizabeth Pease of Darlington was dubbed "ungenteel" and "vulgar" on account of her support for universal suffrage.[3] Active involvement in certain reform campaigns, such as those regarded as essentially pacifist, or educational, was considered an appropriate arena for women to dispense their innate humanitarian impulses. Those who challenged the status quo on suffrage often attracted censure from their meetings and family members. Nonetheless, some Quaker women were prepared to defend their commitment to natural justice and gender equality. As the century progressed, they were more visibly engaged in social, political, and cultural reform.

Literacy and education were always greatly valued by Quakers, and they exploited developments in print culture, producing tracts, pamphlets, periodicals, testimonies, and memoirs. These diverse texts afford rare insights into women's activism. Drawing on Quaker and non-Quaker materials, this chapter documents the networks that shaped Quaker women's spectrum of social and cultural reforms. It considers the obstacles they encountered and the extent to which they acted as a brake on their public participation. It also establishes the extent to which Quaker women made common cause with other nonconformists, especially Unitarians and Methodists, by working together cooperatively to achieve their objectives.[4]

By the late eighteenth century, as Sheila Wright observes, Quaker women's ministry had "little of its original verve and vigour ... [and] had given way to a more seemly and quiet style of preaching."[5] Thereafter, radical female Quaker reformers increasingly worked independently of their meetings, though others remained within the Society and felt able to promote a radical agenda.[6] There was, however, an expectation that Quakers would ensure that "their education and socialization did not include frivolous or time-wasting pleasures. ... Efforts were to be channeled into worthwhile and productive activities."[7] Indeed, being part of a religious community did not necessarily confine women to the domestic sphere. Rather, it gave them "the chance to exercise real historical agency and power."[8]

The impulse to humanitarianism and the desire to tackle the social problems of the age contrasts with the alleged quietism of the Quakers, challenging the assumption that they withdrew from the wider society.[9] Many social reform campaigns from the late eighteenth century onward elicited other responses. Priscilla Wakefield of London became well known for her children's books and philanthropic ventures, including the Lying-In Charity for Women, which she began in 1791, and the School for Industry in Tottenham, founded in 1791. This school taught girls to read and write as well as practical skills such as sewing and knitting. An advocate for economic self-sufficiency, Wakefield was also instrumental in establishing the Penny Savings Bank in Tottenham in 1798. Its aim was to provide a pension for the elderly or those incapacitated by sickness, while children were encouraged to save their pennies for an apprenticeship or clothing. There were limits to such initiatives, as Wakefield "did not contest the division of society into social classes," as Ann B. Shteir notes, but "directed her ideas about female improvement to women of the nobility, the middle classes, and the labouring poor." Significantly, she did not challenge "gendered ideas about the 'female character.'" As Wakefield observed in 1797, "there are many branches of science, as well as useful occupations, in which women may employ their time and their talents, beneficially to themselves and to the community, without destroying the peculiar characteristic of their sex, or exceeding the most exact limits of modesty and decorum."[10] Even so, these ideas caused divisions in many meetings. As the century progressed, women's activism changed, and they gained ever greater freedom to express themselves.[11]

Traditionally, Quaker women assisted the needy. Caroline Parken of Bournemouth distinguished between her privileged childhood and the difficulties she encountered as a young woman and later in life. Living with her brother William, a London barrister, she was "exposed to the attractions of worldly society" but found them unrewarding. Instead, she devoted herself to helping the poor, particularly those confined to the workhouse at Gray's Inn and the indigent of St. Albans parish. Jane Richardson of Newcastle was also committed to charitable works. In 1853 Richardson put aside her own fears to help the victims of the cholera pandemic. As she recalled, fifteen hundred people had died in Newcastle and Gateshead over the course of a single month, but "to rise in the morning, and find all the household [of the poor] well, was a daily cause for unspeakable thankfulness."[12] In addition to this humanitarian work, women Friends championed a myriad of other causes.

From the 1660s, Quakers were recognized for their peace testimony, and meetings called upon members to stand firm against bearing arms, providing military substitutes, or financing county militias.[13] Clearly, female

Quakers who became involved in the peace movement often had different experiences and expectations; their response was not uniform, as some have inferred.[14] Eliza Wigham of Edinburgh and Dublin was a devout pacifist who promoted arbitration instead of conflict. This approach to conflict was nowhere more marked than during and after the Franco-Prussian War (1870–71). Wigham distributed clothes and assisted the wounded during the Herzegovina uprising (1875–77); she also established a school for orphans. She spared no effort to help the Armenians after the massacre of many civilians by the Turks between 1894 and 1896. So committed was she to rescuing the victims that she cared for an orphaned Armenian girl in her own home in Edinburgh.[15]

Anna Maria Priestman of Newcastle attended the International Peace Bureau's first congress in 1892, while Isabella Ford of Leeds supported the Women's International League for Peace and Freedom well into the twentieth century.[16] In contrast, Ellen Robinson of Liverpool promoted her pacifist views in Quaker meetings and in eighty public appearances in 1898. In some quarters, this activism has been interpreted as "Friendly patriotism"—a gesture in support of British imperialism.[17] Nevertheless, Priestman and Robinson were critical of the wars in South Africa, and in 1900 Robinson called on the London Yearly Meeting to oppose "the monstrous yoke of militarism." She was not alone; Emily Hobhouse of London published a damning critique of the war in 1902, particularly the concentration camps used against the Boers.[18] She denounced the camps as "needless cruelty" and argued that "to keep these camps going is murder to the children." As for the female captives, she wrote, "the very magnitude of their sufferings, their indignities, loss and anxiety seems to lift them beyond tears." Her impassioned appeals led to an investigation of the atrocities.[19]

In other regions of the world, the presence of Quaker women was felt. Charlotte Hanbury of Richmond had a privileged background and was influenced in her earlier years by the religious, scientific, and philanthropic work that emanated from Plough Court in London. Hanbury enjoyed the company of "the elite in the Christian life of England and the continent." Yet she embarked on risky journeys to Morocco and visited "the chained prisoners of its dreary dungeons," providing inmates with food, water, and clothing. Charlotte wanted not only to reform the inhumane system of imprisonment but also to bring "the prospect of liberty, and always some claim of heavenly help and love to brighten the darkness of their lot."[20]

The abolition of slavery was a central objective for many Quaker women. From the seventeenth century onward, some Quakers had opposed the slave trade, yet slaveholding persisted.[21] Increasingly, Friends and other reformers campaigned for the end of slave labor, and Quaker women were involved in this effort at the highest level. Notably, they supported William Wilberforce, which led, in 1807, to the abolition of the slave trade. Despite this legislation, merchants, including some Quakers, remained wedded to the advantages of slaveholding.[22] Female abolitionist Quakers were not always supported by their meetings, which used "their extended powers to silence dissent." Consequently, some were disowned or forced to work outside their meetings.[23] Others worked within the Society's restrictions but were frustrated by their limited progress.

Sarah Hoare of Bath wrote in 1826 of her distress at the "cruelly oppressed slaves," particularly "the cries of one poor woman ... who had been deprived of her two children," which, she wrote, "seemed to follow me, and pierce my very heart; but I was enabled to raise my feeble cries for her, and for the whole injured race, and it relieved me." Junia Price from Neath shared Hoare's concern for "the temporal and spiritual welfare of mankind" and was "ready to relieve the distressed." For many years, Price refused to use the products of slave labor but believed there should be a more extensive adoption of the boycott.[24] Some women took practical steps to oppose the slave trade. On April 8, 1825, Lucy Townshend, an Anglican, hosted a meeting with Quaker and non-Quaker women that resulted in the establishment of the Birmingham Ladies Society for the Relief of Negro Slaves.[25] Two years later, the Retreat Asylum in York agreed to boycott West Indian sugar because "eight hundred thousand slaves in these Dominions ... work hard all the day and frequently half the night and some times the whole Night and live on a scanty subsistence; and [are] killed off like old Horses, and are sold as beasts in the markets both men and Women and their hard Task Masters standing over them with a whip and flog them at their Pleasure."[26]

The Retreat Asylum's decision was endorsed by more than a dozen Quaker women, and similar efforts were orchestrated in Scotland by Jane Smeal and her stepdaughter Eliza Wigham. Jane established the Glasgow Ladies' Emancipation Society, which backed the 1833 Slavery Abolition Act and the controversial payment of £20 million to compensate the slave owners in the British Empire. She continued her fight to eradicate slavery, and in 1840 was a delegate at the World Anti-Slavery Convention held in

London.[27] Eliza was influenced not only by her stepmother but by the philanthropic and political interests of John Wigham Jr., her Edinburgh cousin. Consequently, she met some leading abolitionists, particularly those who wanted to end slavery in the Caribbean. Thereafter, Eliza and other "young people at South Gray Street entered eagerly into the work." Others, including Eliza Wigham, treasurer of the Edinburgh Ladies' Emancipation Society, continued to condemn slavery. She and Anna Harrison of Bournemouth educated the British public about the American Civil War, notably the oppression of slaves. They promoted support of the Union cause as being one of "justice and true progress."[28]

Quakers sought to provide a good education for their offspring and for orphans in their religious community. Quaker parents encouraged children to adopt their principles. Quaker schools in Britain and Ireland strengthened the "habits of regularity, of decency, and respectful subordination to their superiors, of forbearance, affection, and kindness."[29] Women were frequently at the forefront of educational initiatives,[30] among them Susanna Corder, who attended Ackworth School in Yorkshire and turned to teaching when she was thirty. Corder's first teaching post was at the school on Suir Island established by Sarah and Robert Grubb of Clonmel, Ireland. The Grubbs wanted pupils to be taught "useful skills,"[31] and Corder remained there for seven years before returning to England. With the help of the Quaker pharmacist, pacifist, and abolitionist William Allen and other Quaker stakeholders, Corder established the (Stoke) Newington Academy for Girls. Although it adhered to many Quaker tenets, especially the dress code, the school delivered a progressive curriculum that included astronomy, experimental philosophy, physics, and natural history.[32] Ann Capper's journals give an insight into Newington's syllabus. In December 1827, Capper described attending several lectures with her governess.[33]

Young Quakers also took up the challenge. Anna Maria Fox and her siblings Barclay and Caroline, of Falmouth, valued education. In 1832 the Foxes promoted the idea of a Cornwall polytechnic society, which became a successful venture. Martha Storr of Leominster was equally pioneering. In 1864 Storr launched an evening class for young women in Bury St. Edmunds meetinghouse, where she taught reading and writing alongside practical skills such as sewing. Shortly afterward, she taught at a ragged school in the town. Her charitable work included visiting the poor and sick, and "anything else that her hands found to do," garnering considerable respect from all quarters "irrespective of denomination." Equally, Rebecca

Alexander of Essex, despite being deaf, was an advocate for temperance and education. She regularly attended Band of Hope meetings and visited the homes of "rough boys and girls," where she distributed tracts and "endeavoured to awaken an interest in the parents not only in temperance but in still higher things." Moreover, Alexander provided small meetings, classes for girls, and evening schools for boys, which had a lasting impact.[34]

As part of Quakers' wider commitment to education, they engaged with mechanics' institutes and philosophical societies to promote educational, technological, and scientific advancement.[35] Mary Anne Galton-Schimmelpenninck, whose father was a member of the Lunar Society, was introduced to educationalists, inventors, and noted philosophers, among them William Herschel, James Watt, Joseph Priestley, and David Hartley.[36] Quakers and Unitarians judged involvement in such matters "an important part of their children's education." The teenage Rachel Gurney of Tottenham spent several months in 1807 in northern England, where she was encouraged to visit docklands, leadworks, and glass manufactures. Scientific instruction was also considered important for Quaker children. This could take the form of reading works that improved mental agility and the knowledge of manufacturing and science more generally or attending public lectures on science. Other members taught female Quakers about the natural world, politics, and reform in Quaker schools, notably that established by Sarah and Harriet Hoare of Bristol. In 1856 Sarah, a poet and botanist, was considered "gifted with superior mental powers, and possessed much refinement of mind ... her literary and scientific attainments were also considerable."[37] Indeed, in 1837 the Friends Educational Society encouraged "expansion of the mind, [and] the cultivation of the intellectual faculties."[38] Not all Quakers accepted these liberal steps, and Joseph Pease of Darlington, although appreciative of educational progress, dubbed Susanna Corder's academy the "N[ewington] Nunnery."[39]

Similar humanitarian impulses were shown by Felicia Hopkins of Bocking, who emigrated in 1862 to Brisbane, where she established an orphanage in the late 1860s and in 1888 founded the interdenominational Young Women's Christian Association at Rockhampton and five other branch institutions throughout Queensland. Also in 1862, Ann Mary Burgess of Norfolk provided medical assistance, religious education, and employment for a small community of Armenians living in eastern Anatolia. By the turn of the twentieth century, there were four hundred women workers there with an annual income of between £8,000 and £10,000 producing rugs, embroideries, toys, and confectionery. Burgess's assistance to widows and orphans via the Friends' mission hospital in Constantinople lasted for nearly half a century and exemplifies the scope and geographical reach of the networks that humanitarians and evangelists established.[40]

The temperance movement attracted many women Friends,[41] including Mary Waterhouse of Reading, who advocated total abstinence. She helped establish and pay for a coffeehouse "in one of the poorest streets" to counteract the large number of local public houses. Familiar names appear at the forefront of such campaigns. Eliza Wigham became the vice president of the Scottish Woman's Christian Temperance Union and used her "persuasive charm" to recruit a significant number of campaigners.[42] London-based Quaker Margaret Bright Lucas, the sister of John Bright, MP, advocated women's rights from the 1860s onward. In 1870, Margaret went to Nova Scotia and then to northeastern America, where she was warmly welcomed by suffragists and temperance campaigners. Her credentials as "John Bright's sister" introduced her to high-profile transatlantic Quaker networks. A lifelong temperance campaigner, Margaret joined the Independent Order of Good Templars while in America in 1872 and two years later was elected a vice templar. At the same time, she became active in the World's Woman's Christian Temperance Union (WWCTU) and addressed the 1876 Newcastle upon Tyne temperance meeting. This led to the creation of the White Ribbon Association and the British Women's Temperance Association— another organization of which she was elected president (ca. 1878). Although more conservative in her approach than her American colleagues, Margaret nonetheless rallied supporters to petition Parliament for the closing of pubs on Sunday, and in 1879 she took the first women's petition on this issue to the House of Commons.[43] Her memoir reveals that she increasingly favored direct action. She became convinced that petitions, although laudable, needed to be "effectual." She observed that women should secure the franchise alongside temperance. Her transatlantic campaigning continued into the 1880s. In 1886 she attended the Minneapolis convention of the WWCTU as its president, demonstrating Quaker women's contribution to social movements and their ability to network with like-minded individuals across the world.[44]

Political activism, however, represented a greater challenge. For much of the nineteenth century, prevailing gender ideology made it extremely difficult for women to be active in politics. Indeed, "public space" was "dangerous territory" for women activists, as it undermined their assigned role as spiritual guardians of home and family.⁴⁵ While the extensive historiography of Chartism has enhanced our understanding of the movement's geographical and cultural reach, too little is known about women's engagement in electoral reform in this earlier period.⁴⁶ New histories have rebalanced the emphasis on male leadership by acknowledging the contribution of men *and* women who were active in small towns and villages. Yet recovering women's engagement with Chartism has proved remarkably elusive; too often the question of class has assumed greater precedence. In the 1980s, historians like David Jones were hindered by the limitations of surviving sources. Jones was convinced that women's participation in Chartism had been "underestimated," but demonstrating this proved difficult.⁴⁷ Subsequently, historians have identified more female reform groups, though their studies have not strayed much beyond the industrial north and midlands, or the mid-1840s, when these associations seemed to disappear.⁴⁸ Digitization of the press has helped, but newspaper reports often carry only the initials of association officers and document speeches made by invited male speakers. Women subscribed to the Chartist Land Plan or to the John Frost defense fund in significant numbers but deliberately withheld their addresses and occupations, possibly to avoid identification and censure.⁴⁹ Their reticence has complicated attempts to identify Quaker women who engaged with Chartism, unless they were high-profile individuals or involved in related causes, such as the Anti-Corn Law League.

Between 1837 and 1842, when mass meetings brought together entire communities, a veritable army of unidentified women attended Chartist demonstrations and rallies and joined women's reform associations. Dorothy Thompson has traced more than a hundred active women's groups in 1838–39 alone. Nottingham was one of the first towns to establish a women's chartist association, led by Mary Savage. Many groups were galvanized by the punitive provisions of the Poor Law Amendment Act (1834), which disproportionately affected women and children. As this was a humanitarian cause, it is not surprising to find Quaker women involved. Malcolm Chase argues that Thomas Salt's formal "Address to the Women of Birmingham" in 1838 was a significant moment in the growth of female activism. The Birmingham Female Political Union, one of the largest such groups, had more than three thousand members, and branches rapidly appeared in the major urban areas of eastern Scotland.⁵⁰ At the first Chartist convention in 1839, when Feargus O'Connor specifically appealed to "virtuous women" to pledge their support, twenty-four thousand women signed the first national petition.

O'Connor's words would not have been lost on Quaker women. In some areas—Ashton-under-Lyne and Carlisle, for instance—one-fifth of signatories were women.[51]

The familial culture of radical politics enabled the involvement of women, and they were not always limited to the role of helpmeet. The *Halifax Guardian* reported that the meeting at Skircoat Moor in August 1842 was attended by upward of fifteen thousand people, including many women. These women urged their men to rescue imprisoned Chartists: "ye're soft, if you don't fetch them oot."[52] Inevitably, northeast women were active in Chartism, as this was a region where many Quaker women strongly supported abolition. As Clare Midgley argues, the abolition campaign succeeded because men and women worked together, and this applied to other causes, not least Chartism and the Anti-Corn Law League.[53] In February 1839, the Newcastle upon Tyne Female Political Union published an "Address to Their Fellow Countrywomen" in the leading Chartist newspaper, the *Northern Star*. The sheer ambition of the Newcastle address, and its unequivocal assertion of women's rights, is impressive. It boldly appealed to women to work with their male relatives, "to free themselves from political, physical and mental bondage." And it rejected the idea that women should "leave politics to the men," cautioning shopkeepers who had been enfranchised in 1832 to "remember that our pennies make their pounds, and that we cannot in justice spend the hard earnings of our husbands with those that are opposed to their rights and interests."[54] This reference to "exclusive dealing" would have struck a chord with Quaker abolitionists whose sugar boycott had been so effective. Borrowing the rhetoric of abolition became common in Chartist speeches too, whether denouncing the punitive factory system or condemning the pauperization of those forced into workhouses. As the Chartist activist Abram Hanson declared, working men and women were "slaves in the land called free and starving in the land of plenty."[55] Even if Quaker women are still largely invisible in the record of Chartism, the stark comparisons drawn between slavery at home and slavery abroad is highly suggestive of Quaker influence.

The leader of the women's abolition campaign in Darlington, a town with a politically dominant Quaker group, was Elizabeth Pease, "the most influential anti-slavery activist in Britain in the 1840s," who built a considerable transatlantic network, especially in America. Her father, Joseph, was the first Quaker MP, and she held radical beliefs, including free trade and Chartism.[56] The Darlington women established their own Female Radical

Association in 1839 and Elizabeth helped distribute pamphlets. Elizabeth drew a direct correlation between slavery in the colonies and the "white slavery" of British factory workers, denied their political rights. The idea that they were not fit for the vote she dismissed as "a slaveholder's argument."[57] She openly promoted the Chartist cause among her abolitionist friends in America, though she always positioned herself as a supporter of the "moral force" branch of the movement. Even so, Elizabeth willingly acknowledged the "forbearance" of Chartists who abjured violence and was not intimidated by the scorn of those who considered her advocacy of Chartism to be scarcely respectable, even "vulgar."[58] There were many Quaker women in the region, such as the Newcastle abolitionist Anna Richardson, who sought a less confrontational outlet for their humanitarianism. They distributed food and essentials to the needy rather than campaigning against the system of poor relief.[59] The turn to physical force that culminated in the Newport Rising in 1839 hardened the divide between the two Chartist factions, inevitably making it more difficult for women to participate openly.

Although female Chartism is held to have declined in the mid-1840s, there is new evidence that their activism revived in the early 1850s.[60] Dorothy Thompson has attributed this decline to the intimidatory policing of mass demonstrations, as well as women's growing commitment to temperance. After 1848, smaller Chartist gatherings met indoors, mostly outside working hours in taverns and inns. These male-dominated drinking venues were out of bounds to respectable women and a definite barrier to women's involvement. Equally, the movement's loss of commitment to female suffrage left women with little to fight for. When Reginald Richardson, the Manchester Chartist, wrote an 1840 pamphlet titled *The Rights of Women*, he vindicated female participation in politics but drew a sharp distinction between married and single women.[61] This affirmation that women should be protected from exploitation and degradation in the factory or workhouse, should dedicate their lives to the care of the family and the proper nurturing of children, was the view that held sway. As Jutta Schwarzkopf argues, improving the lives of women became central to the vision of a democratic future, ironically confirming their subordinate status.[62] Chartist women were invariably viewed as transgressors by clerics, and their public role was increasingly circumscribed by male Chartists.

In early 1851, when the Chelmsford Quaker Anne Knight set out to revive female enfranchisement, she appealed to Mrs. Rooke, a member of the Sheffield Female Radical Association, which had been active since

1839.⁶³ Knight is best known as the author of an anonymous broadside that aggressively asserted equal rights in 1847.⁶⁴ As Gail Malmgreen argues, Knight was not breaking new ground here, though she can be counted as an early feminist.⁶⁵ Knight led a new campaign for women's suffrage at a time when Chartism was in marked decline and few women were advocating reform. In March 1851, she unsuccessfully attempted to persuade the prominent London Chartist Julian Harney to promote women's suffrage in his periodical *Friend of the People*. By foolishly referring to Chartism as "a dead letter" and its supporters as "superannuated," her strident letter seems only to have irritated Harney. Although he promised to publish "selections" of the several papers she sent him, he insisted that the demand for universal suffrage was "premature," that the time was not "ripe." She sent the same blunt letter to Feargus O'Connor's *Northern Star*. Undaunted, Knight appealed to Harney again in May, this time from her residence in Paris, where she once again couched her overtures in a sarcastic tone, accusing the Chartists of "selfishness" in "persisting in their infatuation of calling that universal which is only half."⁶⁶ Chartist leader Ernest Jones was more receptive, publishing an anonymous serialized novel titled *Woman's Wrongs* in his periodical *Notes to the People* and pledging support for the newly formed Sheffield Women's Right's [sic] Association, following a polite appeal by the secretary, Abiah Higginbotham. Jones conceded that women's voices were not "sufficiently heard" and agreed that the tradition of meeting in "pothouses" obstructed their attendance. He swiftly prohibited branch meetings in public houses.⁶⁷ Given her status as a well-educated single woman, Knight's early engagement with international abolitionist circles and frequent trips to France, which introduced her to utopian socialists such as Flora Tristan, meant that she had no qualms about writing to leading thinkers and reformers. She was in France during the revolutionary days of 1848 and was a close associate of the French socialist Jeanne Deroin, who sent supportive letters to the women of Sheffield, almost certainly at Knight's instigation.⁶⁸ Knight can be viewed as a propagandist and a progressive thinker who inspired others, rather than as an activist engaged in day-to-day campaigning.

The relative invisibility of Quaker women in Chartism contrasts with their clear presence in the Anti-Corn Law League. In the early 1840s, Quaker women such as Margaret Priestman and her sisters Anna Maria and Mary were more likely to identify themselves as members of the League than as Chartists.⁶⁹ This posed little threat to their respectability, for free trade was presented as an altruistic reform that would reduce the price of the "people's bread," thereby alleviating poverty.[70] With membership cards emblazoned with the Lord's Prayer ("Give us this day our daily bread"), the League trumpeted its Christian values, promoting the idea that repealing the "sinful" Corn Laws was a moral responsibility. Nor was it insignificant that the established church ("the thief of the poor man's bread") was denounced as having a selfish and cruel interest in keeping corn and grain prices high.[71] Sandra Holton has drawn attention to the "Bright Circle," a network of interrelated Quaker families in Manchester and Newcastle that collaborated closely on reform questions, notably the Anti-Corn Law League, and later championed women's rights. Their dynamic correspondence legitimized the construction of a powerful dialogue that linked "household economy and political economy."[72]

Margaret Priestman was related by marriage to John Bright, a leading League campaigner, and shared his commitment to educational reform and pacifism. Like abolition, this was a familial campaign in which leading "liberal" Quakers such as Bright and Henry Ashworth collaborated with other nonconformists, notably Edward Miall, the founder of the highly influential weekly periodical the *Nonconformist*.[73] Quaker manufacturers contributed to the League's lecture series and pamphlet campaign, contributed generously to its coffers, and occupied 15 percent of the seats on the League's council. Richard Cobden made every effort to draw leading Friends to the cause. He persuaded the prominent Birmingham abolitionist Joseph Sturge to cultivate working-class Chartists and persuade them to prioritize the Anti-Corn Law League, while studiously avoiding any "formal & official coalition" between the two movements.[74] However, until repeal was secured in 1846, relations between Leaguers and Chartists remained tense, with neither side completely trusting the other. In 1842 Sturge became more committed to electoral reform and established his own Complete Suffrage Union.[75]

Scrutiny of the League's Association Council in 1839 and 1840 captures the scale of Quaker women's involvement, notably their organization of the League's fundraising bazaars.[76] The bazaars were so successful that they are believed to have exerted as great an influence on Parliament as all the speeches in favor of free trade.[77] Peter Gurney argues that the contribution of women was "vital," not merely in their fundraising work but in "moralising the capitalist market."[78] The 1842 bazaar, held in Manchester's opulent Theatre Royal, raised £10,000, thereby rescuing the League's finances from near bankruptcy.⁷⁹ The revenue-raising efforts of Quaker women thus contributed to the League's ability to secure repeal of the Corn Laws. Sturge was ably supported by his sister, Sophia, a leading member of the Birmingham Ladies Society for the Relief of Negro Slaves and a committed pacifist.⁸⁰ John Bright's sister Margaret and her husband, Samuel Lucas, campaigned tirelessly for free trade. Like other Quaker women, Margaret gained invaluable experience in her abolitionist campaigning and dedicated herself to the fundraising effort, drawing an attendance of more than 170,000 and raising some £25,000 at the Grand Bazaar in Covent Garden in 1845.⁸¹ As *Punch*'s graphic depiction revealed, the event had been organized by a committee of "one thousand ladies" whose "pretty politicians" presided over the proceedings for more than three weeks. Even as it celebrated their achievement, *Punch*'s deprecating tone exposed the gendered attitudes that held women back.⁸² Nonetheless, in empowering the representatives of local towns across Britain, the bazaar became a national phenomenon and, crucially for future activism, unified women reformers behind a successful campaign. The epitaph on Margaret's grave paid due tribute to her international standing as a temperance activist and a life that was "simple, beneficent, noble."⁸³ In much the same way, Henry Ashworth, editor of the *Anti-Corn Law Circular*, relied on his wife, Letitia, who had built close links with Edwin Chadwick and his campaign to improve national sanitation and public health. Cobden was convinced that pacifism and free trade were linked and sought to persuade Ashworth that "they are one & the same cause," proposing that he might secure the backing of London Friends who had "a good deal of influence over the City moneyed interest which has the ear of government."⁸⁴

Quaker women emerged from the League's successful campaign with newfound confidence as members of a nationwide network of committed activists, convinced that their united efforts could deliver positive change. Younger daughters and siblings had gained considerable experience, and this new generation of Quaker activists was less reticent about engaging in the political sphere. Intergenerational continuities meant that female Friends were increasingly prepared to challenge the strictures of their meetings and the authority of their male relatives. When the debate about women's rights gathered new strength in the late 1850s, Quaker women like the abolitionist Mary Howitt worked alongside feminists of the London Langham circle to secure reform of the iniquitous married women's property laws.⁸⁵ By then, well versed in the arguments, they more willingly joined suffrage societies and signed petitions in favor of electoral reform.[86] The "strong-minded" secretary of the Manchester National Society for Women's Suffrage (NSWS), Lydia Becker, appealed in January 1868 directly to Anne Knight to "use your influence to include others."[87] The NSWS already had two other independent branches, in London and Edinburgh, where prominent Quakers such as Jacob and Ursula Bright, Eliza Wigham, and Margaret Bright Lucas were serving on the executive committee alongside leading nonconformists.[88] It was Jacob who represented the NSWS in Parliament, introducing the unsuccessful Women's Disabilities Removal Bill in May 1870 in a bid to enfranchise female ratepayers.[89] Mary Howitt, Helen Bright Clark, and Lilias Ashworth were among many Quaker women members who were tasked with organizing local affiliated branches elsewhere.

Cooperative efforts to advance women's rights were tested after 1872, as the NSWS split over enfranchising married middle-class women only, making class, not gender, the critical dividing line. Ideological differences were compounded when key officers, notably Millicent Fawcett, argued against members' participation in the controversial movement to repeal the Contagious Diseases Acts (CDA).[90] Fawcett feared damaging chances of electoral reform. It would be hard to underestimate the extent to which the CDA campaign was forbidden terrain, not just jeopardizing the respectability and moral standing of Quaker women but threatening all women repealers. The 1864 CDA and subsequent extensions (1866, 1869) regulated prostitution in Britain and its colonies to suppress sexually transmitted diseases in the army and navy. Initially, it targeted women in garrison towns and ports, but later it applied to major British towns and cities as well; women suspected of disease were subjected to summary arrest, forcible examination, and treatment. They could be fined and imprisoned for noncompliance. Poor women could be accused of "consorting with prostitutes" or of living in a brothel solely on the basis of an address in the wrong part of town. Seventeen-year-old Caroline Wybrow typified the pitfalls such women encountered. Her ill treatment in 1875 was presented to Richard Cross, the home secretary, by the Quaker lawyer Frederick Wheeler. A storm of public protest followed when it was revealed that she had been forcibly detained at Chatham Lock Hospital even though she was not infected by venereal disease.[91] Addressing the Royal Commission in 1870, John Stuart Mill protested that the CDA undermined the "personal liberty" of a "particular class of women intentionally and . . . unintentionally of all women."[92]

The records of the Ladies National Association for the Repeal of the Contagious Diseases Acts (LNA) in 1871 reveal that Quaker women were prepared to risk public opprobrium. The executive committee, which denounced the CDA as "utterly corrupt and indefensible," included younger and older Quakers, notably Miss Jacob Bright, Mrs. McLaren, Miss Wigham, and Mrs. E. Backhouse. Every constitutional strategy was deployed. The LNA repeatedly petitioned Parliament, convened major demonstrations and meetings, and published a stream of books and pamphlets to expose the way the CDAs "violated the principle of English jurisprudence," constituting "an insult and an outrage to every woman in the land."[93] They lobbied electoral candidates and called on voters to vote against those who refused to support repeal.[94] The men's parliamentary campaign failed to secure repeal. The LNA branches continued to agitate for repeal in local and national meetings and fundraising events. In March 1873, Quaker women established the Society of Friends Repeal Committee to raise the £10,000 needed to back Fowler's repeal bill, but it failed at the second reading by 251 to 128 votes.[95] LNA accounts show that Quaker women frequently made larger donations as well as regular subscriptions in their own name. Occasionally, generous donations were made by "A Friend," signaling that some women were still inhibited about declaring their support publicly.[96] As ever, they deployed the rhetoric of slavery to highlight how the acts deprived women of their liberty, dignity, and autonomy. To counter the influence of the Church of England, they always stressed that the LNA included members of all nonconformist bodies, including "the Friends."[97]

After repeal was finally secured in 1883, the movement sought to halt the acts in the imperial territories, where race *and* gender perniciously shaped women's encounters with the law.[98] Perhaps the most impressive aspect of Quaker women's activism was the extent to which they campaigned on a myriad of different fronts. Quakers in the LNA still found time to serve their communities, helping the needy, improving women's working conditions, and supporting the Peace Society, the Women's Temperance Association, and the National Vigilance Association for the Defence of Personal Rights. Several were founding members of the Women's Liberal Federation in their own localities.[99] The Irish activists Anna and Thomas Haslam exemplify Friends' commitment to humanitarianism and pacifism, which was complemented by an unshakeable belief in equal rights. Although the Haslams ceased to be members of the Society, Anna always attributed her egalitarian convictions to her Quaker upbringing.[100]

Thomas Haslam's writings on birth control and sexual morality, notably his anonymous work *The Marriage Problem* (1868), were ahead of the times. The Haslams campaigned to repeal the CDAs, albeit as members of separate gendered committees. While Thomas delivered speeches and wrote pamphlets, Anna's high-profile role as secretary of the Dublin branch was more demanding. She never wavered in her commitment to the NSWS or, crucially, in her advocacy of education for women. She worked alongside other prominent Irish female Quakers on the LNA, including Mrs. Addey, the Cork secretary, and members of the Webb, Edmundson, Shackleton, and Wigham families. In 1876, the Haslams established the Dublin Women's Suffrage Association and persistently advanced women's role in local and national politics. Yet Anna never contemplated neglecting other campaigns, and in 1880 she was appointed to the LNA London Executive Committee. Arguably, she acted as a vital bridge between English and Irish suffragists, connecting activists in Britain and America and encouraging an international exchange of feminist ideas.[101]

The World Anti-Slavery Convention in London (1840) was a seminal moment in Quaker women's international activism. While the success of the campaign was undoubtedly a source of satisfaction, the exclusion of so many of their number from the official commemorative portrait exposed their subordinate, disempowered status, prompting many to invest their energies in the struggle for equal rights and other humanitarian work. For some Quaker women, their work with pauperized, ill-educated, and criminalized communities inspired them to press for progressive social and economic reforms. They had to face hard choices: to limit their activism to their proscribed domestic roles and thereby remain respected members of their meetings; to operate surreptitiously, anonymizing their donations and support for radical reforms and limiting their involvement in more risky campaigns; or to challenge the status quo by publicly campaigning for sexual, cultural, and political rights for all women. Women did not give up their Quaker fellowship easily. In the early 1870s, many questioned the persistence of attitudes that forced women to choose between their deeply held religious values and their principled stand for equal civil rights. Their arguments gained traction slowly but inexorably, and by the end of the 1890s, Friends began to embrace a more liberal view of the world and the place of women within it.

NOTES

1. Patricia Hollis, ed., *Pressure from Without in Early Victorian England* (London: Edward Arnold, 1974).
2. Annemieke van Drenth and Francisca de Haan, *The Rise of Caring Power: Elizabeth Fry and Josephine Butler in Britain and the Netherlands* (Amsterdam: Amsterdam University Press, 1999); Emmanuelle Morne, "Glorious Auxiliaries? Gender Participation and Subordination in the Chartist Movement (1838–1851)," *Labour History Review* 85, no. 1 (2020): 8.
3. Sandra Stanley Holton, *Quaker Women: Personal Life, Memory, and Radicalism in the Lives of Women Friends, 1780–1930* (London: Routledge, 2007), 5; Clare Midgley, *Women Against Slavery: The British Campaigns, 1780–1870* (London: Routledge, 1992), 151.
4. Hilary Hinds, *God's Englishwomen* (Manchester: Manchester University Press, 1996); Ruth Watts, *Gender, Power, and the Unitarians of England, 1760–1860* (Harlow, UK: Longman, 1998); M. Hilton and P. Hirsch, eds., *Practical Visionaries: Women, Education, and Social Progress, 1790–1930* (Harlow, UK: Pearson, 2000).
5. Sheila Wright, "Quakerism and Its Implications for Quaker Women: The Women Itinerant Ministers of York Meeting, 1780–1840," *Studies in Church History* 27 (1990): 403–4.
6. Elizabeth A. O'Donnell, "'Woman's Rights and Woman's Duties': Quaker Women in the Nineteenth Century, with Special Reference to Newcastle Monthly Meeting of Women Friends" (PhD diss., University of Sunderland, 2000); Mijin Cho, "British Quaker Women and Peace, 1880s to 1920s" (PhD diss., University of Birmingham, 2010).
7. Wright, "Quakerism and Its Implications," 412.
8. Sue Morgan, "Introduction," in *Women, Religion, and Feminism in Britain, 1750–1900*, edited by Sue Morgan (Basingstoke: Palgrave Macmillan, 2010), 10; Robynne Rogers Healey, "Quietist Quakerism, 1692–c. 1805," in *The Oxford Handbook of Quaker Studies*, edited by Stephen W. Angell and Pink Dandelion (Oxford: Oxford University Press, 2013), 47–62.
9. Elizabeth Isichei, *Victorian Quakers* (Oxford: Oxford University Press, 1970), 150.
10. Ann B. Shteir, "Wakefield [née Bell], Priscilla (1750–1832)," in *Oxford Dictionary of National Biography* (Oxford: Oxford University Press, 2004) (*ODNB*); Patricia Wakefield, *Reflections on the Present Condition of the Female Sex* [. . .], 2nd ed. (London: printed for Darton, Harvey, and Darton, 1817), 8–9; see also Camilla Leach, "Religion and Rationality: Quaker Women and Science Education, 1790–1850," *History of Education* 35, no. 1 (2006): 79–89.
11. Pam Lunn, "'You Have Lost Your Opportunity': British Quakers and the Militant Phase of the Women's Suffrage Campaign, 1906–1914," *Quaker Studies* 2, no. 1 (1997): 52.
12. Quoted in *Annual Monitor* 33 (1875): 113–16, 126–27, 145 (quotation).
13. Meredith B. Weddle, *Walking in the Way of Peace: Quaker Pacifism in the Seventeenth Century* (Oxford: Oxford University Press, 2001).
14. Thomas C. Kennedy, *British Quakerism, 1860–1920: The Transformation of a Religious Community* (Oxford: Oxford University Press, 2001), chap. 6.
15. *Annual Monitor* 59 (1901): 176–77.
16. *Annual Monitor* 104 (1916): 112; Sandra Holton, "Priestman, Anna Maria (1828–1914)," *ODNB*; June Hannam, "Ford, Isabella Ormston (1855–1924)," *ODNB*; Heloise Brown, *The*

Truest Form of Patriotism: Pacifist Feminism in Britain, 1870–1902 (Manchester: Manchester University Press, 2003), 118.

17. *Annual Monitor* 101 (1913): 111, 113; Cho, "British Women," 64; Kennedy, *British Quakerism*, 263; B. D. Phillips, "Friendly Patriotism: British Quakerism and the Imperial Nation, 1890–1910" (PhD diss., University of Cambridge, 1989), 74.

18. Cho, "British Women," 76–77; Kennedy, *British Quakerism*, 252, 260.

19. Emily Hobhouse, *Report of a Visit to the Camps [. . .] in the Cape and Orange River Colonies* (London: Friars, 1901), 108, 109. For additional details, see Emily Hobhouse, *The Brunt of the War, and Where It Fell* (London: Methuen, 1902); and for a modern analysis, see Birgit Susanne Seibold, *Emily Hobhouse and the Reports on the Concentration Camps During the Boer War, 1899–1902: Two Different Perspectives* (Stroud: History Press, 2015).

20. Quoted in *Annual Monitor* 59 (1901): 59–63.

21. J. William Frost, ed., *The Quaker Origins of Antislavery* (Norwood, PA: Norwood Editions, 1980); Julie L. Holcomb, *Moral Commerce: Quakers and the Transatlantic Boycott of the Slave Labor Economy* (Ithaca: Cornell University Press, 2016).

22. S. Farrell, M. Unwin, and J. Walvin, eds., *The British Slave Trade: Abolition, Parliament, and People* (Edinburgh: Edinburgh University Press, 2007).

23. K. I. Halbersleben, "Elizabeth Pease: One Woman's Vision of Peace, Justice, and Human Rights in Nineteenth Century Britain," *Quaker History* 84 (Spring 1995): 27–28; Jennifer Rycenga, "A Greater Awakening: Women's Intellect as a Factor in Early Abolitionist Movements, 1824–1834," *Journal of Feminist Studies in Religion*, 21, no. 2 (2005): 33.

24. *Annual Monitor* 14 (1856): 95–96; *Annual Monitor* 4 (1846): 98–100.

25. Adam Hochschild, *Bury the Chains: The British Struggle to Abolish Slavery* (London: Macmillan, 2005), 326.

26. Borthwick Institute for Archives, University of York, "An Humble Petition from the Retreat Servants to the Retreat Committee [. . .], 1st Month 16th 1827," https://www.york.ac.uk/borthwick/holdings/research-guides/race/quakers-and-slavery/retreat-petition/.

27. Midgley, *Women Against Slavery*, 135–37, 171, 175; Glasgow Ladies' Auxiliary Emancipation Society, *Three Years' Female Anti-Slavery Effort, in Britain and America [. . .]* (Glasgow: Aird & Russell, 1837); Lesley M. Richmond, "Wigham, Eliza (1820–1899)," *ODNB*.

28. Quoted in *Annual Monitor* 59 (1901): 167, 72.

29. John Coakley Lettsom, *Memoirs of John Fothergill M.D., &c.*, 4th ed. (London, 1786), 137; see also Alexandra Walsham, "Nature and Nurture in the Early Quaker Movement: Creating the Next Generation of Friends Studies," *Church History* 55 (2019): 161–76.

30. Gillian Mason, "Quaker Women and Education, 1642–1840" (MA thesis, University of Lancaster, 1987), 40–56; Kerri Allen and Alison Mackinnon, "'Allowed and Expected to Be Educated and Intelligent': The Education of Quaker Girls in Nineteenth-Century England," *History of Education* 27, no. 4 (1998): 391–402.

31. Gil Skidmore, *Strength in Weakness: Writings of Eighteenth-Century Quaker Women* (Walnut Creek, CA: Altamira, 2003), 85.

32. Rosemary Mitchell, "Corder, Susanna (1787–1864)," *ODNB*.

33. Anne Capper's journals, 1824–30, Temp MSS 310, LSF.
34. Thomas Hodgkin, "Anna Maria Fox," *Friends Quarterly Examiner* 125 (1898): 115–36; *Annual Monitor* 46 (1888): 1–4, 97–107. See also Allen and Mackinnon, "Allowed and Expected," 394–97.
35. Leach, "Religion and Rationality"; Geoffrey N. Cantor, *Quakers, Jews, and Science: Religious Responses to Modernity and the Sciences in Britain, 1650–1900* (Oxford: Oxford University Press, 2005).
36. Leach, "Religion and Rationality," 75; Elizabeth Lee, revised by K. D. Reynolds, "Schimmelpenninck [née Galton], Mary Anne (1778–1856)," *ODNB*; Christina C. Hankin, ed., *Life of Mary Anne Schimmelpenninck* (London: Longman, 1860), 30–33.
37. A. E. Pease, *Rachel Gurney of the Grove* (London: Hadley Brothers, 1907), 38, 42; Leach, "Religion and Rationality," 76, 79–89; *Annual Monitor* 14 (1856): 88; Sarah Hoare, *Poems on Conchology and Botany* (London: Simpkin & Marshall, 1831); Ann B. Shteir, *Cultivating Women, Cultivating Science: Flora's Daughters and Botany in England, 1760 to 1860* (Baltimore: Johns Hopkins University Press, 1996).
38. Leach, "Religion and Rationality," 76, 78 and n. 48; *Reports and Essays of the Friends Educational Society 1837–1845* [. . .] (London: n.p., 1845).
39. MS box 10 (13), 2, LSF; Mitchell, "Corder, Susanna."
40. Ellen Jordan, "Hopkins, Felicia (1841–1933)," in *Australian Dictionary of Biography*, vol. 9 (Melbourne: Melbourne University Press, 1983); Edward Annett, *Fifty Years Among the Armenians: A Brief Record of the Work of Ann Mary Burgess* (London: Friends Armenian Mission, 1939); Michelle Tusan, "The Business of Relief Work: A Victorian Quaker in Constantinople and Her Circle," *Victorian Studies* 51, no. 4 (2009): 633–61.
41. Brian Harrison, *Drink and the Victorians: The Temperance Question in England, 1815–1872*, 2nd ed. (Keele: Keele University Press, 1994), 156.
42. *Annual Monitor* 39 (1881): 124; *Annual Monitor* 59 (1901): 174–75.
43. "Circular from Margaret Lucas [. . .] Petition in Favour of Women's Suffrage," February 12, 1879, M50/1/10/168, Manchester Archives and Local Studies, Manchester, England.
44. British Women's Temperance Association, *Memoir of Margaret Bright Lucas: President of the British Women's Temperance Association* (London: BWTA, 1890); Ian Tyrrell, "Lucas, Margaret Bright, 1818–1890," *ODNB*. See also Ian R. Tyrrell, *Woman's World, Woman's Empire: The Woman's Christian Temperance Union in International Perspective, 1880–1930* (Chapel Hill: University of North Carolina Press, 1991); Sandra S. Holton and Robert J. Holton, "From the Particular to the Global: Some Empirical, Epistemological, and Methodological Aspects of Microhistory with Regard to a Women's Rights Network," in *Performing Global Networks*, edited by Karen Fricker and Ronit Lentin (Newcastle: Cambridge Scholars, 2007), 14–15.
45. Eileen Yeo, "Introduction: Some Paradoxes of Empowerment," in *Radical Femininity: Women's Self-Representation in the Public Sphere*, edited by Eileen Janes Yeo (Manchester: Manchester University Press, 1998), 1; Tom Scriven, "Humour, Satire, and Sexuality in the Culture of Early Chartism," *Historical Journal* 57, no. 1 (2014): 158, 165.
46. Joan Allen and Owen R. Ashton, "Radicals, Chartists, and Internationalism," *Labour History Review* 78, no. 1 (2013): 1.
47. David Jones, "Women and Chartism," *History: The Journal of the Historical Association* 68, no. 222 (1983): 9.
48. Dorothy Thompson, *The Early Chartists* (London: Macmillan, 1971); Jutta Schwarzkopf, *Women in the Chartist Movement* (Basingstoke: Macmillan, 1991); Alice Clark, *The*

Struggle for the Breeches: Gender and the Making of the British Working Class (Berkeley: University of California Press, 1995); W. Hamish Fraser, *Chartism in Scotland* (Pontypool, UK: Merlin, 2010), 194–200.

49. Chartists Ancestors Databank, http://chartistancestors.co.uk/chartist-ancestors-databank/.

50. F. C. Mather, *Chartism and Society: An Anthology of Documents* (London: Bell and Hyman, 1980), 114; Thompson, *Early Chartists*, 134; Malcolm Chase, *Chartism: A New History* (Manchester: Manchester University Press, 2007), 42; Fraser, *Chartism in Scotland*, 194.

51. Thompson, *Early Chartists*, 120; Chase, *Chartism*, 42.

52. Mather, *Chartism and Society*, 116.

53. Midgley, *Women Against Slavery*, 206–7; Clare Midgley, "Women Anti-Slavery Campaigners, with Special Reference to the North East," *North East History Society Bulletin* 29 (1995): 19–39. Durham, Darlington, and Newcastle upon Tyne all had Ladies Anti-Slavery associations (1825–68). For Abram and Elizabeth Hanson's campaign against the Poor Law Amendment Act in Yorkshire, see Chase, *Chartism*, 22–29.

54. "Address to Their Fellow Countrywomen," *Northern Star*, February 2, 1839. See also Eileen Yeo, "Radical Femininity: Women's Self Representation in Labour Movements in the 19th and 20th Centuries," *North East Labour History Society Bulletin* 29 (1995): 10.

55. Quoted in Chase, *Chartism*, 22.

56. Midgley, "Women Anti-Slavery Campaigners," 22; Midgley, *Women Against Slavery*, 77–78; T. J. Nossiter, *Influence, Opinion, and Political Idioms in Reformed England: Case Studies from the North East, 1832–1874* (Brighton, UK: Harvester Press, 1975), 129–32.

57. Elizabeth Pease to J. A. Collins, Darlington, May (1841?), quoted in Midgley, "Women Anti-Slavery Campaigners," 27n31.

58. Elizabeth Pease to A. W. Weston, June 24, 1841, quoted in Chase, *Chartism*, 193.

59. Midgley, "Women Anti-Slavery Campaigners," 26–32.

60. Morne, "Glorious Auxiliaries," 7–32.

61. Thompson, *Early Chartists*, 115, 125.

62. Schwarzkopf, *Women in the Chartist Movement*, 77.

63. Ibid., 248–51.

64. Midgley, *Women Against Slavery*, 157.

65. Gail Malmgreen, "Anne Knight and the Radical Subculture," *Quaker History* 71, no. 2 (1982): 101.

66. Anne Knight, letter to the editor, "Correspondence, Universal Suffrage," *Friend of the People*, March 6, 1851, 102; Knight's letter also appeared in the *Northern Star*, March 29, 1851; Anne Knight, letter to the editor, "Correspondence, 'Rights of Woman,'" *Friend of the People*, May 31, 1851, 216.

67. *Woman's Wrongs*, serialized novel that ran from May 1851 (p. 515), to December 17, 1851 (p. 709), in Ernest Jones, ed., *Notes to the People, May 1851–May 1852*, vol. 2 (n.p.: Barnes & Noble, 1968); Ernest Jones, "Pothouse Localities," January 1852, ibid., 728.

68. Malmgreen, "Anne Knight," 103–6, 108–9; Schwarzkopf, *Women in the Chartist Movement*, 252–53.

69. Sandra Stanley Holton, "Kinship and Friendship: Quaker Women's Networks and the Women's Movement," *Women's History Review* 14, nos. 3–4 (2005): 375.

70. Midgley, *Women Against Slavery*, 82.

71. Paul Pickering and Alex Tyrrell, *The People's Bread: A History of the Anti-Corn Law League* (London: Leicester University Press, 2000), 88; Norman McCord, *The Anti-Corn Law League, 1838–46* (London: Allen and Unwin, 1958), 26.

72. Holton, "Kinship and Friendship," 375.

73. Pickering and Tyrrell, *People's Bread*, 99.

74. Cobden to Sturge, October 29, 1841, in *The Letters of Richard Cobden, vol. 1, 1815–1847*, edited by Anthony Howe (Oxford: Oxford University Press, 2007), 243–44; Tom Scriven, "Chartism's Electoral Strategy and the Bifurcation of Radicalism, 1837–1852," *Labour History Review* 85, no. 2 (2020): 115.

75. Alex Tyrrell, *Joseph Sturge and the Moral Radical Party in Early Victorian England* (London: Christopher Helm, 1987), 120; Scriven, "Chartism's Electoral Strategy," 115.

76. Pickering and Tyrrell, *People's Bread*, appendix 4, 272–83.

77. "The Anti-Corn Law Bazaar," *Manchester Guardian*, January 22, 1842; "The Anti-Corn Law Bazaar," *Manchester Guardian*, February 5, 1842; Richard Cobden to Catherine Cobden, February 1, 1842, in *Letters of Richard Cobden*, 1:256; Peter J. Gurney, "'The Sublime of the Bazaar': A Moment in the Making of Consumer Culture in Mid-Nineteenth Century England," *Social History* 40, no. 2 (2006): 385–405.

78. Gurney, "Sublime of the Bazaar," 400.

79. Wendy Hinde, *Richard Cobden: A Victorian Outsider* (New Haven: Yale University Press, 1987), 96–98.

80. Obituary of Sophia Sturge, *Birmingham Pilot*, June 14, 1845; Alex Tyrrell, "Sturge, Sophia (1795–1845)," *ODNB*.

81. "Anti-Corn Law Bazaar in Covent Garden," *Manchester Guardian*, March 29, 1845; Ian Tyrrell, "Lucas, Margaret Bright (1818–1890)," *ODNB*; Gurney, "'Sublime of the Bazaar,'" 390.

82. "The Anti-Corn Law League Bazaar," *Punch* 8, 1845, 216.

83. See "The Tomb of Samuel Lucas and Margaret Bright Lucas in Highgate (Western) Cemetery," https://historicengland.org.uk/listing/the-list/list-entry/1392350.

84. Cobden to Catherine Williams (Cobden), April 24, 1840; Cobden to Henry Ashworth, April 12, 1842, both in *Letters of Richard Cobden*, 1:189, 267, respectively.

85. Barbara Caine, *English Feminism, 1780–1980* (Oxford: Oxford University Press, 1997), 77, 95; Mary Howitt to Julian Harney, 1848, in Frank Gees Black and Renee Metivier Black, eds., *The Harney Papers* (Assen, Netherlands: Van Gorcum, 1969), 23n1.

86. Harriet B. Applewhite, *Women's Representatives in Britain, France, and the United States* (Basingstoke: Palgrave Macmillan, 2015), 14; Holton, "Kinship and Friendship," 366.

87. Lydia Becker to Anne Knight, January 31, 1868, MSS W2/2/17a, LSF; Caine, *English Feminism*, 118; Laura E. Nym Mayhall, *The Militant Suffrage Movement: Citizenship and Resistance, 1860–1930* (Oxford: Oxford University Press, 2003), 90.

88. NSWS membership list, W2/2/17c., LSF.

89. Mayhall, *Militant Suffrage Movement*, 15.

90. Ibid., 15–19; Patricia Ward D'Itri, *Cross Currents in the International Women's Movement, 1848–1948* (Bowling Green: Bowling Green State University Press, 1999), 31.

91. Anne-Marie Kilday and David Nash, eds., *Law, Crime, and Deviance Since 1700: Micro-Studies in the History of Crime* (London: Bloomsbury Academic, 2017), 61–77.

92. *Evidence of John Stuart Mill* [. . .] *Royal Commission of 1870* [. . .] (London: National Association for the Repeal of the Contagious Diseases Acts, [1870]), 860, National Library of Australia, RB Ec, PV/36.

93. *Report of the Ladies National Association for the Repeal of the CDAs*, November 14, 1871, 937, 379, National Library of Australia, RB Ec, PV/36.

94. Scottish National Association for the Repeal of the Contagious Diseases Acts, "A Few Words to Electors," Wellcome Library, London, MS C_Rb2145047.

95. "Appeal Signed by 12 Women 'Friends,'" March 1873, Women's Library, London, MS LSE/3JBL/07/38.

96. *Third Annual Report of the Ladies National Association for the Repeal of the CDAs*, 1872, 17–26, National Library of Australia.

97. Ibid., 12, 13; for membership lists, see 1–6.

98. Philip Howell, *Geographies of Regulation: Policing Prostitution in Nineteenth-Century Britain and the Empire* (Cambridge: Cambridge University Press, 2009); E. M. Sigsworth and T. J. Wyke, "A Study of Victorian Prostitution and Venereal Disease," in *Suffer and Be Still: Women in the Victorian Age*, edited by Martha Vicinus (London: Methuen, 1972), 77, 95–98.

99. Holton, "Kinship and Friendship," 376–77.

100. Carmel Quinlan, *Genteel Revolutionaries: Anna and Thomas Haslam and the Irish Women's Movement* (Cork: Cork University Press, 2002), 3.

101. Ibid., 52, 75, 90, 97–98, 101, 106; Ladies National Association, *Eleventh Annual Report* (1880), 133–34.

CHAPTER II

"We Must Hope That the Moderates with Their Quiet Attire Are the Rising Section"
British Women Friends' Relinquishment of Plain Dress

HANNAH RUMBALL

On November 5, 1910, Lionel Monkton's production *The Quaker Girl* exploded onto the stage at London's Adelphi Theatre. The popular actress and singer Gertie Millar played the lead role of Prudence Pym, a plain Quaker stereotypically attired in "white Quaker kerchief . . . white turned-back cuffs and apron and white Quaker bonnet" over a "dainty" brown dress.[1] After scandalizing relatives by sipping champagne at a wedding, she is whisked away to Paris, where she becomes enraptured by the lavish array of fashionable gowns. Meanwhile, her own peculiar Quaker plain dress, ironically, becomes the craze of the city. The musical charted how "a fascinating damsel . . . chafes under the stern repression of Quaker life," in a quaint and humorous parody of the Quaker religion and its distinctive, once religiously prescribed, plain attire.[2]

Readers today may assume that a play based on the niche practice of plain dress once prescribed by the Religious Society of Friends would have distinctly limited appeal. At the time of its production, however, *The Quaker Girl* was an outright success, enjoying a five-month run in London and thereafter moving to the Park Theatre on Broadway in New York City. British audiences were enraptured by the fashion content of the production. The theater review journal the *Play Pictorial* even ran an article titled "Frocks and Frills," documenting and celebrating the lavish array of fashionable costumes created by the British couturier Lucile (Lady Duff Gordon) for the show.

The Quaker Girl illustrates how plain Quaker attire by this date had become a stereotype in the minds of the British public, ripe for parody. By 1910, popular representations of British Quaker plain dress illustrated the style as a long-fossilized form of religious garb, which had been rapidly swept away in the mid-nineteenth century in the face of progress and in an attempt by the Society of Friends to modernize. But research into the lives of British Quaker women in the second half of the nineteenth century challenges these stiflingly stereotypical portrayals of Quaker women's dress.

After the revision of the Quaker testimonies in 1860 by the London Yearly Meeting (LYM), especially that which governed plainness in speech and apparel, there was no consensus as to the manner in which British Quaker women should attire themselves. Thereafter, this question was guided by a personal negotiation of the extent to which religious and fashionable identity was most appropriately illustrated by their clothes. Thus attitudes toward clothing by British Quaker women were nuanced and conflicted. This chapter illustrates the three distinctive styles of dress adopted by British Quaker women in the late nineteenth century in response to this individual negotiation. These three styles are exemplified in three case studies of high-profile, relatively wealthy British Quaker women—Elizabeth Petipher Cash (1796–1894), Geraldine Cadbury (1865–1941), and Lucretia Seebohm (1841–1936)—each of whom chose to adopt a differing interpretation of clothing to illustrate her personal sense of religious self, alongside the newly found freedom to present a fashionable identity.

For adult Quakers, plain dress was historically a physical visual signifier through which they and their ancestors had long illustrated their religious affiliation. Early Quakers condemned any aspect of dress that could be interpreted as superfluous. Over the centuries, the generalized recommendations on followers' dress became increasingly prescriptive in Britain.[3] By the nineteenth century, plain dress for women had come to be understood as full-length gathered skirts without a crinoline or bustle and close-fitting bodices with long sleeves, made in plain unpatterned cloth in muted color palettes. Large undecorated shawls and pale undecorated white muslin or linen caps with a high crown, tied under the chin, accompanied these.

Enforced through religious prescription and community peer pressure, the failure to dress plainly before 1860 was a serious breach of custom and could result in ostracism in the religious community. Many elderly members of the society, especially those of a conservative bent, represented in this chapter by Elizabeth Petipher Cash, therefore quaked at the prospect of losing such a fundamental religious marker. Conservative voices continued to decry fashionable dress in British Quaker meetings in the mid- to late nineteenth century and in Quaker-circulated publications such as the *Friend* and *British Friend*, where women's fashionable dress was most frequently marked out for censure. Despite this opprobrium, many women of the Society threw off the "uniform" of plainness, especially those of the younger demographic, such as Lucretia Seebohm, who relished the effervescent Paris fashions available to them through their newfound religious freedoms. This decision exposed them to criticism and was not without its detractors. In reaction, a quietly fashionable third interpretation appeared, as exemplified by the clothing choices of Geraldine Cadbury. Neither showily fashionable nor ascetic, it was this third interpretation that became the most prominent, especially among the younger generation of Quaker women.

In considering the clothing these women wore, material culture analysis is crucial in both supporting and informing Quaker dress history. As Ann Smart Martin has noted, "material objects matter because they are complex, symbolic bundles of social, cultural, and individual meanings fused onto something we can touch, see, and own."[4] Thus surviving garments with a verifiable British Quaker derivation provide key evidence of how these three ideological standpoints were manifested in Quaker women's clothing. Housed in some of Britain's most important costume collections, garments belonging to these three Quaker women illustrate these three distinct sartorial interpretations.[5] Along with historical letters, religious texts, department store catalogues, photographs, and fashionable women's magazines of the period, these sources build a picture of how three British Quaker women negotiated the public display of their sincere religious affiliation alongside fashionability between 1860 and 1914.

THE PLAIN DEBATE

As early as the seventeenth century, concern was expressed from within the Society of Friends that emphasis on outward presentation, specifically clothing, could become "a distraction from or even a substitute to piety."[6] To this day, *Quaker Faith and Practice*, which seeks to outline the main beliefs of the religion and its structure, includes Quaker Margaret Fell's 1698 warning that "it is a dangerous thing to lead young Friends much into the observation of outward things which may be easily done. For they can soon get into an outward garb, to be all alike outwardly. But this will not make them true Christians: it's the spirit that gives life."[7] By the beginning of the nineteenth century, appropriate dress for Quakers had become a serious topic of contemplation for many members of the Society. These agitators sought to contest the query of plainness, which regularly asked whether Friends "who have children and servants under their care . . . endeavour to train them up in a religious life and conversation, consistent with our Christian profession; in the frequent reading of the Holy Scripture and in plainness of speech, behavior and apparel."[8] It is striking that as early as the 1830s, Quaker publications denounced the practice of religiously encouraged plain dressing, which they "felt to be a weak point, scarcely susceptible to defense at all."[9] Several high-profile Quakers, including the banker and Quaker minister Joseph John Gurney, spoke of the lack of "moral virtue" in the adoption of the Quaker "uniform," and noted that to be adamant about plain dress was to impede genuine Christian simplicity. Some Quakers even felt that the continued use of these peculiarities was not motivated by "true Christian simplicity and plainness."[10] Instead, one anonymous writer, in *Observations of the Quaker-Peculiarities of Dress and Language*, argued that most Quakers observed plain living from both fear of ostracism and anxiety about criticism of their attire from their peers. As the anonymous writer put it as early as 1836, Quakers who maintained all other Quaker principles were still made to feel social discomfort if they failed to adhere to plain-dress practices: "From the moment they throw off the badge of Quakerism, they are looked upon as delinquents and treated as such. Thus the advantages of membership,—namely, communion and co-operation with men of kindred opinions and feelings, are lost to them:— they feel, that although attached in other respects to the principles of the society, yet having violated these minor peculiarities, they are accounted to have passed the Rubicon, and henceforth have no alternative but to join in fellowship with some body of Christians who will look more charitably upon their conduct."[11] These criticisms, which contested and eventually led to the relaxation of certain ritualistic practices that distinguished Friends, characterized the faith throughout the nineteenth century. Debate on Quakerism's peculiar practices were never so heated than during the LYM of 1859. John Stephenson Rowntree's account of that all-male yearly meeting is particularly revelatory, his notes illustrating a microcosm of the debates raging in the wider religious community.

On a hot May afternoon in 1859, thirty to forty male friends gave their opinions of the "proposal to make the peculiarity of dress and speech optional." There was a difference of opinion on amending the query, as many "thought the 'peculiarities' had been useful in many ways and should be sorry to see them given up," according to Rowntree's account of the meeting. These plain-dress advocates argued that they acted as "a hedge, as a convenience, as a good thing."[12]

As Marcia Pointon has noted, Quakers, like other Christian denominations, have historically connected the actions and presentation of the body with the expression of spirituality, which resulted in their adoption of "a Plain outward appearance."[13] The sociologist Daniel Miller, meanwhile, has sought to challenge myths surrounding historical consumption practices, and has argued that consumerism has long been represented as a "misleading act, which mystified the true nature of personhood which lay deep within." Miller notes that this "myth" is based on the idea that a perfect spirituality, uncorrupted by consumerism, once existed.[14] Likewise, many Quakers opposed making plainness in dress and speech optional because of its association with ancestral religious practices, alongside its apparent ability to shield wearers from the corruption of the wider world in their quest for a perfect spiritual state.[15] It is clear that some Quakers held an idealized belief that a historical state of "pure sociality" had once existed, and that their ancestors had rejected consumerism outright and unequivocally.

During the 1859 yearly meeting, the tide appeared to turn in favor of an amendment to the plainness query, and Rowntree noted that "the assertion that 'plainness' did mean a costume was felt to be so objectionable that it appeared to me, many friends now felt that what to begin with was an alteration of detail not very important—now became one of principle, as there were not many who deemed it the duty of the Church to impose a costume per se."[16] While traditionalist dissenters made the revision of the query impossible that year, in 1860 a committee made "peculiarity of dress and speech ... optional," and it was formally written into *Christian Doctrine, Practice, and Discipline* in 1861.[17] In practice, this meant that for the first time since the adoption of plain dress in the late seventeenth century, Quaker men and women were granted individual freedom of choice in the style of their attire. Such queries thus shifted from serving a disciplinary function to one of self-examination, and the function of dress as a symbolic communicator of faith in the Quaker community continued to be a matter of debate for many decades.

Women Friends' opinions on these sartorial revisions were absent, even though women were equally governed by the traditional practice of plain attire. As Thomas C. Kennedy explains, Quaker "males ... decided every important local and national question without reference to Women's Meetings or women's opinions."[18] When the motions were passed, however, it was the women of the religious community who were most acutely exposed to the minefield of etiquette, which underpinned mainstream nineteenth-century fashionable dress.

As dress historian Diana Crane has noted, during the nineteenth and early twentieth centuries, "for a costume to be considered elegant, every detail had to be correct." Any departure from socially accepted fashionable attire would have been immediately recognizable to the fashionable classes and read as inappropriate, defiant, or even subversive of established etiquette and the social order.[19] Clearly, formerly plain Quaker women wishing to embrace de rigueur fashions in capitulation to British society's social expectations had to navigate a minefield of fashion and etiquette.

REMAINING PLAIN

Nonetheless, proponents of plain dress were far from appeased. Many men and women of the elder generations, who had observed plain practices their whole adult lives, spurned and even actively disapproved of the option of fashionable dress and habits. As Elizabeth Isichei has shown, these opponents of change often represented those seeking to modernize as "lowerers of standards, shrinking from the rigors of true religion."[20]

Elizabeth Petipher Cash (1796–1894) was one such Quaker who remained plain and thus continued deliberately to mark herself out as socially separate by her appearance after 1861. Even in her letters, Cash continued to observe the customs of plain speech, systematically using the ritualized Quaker "thee," "thy," and "thou" when writing to family.[21] In many ways, such reticence is understandable, given Cash's mature age of sixty-five in 1861, when the revisions were adopted. Although little has been written about older women's dress from this period, it is commonly accepted that the etiquette and styles of youth continued to be of influence as women grew older. In

Cash's youth, plain dressing was unwaveringly observed in her community and at the Friends' school in London, which she attended between 1808 and 1811.[22] The school's enforcement of plain dress emphasized frugality, mandating limited spending on clothes, advocating mending rather than purchasing new clothing, and restricting the amount of time spent on dressing. The school's rules advocated clothes that were "plain, strong, without ornamental trimmings" well into the 1870s.[23] The environment in which Cash received her sartorial training would have had a great influence on her future negotiation of fashionable dress.

A number of Cash's garments dating from the second half of the nineteenth century survive in the collection of Killerton House National Trust. They illustrate her resolute refusal to follow the dictates of fashion and her determination to remain plain. These garments provide material evidence of Cash's religious beliefs and self-presentation through dress. Their most striking feature is the absence of embellishment, given the fastidious attention to the high quality of the materials and construction. The hemming stitches of Cash's plain white cotton-muslin kerchiefs are so fine that they are barely perceptible. A huge pale blue silk shawl is constructed of two layers of costly fabric. All of these garments have an absence of decay that belies their antique age and indicates their exceptional quality. Two plain Quaker poke bonnets, one deep navy blue and one of black silk, are notable for their want of accoutrements, especially since Quaker women's adoption of bonnets with lavish trim would be expected after 1860.

Cash's dismissal of fashionable clothing is perhaps nowhere as noticeable as in a portrait of her with two of her adult daughters, Caroline (1838–1924) and Ann (1835–1895), taken around 1860–65 (fig. 11.1). Cash, seated to the right, wears full plain garb: a full silk skirt without the fashionable crinoline, pale muslin kerchief, silk shawl, and high-peaked muslin cap, all devoid of embellishments. Her daughters' ensembles, by contrast, quietly observe the fashions of the period. Caroline, the more fashionable, holds an a la mode bonnet heavily trimmed with ribbon and flowers; her bodice features decorative braiding at the cuffs and her stance illustrates her use of a crinoline to achieve the fashionable wide skirt. Cash thus marks herself as separate through her sartorial choices, even from her own daughters.

Cash's commitment to a plain aesthetic was no anomaly. A collection of Quaker photographic portraits, titled the Friends' Institute London albums and held by the Library of the Society of Friends, contains multiple examples of elderly Quaker women wearing plain attire long after 1860. Nowhere

FIG. 11.1 Photograph of (*left to right*) Caroline Barrow, Ann Cash, and Elizabeth Petipher Cash, ca. 1860–65. Papers of the Cadbury Family of Birmingham, Birmingham Library, MS466/8a/9. Photo © Cadbury Archive, Mondelēz International.

is it easier to see the "uniform" of plainness than in this series of images of elderly women all in plain dress. Each observes the composite elements of Cash's garb—kerchief, silk shawl, and muslin cap, all in unpatterned fabrics. One even stands beside her distinctive plain Quaker bonnet. These portraits demonstrate that Elizabeth Cash's appearance was typical of a subset of traditionalist Quakers who opted to remain plain well into the late nineteenth century.

Despite Quaker women's apparent liberty in their clothing choices after 1860, conservatives continued to voice their discontent at "the tyranny of ever changing fashion," heard in British Quaker meetings and in Quaker-circulated publications such as the *Friend*, *British Friend*, and the *Friends Quarterly Examiner*.[24] In 1866, an anonymous "female member" wrote a letter to the *Friend* protesting the "departure from simplicity amongst our younger Friends, particularly in the attire of a large proportion of our female members." While she sought to reassure the reader of her disapproval of traditional plain dress, she castigated the wearing of what she deemed to be capricious fashions by Quaker women in meetings. She asserted that although plain dress had been relaxed, the incorporation of fashionable features was still inappropriate for Quaker women: "it gives no license for the extravagantly wide and costly ribbons which are exhibited in our meetings, the expanded dresses [i.e., crinoline], and the indulgence in almost every unbecoming and ever-varying fashion of the day."[25]

Likewise, in 1869, the Quaker William Pollard wrote a letter to the *Friends Quarterly Examiner* decrying the fashionable bonnets increasingly worn by women Friends, especially those who attended meetings with "fantastic structures upon their heads." While Pollard's reproof of mainstream fashions worn by British women Friends echoes the criticisms voiced by other conservative detractors, his letter is notable in its detailed description of women's dress. Pollard identifies the three distinct factions into which British Quaker women had coalesced with respect to fashion in dress:

> The empty-headed French milliners rule the female world. But let us be thankful, all are not under their cruel sway. The problem has been thoroughly solved (and there were abundant instances of its solution at this Yearly Meeting) how to dress with beautiful taste and neatness and simplicity combined; how to avoid singularities and oddities, and to be attired both with grace and Christian moderation. We must hope that the moderates with their quiet attire are the rising section,

and that the extreme reds among us will soon, even for the sake of appearance, if for no higher motive, be all converted to their view.²⁶

Pollard's letter makes it clear that as a result of conflicting views on Quaker women's self-presentation, between apparent liberty in fashion and blustering conservatism, a fracturing of practices had occurred among women Friends. Conservative plain dressers, mostly the elder generations, sat side by side with women Friends who embraced fashionable dress to varying degrees. Pollard, and others who felt compelled to criticize fashionable dress in the pages of Quaker publications, reserved the deepest disdain for women who conspicuously embraced mainstream fashionable dress, with its wide-skirted silhouette, profusion of lace and ribbons, and garish colors, achieved using newly discovered aniline dyes. Thus women Friends who endeavored to relinquish plain attire without riling the conservative traditionalists were finding a third way. These "moderates" looked to simplicity as a guiding principle, under which they adopted fashionable clothing plainer than the styles that were the height of fashion.

"FRILLINGS AND TRIMMINGS"

One such moderate was Geraldine Cadbury (1865–1941). Despite being born in Birmingham four years after the revision of the plainness query, Cadbury learned about Quaker plainness from her father, Alfred Southall. A chemist, druggist, and fellow of the Chemical Society, Southall maintained the habits of plainness all his life, spurning the use of overcoats and refusing curtains or carpet in his bedroom, despite the fact that he became "exceedingly well-to-do."²⁷

However, the Southalls were far from traditionalists. According to Cadbury's biographer Janet Whitney, in the Southall family home, discussions often focused on progressive social ideas, particularly concerning the new women's movements. Forward thinking in her attitudes toward women's position in society, Cadbury's mother, the Irish Quaker Mrs. Anna Southall (née Strangman Grubb), moved in a busy religious and social lecturing circuit, where she "was a pioneer in candid health talks to girls, and started reform of girls' dress for drill and activity, bloomers, etc."²⁸ Whitney's allusion to "bloomers" refers to the wearing of loose pantaloons gathered at the ankle under short dresses. They are an early example of the dress advocated by a progressive niche movement, known as the dress reform movement, championed by a band of radical female progressives in America and Britain. Originating in the United States, bloomers were closely associated with encouraging women to participate in more outdoor exercise but also, in their earliest incarnations, with the fight for women's emancipation. Thus heterodox clothing choices were accepted, if not keenly encouraged, in Cadbury's family home during her formative years.

Cadbury would have been familiar with the community's conflicting opinions on the plainness issue through frequent letters in the *Friend*, from which her mother read extracts to her children every Sunday.[29] Cadbury would have heard the vocal criticisms that conservative Quakers continued to level at women's fashionable dress. In one 1870 letter, T. Swann criticized the "absurd" and "gaudy" colors worn by female Friends and stated that "too much colour in dress looks like an eruption of folly."[30] Instead, Swann advocated that Quaker women limit the colors of their garments to natural tints. Even in the final decade of the century, conservative Quakers' preoccupation with the suitability of certain fashionable fabrics, especially bright colors, continued. As late as May 1898, one anonymous Quaker writer chided the "confusion of colours" worn by attendees at LYM.[31]

In that final decade of the century, Cadbury purchased a beautiful but rather unorthodox dress from the "Historic and Artistic Costume Studio" of the fashionable London department store Liberty & Co. for her marriage to Barrow Cadbury, of the chocolate-manufacturing family. Today, it survives in the archives of the Birmingham Museum and Art Gallery (fig. 11.2). Extant Liberty & Co. catalogues from the period demonstrate that Liberty's garments were expensive for fashion retailing in 1890s Britain. Cadbury's choice of dress, therefore, was a symbol of her family's prosperity and upper-middle-class status. That her parents could afford, and were willing to pay for, such a high-priced garment indicates both their approval of the complex subtleties of their daughter's clothing choices and their upper-middle-class income. Clearly, her family's affluence gave Cadbury access to fashion opportunities that would not have been available to Quaker women whose clothing choices were curtailed by cost.

Cadbury's wedding ensemble, far from being either ascetically plain or highly fashionable, was described in the *South Birmingham News* as "a Grecian gown of white pongeé silk, with tulle veil, and flowers."[32] Most unusually, the gown was made in the form of a traditional Grecian chiton (a long tunic) and himation (a Grecian outer garment draped over the shoulder).

FIG. 11.2　Grecian-style aesthetic wedding gown worn by Geraldine Cadbury, 1891. Pongée silk lined with cotton. Birmingham Museum and Art Gallery, 1968M68. Photo by Birmingham Museums Trust (licensed under CC0).

Made of a luxurious, lightweight, butter-colored silk, it drapes the shoulders in layers of extravagant folds that envelop the silhouette, hiding the hook-and-eye closure at the rear of the dress. Thus Cadbury's dress for her wedding at the Bull Street Friends' Meeting House in 1891 is radical in its rejection of the cut and style of conventional fashionable wedding dresses of the period, which emphasized tightly corseted fitted bodices and lavish embellishment.

Apart from the discrete rows of handmade lace concealed inside the train and peeking out at the cuffs, Cadbury's dress is notable for its absence of embellishments. This lack of ornament is characteristic of the quiet attire of Quaker moderate dressers, who favored the "neatness," "simplicity," and "moderation" so lauded by conservatives.[33] Such simplicity, however, was applied to highly fashionable, and in Cadbury's case unconventional, silhouettes. Their omission of embellishment reflects their respect for the advice of the Yearly Meeting of Women Friends in 1872, which, despite followers' freedom to dress as they saw fit, continued to encourage "self-denial" in dress and to discourage "thoughtless expenditure or needless superfluities."[34]

Cadbury's wedding attire, while moderate, was far from antiquated. Instead, it illustrated her appreciation of the unconventional and artistic fine art movement emerging in Britain, the Pre-Raphaelites, who had invented a radical loose style of artistic dress, later termed aesthetic dress, in the middle of the century. Originally made by the artists for their female sitters and relations, the style looked to antiquated dress forms from the medieval period and ancient Greece for inspiration. Inspired by the writings of art critic John Ruskin, these artists studied nature and historicism. Idealized, loosely draped classical robes, often realized in flowing silks, can be seen on fiery-haired heroines in the works of Pre-Raphaelite painters Dante Gabrielle Rossetti, William Holman Hunt, and Albert Joseph Moore. Considered radical in their day, these simple dresses developed into a style adopted by artistically minded women, which featured modest embroidery and smocking, dyed in soft hues without the crude aniline dyes popular in mainstream fashions, and sometimes worn, by the most radical women, without corsets. They are distinctive for their rejection of the close-fitting and tightly corseted silhouette of mainstream late nineteenth-century fashions originating in Paris. The female adherents of aestheticism, including Geraldine Cadbury for her bridal ensemble, copied the heterodox draped Grecian or medieval-inspired gowns (fig. 11.3). In fashion and décor, this copying of Pre-Raphaelite paintings in daily life became a way to define

FIG. 11.3 Photograph of the wedding of Geraldine Southall and Barrow Cadbury, September 8, 1891. Birmingham Museum and Art Gallery, 1968M68(2). Photo by Birmingham Museums Trust (licensed under CC0).

oneself as a devotee of the aesthetic movement. Despite its unconventionality, the style was adopted and disseminated by high-class members of society affiliated with the arts, such as Oscar Wilde and the popular actor Ellen Terry. British newspapers and social commentary often derided the unorthodox and instantly recognizable style, with caricatures of aesthetes regularly appearing in the popular satirical magazine *Punch*.

Liberty & Co.'s Historic and Artistic Costume Studio, which produced Cadbury's dress, designed many aesthetic-style garments during the 1880s and 1890s. Prior to the studio's founding, Arthur Liberty's store was most famous for selling exquisite materials such as "supple cashmeres, delicate pongee, and matt-surfaced slubby wild-silk tussores ... shown in infinitely nuanced ranges of delectable new colors" that were manufactured exclusively using natural dyes.[35] Thus the emphasis on high quality and beautifully draped silk for Cadbury's wedding dress was decidedly in keeping both with Liberty's specialty and also with traditional plain Quaker notions of appropriate consumption habits. Sober colors were universal among plain Quakers, while early Quakers had long harbored uneasiness about brightly colored textiles. The eighteenth-century Quaker John Woolman believed that dyed cloth was a signal of vain and environmentally destructive habits.[36] Furthermore, the high quality of plain Quaker women's garments was a characteristic so widely acknowledged as to appear in the popular press. An 1858 article titled "The Decline of Quakerism," which has a distinctly anti-Quaker undertone, leveled a charge of hypocrisy at Quaker plain-dress practices as a result of Quakers' choice in fabrics. The anonymous author stated that "the Quaker ladies have always been famous for the exquisite delicacy of their materials."[37] The piece criticized the Quaker trait of adopting fine fabrics, arguing that the "demon of finery," far from vanishing in plain dress, could be seen in the high-quality expensive material. Such sartorial compromises, identifiable by their restrained and somewhat simplified interpretation of fashion, were realized in the highest-quality textiles before the plainness query became optional. Yet even after its relaxation, fashionability and luxury were to be found in the quality of materials, rather than in style or color, among Quaker moderate dressers and plain dressers after 1860.

Liberty's materials had long been acknowledged as the most suitable for the increasingly voguish, though often ridiculed, aesthetic dress. Thus the establishment of an in-house design studio, where garments were made in the aesthetic style, was an obvious extension of his commercial venture. Employed to direct the studio and oversee its designs was the lauded theater-costume designer E. W. Godwin. Under his guidance, it maintained a distinctive "sartorial identity," which was justified by a series of principles printed in the studio's catalogues.[38] These principles, which rejected "exaggeration and needless extravagance" and felt it "better to ignore the present mode" and instead adopt a "more slowly perfected earlier style" of dress, set Liberty's designs radically apart from the seasonally changing and highly decorative mainstream fashions.[39]

Such sentiments were shared by the champion of Pre-Raphaelitism John Ruskin, whom Liberty's Studio quoted in its catalogue *Evolution in Costume*. Ruskin observed that "the fond and graceful flattery of each master does in no small measure consist in his management of frillings and trimmings, cuffs and collarettes."[40] This preference for simplicity in dress and respect for historical garment styles, from both Liberty's and Ruskin, are important for two reasons. First, Ruskin's statement would undoubtedly have appealed to Cadbury, who held Ruskin in high regard.[41] Writing to her mother while on vacation in France in 1894, Cadbury esteemed Ruskin's description of Amiens Cathedral over her own descriptive abilities, saying, "as I believe Ruskin has already (and possibly better than I can) described the scene I will refer you to him."[42] In keeping with Ruskin's advice, Cadbury did indeed manage the "frillings and trimmings" on her wedding dress by restricting embellishments to the discrete rows of handmade lace concealed inside the train and at the cuffs. Second, and illuminatingly, such language and sentiment is consistent with that used by conservative traditionalist Quakers. Strikingly, recommendations to spurn "needless" extravagance or superfluity in a garment appear in both Liberty's principles and the advice of the Yearly Meeting of Women Friends in 1872, which, as mentioned above, continued to be respected by many female Friends throughout the late nineteenth century.

Cadbury would also have been mindful of respecting simplicity and shunning "needless extravagance" on the very public and sacred occasion of her marriage. Day-to-day plainness may have been relaxed, but the yearly meeting's directions concerning marriage ceremonies remained austere. The LYM singled out marriage ceremonies as specific occasions on which simplicity in dress was encouraged. Quaker guidance from 1857 continued to be published for Friends well into the twentieth century. Advices published in 1911 regarding "simplicity at weddings" advised that "at such a time, let there not be, either in the attire of the contracting parties or in that of their relatives and friends any display unbecoming an assembly of worshippers; and let the general proceedings of the marriage day . . . never pass the bounds of Christian moderation."[43] It was not merely formal religious guidance that encouraged reserve in clothing, as the sentiment also endured among the religious community. Even in the late 1890s, letters still appeared in the *Friend* criticizing the styles of clothing adopted by Quaker women, especially at meetings. As late as April 1898, one anonymous letter suggested "that Friends attending Yearly Meeting next month should not indulge in such brilliant head-gear and other habiliments as have been the increasing custom of late years."[44] Within such an environment, it is a wonder that any Quaker woman felt able to embrace fashionable dress. Yet it is clear from the regularity with which fashionable women's dress was castigated by social commentators, and from the highly fashionable garments that survive, that they not only managed to but relished doing so.

"THIS WILL NOT MAKE THEM TRUE CHRISTIANS"

Two decades before Cadbury's wedding, and only a decade after the relaxation of the plainness query, Lucretia Seebohm (née Anson Crouch) chose a highly fashionable ensemble for her marriage to the wealthy widowed banker Benjamin Seebohm Jr. at the Clevedon Friends Meeting House in Somerset in 1874.

Lucretia Seebohm's wedding outfit, now housed at the Victoria and Albert Museum in London, features a boned bodice, bustle-backed skirt, sash, collar, and matching cape, produced from a fine ivory-colored silk gauze with an opaque silk stripe, all trimmed with blonde silk net lace and cream silk satin rouleaux and bows (fig. 11.4). Once again, the exquisite delicacy of the materials is evident. Significantly, not only was the textile of exceptional quality, but Seebohm's choice of fabric was also of the utmost fashionability for its time. The leading British fashion journals of the day, including the *Englishwoman's Domestic Magazine* and Samuel Beeton's *Young Englishwoman*, illustrate how silk gauze, especially when it featured a stripe, was "particularly admired." One ensemble described at length that year featured "striped gauze over a silk slip. The gauze is a fabric consisting of clear white gauze and coloured satin."[45]

Fashionable silhouettes of the early 1870s for middle- and upper-class women were distinctive for their exaggerated bustle at the rear of the skirt, the addition of a polonaise,[46] and a profuse effervescence of materials and trimmings. Lightweight fabrics applied in layers, such as gauzes, were romantically draped and then embellished with an abundance of bows, lace, and ribbons, as can be seen on Seebohm's gown in the buff-colored silk bows at the cuffs, bust, and sash. On fashionable dresses of the era, every edge was decoratively bordered. Seebohm's gown features blonde silk lace in a leaf motif at the hem of the skirt, polonaise, cuffs, and collar. It epitomizes these design features and is fashionably accurate in every respect. Even the choice of ivory and cream colors was highly appropriate for her wedding, as white had been generally accepted as the customary bridal color since the eighteenth century.[47] Clearly, Lucretia, despite her provincial address (first in Clevedon in Somerset and later in Luton in Bedfordshire), closely observed the latest fashions from Paris and London, probably through the fashionable magazines of the day, and could afford to adopt them.

With the persistent denunciation of fashionable dress by conservative traditionalist Quakers during this decade, we might assume that Seebohm's

FIG. II.4 Fashionable wedding dress worn by the Quaker Lucretia Seebohm (née Anson Crouch), 1874. Silk gauze trimmed with silk-embroidered net lace and silk satin and lined with silk. Victoria and Albert Museum, London, T.68 to E-1962. Photo © Victoria and Albert Museum, London.

embrace of mainstream fashion signified what they decried as a "lowering of standards." In fact, it can be argued that Seebohm's choice of dress reveals a historic precedent in the Quaker community, attesting that attire was not an appropriate marker of religious devotion. As Joan Kendall has noted, from the genesis of the Society, "there were Friends who never adopted the plainest form of dress. These became known as 'gay Friends.'"[48] Clearly, the use of clothing as a signifier of religiosity was always a contested practice. In part, this was because of established social expectations that clothing communicated a person's class and wealth, a practice that some wealthier Quakers believed was perfectly proper. High-profile Quakers such as Robert Barclay (1648–1690) had argued since the founding of the religion that wearing clothing denoting class and status was appropriate, "for we know that as it hath pleased God to dispense it diversely, giving to some more, and some less, so they may use it accordingly."[49] Margaret Fell (1614–1702), by contrast, cited New Testament passages that condemned the use of "outward ceremonies." Her 1698 epistle condemned the wearing of "an outward garb," warning those who wore it that "this will not make them true Christians." In her best-known statement, she made it completely clear that the wearing of a uniform was "a silly poor Gospel."[50] Clearly, Quakers throughout the history of the religion had publicly undermined the Quaker advices concerning plainness of apparel.

It is important to note that Fell and Barclay, like the three women who are the subjects of this chapter, represent wealthier Quakers who could afford to purchase the finest garments and materials in their style of choice. Cash, Cadbury, and Seebohm occupied similar upper-middle-class positions and were comparably wealthy. Thus, whether plain or fashionable, their garments illustrate a self-presentation born of careful consideration of their Quaker identity, rather than one born of utility or financial constraint. The exceptional quality of the textiles of these women's surviving garments (and in Seebohm's and Cadbury's cases their fashionability) is a crucial justification for their preservation in the rarefied stores of a costume collection. It is probable that for many Quaker women, both class and wealth were contributing factors in clothing decisions. Perhaps plain dress was retained far longer than individually desired for the sake of economic expediency. Far more research is needed into the intersections of status, class, and Quaker religiosity in the debate on plainness during this period.

In consequence of "gay" Friends' attitudes, incorporating fashionable mainstream attire into the wardrobe of Quakers had occurred since the seventeenth century. Seebohm's choice to wear an ensemble that would have been read as highly fashionable by her fellow Quakers exemplifies how women Friends negotiated wearing fashionable clothing given the tension between notional liberty in their choices and blustering vocal opposition from conservatives. While such tension between fashionable modernizers and traditionalist conservatives reached its apogee in the late nineteenth century, it had been a concern for all three centuries of the religion's existence.

CONCLUSION

By the time Prudence Pym trod the boards in *The Quaker Girl*, the "stern repression of Quaker life" had in fact been in retreat for fifty years. The large number of men who supported the amendment to the query on plainness at LYM reveals the extent to which the practice was viewed by many, as early as 1859, as "absurd" and "objectionable" because it "failed to attain its object."[51] Furthermore, the attitudes of early "gay Friends," including Fell, illustrate how clothing as a marker of religious devotion and piety had always been contested. It is unsurprising, therefore, that some young middle-class women with financial means, such as Lucretia Seebohm, enthusiastically adopted the bustle-backed silhouettes and lavish trappings of high-fashion ensembles of the day, when the query on plainness shifted from a disciplinary function to one of self-examination.

Women who embraced mainstream fashionable dress, with its wide-skirted silhouette, abundance of accoutrements, and garish colors, bore the brunt of the blustering vocal criticism of their conservative co-religionists. Traditionalist Quakers, especially elders, remained outspokenly opposed to "the tyranny of ever changing fashion"; their thoughts on the matter were expressed in British Quaker meetings and in letters in Quaker publications to the end of the nineteenth century. Their opposition to change was manifested in their maintenance of the Quaker plain dress of their youth; conservative Quaker women like Elizabeth Petipher Cash wore the full silk skirt without crinoline, pale muslin kerchief, silk shawl, and high-peaked muslin cap in plain solid fabrics and muted shades, barren of embellishments or trimmings, until death. Their widely disseminated critiques and ascetic ensembles appear to have tempered the clothing choices of the younger demographic of middle-class Quaker women of means.

Among a community wrestling with conflicting opinions, most British Quaker women opted for a quietly fashionable form of dress. For the very public occasion of her marriage, Geraldine Cadbury turned away from the mainstream fashions of Parisian couturiers and looked to the British store Liberty & Co. for the "neatness," "simplicity," and "moderation" lauded by conservative Quakers. Liberty's rejection of seasonally changing fashions, exaggeration, and needless extravagance was reflected in gowns typified by loose silhouettes, adaptation from historic styles, and fabrics of muted colors made from natural dyes. Cadbury's gown was carefully selected as a design that negotiated her Quaker beliefs and her desire for a simple, moderately fashionable, yet contemporary dress. As early as 1869, William Pollard hoped that such women would win the sartorial battle occurring in the British Quaker community and become "the rising section." Pollard's wish came to fruition in the consensus that Quakers should "appear well-dressed but unobtrusive."[52]

NOTES

1. Rita Detmold, "Frocks and Frills," *Play Pictorial: An Illustrated Monthly Journal* 17, no. 104 (1911): 118–19.

2. B. W. Findon, "The Quaker Girl," ibid., 98–99.

3. Peter Collins, "Ethical Consumption as Religious Testimony: The Quaker Case," in *Ethical Consumption, Social Value, and Economic Practice*, edited by James G. Carrier and Peter G. Luetchford (Oxford: Berghahn Books, 2012), 184.

4. Ann Smart Martin, "Makers, Buyers, and Users: Consumerism as a Material Culture Framework," *Winterthur Portfolio* 28, nos. 2–3 (1993): 141.

5. Their clothes are housed in the Victoria and Albert Museum London, Killerton House National Trust, and the Birmingham Museum and Art Gallery.

6. Emma Lapsansky, "Past Plainness to Present Simplicity: A Search for Quaker Identity," in *Quaker Aesthetics: Reflections on a Quaker Ethic in American Design and Consumption*, edited by Emma Jones Lapsansky and Anne A. Verplanck (Philadelphia: University of Pennsylvania Press, 2003), 2.

7. *Quaker Faith and Practice: The Book of Christian Discipline of the Yearly Meeting of the Religious Society of Friends (Quakers) in Britain* (London: Britain Yearly Meeting, 1995), 20.3.

8. "Cumberland and Northumberland Quarterly Meetings Answers to Queries," March 31, 1814, YM/YMWF, file 1, LSF.

9. *Observations of the Quaker-Peculiarities of Dress and Language* (London: Effingham Wilson, Royal Exchange, 1836), 5.

10. Ibid., 12, 18.

11. Ibid., 17.

12. John Stephenson Rowntree, "Personal Written Accounts of the Men's Yearly Meeting," 1859, YM/MSS/vol. S 368, LSF.

13. Marcia Pointon, "Quakerism and Visual Culture, 1650–1800," *Art History* 20, no. 3 (1997): 407.

14. Daniel Miller, "Consumption as the Vanguard of History: A Polemic by Way of an Introduction," in *Acknowledging Consumption: Reviewing New Studies*, edited by Daniel Miller (London: Routledge, 1995), 23, 25.

15. Pointon, "Quakerism and Visual Culture," 412.

16. Rowntree, "Personal Written Accounts."

17. Elizabeth Isichei, *Victorian Quakers* (Oxford: Oxford University Press, 1970), 159; Thomas C. Kennedy, *British Quakerism, 1860–1920: The Transformation of a Religious Community* (Oxford: Oxford University Press, 2001), 216.

18. Kennedy, *British Quakerism, 1860–1920*, 217.

19. Diana Crane, "Clothing Behaviour as Non-Verbal Resistance: Marginal Women and Alternative Dress in the Nineteenth Century," *Fashion Theory* 3, no. 2. (1999): 242.

20. Isichei, *Victorian Quakers*, 161.

21. Elizabeth Petipher Cash, *A Dear Memory: Pages from the Letters of Mary Jane Taylor*, edited by Elizabeth Mary Cadbury (Birmingham: Cornish Brothers Ltd., 1914), 214.

22. W. Robinson, *Annual Monitor for 1895, or Obituary of the Members of the Society of Friends in Great Britain and Ireland for the Year 1894* (London: Headley Bros., 1895), 51.

23. *Rules and General Regulations for the Government of Croydon School* [...] (London: E. Newman, 1870), 25.

24. See, for example, "Plainness of Apparel," *British Friend*, August 1867, 189.

25. "On Christian Simplicity," *Friend* 6, no. 65 (January 1866): 99.

26. William Pollard, "Colloquial Letters, no. 9: My Unspoken Speeches in the Late Yearly Meeting," in *The Friends' Quarterly Examiner* (London: F. Bowyer Kitto, 1869), 443–44.

27. Janet Whitney, *Geraldine S. Cadbury, 1865–1941: A Biography* (London: George Harrap and Co., 1948), 30.

28. Ibid., 31.

29. Ibid., 24.

30. T. Swann, "Correspondence: On Dress," *Friend* 10, no. 119 (November 1870): 275.

31. Another Man Friend, "Dress at London Yearly Meeting (To the Editor of the Friend)," *Friend* 38, no. 19 (May 13, 1898), in *The Friend: A Religious, Literary, and Miscellaneous Journal* (London: Headley Brothers, 1898), 294.

32. *South Birmingham News*, September 12, 1891, MS 466A/169, Library of Birmingham, Birmingham, UK.

33. Pollard, "Colloquial Letters, no. 9," 443–44.

34. "Yearly Meeting of Women Friends Held in London by Adjournment from the 22nd of the Fifth Month to the 31st of the Same, Inclusive, 1872, to the Quarterly and Other Meetings of Discipline of Women Friends in Great Britain and Ireland," YM/YMWF, LSF.

35. Geoffrey Squire, "E. W. Godwin and the House of Liberty," *Costume* 34 (2000): 91.

36. Pointon, "Quakerism and Visual Culture," 415.

37. "The Decline of Quakerism," *Chester (UK) Chronicle*, December 24, 1858, 2.

38. Judith Watt, "Costume," in *Liberty of London: Masters of Style and Decoration*, edited by Stephen Calloway (London: Thames and Hudson, 1992), 34.

39. Squire, "E. W. Godwin," 95.

40. Quoted in *Evolution in Costume, Illustrated by Past Fashion Plates and Present Adaptations of the Empire and Early Victorian Period* (London: Messrs. Liberty, 1893), 4.

41. Whitney, *Geraldine S. Cadbury*, 32.

42. Geraldine Cadbury to Mrs. Anna Southall, 1894, MS 466A/510/1, Library of Birmingham.

43. *Christian Discipline of the Religious Society of Friends of London Yearly Meeting, Part II* (London: Headley Brothers, 1911), 58.

44. A Man Friend, "Dress at London Yearly Meeting (To the Editor of the Friend)," *Friend* 38, no. 17 (April 29, 1898), in *The Friend: A Religious, Literary, and Miscellaneous Journal*, 263.

45. "Fashions for September," in *Young Englishwoman: A Volume of Pure Literature, New Fashions, and Pretty Needlework Designs* (London: Ward, Lock, and Tyler, 1874), 514.

46. A matching overskirt, looped up at the sides into a soft puff behind to reveal the underskirt.

47. Edwina Ehrman, *The Wedding Dress: 300 Years of Bridal Fashions* (London: V&A Publishing, 2011), 65.

48. Joan Kendall, "The Development of a Distinct Form of Quaker Dress," *Costume: The Journal of the Costume Society* 19, no. 1 (1985): 58.

49. Robert Barclay, *An Apology for the True Christian Divinity: Being an Explanation and Vindication of the Principles and Doctrines of the People called Quakers* (Dublin: L. Flin, 1780), 516.

50. *Quaker Faith and Practice*, 20.3.

51. Rowntree, "Personal Written Accounts."

52. Ehrman, *Wedding Dress*, 82.

CHAPTER 12

"The Joy of Doing Right"
The Humanitarian Work of Doctor Hilda Clark During the First World War

LINDA PALFREEMAN

Hilda Clark (1881–1955), a bright, determined child of "sparkling vitality," grew up in the village of Street, Somerset, in the heart of a large and loving Quaker family who considered her "good-humoured, always up to fun, delighting in outdoor life and exercise and the loveliness of the world, a good companion in everything." There were also early indications of Hilda's caring nature. As the editor of her letters notes, "any wild or tame living thing, bird, snake, cat, dog, horse, appealed to her, and she would give it joyful companionship as well as care."[1]

Hilda was the youngest of the six children of William Stephens Clark (1839–1925), shoe manufacturer and social reformer,[2] and Helen Priestman Bright Clark (1840–1927), daughter of renowned Liberal politician John Bright. She was educated at Brighthelmston and the Mount, a Quaker schools for girls, and went on to study medicine at Birmingham University. In Birmingham, she stayed with her aunt Dr. Anne Elizabeth (Annie) Clark (1844–1925), pioneering physician and just one of a long line of strong female family role models for the aspiring young doctor. Annie Clark followed the example of Elizabeth Garrett in her pursuit of a medical career. When Annie went to the United States to complete her studies, Helen Clark wrote of her great sadness: "I shall try to comfort myself by thinking of you as one who is really doing something definite for women."[3] It is hardly surprising, then, that she would give her blessing and encouragement when one of her own daughters later expressed an interest in becoming a physician.

Hilda Clark descended from a long line of stalwart Quaker women, champions of women's rights and committed to social reform. She was close to her paternal grandmother, the philanthropist and antislavery campaigner Eleanor Stephens Clark (1812–1879), and to her maternal relations, among whom there were several leading women's rights campaigners, including her great aunt Priscilla Bright McLaren (1815–1906) and her aunts Anna Maria Priestman (1828–1914) and Margaret Priestman (1817–1905). Her mother, Helen Clark, was at the forefront of national campaigns for welfare, education, temperance, and women's suffrage, taking a public stand against her father's opposition to the vote for women.

As Anna Vaughan Kett explains in her chapter in this volume, despite the Quaker philosophy of developing women's independence, an idea permeated Quaker culture that females had the essential characteristics to be homemakers in the private sphere, rather than workers in the public sphere. Sandra Stanley Holton contends that "Quaker women as a generality were better known at this time for the nicety of their domestic arrangements, for their good works, for their thorough if practical education and for notions of female modesty that led them in general to shun the public eye." However, none of the Priestman-Bright-Clark circle represented the stereotypical "domestic, retiring and modest woman Friend."[4] Helen Clark helped found a range of women's organizations and joined in the effort to gain equality for women within the Society of Friends. Along with her sister-in-law, Sophia Sturge Clark (1849–1933), she was appointed to a committee of the Bristol, Somerset, and Dorset Women's Quarterly Meeting to look into the question of the nonrepresentation of women at the men's London Yearly Meeting and the Meeting for Sufferings. The committee concluded that the arrangements for separate men's and women's yearly meetings were "incompatible with the views of religious equality held by our Society."[5] Clark advocated the need for Quakers to examine the gendered hierarchy governing their own religious society, and to work toward equality. It was in this climate that Hilda Clark was raised.

Imbued with the same spirit as their female forbears, Hilda and her sisters, Alice, Esther, and Margaret, all became suffragists. They were members of the Women's Liberal Federation and of the National Union of

Women's Suffrage Societies. Hilda was also a member of the Women's Social and Political Union. However, none of them became involved in acts of radical civil disobedience or in the violent protests staged by more extremist suffragette groups led by the Pankhursts. Nevertheless, in a moment of belligerent frustration (albeit of verbal rather than physical expression) at the Liberal government's persistent political obstruction of their cause, Hilda's sister Alice wrote from her sickbed to one of her elderly aunts, "I rather long to go break some windows. I am not sure whose, but I think any Liberal offices would answer the purpose."[6]

Twentieth-century Britain would witness changes in almost every aspect of the day-to-day lives of women in society. The women's movement promoted the emergence of a new generation of females set to challenge established societal norms; Hilda Clark carved her niche very firmly among them. Like her mother and grandmother before her, she refused to be bound by the confines of the home or to accept the myth of male superiority. The advent of the First World War would see these social shifts developed further, as women were impelled into the workforce and into the previously male-dominated professional and political arenas, reshaping the identity of women and marking a turning point in relation to their presence in the public sphere. At the turn of the century, however, as an unmarried female doctor, Clark was still something of a novelty. It is later evident from Clark's wartime correspondence that she was very much aware that she did not conform to the expectations of "the fairer sex," particularly those concerning family life, and she did experience some internal conflict over her situation. For instance, amid the unrelenting demands of wartime medical work in France, into which Clark threw herself with characteristic fervor, she confessed to feeling guilty about "abandoning" her parents. While this kind of commitment was accepted—indeed, expected—from male counterparts, Clark wrestled with the feeling that she was being selfish and inconsiderate.[7] Nevertheless, her letters to her mother and sisters reveal their complicity. She does not hesitate to share her opinions as to the failings of certain men and on the general folly of "male rule"—sentiments that she knew would be reciprocated.

Clark completed her medical training at the Royal Free Hospital, London, in 1908. It was there that she met Edith Pye (1876–1965), the midwife who would become her lifelong friend and soulmate. Pye had just moved to London to take an appointment as superintendent of district nurses when she met Clark. It was a meeting that profoundly shaped her future destiny. Soon afterward, she became a member of the Society of Friends and, like Clark, dedicated her life to helping those in need.

After an exhausting period of final examinations, Clark went home to Street for a holiday, but while driving a pony and cart, she suffered a serious accident. A short while later, she suffered emotional trauma when her elder brother's wife, Clara, died giving birth to a son. In a letter to Edith Pye, Clark revealed how Clara's death would play a crucial part in her personal and professional future: "I feel as if my whole life might be better and more use to others from those two days, but what an awful price it is to pay.... And if I ever have to hold such a cold hand and feel such a death-stricken pulse, I think a little of the love I have for Clara will go out to the victim, whoever it may be." This sad event was, indeed, something of a cathartic experience. Clark affirmed, "one thing I understand now is that one's intellect alone won't pull one through, and that the greatest service it can perform is to open a window for that thing that we call the divine spirit."[8]

Clark fully embraced the Quaker philosophy toward helping others, which involved much more than simple charity. "How straightforward it would be," she wrote, "if 'sell all that thou hast and give to the poor' were the panacea—but the important thing was 'follow me' and that is so much more complicated."[9] Inspired throughout life by her strong religious beliefs and family role models, in true Quaker spirit, Clark sought to "do right" by others: "I think love is the only thing that carries one beyond the boundary of this life. No, I can't separate it from the joy of 'doing right,' they are two wonderful fundamental essentials of the soul's existence. We cannot grow unless we do right, we cannot grow unless we understand the meaning of love, and just as I have to learn to 'do right' by doing right the duties that this outward world brings, so do I learn to love."[10]

Though Clark was explicit about her need for love and friendship, she was equally certain that, for her, this did not include marriage. Here, she was perfectly at one with the flouting of social expectation. "I do not feel nearly so dependent on marriage to complete myself—though I know it would bring one a world of new experiences and teach one to understand things that perhaps one will not fully understand without, but I am quite sure that I do not depend upon it or require it."[11] Clark did not understand her relationship with Edith Pye in sexual terms but believed it to be "true spirit love,"[12] which Holton describes as "a selfless kind of loving, spiritually and morally elevating to the giver, especially as it developed a more general capacity for loving humankind."[13]

In 1909, recovered from her accident, Clark took up an appointment at the Birmingham Maternity Hospital. The following year, however, she resigned her post and set up a tuberculosis dispensary in her hometown of Street, combining her practice with exhaustive research into the disease and its treatment. Her success was followed by her appointment as tuberculosis officer in the county borough of Portsmouth, a post she held from 1911 to 1913.[14] At the age of thirty-three, Clark was ready for a new challenge. She established a general practice in London, with a view to providing medical care for the working class, but war upset her plans.

WAR IN EUROPE

When war broke out in Europe in the summer of 1914, it had been almost forty years since British women became eligible to study and practice medicine. Even so, their work was still largely confined to general practice and to the hospitals women had founded to treat women and children. Clark's practice was no exception. The demands of war would bring significant change. The first women determined to create medical facilities and to treat the war-wounded had an ulterior motive—to prove that women were as able and as courageous as men and thus deserved the right to vote.

The outbreak of war presented a serious moral dilemma for Quakers. Many felt the urge to perform their duty for their country, but they struggled to reconcile this impulse with their duty to God to promote peace and oppose war. Friends were by no means unanimous about their stance, and heated debate would continue throughout the conflict.[15] Irrespective of their views regarding enlistment, many Quakers devoted themselves to alleviating the suffering of the civilian victims of the war, as they had done in previous conflicts such as the Crimean War, the Second Boer War, and the Balkan Wars. The most extensive and most notable Friends' relief work, however, was that begun in 1870, during the Franco-Prussian War, and continued in France and Alsace-Lorraine. This set the precedent for the relief work that would be undertaken in 1914 in Europe and, consequently, would afford Quakers access to war zones from which the French authorities barred other voluntary organizations.

During the first weeks of war, as the German army began its invasion of Belgium, thousands of people fled their homes. Some escaped into France or Holland and others to Britain, at the invitation of the British government. In what was the largest relief operation ever seen in British history, the Society of Friends joined other aid organizations in giving voluntary assistance on a massive scale to supplement government aid.[16] The presence of the first refugees to reach Britain also provided tangible evidence of the plight of many thousands more homeless civilians trapped in the war zones in desperate need of help. Relief worker J. T. Elliott described the response of the British Friends: "As the tragedy unfolded in the first few weeks of the war, English Friends burned with the desire to do something—anything—to relieve anguish and misery which, it was only too clear, would exist on a scale so appalling as to constitute the supreme call of a lifetime."[17]

Hilda Clark wasted no time in converting that desire into action. She knew that the efforts of the existing medical services would be focused on the overwhelming needs of the military, to the detriment of civilians caught up in the war through no fault of their own. Together with prominent Quaker T. Edmund (Ted) Harvey, MP (1875–1955), she set about mustering the support of Friends and sympathizers disposed to go to France and Belgium to administer aid. At the September 1914 Meeting for Sufferings, she put forward the motion that Friends should undertake relief work for civilians in war-torn France and Belgium. The motion passed, and a small committee was appointed to get the work under way.[18]

The committee adopted the name used by the organization that had administered relief in the Franco-Prussian War—the Friends' War Victims' Relief Committee (FWVRC); volunteers would wear the same brassards bearing the famous black and red Quaker star. As the FWVRC's aim was to administer aid to noncombatant victims of the war, it was afforded the full and immediate backing of the Society of Friends.[19] William A. Albright (1853–1942) was appointed chairman of the committee and Hilda Clark and Ted Harvey acted as joint honorary secretaries. When Clark and Harvey left for France in November 1914, Edmund Wright Brooks (1834–1928) and Ruth Fry (1878–1962) took over as executive secretaries.

The organization expanded, eventually developing into an enterprise of vast dimensions, operating in at least nine European countries and enduring for more than nine years. FWVRC workers were by no means all members of the Society of Friends, and they came from every professional sphere, social class, and background.

Initially, the British War Office, believing that it had sufficient reserves of male medical personnel, refused to employ women doctors in war zones. However, the desperate French authorities welcomed into the Service de Santé anyone—including women—able to raise the necessary funds and staff.

On September 26, 1914, after the devastation caused by the first bloody Battle of the Marne, Edith Pye traveled to Paris to assess the need for medical and nursing assistance. The battle had been fought from September 5 to 12 and had resulted in an Allied victory against the German armies in the west. Victory, however, came at a cost, especially for civilians trapped in the war zone. A large section of eastern France lay in ruins, and an even larger part was occupied by the Germans. With most of their menfolk called to arms, the inhabitants of these areas were now mostly women, children, the elderly, and the infirm.

Pye was warmly received by Renée de Montmort, founder and honorary secretary of the Association des Infirmières Visiteuses de France. De Montmort showed great enthusiasm for Clark's plan to send a medical team into the devastated district. Furthermore, she thought that the spiritual help the Friends would bring to suffering civilians could be invaluable. War Office officials, including the government minister Leon Bourgeois, also pledged support.[20] While negotiations continued, Hilda Clark contacted banker Gaston Verdé-Delisle, who was visiting London to organize help for the French Red Cross. Impressed by Friends' previous history of relief work, Verdé-Delisle determined to do all he could to help send a mission to France. With his assistance, the enterprise was finally authorized by the French Ministry of War. The FWVRC functioned under the auspices of the Association des Infermières Visiteuses de France under the overall authority of the Santé Militaire.[21] The work fell into four main divisions: (1) general relief work, including provision of food, clothing, medical supplies, and furniture, (2) building of housing and repair of ruined homes, (3) agricultural work, and (4) medical work and nursing.[22]

On November 1, 1914, Renée de Montmort wrote to Hilda Clark from Paris, "Our negotiations have at last been wholly successful, as Mr. Harvey will tell you. . . . The expedition will very probably be able to begin active work in the Marne district by Monday next."[23] The first team set out for France on November 5 under the leadership of Hilda Clark and Ted

Harvey. The group included two doctors and a medical student, two pharmacists, a dozen or so trained nurses (including midwives and district nurses), an experienced female relief worker, and a sanitary inspector, along with other men prepared to work as drivers, orderlies, and general laborers.[24] Far from launching themselves into their anticipated mission when they arrived in Paris, the volunteers met with an avalanche of frustrating bureaucratic obstacles. While Clark and Harvey engaged in a seemingly endless round of consultations and permit seeking, the rest of the group familiarized themselves with their surroundings and practiced their French.

Finally, after protracted negotiations with the French military authorities, the Friends obtained the necessary permits to proceed. Clark wrote to her family that the lengthy discussions had been in no small part due to Harvey's "excessive politeness." She was even less impressed by the attitude of General Azibert, commanding DES (directorate of emergency services) of the Fifth Army, who assigned the Quaker mission to Marne. The general expressed some annoyance at the number of nurses in the group; in his opinion, the war zone was no place for women. "He was not such a good type as the general at Châlons," Clark wrote her sister Alice, "and was inclined to think everything was being done and that there was no work for women, etc. Of course, I shall fight that tooth and nail. . . . I shall take jolly good care that I get everywhere the men do."[25]

For the FWVRC, providing aid in the areas devastated by war became a complex and difficult undertaking, as the destruction of towns and villages was irregular: a few were left almost intact, while others were completely razed. There had also been much pillaging and destruction of agricultural tools, small livestock, and crops, and most returning refugees were without any means of livelihood. Harvey led a team of sixteen volunteers in an extensive scheme of general relief, building, and agricultural work and began initiatives such as sewing workshops for women and girls and schooling for children.[26]

Clark directed the provision of medical care in the region, with the town of Châlons as the center of operations. Fortunately, little of the feared outbreak of disease materialized, and apart from numerous cases of scarlet fever and measles, the general health of the people seemed good. "Good climate and sturdy people!" noted Clark.[27] Nevertheless, as most civilian doctors had been mobilized and as civilian hospitals had been requisitioned for military medical needs, Friends turned to providing valuable and welcome medical assistance throughout the region. Clark created a number of vital medical facilities, including hospitals and convalescent homes, country medical practices, and extensive district nursing in the more remote villages. But the FWVRC's first and most enduring medical venture was the maternity hospital at Châlons-sur-Marne. The hospital opened its doors on December 14, 1914. It would be handed over to the French as a permanent memorial of the mission of the Society of Friends in 1922.

LA MATERNITÉ ANGLAISE, CHÂLONS-SUR-MARNE

Châlons-sur-Marne (today Châlons-en-Champagne) is some fifty kilometers southeast of the city of Rheims, which was being mercilessly bombarded by the Germans. The town had been occupied by the Germans for only nine days, during which time it suffered very little. But it lay in the center of the Marne district, now crammed with thousands of refugees from the surrounding villages and from the Meuse and Ardennes further north. About fifteen miles from the front, the town was also overflowing with military personnel.

Situated in an agricultural region flanking the River Marne, the pleasant town boasted several emblematic buildings, including Saint Etienne Cathedral, the Hôtel de Ville, the beautiful Notre Dame church, and the Hôtel Dieu (the hospital). Hidden from view behind the picturesque main streets were numerous hovels. Condemned before the war as unfit for human habitation, these buildings were now teeming with refugees, despite unscrupulous landlords demanding exorbitant rents.[28] Some found shelter in the enormous barracks on the outskirts of the town or in the vast champagne cellars tunneled into the hillside; others sought refuge in barns and sheds, crowded together in unsanitary conditions. The refugees were mostly women and children and were practically all destitute. Thus the immediate relief brought by the FWVRC in the form of food, clothes, and blankets was a vital comfort.

Dr. Hilda Clark, Dr. Dyson Holdsworth, and the party of FWVRC nurses were warmly welcomed when they arrived in Châlons in November 1914. The prefect of the department, Monsieur Chaprón, was seeking accommodation and care for some two hundred maternity cases. Many were living in dreadful conditions and could not easily be reached by French philanthropic agencies. The FWVRC had not planned to undertake maternity work in France, but the need was desperate—most midwives had fled and almost all eligible doctors had been mobilized. Chaprón suggested that Friends open a maternity hospital, and he offered a wing of the town's Asile des Vieillards, the home of "the aged, the imbecile and the epileptics." While Friends were to provide the staff, French authorities would be responsible for the necessary alterations to the building, the provision of food and fuel, and maintenance costs.[29]

The imposing redbrick Asile des Vieillards lay on the northern edge of the town. Edith Pye described her first impressions of the building: "Built in separate blocks, of an ugliness almost unbelievable, like matchboxes set up on edge, within, the wards were light and lofty, ventilation good and adaptation seemed possible. The one offered to us had been the epileptic block, and so the ten-feet windows were caged in with wire netting, but they opened inward, and only to the discontented occasionally suggested a prison."[30] While Clark set up the maternity hospital, it was Edith Pye who ran it. She not only administered the hospital but also trained volunteers and fulfilled her role as midwife. It was she, not Clark, who would later be recognized for her work by the French.

Staff had been depleted by the needs of war, and the state of the wards was well below acceptable standards of the day. Pye described the toilet facilities as "sanitary conveniences of a hair-raising type."[31] After an initial inspection, Clark reported with characteristic candor that conditions were worse than those in the "oldest and dirtiest English Workhouses."[32] Furthermore, the lack of cellars meant that the building could offer no shelter in the event of a bombing raid, making it a less than ideal choice as a hospital. But choice played little part in the matter: these were difficult times and no more appropriate premises were available.[33]

After most of the epileptic women had been housed elsewhere, the FWVRC volunteers set about preparing the hospital. For two solid weeks, observed by the assortment of bewildered inmates who remained in the building, the whole team, including doctors and nurses, scrubbed and scoured from dawn until dusk.

The prefect commissioned a local architect, Monsieur Dupont, to partition the wards to the Friends' requirements, and after some repainting and a final disinfection, the maternity hospital was finally ready. "It was a trying ordeal," declared Edith Pye, "but it ended at last and the building, bare but clean, was ready for the new life that soon surged into it." Hot water had to be heated on stoves or in a large boiler, and lighting was provided by paraffin lamps and a few petrol-burning lamps that, Pye noted, produced less light than a candle. "When in 1917 the American Red Cross paid for an installation of electric light," she added, "we thought we were in paradise."[34] The domestic staff were provided by Monsieur Becq from the least incapable mentally ill female patients. They were very eager to please but presented their own peculiar complications, as Clark wrote to her sister Esther: "The third ward maid is a dipsomaniac ... and more dangerous, really, than any zeppelin."[35]

The first ward at the Maternité Departmentale (or Maternité Anglaise, as it became known) was opened on December 6, 1914, and its first baby was brought into the world just a few days later, on December 9. Marie Louise, otherwise referred to as *la petite Anglaise*, was the ninth child of a refugee mother from Ardennes. With no safe place to leave the rest of her children, the mother had brought them with her to the hospital. There was great need for the provision of care for such children, and a crèche and two dormitories were provided for them on the ground floor.

A second ward was ready to receive patients on January 1, 1915. After a couple of weeks, there were continually more patients than beds. In the first month alone, fifteen babies were delivered in the hospital. After six months in operation, fifty-two births had been recorded.

A motor vehicle was essential for bringing patients to the hospital and transporting them home again, and it was a source of great joy when one was finally obtained. At a time when most people had never traveled in a car, Clark happily assumed the role of driver and mechanic. As the Friends' work increased, she rarely drove fewer than forty miles a day between the different centers and in visiting the various authorities with whom she had constantly to liaise on behalf of the FWVRC.

The local authorities were extremely appreciative of the Friends' work, and the prefect was a frequent visitor to the hospital. He believed that the maternity services available in country districts were inadequate even in times of peace; he was anxious for the new maternity facility to become a permanent institution. Clark expressed a certain satisfaction with what had been achieved: "I am reposing in great bliss as the worst anxiety of failures and muddles are over and we have succeeded both in being of enough use ourselves to justify coming out, and all the expenditure, and in opening up the way to help the awful suffering which we knew all along was here. We have got the confidence of both civil and military authorities and if in the next few weeks we can make this good, I think the limits to our work will be those of the capacities of ourselves and the volunteers who are waiting."[36]

Despite the satisfying aspects of her work in France, Clark struggled with negative emotions, as she revealed in a letter to her sister Alice: "It is a queer and varied life we lead and my natural tendency to moody is horribly exaggerated by the rapidly changing outlook—from depths of depression to quite irrepressible excitement."[37] Toward the end of January, her worst anxieties apparently abated, she announced, "this Maternité is a very satisfactory piece of work."[38] Once the maternity hospital was running properly, Clark turned her attention to other plans, as Edith Pye explained:

> The work of the Châlons Maternité, though it was of immense importance to the French officials with whom we had to deal, was only a small cog in an immense wheel of which Hilda Clark was the hub. It is also true that it proved to be the enduring memorial of the Friends' work in the Marne, but it was only one of the growing points of Hilda Clark's concern. She had a clear vision of what Friends and those who thought as they did could offer to a country at war. Her vision and organizing power outreached the ideas of other workers—she saw what needed to be done and held people to it. Not only did our own workers accept her ideas, but she was able to convince and carry with her French officials at every level. Perhaps it was her simplicity and her conviction that awoke an echo in those she sought to convince—certain it is that she was seldom refused.[39]

Under Clark's instructions, the relief team in Sermaize-les-Bains built a small cottage hospital and then created a convalescent home for children in a chateau at Bettancourt-la-Longue. Country medical practices were established in the more remote towns and villages, and extensive district nursing was begun. This service, an unknown luxury in France at that time, was particularly appreciated. The nurses' services were provided free of charge, and they distributed sheets and bedding along with medicines among their needy patients. Next, Clark secured an Alpine hotel in Samoëns in the Haute-Savoie, which she had converted into a rest and convalescent home for refugees.

Clark personally oversaw the creation and maintenance of each branch of the work and traveled constantly between the different centers and the Paris headquarters, where she also directed medical assistance among some of the hundred thousand refugees. She was particularly concerned with the pretubercular cases she had detected among people crammed into the capital's overcrowded slums, some of whom were sent to Samoëns. She wrote to her mother of the progress being made, "I have got Sermaize hospital very full now—it is a most invaluable place, and it is a wonderful pleasure to be able to take these delicate children straight out of their wretched lodgings to the country they love so dearly.... I hope very much we shall be able to extend the Samoëns place to take boys. Bettancourt also is very full." However, expansion of the FWVRC's activities brought ever-increasing administrative work and endless negotiations with authorities, which began to take their toll on Clark, who complained, "I spend a weary time talking and trying to be nice to people. I never see anything of the refugees themselves."[40]

The issue of new volunteers (or lack thereof) was another cause for dismay and led to troubled relations between Clark and the London committee. In order to be allowed into a war zone, each worker needed, in addition to a passport, a permit from the French Red Cross and a *carnet d'étranger*.[41] The latter could only be obtained from the already overstretched military authorities. This often meant long delays. The bureaucracy was frustrating not only for the workers in France but also for those at London headquarters, where the overworked and overextended Ruth Fry was at the helm. Clark apparently failed to comprehend this fully, or she found it difficult to accept, and relations with Fry became strained. "Things have got so wrong between us and the London Committee," Clark wrote to her cousin Lily Sturge in April, "that if I could be sure of getting out again I should try to get back to see them as soon as the other doctors come."[42] On occasion, Clark's despair led her to bypass protocol and to contact volunteers directly, much to the consternation of the committee; this contravened official procedure and the committee worried that it might jeopardize the FWVRC's future operations. Fry reminded Clark of this, saying, "in our efforts to get the people you need, in spite of your very irregular mode of proceeding, we have got into difficulties."[43]

Katherine Storr suggests that another reason for the tense relationship between Clark and Fry may have concerned the issue of women's suffrage. Edith Pye and Hilda Clark were both members of the militant Women's Social and Political Union, a group of which Fry may have disapproved.[44] Fry appears to have had no connection with suffragist movements, though, so it is more likely that the excessive red tape and the selection process for volunteers were the chief concerns of committee members. It was not an easy task to find candidates for work in France who satisfied the precise prerequisites Clark stipulated. In general, candidates were required to be competent and amiable, physically fit, and capable of living in basic conditions. "We want someone with a good deal of nursing and sanitary experience if possible," Clark explained, "with fluent French and a bicycle. Really, someone with a grip of things and an interest in illness and children and smells and an idea of teaching and sympathy and can do the work quite well without regular hospital training, provided she understands what she ought to get help for and does not think she knows everything!"[45]

Perhaps unsurprisingly, several of the volunteers the committee sent fell short of one or more of Clark's exacting credentials. She told the committee that one volunteer simply "will not do ... she does not cycle, and her French is poor"; another "is of little use," and another "needs too much looking after herself." Clark also made no secret of her opinion of Ted Harvey's skills as mission leader. "I think it's wonderful what good work the party have done," she commented to her mother, "considering what a queer team they are and how queerly they've been led."[46] Later, as the number of volunteers increased, she complained, "Ted Harvey is not capable of bossing one party, let alone several, and yet he will not give anyone else a chance."[47]

In the midst of tremendous activity, Clark wrote to her parents on the occasion of their golden wedding anniversary to acknowledge the importance of their love and support in her own life: "I don't know what one is supposed to write about to one's parents for their golden wedding. But I have it very much in my mind to try to tell you how constantly and deeply grateful I am to you for the possibility of independent development that you have given me.... The love of the child for its parents, which may be called a simple law of nature, has grown into a much greater force which helps me in everything I try to do."[48]

The Châlons maternity hospital continued to flourish, and mothers and babies appeared in a ceaseless and ever-increasing stream. In the three years the hospital remained under the control of the FWVRC, 981 babies were delivered. There was only one maternal death over that period, and that was in the case of a woman requiring caesarean section, who had had a prolonged labor before she entered the hospital. The infant mortality rate was less than 5 percent—better than many prestigious clinics of the day.[49] In 1917, when the United States entered the war, Dr. Morris Slemons, professor of obstetrics at Yale University, inspected the hospital and declared it to be "excellent." "The quality of the work already done by this institution," his report concluded, "the resulting confidence in which it is held by the civil authorities and the devotion of all the patients who have been treated there, together indicate that the institution will become a permanent one. It will also serve as a model for similar institutions which will probably be needed in other localities."[50]

Medical provision, including the Maternité Anglaise, effectively became a joint Anglo-American enterprise, with American money and personnel proving vital to the continued work of the FWVRC. With typical frankness, Clark made clear her views. She thought it was a good idea to welcome American Friends, but not too many of them. She wrote to her mother, "Those who have already joined us seem nice people but not at all decided in their views, and I don't know how many of those waiting in America will really wish to join us when they realise that we expect the men who join us to agree with us."[51] In fact, after initial challenges, the American and British workers united wholeheartedly in providing extensive relief for the civilian victims of the war. Clark's own activity became even more frenetic, as she revealed to her cousin Lily Sturge:

> I went to Paris last Saturday to meet Dr. Kerr and to make arrangements for the new workers coming out. On Monday I went back to see to things at Châlons and Sermaize.... I am now on my way back to Paris.... I have to see the representative of the Rockefeller Foundation, Professor Sabine, about the tuberculosis question, and M. Verde Delisle ... and Friday afternoon I have to see patients for Samoëns. If Dr. Macphail has not come by then I shall have to go to Samoëns myself until she does. Otherwise I shall come back to Châlons and Sermaize on Saturday and go to Troyes on Sunday.[52]

In the summer of 1918, she finally succumbed to the strain and exhaustion, and was obliged to return home to rest.

That winter, as the bombing raids became more intense, the Maternité Anglaise finally had to be evacuated to Méry-sur-Seine, some seventy kilometers south of Châlons. There it remained until early the following year, when it was returned to Châlons, first to the *aisle* and then, eventually, to its own purpose-built facility, which became known as the Maison Maternelle de la Marne, a permanent legacy of the Friends to the people of Châlons.[53] Edith Pye was awarded the Cross of the Legion of Honor by the French government, in recognition for the work she and the Friends had done for the French people. It was really Hilda Clark who should have received this honor, but Clark had left France before the war had ended and was already planning the next stage of her humanitarian work, while recovering at home in England.[54]

After recovering from illness and exhaustion, Clark worked closely with sisters Eglantyne Jebb and Dorothy Buxton to establish the Save the Children Committee[55] before departing for Austria, where postwar conditions were causing tremendous suffering. Clark organized infant feeding programs and set in place schemes to redevelop the country's agriculture. In a novel scheme to provide much-needed milk, she had dairy cows shipped in from other European countries. During this time, Clark published several scientific articles based on her studies on infant development, sickness, and mortality in the country.

In her role as foreign relations secretary for the Women's International League for Peace and Freedom and as the League of Nations' Women's Committee observer, Clark went on to Poland, Greece, Serbia, Bulgaria, Turkey, and the Middle East. During the Spanish Civil War (1936–39) she undertook relief work for Spanish refugees, and during the Second World War she again served the French.

Clark continued to support the League of Nations in its efforts to promote world peace. She was also honorary secretary of the Women's Peace Crusade and worked for the International Commission for the Assistance of Child Refugees and the Friends Service Council. She continued her involvement with social work and with the tuberculosis dispensary until she became too debilitated by Parkinson's disease. In 1952, she and Pye moved to Street, Somerset, where she died on February 24, 1955.

After Clark's death, Edith Pye published *War and Its Aftermath*, an edited collection of Clark's letters. The letters were donated to Friends House Library in London, where today readers can still see Pye's editorial marks.[56] The eye is drawn, inevitably, to the content that Pye chose to exclude from the record—in particular, to the words of endearment exchanged by the two women. Clark's letter to Pye on January 30, 1910, for instance, in which she talks of "the joy of doing right," begins, "Darling, I do long for thee so, precious sweetheart. My whole being craves to find thee in my arms."[57] While such declarations demonstrate the strength of the bond between the two women, it is important to view them within the wider context of the time. During the war and interwar periods, the pacifist and feminist networks to which the two women belonged were crucial to the organization of extensive humanitarian work. Relationships between women active in these organizations often became what we might describe today as partnerships.[58] It is difficult to determine to what extent the forming of such relationships was simply a rejection of the limitations that marriage might impose on intelligent and industrious women. As Sara Delamont argues, "celibacy was often a form of revolt against the traditional female sphere."[59] In the particular case of Clark and Pye, it is clear from their correspondence that Clark understood their love as something different from both sexual love and maternal love; she refers to it as "spirit love," a kind of selfless comradeship "spiritually and morally elevating to the giver, especially as it developed a more general capacity for loving humankind."[60]

CONCLUSION

In evaluating Clark's humanitarian activities during the First World War, it is important to consider her identity as a woman. On the one hand, her indefatigable activism fits that traditionally associated with Quaker women, beginning with the rousing of compassion and the mobilizing of support for civilian victims of the war. This pattern continued in her work with civilians (mostly women and children) in France and, later, on a wider international scale. On the other hand, Clark's activism openly broke with the established gender model, helping to debunk the mythical representation of women in the history of humanitarian relief as "loving angels or compassionate mothers."[61] Clark consciously invaded spaces traditionally reserved for men, not only with respect to the activities involved (doctor, ambulance driver, negotiator) but in the audacity and determination with which these enterprises were carried out. Clark, as a Quaker woman, was part of an incipient gendered solidarity being forged across national and political boundaries.

Clark's female family role models undoubtedly played a critical part in shaping her independent spirit and humanitarian principles. This powerful network of strong and pioneering female support, together with her religious faith, drove Hilda Clark to dedicate her life to political, social, and civic causes in Britain, Europe, and the rest of the world. Her crossing of the domestic threshold was absolute. Gone were the restrictions of the domestic and motherly home-based activism that Anna Vaughan Kett attributes to Hilda's grandmother, Eleanor Clark. Rather than signal a break with tradition, Hilda Clark's involvement in the First World War reflects an inexorable evolution in the place of the Quaker woman in twentieth-century society. The struggle for professional acceptance went hand in hand with the campaign for the vote, and now there was no stopping either cause. Examining such narratives of leadership in humanitarian activism helps us appreciate the part played by women like Hilda Clark in the forging of modern political culture.[62]

NOTES

1. Edith Pye, ed., *War and Its Aftermath: Letters from Hilda Clark, M.B., B.S., from France, Austria, and the Near East, 1914–1924* (London: Clare, Son and Co., 1956), 5. An earlier version of portions of this chapter appeared in my article "The Friends' Ambulance Unit in the First World War," *Religions* 9, no. 5 (2018), https://doi.org/10.3390/rel9050165.

2. It was Hilda's paternal grandfather, James Clark, who along with his brother, Cyrus Clark, founded the famous C. & J. Clark shoe-manufacturing company.

3. Quoted in Sandra Stanley Holton, *Quaker Women: Personal Life, Memory, and Radicalism in the Lives of Women Friends, 1780–1930* (London: Routledge, 2007), 151.

4. Ibid., 4, 5.

5. Sandra Stanley Holton, *Suffrage Days: Stories from the Women's Suffrage Movement* (London: Routledge, 1996), 7, 15.

6. Quoted in Lisa McQuillan, "World War 1 Relief and After: Hilda Clark," *Quaker Connections* 64 (March 2015): 12.

7. Hilda Clark to her parents, July 20, 1916, in Pye, *War and Its Aftermath*, 34.

8. Hilda Clark to Edith Pye, August 1908, ibid., 6.

9. Hilda Clark to Edith Pye, December 1909, ibid., 8.

10. Hilda Clark to Edith Pye, January 1910, ibid., 8.

11. Ibid., 9.

12. H. Clark to E. Pye, July 29, 1908, box 1, folder 1908, Hilda Clark Papers (HCP), Temp MSS 301, LSF.

13. Holton, *Suffrage Days*, 203.

14. Clark published her research on the disease and its treatment in Hilda Clark, *Dispensary Treatment of Pulmonary Tuberculosis* (London: Baillière, Tindall and Cox, 1915). Hilda's TB patients included her sister Alice and, later, Edith Pye.

15. See Linda Palfreeman, *Friends in Flanders: Humanitarian Aid Administered by the Friends' Ambulance Unit During the First World War* (Brighton: Sussex Academic Press, 1917); and David Rubinstein, *A Quaker Dilemma: The Rowntree Family and the Great War, 1914–1918* (York, UK: Quacks Books, 2015), 4.

16. See Peter Grant, *Philanthropy and Voluntary Action in the First World War: Mobilizing Charity* (New York: Routledge, 2014); and Sian Roberts, *Birmingham: Remembering 1914–18* (Stroud: History Press, 2014).

17. Quoted in Charles Evans, "American Friends' Service Committee, First Annual Report of Charles Evans, Chief of Friends' Unit in France," American Red Cross, 1917, 1–2, YM/MfS/FEWVRC/MISSIONS/2/6/5/2, LSF.

18. McQuillan, "World War 1 Relief and After," 11.
19. The Friends' Ambulance Unit was established with the intention of aiding fallen soldiers, thus causing discord between the unit and the Society of Friends, from which it would not receive official backing.
20. A. Ruth Fry, *A Quaker Adventure: The Story of Nine Years' Relief and Reconstruction* (New York: Frank-Maurice, 1927), 5, https://babel.hathitrust.org/cgi/pt?id=mdp.39015014523776&view=1up&seq=10.
21. The Friends attempted to maintain independence from the military, but in practice this was impossible for any organization functioning in the war zone.
22. Fry, *Quaker Adventure*, 2.
23. Quoted in a supplement to *the Friend*, November 6, 1914.
24. Pye, *War and Its Aftermath*, 16.
25. Hilda Clark to Alice Clark, November 19, 1914, HCP, LSF.
26. Pye, *War and Its Aftermath*, 21–22.
27. Hilda Clark, "Society of Friends' War Victims' Relief Committee Medical Report for Non-Combatants in the Departments of the Marne and the Meuse, During the Months December 1914–April 1915," HCP, LSF.
28. Pye, *War and Its Aftermath*, 18.
29. Becq, Archive Châlons, March 23, 1919, Archives Departamentales de la Marne, CEC H dépôt 1321, Maternité "anglaise" departamentale.
30. Pye, *War and Its Aftermath*, 18–19.
31. Ibid.
32. Quoted in Edith Pye, "Report on the Work Undertaken by the War Victims' Relief Committee of the Society of Friends at Châlons-sur-Marne for the Three Months, December 1914–February 1915 Inclusive," YM/MfS/FEWVRC/MISSIONS, LSF.
33. For further details on the establishment and functioning of the Friends' maternity home in Châlons, see Linda Palfreeman, "The *Maternité Anglaise*: A Lasting Legacy of the Friends' War Victims' Relief Committee to the People of France During the First World War (1914–1918)," *Religions* 12, no. 4 (2021): 265–84, https://doi.org/10.3390/rel12040265.
34. Pye, *War and Its Aftermath*, 19.
35. Hilda Clark to Edith Pye, March 10, 1916, HCP, LSF.
36. Hilda Clark to unknown relative, December 1914, in Pye, *War and Its Aftermath*, 23.
37. Hilda Clark to Alice Clark from Paris, November 19, 1914, HCP, LSF.
38. Hilda Clark to unnamed cousin (most probably Lily Sturge), January 22, 1915, HCP, LSF.
39. Pye, *War and Its Aftermath*, 16.
40. Hilda Clark to her mother, May 17, 1916, HCP, LSF.
41. Fry, *Quaker Adventure*, xxii–xxiii.
42. Hilda Clark to Lily Sturge, April 26, 1915, HCP, LSF.
43. Ruth Fry to Hilda Clark, July 29, 1915, HCP, LSF.
44. Katherine Storr, *Excluded from the Record: Women, Refugees, and Relief, 1914–1929* (Bern: Peter Lang, 2010), 156.
45. Hilda Clark to Alice Clark, June 17, 1915, HCP, LSF.
46. Hilda Clark to her mother, January 1915, HCP, LSF.
47. Hilda Clark to her mother, August 1915, HCP, LSF.
48. Hilda Clark to her mother, July 19, 1916, HCP, LSF.
49. "Report on the Medical Work Undertaken by the FWVRC Expedition in France, November 1914 to September 1916," YM/MfS/FEWVRC/MISSIONS, LSF.

50. J. Morris Slemons, "The Maternity Hospital at Châlons, Conducted by the Society of Friends," September 28, 1917, 1, HCP, LSF.

51. Hilda Clark to her mother, July 24, 1917, HCP, LSF.

52. Hilda Clark to Lily Sturge, September 20, 1917, HCP, LSF.

53. The buildings still stand at 47 rue Général Charles de Gaulle in Châlons, with the Quaker star clearly visible in the stonework above the entrance.

54. Pye, *War and Its Aftermath*, 37.

55. Hilda Clark, "Notes on Principles of Relief Work," *Bulletin of the Save the Children Fund: Central Union (Union Internationale de Secours aux Enfants)* 1, no. 17 (June 30, 1920).

56. Some of Clark's correspondence is featured in the Religious Society of Friends' *White Feather Diaries*, a social media project marking the centenary of the First World War, at https://quakerstrongrooms.org/2014/07/31/whitefeatherdiaries/.

57. Hilda Clark to Edith Pye, January 30, 1910, in Pye, *War and Its Aftermath*, 8–9.

58. Rose Holmes, "A Moral Business: British Quaker Work with Refugees from Fascism, 1933–39" (PhD diss., University of Sussex, 2013), http://sro.sussex.ac.uk/54158/1/Holmes%2C_Rose.pdf.

59. Sara Delamont, "The Domestic Ideology and Women's Education," in *The Nineteenth-Century Woman: Her Cultural and Physical World*, edited by Sara Delamont and Lorna Duffin (London: Croom Helm, 1978), 176.

60. Holton, *Suffrage Days*, 203. Hilda Clark and Edith Pye are buried under the same headstone in the Friends' Meeting House in Street, Somerset, after a lifetime of shared devotion to humanitarian causes.

61. Dolores Martín-Moruno, "Tejiendo redes de cuidado: La compasión como conocimiento de las mujeres humanitarias en la guerra (1853–1945)," in *Al servicio de la salud humana: La historia de la medicina ante los retos del siglo XXI*, edited by Alfons Zarzoso and Jon Arrizabalaga (Ciudad Real: QL Printers, 2017), 21 (my translation).

62. Amanda Green, "Humanitarianism in Nineteenth-Century Context: Religious, Gendered, National," *Historical Journal* 57, no. 4 (2014): 1157–75.

Afterword

EMMA LAPSANSKY-WERNER

Lacking a consistent, enduring, and authoritative doctrine and leadership, the Religious Society of Friends has simultaneously celebrated its theological nimbleness (lauded as "continuing revelation") and lamented its theological instability (bemoaned as "schisms" or "separations"). In no aspects of their community life have Quakers been more vexed by this conundrum than in the issue of workable relationships with those whom the wider society has set on its economic and power margins: racial, cultural, economic, and gender "outsiders."

In this provocative exploration of women and the "changing landscape" of the nineteenth century, readers are summoned to contextualize Quakers in the framework of several interrelated modernization phenomena—e.g., liquid capital, relatively efficient transatlantic communication and travel, international social reform movements, and increasingly wide circulation of printed materials, with an expanding literacy to partake of them. The result is the foundation of a broad dynamic and provocative research terrain, or "landscape," that illuminates and adds nuance to both "Quaker studies" and "women's studies." At the same time, the terrain explored here will stimulate future scholars to penetrate more deeply into the nooks and crannies of nineteenth-century minds and behaviors—not just of Quakers, or of Quaker women and their circumstances, but of the outward manifestation of the inner lives of other overlooked religious (and nonreligious) "outsiders."

One can enter this new terrain through many gateways. Where did these women learn to read and write? At the network of Quaker schools that began to spring up in the British and North American "landscape"? In their Quaker families, or in their Quaker meetings? Is there any discernible pattern—education? family "role models"? geographic, economic, or social networks?—among the "audacious" women who challenged the norms of their communities? To what degree was Lucretia Mott "radicalized" by her education in the abolitionist cauldron of northern New York's Nine Partners School? To what degree did Mott arrive at Nine Partners, in 1806, at age thirteen, already primed to hear and absorb Elias Hicks's antislavery ministry? Were Mott and others inspired by the example and legend of the fabled "recorded minister" Hannah Barnard, who had been encouraged by her husband, and by Nine Partners Meeting, to follow her calling, to leave her children and to embark on extended ministry travel through England and Ireland? What can we learn from Mott's poignant eulogy of Barnard: "I have always regretted," Mott wrote in one of her last letters, "that so little has been published of the sad experience of that remarkable woman, Hannah Barnard."[1]

What, if anything, can we infer from the median age at which nineteenth-century Quaker women agitators hit their leadership stride? Many outspoken seventeenth-century Quaker women embraced leadership when they were barely out of their teens. But Hannah Barnard, Lucretia Mott, Susan B. Anthony, Elizabeth Pease, Eleanor Stephens Clark, Anne Knight, and Hilda Clark do not seem to have blossomed much earlier than middle age. Might this phenomenon be related to expanded educational possibilities for women such as Hilda Clark and Sarah Hoare? Did the nineteenth century usher in broader knowledge and acceptance of contraception that allowed women more options? The essays gathered here invite a cluster of new questions about intersections in women's family life, biology, education, life expectancy, self-identity, career possibilities—and the pursuit of suffrage. When Elizabeth Robson went traveling—leaving babies at home—how was day-to-day life managed in the Robson household? What were the practical systems by which comrades from meeting fed, clothed, and delivered nurture and medical care to what were essentially orphans? What were the contours of Elizabeth Sykes Taylor's life like when her journal went quiet for more than a decade during her marriage to George Taylor?

And the troupe of women who cast large shadows across the Hicksite-Orthodox landscape entice scholars to explore—even more than Allen and Allen do here—some relationships and interconnections between Quaker women and the women of other denominations (e.g., the simultaneous convulsions among Methodists in both England and America). Might future researchers expand what Allen and Allen describe here as "radicalism within boundaries," and thus explore how women reconfigured their roles in both religious and nonreligious spheres?[2]

As future scholars pursue these questions, it will be interesting to see broader and deeper explorations of some of the underlying themes exposed in the essays presented here—for example, the continuing tension between upper-class norms and Quaker "simplicity," and how to navigate the narrow corridor of "well-dressed but unobtrusive." And then there is Quakers' long-standing ambivalence about "authority": scripture versus Inward Light; meeting community versus individual; conscience versus statutes; patriarchs' control versus wives, households, and finances.[3]

An exciting and inspiring aspect of this collection of essays—ostensibly "about women"—is its stunning breadth of evidence, footnotes, and references, reflecting a diversity not only of interdisciplinary scholarship but also of the multiplicity of Quaker experiences across time, continent, region, gender, subdivision of Quaker theology and culture, and sources (material culture and economic records, local and regional organizational records, periodicals, public records, diaries, journals, memoirs, poetry, images, and intimate correspondence). Future scholars are invited—and challenged—to bring additional offerings to this sumptuous intellectual feast.

NOTES

1. Anna Davis Hallowell, ed., *James and Lucretia Mott: Life and Letters* (Boston: Houghton Mifflin, 1884), 478, quoted in David Maxey, "New Light on Hannah Barnard, a Quaker 'Heretic,'" *Quaker History* 78, no. 2 (1981): 61.

2. See, for example, Carl J. Guarneri, "Reconstructing the Antebellum Communitarian Movement: Oneida and Fourierism," *Journal of the Early Republic* 16, no. 3 (1996): 463–88.

3. Martha Blauvelt, *The Work of the Heart: Young Women and Emotion, 1780–1830* (Charlottesville: University of Virginia Press, 2007).

SELECTED BIBLIOGRAPHY

Allen, Kerri. "Representation and Self-Representation: Hannah Whitall Smith as Family Woman and Religious Guide." *Women's History Review* 7, no. 2 (1998): 227–39.

Allen, Kerri, and Alison Mackinnon. "'Allowed and Expected to Be Educated and Intelligent': The Education of Quaker Girls in Nineteenth-Century England." *History of Education* 27, no. 4 (1998): 391–402.

Angell, Stephen W. "The Early Period." In *Black Fire: African American Quakers on Spirituality and Human Rights*, edited by Harold D. Weaver Jr., Paul Kriese, and Stephen W. Angell, 1–43. Philadelphia: Quaker Press of FGC, 2011.

Angell, Stephen W., and Pink Dandelion, eds. *The Cambridge Companion to Quakerism*. Cambridge: Cambridge University Press, 2018.

———, eds. *The Oxford Handbook of Quaker Studies*. Oxford: Oxford University Press, 2013.

Bacon, Margaret Hope. *Abby Hopper Gibbons: Prison Reformer and Social Activist*. Albany: SUNY Press, 2000.

———. *Mothers of Feminism: The Story of Quaker Women in America*. San Francisco: Harper and Row, 1986.

———. "New Light on Sarah Mapps Douglass and Her Reconciliation with Friends." *Quaker History* 90, no. 1 (2001): 28–49.

———. *Sarah Mapps Douglass, Faithful Attender of Quaker Meeting: View from the Back Bench*. Philadelphia: Quaker Press of FGC, 2003.

———. *Valiant Friend: The Life of Lucretia Mott*. New York: Walker and Co., 1980.

Barbour, Hugh, Thomas Bassett, Christopher Densmore, H. Larry Ingle, and Alson D. Van Wagner. "The Orthodox-Hicksite Separation." In *Quaker Crosscurrents: Three Hundred Years of Friends in the New York Yearly Meetings*, edited by Hugh Barbour, Christopher Densmore, Elizabeth H. Moger, Nancy C. Sorel, Alson D. Van Wagner, and Arthur J. Worrall, 100–130. Syracuse: Syracuse University Press, 1995.

Barbour, Hugh, Christopher Densmore, Elizabeth H. Moger, Nancy C. Sorel, Alson D. Van Wagner, and Arthur J. Worrall, eds. *Quaker*

Crosscurrents: Three Hundred Years of Friends in the New York Yearly Meetings. Syracuse: Syracuse University Press, 1995.

Barbour, Hugh, and J. William Frost. The Quakers. Westport, CT: Greenwood Press, 1988.

Benjamin, Philip S. The Philadelphia Quakers in the Industrial Age, 1865–1920. Philadelphia: Temple University Press, 1976.

Bouldin, Elizabeth. "'The Days of Thy Youth': Eighteenth-Century Quaker Women and the Socialization of Children." In New Critical Studies on Early Quaker Women, 1650–1800, edited by Michele Lise Tarter and Catie Gill, 202–20. Oxford: Oxford University Press, 2018.

Bressey, Caroline. Empire, Race, and the Politics of Anti-Caste. London: Bloomsbury, 2013.

Bronner, Edwin B. "The Other Branch": London Yearly Meeting and the Hicksites, 1827–1912. London: Friends Historical Society, 1975.

Cadbury, Henry J. "Negro Membership in the Society of Friends." Journal of Negro History 21, no. 2 (1936): 151–213.

Campbell, Debra. "Hannah Whitall Smith (1832–1911): Theology of the Mother-Hearted God." Signs: Journal of Women in Culture and Society 15, no. 1 (1989): 79–101.

Cantor, Geoffrey N. Quakers, Jews, and Science: Religious Responses to Modernity and the Sciences in Britain, 1650–1900. Oxford: Oxford University Press, 2005.

Carey, Brycchan, and Geoffrey Plank, eds. Quakers and Abolition. Urbana: University of Illinois Press, 2014.

Caton, Mary Anne. "The Aesthetics of Absence: Quaker Women's Plain Dress in the Delaware Valley, 1790–1900." In Quaker Aesthetics: Reflections on a Quaker Ethic in American Design and Consumption, edited by Emma Jones Lapsansky and Anne A. Verplanck, 246–71. Philadelphia: University of Pennsylvania Press, 2003.

Cavey, Verna M. "Fighting Among Friends: The Quaker Separation of 1827." In Social Conflicts and Collective Identities, edited by Patrick G. Coy and Lynn M. Woehrle, 133–48. Lanham, MD: Rowman and Littlefield, 2000.

Chase, Malcolm. Chartism: A New History. Manchester: Manchester University Press, 2007.

Clark, Roger. Somerset Anthology. York, UK: Sessions Books, 1975.

Collins, Peter. "Ethical Consumption as Religious Testimony: The Quaker Case." In Ethical Consumption, Social Value, and Economic Practice, edited by James G. Carrier and Peter G. Luetchford, 181–97. Oxford: Berghahn Books, 2012.

Crane, Diana. "Clothing Behaviour as Non-Verbal Resistance: Marginal Women and Alternative Dress in the Nineteenth Century." Fashion Theory 3, no. 2 (1999): 241–68.

Cromwell, Otelia. Lucretia Mott. Cambridge: Harvard University Press, 1958.

Cross-Hansen, Jody L. The Contribution of Quaker Women to the Political Struggle for Abolition, Women's Rights, and Peace: From the Hicksite Schism to the American Friends Service Committee. Lewiston, NY: Edwin Mellen Press, 2014.

Crothers, A. Glenn. Quakers Living in the Lion's Mouth: The Society of Friends in Northern Virginia, 1730–1865. Gainesville: University Press of Florida, 2012.

Dales, Joanna. The Quaker Renaissance and Liberal Quakerism in Britain,

1895–1930: Seeking a Real Religion. Leiden: Brill, 2020.

Dalton, Russell. "The American Children's Bible." In *The Oxford Handbook of the Bible in America*, edited by Paul J. Gutjahr, 19–38. Oxford: Oxford University Press, 2017.

Densmore, Christopher. "Swarthmore College." In *Founded by Friends: The Quaker Heritage of Fifteen American Colleges and Universities*, edited by John W. Oliver Jr., Charles L. Cherry, and Caroline L. Cherry, 57–68. Lanham, MD: Scarecrow Press, 2007.

Densmore, Christopher, Carol Faulkner, Nancy Hewitt, and Beverly Wilson Palmer, eds. *Lucretia Mott Speaks: The Essential Speeches and Sermons*. Urbana: University of Illinois Press, 2017.

Divine, John E., Bronwen C. Souders, and John M. Souders, eds. *"To Talk Is Treason": Quakers of Waterford, Virginia, on Life, Love, Death, and War in the Southern Confederacy*. Waterford, VA: Waterford Foundation, 1996.

Doherty, Robert W. *The Hicksite Separation: A Sociological Analysis of Religious Schism in Early Nineteenth Century America*. New Brunswick: Rutgers University Press, 1967.

Dunicliff, Joy. *Mary Howitt: Another Lost Victorian Writer*. London: Excalibur Press, 1992.

Elliott, Errol T. *Quakers on the American Frontier*. Richmond, IN: Friends United Press, 1969.

Enyart, Paul. *Friends in Central America: A History of Church Growth*. Pasadena: William Carey Library, 1970.

Fager, Chuck. *Remaking Friends: How Progressive Friends Changed Quakerism and Helped Save America*. Durham, NC: Kimo Press, 2014.

Faulkner, Carol. *Lucretia Mott's Heresy: Abolition and Women's Rights in Nineteenth-Century America*. Philadelphia: University of Pennsylvania Press, 2011.

———. *Women's Radical Reconstruction: The Freedmen's Aid Movement*. Philadelphia: University of Pennsylvania Press, 2004.

Flexner, Helen Thomas. *A Quaker Childhood*. New Haven: Yale University Press, 1940.

Frost, J. William, ed. *The Quaker Origins of Antislavery*. Norwood, PA: Norwood Editions, 1980.

Garman, Mary, Judith Applegate, Margaret Benefiel, and Dortha Meredith, eds. *Hidden in Plain Sight: Quaker Women's Writings, 1650–1700*. Wallingford, PA: Pendle Hill Publications, 1996.

Graber, Jennifer. *The Gods of Indian Country: Religion and the Struggle for the American West*. New York: Oxford University Press, 2018.

Haines, Deborah L. "Friends General Conference: A Brief Historical Overview." *Quaker History* 89, no. 2 (2000): 1–16.

Hamm, Thomas D. "George F. White and Hicksite Opposition to the Abolitionist Movement." In *Quakers and Abolition*, edited by Brycchan Carey and Geoffrey Plank, 43–55. Urbana: University of Illinois Press, 2014.

———. "Hicksite, Orthodox, and Evangelical Quakerism, 1805–1887." In *The Oxford Handbook of Quaker Studies*, edited by Stephen W. Angell and Pink Dandelion, 63–77. Oxford: Oxford University Press, 2013.

———. "Hicksite Quakers and the Antebellum Nonresistance Movement." *Church History* 63, no. 4 (1994): 557–69.

———. *Liberal Quakerism in America in the Long Nineteenth Century, 1790–1920*. Leiden: Brill, 2020.

———. "Quakerism, Ministry, Marriage, and Divorce: The Ordeal of Priscilla Hunt Cadwalader." *Journal of the Early Republic* 28, no. 3 (2008): 407–31.

———. "The Radical Hicksite Critique of the Emerging Capitalist Order: Cornelius C. Blatchly, Benjamin Webb, and Friends, 1827–1833." In *Quakers, Politics, and Economics*, edited by David R. Ross and Michael T. Snarr, 214–34. Philadelphia: Friends Association for Higher Education, 2018.

———. *The Transformation of American Quakerism: Orthodox Friends, 1800–1907*. Bloomington: Indiana University Press, 1988.

Hamm, Thomas D., Margaret Marconi, Gretchen Kleinhen Salinas, and Benjamin Whitman. "The Decline of Quaker Pacifism in the Twentieth Century: Indiana Yearly Meeting of Friends as a Case Study." *Indiana Magazine of History* 96, no. 1 (2000): 44–71.

Healey, Robynne Rogers. *From Quaker to Upper Canadian: Faith and Community Among Yonge Street Friends, 1800–1850*. Montreal: McGill-Queen's University Press, 2006.

———, ed. *Quakerism in the Atlantic World, 1690–1830*. University Park: Penn State University Press, 2021.

Hewitt, Nancy A. "The Fragmentation of Friends: The Consequences for Quaker Women in Antebellum America." In *Witnesses for Change: Quaker Women over Three Centuries*, edited by Elisabeth Potts Brown and Susan Mosher Stuard, 93–108. New Brunswick: Rutgers University Press, 1989.

———. *Radical Friend: Amy Kirby Post and Her Activist Worlds*. Chapel Hill: University of North Carolina Press, 2018.

Hewitt, Nancy A., Margaret Hope Bacon, Christopher Densmore, Thomas D. Hamm, Sabron Reynolds Newton, Katherine Sorel, and Alson D. Van Wagner. "Women's Rights and Roles." In *Quaker Crosscurrents: Three Hundred Years of Friends in the New York Yearly Meetings*, edited by Hugh Barbour, Christopher Densmore, Elizabeth H. Moger, Nancy C. Sorel, Alson D. Van Wagner, and Arthur J. Worrall, 165–82. Syracuse: Syracuse University Press, 1995.

Hirst, Margaret E. *Quakers in Peace and War: An Account of Their Peace Principles and Practice*. London: Swarthmore Press, 1923.

Holcomb, Julie L. *Moral Commerce: Quakers and the Transatlantic Boycott of the Slave Labor Economy*. Ithaca: Cornell University Press, 2016.

Holton, Sandra Stanley. "Kinship and Friendship: Quaker Women's Networks and the Women's Movement." *Women's History Review* 14, nos. 3–4 (2005): 365–84.

———. *Quaker Women: Personal Life, Memory, and Radicalism in the Lives of Women Friends, 1780–1930*. London: Routledge, 2007.

Hood, James W. "'Novel Reading and Insanity': Nineteenth-Century Quaker Fiction Reading Practices." *Quaker Studies* 23, no. 1 (2019): 3–24.

———, ed. *Quakers and Literature*. Philadelphia: Friends Association for Higher Education, 2016.

Howlett, Charles F. "Quaker Conscience in the Classroom: The Mary S. McDowell Case." *Quaker History* 83, no. 2 (1994): 99–115.

Ingle, H. Larry. *Quakers in Conflict: The Hicksite Reformation*. Knoxville: University of Tennessee Press, 1986. Reprint, Wallingford, PA: Pendle Hill Publications, 1998.

Isichei, Elizabeth. *Victorian Quakers*. Oxford: Oxford University Press, 1970.

Ives, Kenneth. *Black Quakers: Brief Biographies*. Chicago: Progresiv Publishr, 1991.

Jackson, Helen Hunt. *A Call for Reform: The Southern California Indian Writings of Helen Hunt Jackson*. Edited by Valerie S. Mathes and Phil Brigandi. Norman: University of Oklahoma Press, 2015.

Jeffrey, Julie Roy. *The Great Silent Army of Abolitionism: Ordinary Women in the Antislavery Movement*. Chapel Hill: University of North Carolina Press, 1998.

Johnson, Dale A. "From Pilgrimage to Discipleship: Quaker Women's Ministries in Nineteenth-Century England." *Quaker History* 91, no. 2 (2002): 18–32.

Johnson, Lee A. *Mary Hallock Foote*. Boston: Twayne, 1980.

Jones, David. "Women and Chartism." *History* 68, no. 222 (1983): 1–21.

Jordan, Ryan P. *Slavery and the Meetinghouse: The Quakers and the Abolitionist Dilemma, 1820–1865*. Bloomington: Indiana University Press, 2007.

Kendall, Joan. "The Development of a Distinctive Form of Quaker Dress." *Costume* 19, no. 1 (1985): 58–74.

Kennedy, Thomas C. *British Quakerism, 1860–1920: The Transformation of a Religious Community*. Oxford: Oxford University Press, 2001.

Kett, Anna Vaughan. "Quaker Women and Anti-Slavery Activism: Eleanor Clark and the Free Labour Cotton Depot in Street." *Quaker Studies* 19, no. 1 (2014): 137–56.

———. "'Without the Consumers of Slave Produce There Would Be No Slaves': Quaker Women, Antislavery Activism, and Free-Labor Cotton Dress in the 1850s." In *Quakers and Abolition*, edited Brycchan Carey and Geoffrey Plank, 56–72. Urbana: University of Illinois Press, 2014.

Lapsansky, Emma. "Past Plainness to Present Simplicity: A Search for Quaker Identity." In *Quaker Aesthetics: Reflections on a Quaker Ethic in American Design and Consumption*, edited by Emma Jones Lapsansky and Anne A. Verplanck, 1–15. Philadelphia: University of Pennsylvania Press, 2003.

Leach, Camilla. "Religion and Rationality: Quaker Women and Science Education, 1790–1850." *History of Education* 35, no. 1 (2006): 69–90.

Lindman, Janet Moore. "'Deluded Women' and 'Violent Men': Women, Gender, and Language in the Hicksite Schism." *Quaker History* 109, no. 1 (2020): 1–26.

Lunn, Pam. "'You Have Lost Your Opportunity': British Quakers and the Militant Phase of the Women's Suffrage Campaign, 1906–1914." *Quaker Studies* 2, no. 1 (1997): 30–55.

Mabee, Carleton. *Black Freedom: The Nonviolent Abolitionists from 1830 Through the Civil War*. New York: Macmillan, 1970.

Mabee, Carleton, and Susan Mabee Newhouse. *Sojourner Truth: Slave, Prophet, Legend*. New York: New York University Press, 1995.

Maguire, James H. *Mary Hallock Foote*. Boise: Boise State College, 1972.

Mather, F. C., ed. *Chartism and Society: An Anthology of Documents*. London: Bell and Hyman, 1980.

McDaniel, Donna, and Vanessa Julye. *Fit for Freedom, Not for Friendship: Quakers, African Americans, and the Myth of Racial Justice*. Philadelphia: Quaker Press of FGC, 2009.

McIntyre, W. John. *Children of Peace*. Montreal: McGill-Queen's University Press, 1994.

McQuillan, Lisa. "World War I Relief and After: Hilda Clark." *Quaker Connections* 64 (March 2015): 6–15.

Midgley, Clare. *Feminism and Empire: Women Activists in Imperial Britain, 1790–1865*. London: Routledge, 2007.

———. *Women Against Slavery: The British Campaigns, 1780–1870*. London: Routledge, 1992.

Milligan, Edward. *Biographical Dictionary of British Quakers in Commerce and Industry, 1775–1920*. York, UK: Sessions Books, 2007.

———. *Quakers in Commerce and Industry, 1770–1920*. York, UK: Sessions Book Trust, 2007.

Nuermberger, Ruth Ketring. *The Free Produce Movement: A Quaker Protest Against Slavery*. New York: AMS Press, 1942.

Painter, Nell Irvin. "Representing Truth: Sojourner Truth's Knowing and Becoming Known." In *This Far by Faith: Readings in African-American Women's Religious Biography*, edited by Judith Weisenfeld and Richard Newman, 262–99. New York: Routledge, 1996.

Parker, Rozsika. *The Subversive Stitch: Embroidery and the Making of the Feminine*. London: Women's Press, 1984.

Phillips, Kate. *Helen Hunt Jackson: A Literary Life*. Berkeley: University of California Press, 2003.

Plank, Geoffrey. *John Woolman's Path to the Peaceable Kingdom: A Quaker in the British Empire*. Philadelphia: University of Pennsylvania Press, 2012.

Plant, Helen. "Patterns and Practices of Women's Leadership in the Yorkshire Quaker Community, 1760–1820." *Quaker Studies* 10, no. 2 (2006): 223–42.

———. "'Subjective Testimonies': Women Quaker Ministers and Spiritual Authority in England, 1750–1825." *Gender and History* 15, no. 2 (2003): 296–318.

Pointon, Marcia. "Quakerism and Visual Culture, 1650–1800." *Art History* 20, no. 3 (1997): 397–431.

Post Abbott, Margery, Mary Ellen Chijioke, Pink Dandelion, and John William Oliver Jr. *The A to Z of the Friends (Quakers)*. Lanham, MD: Scarecrow Press, 2006.

Rubinstein, David. *A Quaker Dilemma: The Rowntree Family and the Great War, 1914–1918*. York, UK: Quacks the Printer, 2015.

Schmudde, Carol E. "Sincerity, Secrecy, and Lies: Helen Hunt Jackson's No Name Novels." *Studies in American Fiction* 21, no. 1 (1993): 51–66.

Schrauwers, Albert. *Awaiting the Millennium: The Children of Peace and the Village of Hope, 1812–1889*. Toronto: University of Toronto Press, 1993.

Skidmore, Gil. *Strength in Weakness: Writings of Eighteenth-Century Quaker Women*. Walnut Creek, CA: Altamira, 2003.

Smith, Christine H. *Social Class in the Writings of Mary Hallock Foote*. Reno: University of Nevada Press, 2009.

Smith, Logan Pearsall, ed. *Philadelphia Quaker: The Letters of Hannah Whitall Smith*. New York: Harcourt, Brace, 1950. Published in England as *A Religious Rebel: The Letters of "H. W. S." (Mrs.*

Pearsall Smith). London: Nisbet, 1949.

Soderlund, Jean R. "Priorities and Power: The Philadelphia Female Anti-Slavery Society." In *The Abolitionist Sisterhood: Women's Political Culture in Antebellum America*, edited by Jean Fagan Yellin and John C. Van Horne, 67–89. Ithaca: Cornell University Press, 1994.

Spencer, Carole D. "Hannah Whitall Smith and the Evolution of Quakerism: An Orthodox Heretic in an Age of Controversy." *Quaker Studies* 18, no. 1 (2013): 7–22.

———. "Hannah Whitall Smith's Highway of Holiness." In *Quakers and Mysticism: Comparative and Syncretic Approaches to Spirituality*, edited by Jon R. Kershner, 141–60. London: Palgrave, 2019.

———. *Holiness: The Soul of Quakerism*. Colorado Springs: Paternoster, 2007.

Stansell, Ron. *Missions by the Spirit: Learning from Quaker Examples*. Newberg, OR: Barclay Press, 2009.

Stetson, Erlene, and Linda David. *Glorying in Tribulation: The Lifework of Sojourner Truth*. East Lansing: Michigan State University Press, 1994.

Stokes, Christopher. "Poetics at the Religious Margin: Bernard Barton and Quaker Romanticism." *Review of English Studies* 70 (June 2019): 509–26.

Strachey, Barbara. *Remarkable Relations: The Story of the Pearsall Smith Women*. New York: Universe Books, 1982.

Strachey, Barbara, and Jayne Samuels, eds. *Mary Berenson: A Self-Portrait from Her Letters and Diary*. London: Hamish Hamilton, 1983.

Tarter, Michele Lise. "Written from the Body of Sisterhood: Quaker Women's Prophesying and the Creation of a New Word." In *New Critical Studies on Early Quaker Women, 1650–1800*, edited by Michele Lise Tarter and Catie Gill, 69–87. Oxford: Oxford University Press, 2018.

Tarter, Michele Lise, and Catie Gill, eds. *New Critical Studies on Early Quaker Women, 1650–1800*. Oxford: Oxford University Press, 2018.

Taylor, Marion Ann, and Heather E. Weir, eds. *Let Her Speak for Herself: Nineteenth-Century Women Writing on Women in Genesis*. Waco: Baylor University Press, 2006.

Thompson, Dorothy. *The Early Chartists*. London: Macmillan, 1971.

Tolles, Frederick B. "The New Light Quakers of Lynn and New Bedford." *New England Quarterly* 32, no. 3 (1959): 291–319.

Van Drenth, Annemieke, and Francisca de Haan. *The Rise of Caring Power: Elizabeth Fry and Josephine Butler in Britain and the Netherlands*. Amsterdam: Amsterdam University Press, 1999.

Van Wagner, Alson D., and Hugh Barbour. "Reunion." In *Quaker Crosscurrents: Three Hundred Years of Friends in the New York Yearly Meetings*, edited by Hugh Barbour, Christopher Densmore, Elizabeth H. Moger, Nancy C. Sorel, Alson D. Van Wagner, and Arthur J. Worrall, 257–75. Syracuse: Syracuse University Press, 1995.

Walsham, Alexandra. "Nature and Nurture in the Early Quaker Movement: Creating the Next Generation of Friends." *Studies in Church History* 55 (2019): 161–76.

Walvin, James. *The Quakers: Money and Morals.* London: John Murray, 1997.

Washington, Margaret. *Sojourner Truth's America.* Urbana: University of Illinois Press, 2009.

Winch, Julie. "'You Have Talents—Only Cultivate Them': Philadelphia's Black Female Literary Societies and the Abolitionist Crusade." In *The Abolitionist Sisterhood: Women's Political Culture in Antebellum America,* edited by Jean Fagan Yellin and John C. Van Horne, 101–18. Ithaca: Cornell University Press, 1994.

Wright, Sheila. "Quakerism and Its Implications for Quaker Women: The Women Itinerant Ministers of York Meeting, 1780–1840." *Studies in Church History* 27 (1990): 403–14.

CONTRIBUTORS

JOAN ALLEN is a visiting fellow at Newcastle University, UK, where she was formerly head of the History Department. Her research interests coalesce around nineteenth-century British radicalism, Irish nationalism, and the popular press. She is chair of the Society for the Study of Labour History and has served as an editor of *Labour History Review*. She is the author of *Joseph Cowen and Popular Radicalism on Tyneside, 1829–1900* (2007) and has coedited several volumes, including *Faith of Our Fathers: Popular Culture and Belief in Post-Reformation England, Ireland, and Wales* (2009), *Histories of Labour: National and International Perspectives* (2010), and *Papers for the People: A Study of the Chartist Press* (2005). She is the co-convenor (with Richard C. Allen) of the annual Chartist studies conference.

RICHARD C. ALLEN, a fellow of the Royal Historical Society, holds visiting fellowships at the Australian National University, Canberra, and Newcastle University. He is also a former reader in early modern cultural history at the University of South Wales. He has published extensively on Quakerism, migration, and identity. His most recent works are *Quaker Communities in Early Modern Wales: From Resistance to Respectability* (2007), and the coedited *Irelands of the Mind: Memory and Identity in Modern Irish Culture* (2008), *Faith of Our Fathers: Popular Culture and Belief in Post-Reformation England, Ireland, and Wales* (2009), *The Religious History of Wales: A Survey of Religious Life and Practice in Wales from the Seventeenth Century to the Present Day* (2014), and *The Quakers, 1656–1723: The Evolution of an Alternative Community* (2018). He is currently writing *Welsh Quaker Emigrants and Colonial Pennsylvania*, and cowriting, with Erin Bell, *Quaker Networks and Moral Reform in the North East of England*.

STEPHEN W. ANGELL is the Geraldine C. Leatherock Professor of Quaker Studies at the Earlham School of Religion. His recent publications include *Shattered by the Light, or The Ruins and the Green: Quaker Churches in the Northwest and Midwest Clash and Divide over LGBTQ Issues* (2021, with Chuck Fager and Jade Souza), *Indiana Trainwreck: Divisions in Indiana Quaker Communities over Inclusion of Homosexuals, Church Authority, Christ, and the Bible* (with Chuck Fager, 2020), *The Cambridge Companion to Quakerism* (with Pink Dandelion, 2018), *Early Quakers and Their Theological Thought, 1647–1723* (coedited with Pink Dandelion, 2015), *The Oxford Handbook of Quaker Studies* (coedited with Pink Dandelion, 2013), and *Black Fire: African American Quakers on Spirituality and Human Rights* (with Harold D. Weaver Jr. and Paul Kriese, 2011). Forthcoming in 2023 from Penn State University Press, as part of the New History of Quakerism series, is *The Creation of Modern Quaker Diversity, 1830–1937*, coedited with Pink Dandelion and David Harrington Watt.

JENNIFER M. BUCK is an associate professor of practical theology at Azusa Pacific University. She holds a PhD in philosophy of religion and theology from Claremont Graduate University and an MDiv from Fuller Theology Seminary. She is the author of multiple articles and books, including *Reframing the House: Constructive Feminist Global Ecclesiology for the Western Evangelical Church* (2016) and *Distinct: Quaker Holiness in Everyday Life* (2022), and a forthcoming book on fashion and theology. She has served as a licensed Quaker minister for many years.

NANCY JIWON CHO is a research associate at the Centre for Baptist Studies at Regent's Park College, University of Oxford. She was previously an associate professor of English literature at Seoul National University in South Korea. Her research spans the intersection of literature, religion, and gender during the long nineteenth century. She has published widely on British women's hymn writing, dissenting women's writings, Romantic era prophecy, Anglican fiction, women's biblical exegesis, and Quaker imaginative writing. Recent publications include chapters in *The Cambridge Companion to Quakerism* (2018), *Anglican Women Novelists: Charlotte Brontë to P. D. James* (2019), and *Religion and Life Cycles in Early Modern England*

(2021). She is currently researching the writings of Baptist women, including Anne Steele and Mary Anne Hearn (pseudonym Marianne Farningham).

ISABELLE COSGRAVE is a part-time independent researcher, formerly affiliated with the University of Exeter (UK), where she earned her PhD in English in 2014. She has published on Amelia Opie, biography, and the archive and is currently working on shifting Quaker attitudes toward fiction in the long nineteenth century. She is coeditor of The Correspondence of Amelia Alderson Opie: A Digital Archive (ameliaopieletters.com) with Roxanne Eberle (University of Georgia), for which Cosgrave is preparing the publication of Opie's letters to her Quaker mentor, Joseph John Gurney. Cosgrave's research interests include women's writing and nineteenth-century religious belief, biography and correspondence, and archives and their construction.

THOMAS D. HAMM is a professor of history and Quaker scholar in residence at Earlham College in Richmond, Indiana, where he has been on the faculty since 1987 and holds the Trueblood Chair in Christian Thought. He received his PhD in history from Indiana University and is the author of numerous books and articles on Quaker history, including *The Transformation of American Quakerism: Orthodox Friends, 1800–1907* (1988), *God's Government Begun: The Society for Universal Inquiry and Reform, 1842–1846* (1995), *Earlham College: A History, 1847–1997* (1997), *The Quakers in America* (2003), *Liberal Quakers in America in the Long Nineteenth Century, 1790–1920* (2020), and the editor of *Quaker Writings: An Anthology, 1650–1920* (2011).

ROBYNNE ROGERS HEALEY is a professor of history and the codirector of the Gender Studies Institute at Trinity Western University in British Columbia, Canada. She is an associate editor (history) of the series Brill Research Perspectives in Quaker Studies. She also convened the Conference of Quaker Historians and Archivists, and served as publications chair for the Canadian Friends Historical Association. Her publications include *From Quaker to Upper Canadian: Faith and Community Among Yonge Street Friends, 1801–1850* (2006), *Quaker Studies: An Overview—The Current State of the Field* (2018, with C. Wess Daniels and Jon Kershner), *Quakerism in the Atlantic World, 1690–1830* (2021), and many articles and chapters in the field of Quaker history. She is currently working on a monograph on Quaker quietism.

JULIE L. HOLCOMB is an associate professor of museum studies at Baylor University, where she teaches undergraduate and graduate courses in museum, library, and archival collections management, collections ethics, and book history. Holcomb's research interests include Quakers, abolition, and the Civil War as well as library, archival, and museum collections. She has written three books, most recently *Moral Commerce: Quakers and the Transatlantic Boycott of the Slave Labor Economy* (2016) and *Exploring the American Civil War Through 50 Historic Treasures* (2021). Holcomb's work has also appeared in academic journals, edited collections, and online publications. She has held faculty research fellowships at Haverford College and the Gilder Lehrman Center for the Study of Slavery, Resistance, and Abolition at Yale University. She also serves as editor of *Quaker History*, the scholarly publication of the Friends Historical Association. She is at work on a biography of nineteenth-century Quaker reformer George W. Taylor.

ANNA VAUGHAN KETT is a senior lecturer in the history of art and design, formerly at the University of Brighton and the University of Sussex in the UK. Her interests lie in the eighteenth and nineteenth centuries in the areas of textiles and dress among Quakers, cotton and gingham cloth, the signification of ethical practices in clothing and jewelry, dress worn by abolitionists and the enslaved, and the humanitarian work of Quaker women. Recent publications include the chapter "Dressing Abolitionists and the Enslaved: Free-Labour and Slave-Labour Cotton Gingham Cloth in Carlisle in the 1850s," in *Clothing the Enslaved in the Eighteenth-Century Atlantic World*, edited by Chris Evans and Naomi Preston (forthcoming) and "'Without the Consumers of Slave Produce There Would Be No Slaves': Quaker Women, Antislavery Activism, and Free-Labor Cotton Dress in the 1850s," in *Quakers and Abolition*, edited by Brycchan Carey and Geoffrey Plank (2014). She is currently researching the Wedgwood Slave Medallion and its impact on abolitionism.

EMMA LAPSANSKY-WERNER is professor emerita of history and curator emerita of the Quaker Collection at Haverford College, where she continues to lecture and to publish on various Quaker and African American history topics. She has published many articles and chapters on Quaker history. With Gary Nash and Clayborne Carson, Lapsansky wrote *The Struggle for Freedom*, a college text on African American history, the third edition of which appeared in 2018. She is also a coauthor on the Pearson Education high school American history text. She is currently at work on a history of a Bryn Mawr Quaker family and a study of a mid-twentieth-century Philadelphia multicultural intentional community.

LINDA PALFREEMAN is a lecturer in the Department of Humanities at the CEU Cardenal Herrera University, Elche, Spain. Her chief areas of research are the history of medicine and the administration of medical assistance and humanitarian aid in wartime, particularly during the First World War and the Spanish Civil War. Her recent work focuses on achievements in this field by members and associates of the Religious Society of Friends. This research has led to publications and participation in seminars, conferences, and other events at both the national and international levels. Her publications include *Friends in Flanders: Humanitarian Aid Administered by the Friends' Ambulance Unit During the First World War* (2017) and *Diary of a Ypres Nun, October 1914–May 1915: The Diary of Soeur Marguerite of the Sisters of Lamotte—Suffering and Sacrifice in the First World War* (2017).

HANNAH RUMBALL is a senior lecturer at the University of Brighton. She specializes in nineteenth- and early twentieth-century dress, material culture, and women's studies, with a focus on Quaker plain dress and its fashionable adaptation. As a founding member of the research network 19th Century Dress and Textiles Reframed, Rumball is interested in challenging myths and misinterpretations surrounding historical women's garments. She is currently working with the EU research body Groupement d'Intérêt Scientifique Apparences, Corps et Sociétés (ACORSO) on fashionable tailoring for women. This is a comparative study of the material culture, design, manufacture, retailing, and consumption of tailored garments for and by women at all market levels in the period from 1750 to 1930.

JANET SCOTT was the head of religious studies and director of Studies in Theology at Homerton College, Cambridge University, and a member of the faculties of Divinity and of Education at the university. She has also worked as director of the Centre for Ecumenical Studies at Westcott House in the Cambridge Theological Federation. She was a member of the World Council of Churches Faith and Order Plenary Commission and a trustee and moderator of Churches Together in England. She gave the Swarthmore Lecture at Britain Yearly Meeting in 1980.

CAROLE DALE SPENCER was an associate professor of Christian spirituality at the Earlham School of Religion from 2010 to 2016. She also served as an adjunct professor of spiritual formation at Portland Seminary at George Fox University for many years. She received her PhD from the University of Birmingham, UK. She is author of *Holiness: The Soul of Quakerism; An Historical Analysis of the Theology of Holiness in the Quaker Tradition* (2007) and numerous book chapters and articles on Quaker history, theology, and spirituality.

INDEX

Abel, William 130
abolition, 4–6, 7–8, 89, 102, 203–4
   anti-slavery fairs, 110–11
   in Britain, 103, 208–9
   consumer-based activism, 103–5, 208
   criticism of, 92, 144
   and Hicksites, 24, 26, 59, 70
   liberation theology, 81
   literature, 87–88
   movement, 23, 26–27, 95–97
   networks, 79, 86, 97, 104, 100
   societies, 23, 58, 88, 96, 104, 148
   transatlantic influences, 8, 10, 57, 104, 208–11
   See also free-produce movement
Adventism, 89
aesthetic movement, 234–36
African Episcopal Church, 114
   of St. Thoas, 81, 88
African Methodist Episcopal Zion Church, 84, 89
Albright, William A., 250
Alexander, Rebecca, 205
Alexandria Monthly Meeting, 53
Allen, Richard, 94, 204
American Anti-Slavery Society, 23, 58, 88
American Civil War, 6, 18, 26–27, 204
American Free Produce Association, 58
American Revolutionary War, 61
Anthony, Susan B., 26, 31, 266
Anti-Caste, 115

Anti-Corn Law League, 207–8, 210–12
Anti-Slavery Contention (London), 96
Anti-Slavery Convention of American Women, 23
Arch Street Meeting, 95
Armenian massacres (1894–1896), 202
Ashworth, Henry, 211–12
Association des Infermières Visiteuses de France, 251
Augustine Society, 81
Australia, 205
Ayllón, Juan, 130, 133

Bacon, Margaret Hope, 2
Baker, Jane, 19
Ball, Martha, 110
Baltimore Yearly Meeting, 28, 30
baptism, physical, 5, 127
   of the spirit, 182
Band of Hope, 205
Barclay, Robert, 149, 240
Barnard, Hannah Jenkins, 3, 266
Barton, Bernard, 156, 160–61, 170–71
   writings of, 157–60, 162–65
Barton, Lucy, 9, 156–58, 173–74
   Bible Letters for Children, 162–63, 166, 168, 170
   conversion to Anglicanism, 160–61
   gender egalitarianism, 166, 172
   Gospel History of Our Lord, 167
   literary tactics, 170–72

Barton, Lucy (continued)
    Natural History, 171–73
    Quaker writing networks, 169, 171
    The Reliquary, 163–65
    theology and peace, 165, 167–68
Batten, Thomas, 63
Becker, Lydia, 213
Beecher, Henry Ward, 84
Benezet, Anthony, 81, 96
Bettle, Jane, 47, 51
Bettle, Samuel, 67
Bible, 5, 69, 83, 87, 111, 172
    biblical exegesis, 9, 156, 163, 179, 191
    and the Inward Light, 138, 140
    rejection of the, 68
    teachings of the, 158, 162, 171, 179
Birmingham Female Political Union, 207
Birmingham Ladies' Negro's Friend Society, 104, 203, 212
Birmingham Maternity Hospital, 249
Black Quakers, 7, 8, 12
    in Philadelphia, 81–83, 88–89, 91–93
    and prejudice in meetings, 92–96
    (*see also* prejudice, racial)
Black rights campaign, 115
    See also suffrage
Blaugdone, Barbara, 83
Bloomerites, 181
    See also dress reform
Blue River Meeting, 18–19
Boer Wars, 30, 202, 249
Bolivia, 129–30, 133
bonnets, 228, 230
Botham, Anna, 144
Braithwaite, Anna, 18, 39, 40, 43
    in North America, 44, 49, 51, 66
Braithwaite, Isaac, 44
Bright, Jacob, 213
Bright, John (MP), 206, 211
Bringhurst, Deborah, 20
Bristol, Somerset, and Dorset Women's Quarterly Meeting, 246
British and Foreign Anti-Slavery Society, 104-5, 112
British Friend, 114, 224, 230
British War Office, 251
Brown, John, 26–7
Brown, Margaret, 20
Brown, Mary Ann, 26
Buffum, Arnold, 96
Buntin, John, 67
Burgess, Ann Mary, 205–6
Burritt, Elihu, 113
Burrows, Hannah, 93
Bustill, Cyrus, 81
business, 21, 40, 59, 181
    networks, 103–4, 125
business meetings, xii
    separation of, 22, 28
Byberry Monthly Meeting, 53

Cadbury, Barrow, 232
Cadbury, Geraldine Southall, 223–24, 231, 240
    on John Ruskin, 236–37
    wedding attire, 232, 234–35, 242
Cadwalader, Priscilla Hunt, 4, 18–19, 39, 47
California Yearly Meeting, 123, 127
Caln Quarterly Meeting, 22
C. & J. Clark, 102–3
capitalism, attitudes towards, 22, 105
Capper, Ann, 204
Caribbean, 204
Carr, Frances, 19
Cash, Elizabeth Petipher, 223–24, 227, 240
    and plain dress, 228, 230, 241
Catholicism, 124–25, 191
Catt, Carrie Chapman, 31
Central America, 2, 122, 130, 132
Châlons-sur-Marne (Châlons-en-Champagne), 253–54, 258
Chandler, Elizabeth Margaret, 21, 107, 115
Chapman, Joseph B., 21
charity, principle of, 106, 248
Chartist movement, 207–11
Cherry Street Meeting, 17
Chester County, PA, 62
Child, Mary H., 26–27
children, 110, 113, 124, 201, 207
    aid for, 252–53, 255–58
    of disowned Quakers, 61
    and education, 81–82, 88, 92, 94
    orphan care, 202, 204–6
    religious education, 204–5
    writings for, 9, 149, 156, 167, 168–71

Children of Peace, 3
Chiquimula (Guatemala), 123–24, 128–29, 131–32
cholera pandemic, 201
Christ, 3, 64, 90, 125, 130, 166
 atonement, 158, 167
 divinity of, 19
 and love, 107, 186, 188
 within, 89, 182
Christian Doctrine, Practice, and Discipline, 226
Christian Union, 142
Christianity, revivalist, 83–84
Church of England, 157, 160, 165, 171, 214
Clark, Alice, 247
Clark, Anne (Annie), 245
Clark, Eleanor Stephens, 8, 102–3, 116–17, 246
 abolition work, 109–14
 charitable work, 105, 107-8, 114, 116
 free-cotton shop, 111–12
 transatlantic networks, 104, 112
Clark, Helen Priestman Bright, 109, 245–46
Clark, Hilda, 10, 245–49, 261–62, 266
 establishment of district nursing in rural France, 256–57
 maternity hospital at Châlons-sur-Marne, 253–55
 postwar work, 260
 relationship with Edith Pye, 248, 260–61
 war aid, 250–52, 259
Clark, James, 102, 104–5, 108
Clark, William Stephens, 245
Clarkson Anti-Slavery Society, 58
Clarkson, Thomas, 103, 107
Cobden, Richard, 211–12
colonialism, xii, 2, 8, 12, 141
come-outer movement, 89, 96
Comstock, Elizabeth, 91
Confederate States of America, 27, 90
Congregational Friends. *See* Progressive Friends
conscientious objection, 30
 See also pacifism
Contagious Diseases Acts, 213–15
Cooper Union Institute of Design, 145

Corder, Susanna, 204–5
Corn Laws, 211–12
 See also Anti-Corn Law League
Crewdson, Isaac, 5, 158
Cross-Hansen, Jody, 2

De Montmort, Renée, 251
death, life after, 160, 193
"Decline of Quakerism, The," 236
DeGarmo, Rhoda, 24
Delaware Free Press, 22
Deroin, Jeanne, 210
devil, the, 19, 192
discipline, 22, 28, 93, 226
 and disownment, 60–61
 practices of, 4–5, 17, 159
disownment, 7, 22, 60–61, 203
domesticity. *See* separate-spheres ideology
Douglass, Frederick, 111, 115
Douglass, Grace Bustill, 82, 92
Douglass, Robert, 81–82
Douglass, Sarah Mapps, 8, 79
 abolitionist work, 95, 86, 97–98
 early life, 81–83, 85–88
 and Quakerism, 91–93, 96
dress, religious, 10, 85, 116, 144, 162, 225
 conservative expressions of, 227–29, 230, 240–41
 criticisms of, 236
 debates over, 223–27, 230, 232
 fashionable, 231, 234–35, 238
 'gay' Friends, 240–41
 history of, 223–24
dress reform movement, 231–32
Drinker, Henry, 61
Dublin Yearly Meeting, 4, 71
Dumont, John, 80
Dutton, Lizzie and Lida, 27

Edinburgh Ladies' Emancipation Society, 204
education, xii 11, 21, 29
 in Central America, 124, 127–29
 reform, 10, 127, 205
 religious, 168–69
 segregation in schools, 81–82, 86, 88, 92
 of women, 21, 26, 31, 131
Eighteenth Amendment, 31

El Savador, 127
elderly, care of, 201
electoral reform, 206–8, 211, 213–14
　See also suffrage
Ely, Ruth, 47
endogamy, 94, 103
Englishwoman's Domestic Magazine, 238
enslavement, xii, 27, 80–81, 83, 111–12
　self-liberation, 26
　　Quaker involvement in, 66, 95, 203
　See also abolition
Equal Rights Amendment, 32
Evangelicalism, 5, 9, 11, 22, 158, 161
　doctrine of, 3–4
　Evangelical Friends, 5 (see also Crewdson, Isaac)
Evans, Jonathan, 67
Exodusters, 90–91, 114

Farmer's Cabinet, 70
farming, 62, 105, 114
fashion, 222–23, 227–28, 238–39, 241
Fawcett, Millicent, 213
Fell, Margaret, 185, 225, 240
Female Association of Philadelphia for the Relief of the Sick and Infirm Poor with Clothing, 30
Female Literary Association, 87–88
Female Medical College of Pennsylvania, 26
Female Radical Association, 209
feminism, first-wave, 1
　attitudes towards, 11
feminists, Quakers, 26, 31, 180, 185, 210
fiction, attitudes towards, 9, 138, 147, 151
　and Hicksite Quakers, 142
　and Orthodox Quakers, 141
First African Presbyterian Church (Philadelphia), 81–82
First Day School conferences, 29
Fitzgerald, Edward, 156, 159
Flushing, NY, 64
Foote, Arthur De Wint, 145–46, 149
Foote, Mary Hallock, 144–46, 152
　literary work, 148–50
　Reminiscences, 144, 146, 149–50
Ford, Isabella, 202
Forster, William, 39
Forten, James, 81

Foulke, Joseph, 17, 26
Fox, Anna Maria, 204
Fox, George, xii
France, 210, 247, 249–51
Franco-Prussian War (1870–71), 202
Franks, Abigail, 92–93
Free African Society, 81
Free Produce Association of Friends of Philadelphia Yearly Meeting, 57
Free Produce Society of Chester County, 58
free trade, 208, 210–12
freedmen's aid movement, 114
free-produce movement, 8, 57, 85, 104
　community, 105, 112
French Red Cross, 251, 257
Friend (Philadelphia), 70, 93–94, 96, 224
　letters in, 230, 232, 237
Friends Educational Society, 205
Friends Equal Rights Association, 31
Friends General Conference, 29, 31
Friends' Institute London albums, 228
Friends' Monthly Meeting School (New York), 64
Friends Neighborhood Guild, 30
Friends' Preparative Meeting School (Burlington), 69
Friends Quarterly Examiner, 230
Friends' School (Essex), 228
Friends Union for Philanthropic Labour, 29
Friends' War Victims' Relief Committee, 250–52
　issues with, 257
　in Marne district and the Maternité Anglaise, 253–55, 258–59
Friends' Weekly Intelligencer, 87
Fry, Elizabeth Gurney, 5, 139, 169, 199
Fry, Ruth, 250, 257

Galton-Schimmelpenninck, Mary Anne, 205
Gardner, Sunderland P., 53
Garnet, Henry Highland, 112
Garrett, Elizabeth, 245
Garrison, William Lloyd, 83, 87, 110, 111, 114
　abolitionist networks, 79, 95

gender equality, 7, 8, 20–21, 28, 133
   lack of, 246
   in meetings, 27–29
   opposition to, 11
   See also women's rights
Genesee Yearly Meeting, 22, 24
Gibbons, Abby Hopper, 24
Gibbons, Phebe Earle, 28
Gilbert, Olive, 80
Gilder, Helena de Kay, 145, 148, 150
Glasgow Ladies' Emancipation Society, 203
Gloucester, John, 82
Godwin, Edward William, 236
Gould, Stephen, 67
Gradual Emancipation Law (1817), 80
Grand Bazaar in Covent Garden (1845), 211–12
Green, Joshua Joseph, 42–43
Green Plain Monthly Meeting, 24
Green Plain Yearly Meeting of Congregational Friends, 24, 25
Green Street Monthly Meeting, 22
Grimke, Angelina, 95
Grimke, Sarah, 95
Grubb, Sarah, 147, 204
Guatemala, 124, 127–29, 131
Guatemala Band, 123
Guatemala Yearly Meeting, 129
Gummere, Samuel, 69
Gurney, Joseph John, 4–5, 139, 151, 225
   and evangelicalism, 158, 161
      Gurneyites, 5, 8, 11, 180
   Observations on the Religious Peculiarities of the Society of Friends, 40
   opposition to fiction, 140, 146
Gurney, Rachel, 205

Hack, Maria, 169, 171–72
Haiti, Republic of, 83
Hallowell, Benjamin, 66–67
Hanbury, Charlotte, 202
Hancock, Cornelia, 27, 30
Hanson, Abram, 208
Hardenberg, Charles, 80
Hardshaw West Monthly Meeting, 42
Harney, Julian, 210
Harrison, Anna, 204

Harvester (California), 130
Harvey, T. Edmund (MP), 250, 252, 258
Harvey and Darton, 169
Haslam, Anna, 214–15
Haslam, Thomas, 214–15
Hatton, Margaret, 20
Haviland, Laura, 91
Hayley, William, 139
Herzegovina uprising (1875–77), 202
Hicks, Abraham, 19
Hicks, Elias, 3, 18–20, 22, 52
   on anti-slavery, 266
   on doctrine, 66, 138, 140, 151
   opposition to, 42
Hicks, Rachel, 19, 20, 21, 27
Hicksite Friends, 4–7
   and British Friends, 38–39, 40–41, 53–54
   and the Civil War, 26–27
   divisions amongst, 18–19
   gender roles, 21, 28–29, 59
   and reform movements, 22–26, 30–32, 59
   See also Hicksite-Orthodox schism
Hicksite-Orthodox Schism (1827–28):
   aftermath, 38, 41, 93, 97
   and British transatlantic ministry, 39, 42, 46–47, 52–53
   and its impact on fiction, 138, 152
   origins of, 3–5, 22, 64–66
   women's leadership, 17–19, 40
Hoag, Huldah, 47–48
Hoag, Joseph, 47
Hoare, Harriet, 205
Hoare, Sarah, 169, 203, 205, 266
Hobhouse, Emily, 202
Hodgkin, L. V., xi
Holdsworth, Dyson, 253
holiness movement, 5, 126, 131, 180, 182, 192
Holton, Sandra Stanley, 2
Holy Spirit, 20, 83–90, 129, 132, 138
Honduras, 127–28
Hopkins, Felicia, 205
Howitt, Mary Botham, 144, 146, 152, 212–13
   Autobiography, 144
   Desolation of Eyam, 147
   issues with Orthodox Quakerism, 147–48

Howitt, William, 146
  History of Priestcraft, 147
Hughes, Margaretta, 70
Hull, Hannah Clothier, 30
Hull, Henry, 49
Hunt, Jane, 25
Huntington Park Training School, 122–23, 126–27, 131
hymns, 83, 159–60, 164

Illinois Yearly Meeting, 28
Imlay, Maria, 19
imperialism, British, 2, 202
  Western, 127–28, 132
Impey, Catherine, 109, 115
Independent Order of Good Templars, 206
Indiana Yearly Meeting, 4, 19, 24, 28, 184
  schism, 5, 19–20, 22
Indigenous Americans, 12, 91, 126–27
  relationships with Quakers, 130, 138, 143
  treatment of, 141–42
Industrial Revolution, 12
Institute for Colored Youth, 91
International Peace Bureau, 202
Inward Light, 3, 19, 140, 186, 188, 267

Jackson, Helen Hunt, 12, 138, 150, 152
  A Century of Dishonor, 12, 142–43
  literary career, 141–43
  Ramona, 142–43
Jackson, John, 21
Jackson, William S., 141–42
Jackson-Coppin, Fanny M., 91, 97
Janney, Samuel M., 21
Jewett, Susanna, 20, 22
Johnson, Phebe, 19, 23, 47
Jones, Absalom, 81
Jones, Ann, 18, 39, 40, 44, 66
Jones, Ernest, 210
Jones, Rufus, 5
Journal (Philadelphia), 28
Judge, Martha, 47, 52

Knight, Anne, 169, 199, 209–10, 213
Kongo, Kingdom of, 84

Ladies National Association for the Repeal of the Contagious Diseases Act, 214–15
Lady Duff-Gordon, Lucy Christiana, 223
Langham circle, 212
League of Brotherhood, 113
League of Nations, 30, 260
Lee, Jarena, 84–85
Lewis, Enoch, 62, 64, 68
Liberal Party (UK), 247
liberal Quakerism, 5–6, 20, 22, 174, 211, 215
  science, interest in, 5
liberalism, 11, 22
Liberator (Boston), 83, 110
Liberty, Arthur, 235–36
Liberty & Co., 232, 235–36, 242
Lippincott, Mary S., 20, 22
London Yearly Meeting, 4, 5, 18, 147, 223
  criticism of, 202, 246
  on the Hicksite-Orthodox schism, 38, 41, 53–54
  on plainness, 225–26, 241
London Yearly Meeting of Women Friends, 234, 237
Longshore, Joseph S., 26
Lord's Prayer, 211
Lucas, Margaret Bright, 206, 212–13
Lucas, Samuel, 212

Magee family, 59–60, 65
Marietta Monthly Meeting, 29
marriage, xii, 237
Massachusetts Female Emancipation Society, 110
material culture, 224
McClintock, Mary Ann, 24–25
McDowell, Mary S., 30
McLaren, Priscilla Bright, 246
Meeting for Sufferings (London), 250
merchants, 7, 57, 61, 203
  See also Taylor, George W.
Methodism/Methodists, 63, 81, 84, 89, 141
  and Quaker doctrine, 5, 94, 200, 267
  Second Blessing, 182
Methodist Episcopal Church, 81
Middletown Meeting, 19
Miers, Cynthia, 92–93

military service, 6
Mill, John Stuart, 213
ministry:
  equality in, 6, 90, 133
  transatlantic, 39, 47
  travelling, 4, 7, 11, 42, 46–49, 51, 65
  women in, 18, 32, 40, 45, 48, 85, 106, 173, 200
missionaries, 8, 122, 125
  nineteenth-century, 125–26
  twentieth-century, 127, 132
Monkton, Lionel, 222
  The Quaker Girl, 222–23, 241
Moore, Esther, 19
Moore, Lindley Murray, 64, 66
Moore, Mary, 17
Moore, Rachel, 27
Morocco, 202
Mother Bethel Church of the African Methodist Episcopal Church, 81
motherhood, spiritual, 85, 99n29, 261
Mott, Abigail, 64
Mott, James, 23, 25
Mott, Lucretia, 2, 17, 19, 31, 151
  on abolition, 79, 148, 266
  on war, 30
  on women's rights, 23–27, 59
Mott, Richard, 64

Napoleonic Wars, 40
National Anti-Slavery Standard, 24
National Society for Women's Suffrage, 213
National Union of Women's Suffrage Societies, 246–47
National Woman's Party, 31
Neall, Daniel, 70
New England Non-Resistance Society, 23
New England Yearly Meeting, 5
New Garden, PA, 62, 64
New Light Movement, 3
New York Anti-Slavery Society, 145
New York Yearly Meeting, 22, 29
  pre-Hicksite-Orthodox schism, 51
Newcastle upon Tyne Female Political Union, 208
Newington (Stoke) Academy for Girls, 204–5

Newport Uprising (1839), 209
Nine Partners Boarding School, 23, 64, 266
Nineteenth Amendment, 31–32
nonresistance movement, 23
Non-Slaveholder, 57, 70
Northern Star (Leeds), 208, 210
Nottingham, 146, 207
Nova Scotia, 206

oaths, 61
Observations of the Quaker-Peculiarities of Dress and Language, 225
O'Connor, Feargus, 207–8
Ohio Yearly Meeting, 22
Ohio Yearly Meeting of Progressive Friends, 24
Olive Leaf Societies, 113.
Opie, Amelia Alderson, 107, 138–39, 151–52
  fiction and Quakerism, 140–41, 143
  Illustrations of Lying in All Its Branches, 140
  Madeline, 140, 142, 143
  Valentine's Eve, 139, 146
Opie, John, 138
Oregon Yearly Meeting, 130–31
Orthodox Friends, 4, 7, 41, 53
  divisions amongst, 4–5
  doctrine, 13n6, 188
  and literature, 70, 138, 141–43
  and reform movements, 58–59, 96–97
  and revivalism, 181–82
  and schools, 67
  See also Hicksite-Orthodox schism

pacificism, 6, 30, 61, 127, 202, 261
  activism, 10, 200, 211–12, 214
  and anti-slavery, 23, 212
  relief work, 249–50
  See also peace testimony
Palmer, Sarah Hopper, 27
pamphlets, 185, 200, 211, 214
  and the Hicksite-Orthodox schism, 4, 19, 142
  and anti-slavery, 96, 209
Parken, Caroline, 201

Paul, Alice, 31
peace testimony, 2, 6, 30, 127, 157, 201
    teachings, 165, 168
Pease, Elizabeth, 96, 200, 208–9
Pemberton, Philadelphia, 47
Pennsylvania Yearly Meeting of Progressive Friends, 25
Penny Savings Bank (Tottenham), 201
Philadelphia, PA, 17, 23, 30, 57, 69–70
Philadelphia Female Anti-Slavery Society, 23, 88
Philadelphia Yearly Meeting, 4, 22, 26, 28–29
    and the Hicksite-Orthodox schism, 51
    and racial inclusion, 92–93
philanthropy, 29–31, 106, 114
Pike, Mary, 20, 23
plainness, testimony of, 5–6, 10, 223, 241
    at weddings, 237
    See also dress, religious
Plummer, Joseph P., 26
Pollard, William, 230–31, 242
Poor Law Amendment Act (1834), 207
poor relief, 201, 209
Post, Amy Kirby, 24–25, 59, 89
prejudice, racial, 8, 128
    attitudes, 12, 93–94
    instances of, 82–83, 86, 92–96
Pre-Raphaelites, 234–36
Presbyterians, 81–82, 89
Preston, Ann, 26
Price, Junia, 203
Priestman, Anna Maria, 202, 210, 246
Priestman, Margaret, 210–11, 246
print culture, 168, 200
Prior, Margaret, 24
Progressive Friends, 4, 8, 24–26, 59
    religious beliefs, 89–90, 96–97
Protestantism, 5, 125–27
Punch (London), 212, 235
Pye, Edith, 10, 247–48, 260–261
    war relief, 251, 254, 259

Quaker Faith and Practice, 224
Quaker governance, 41
Quaker paternalism, 7, 40

Quietism, 3, 20, 158, 161, 164
    and reform, 200
    and theology, 5, 186
Quinn, William Paul, 92

Radnor Monthly Meeting, 60
Reeder, Elizabeth M., 23
reform: involvement in, 4–5, 158
    disagreements over, 23, 81–82
    humanitarian, 3, 10, 11–12, 40, 58, 68, 200
    and Indigenous cultures, 125
    in meetings, 22
    moral, 83, 125–27
    See also abolition; electoral reform; pacificism; suffrage; temperance
Republican Party, 26
Requited Labor Convention, 58
Retreat Asylum, 203
Richards, David, 60–61
Richards, Elizabeth Magee, 58-61, 65
Richardson, Anna, 209
Richardson, Jane, 201
Richardson, Reginald, 209
Ripley, Dorothy, 52
Robinson, Ellen, 202
Robson, Elizabeth, 7, 18, 39, 40, 266
    and the Hicksite-Orthodox schism, 47
    life and records, 41–46, 56n35
    and personal sacrifice, 49–51
Robson, Thomas, 42–43, 49
Roe, Levi, 80, 88
Romanticism, 11, 158, 163, 169, 183
    influence of, 171, 174
Rowntree, John Stephenson, 225–26
Rowntree, John Wilhelm, 5
Royal Free Hospital, 247
Ruggles, David, 69
Rushmore, Jane P., 29
Ruskin, John, 234, 236–37

Sabin, Lydia, 19
sacraments, Christian, 90, 127
Salt, Thomas, 207
Sansom, Bewlay, 51
Savage, Mary, 207
Save the Children Committee, 260

Schofield, Andrew, 53
Schofield, Martha, 28
School for Industry (Tottenham), 201
science, advancement of, 5, 157, 171–72, 205
Scotland, 42, 203, 207
Scottish Woman's Christian Temperance Union, 206
Seaman, Gideon, 19
Second Great Awakening, 84, 126
Seebohm, Benjamin Jr., 238
Seebohm, Lucretia Anson Crouch, 223–24, 238, 240–41
Seneca Falls Convention, 6, 24–25
separate-spheres ideology, 1–2, 21, 58, 62, 148, 246
    challenges to, 26, 58–59, 178, 200, 246–47
    private sphere, 106
    "third sphere," 11, 59, 102, 106–7, 111, 178
    support of, 6
sewing, 108–9
sex work, 213
Shackleton, Abraham, 3
Sharon Hill Boarding School, 21
Shillitoe, Thomas, 39
Slave; His Wrongs and Their Remedy, 115
Slavery Abolition Act (1833), 203
Slemons, Morris, 258–59
Smeal, Jane, 203
Smith, Hannah Whitall, 9, 178–79
    early life, 180–81
    and the holiness movement, 180
Smith, Martha, 19, 47, 53
Smith, Robert Pearsall, 181–82
Smith, Ruth Esther, 8, 122
    early ministry, 122–23
    in Guatemala, 124, 128–30
    legacy, 131–33
sola fide, 125
Southall, Alfred, 231
Southall, Anna Strangman Grubb, 231
Southey, Robert, 165
Spanish-American War, 30
Stabler, Alice, 27
Stanton, Elizabeth Cady, 25, 31
Steer, Sarah, 27
Stephenson, Isaac, 39, 40

Stephenson family, 41
Stewart, Maria, 84–85
Stowe, Harriet Beecher, 104, 108, 112, 148
Street, town of (in England), 103, 111
Street Free Labour Cotton Depot, 105
Street Sewing Circle, 109–10
Sturge, Hannah Dickinson, 104, 110, 112, 114
Sturge, Joseph, 92, 104, 106, 211–12
Sturge, Sophia, 212, 246
suffrage, 10, 32, 209–10
    activism for, 109, 183–85, 213–15, 246–47
    Black suffrage movement, 94–95
    opposition to, 31, 209, 257
    universal, 200
    See also women's rights
sugar, boycott of, 104, 203, 208
    See also free-produce movement
Sunshine Mission, 123–24
Swarthmore College, 18, 29
Sykes, John, 66

Taylor, Elizabeth Richards, 58–59, 62–66, 69
Taylor, Elizabeth Sykes, 58–59, 66–69, 71–72
Taylor, George W., 7, 57, 64–69, 71–72
Taylor, Jacob, 62, 70–71
Taylor, Thomas, 69–70
temperance movement, 10, 30, 31, 205–6
    grocer, 69, 105
Thomas, Mary F., 26
Thompson, Frances, 49–50
Townshend, Lucy, 203
Training School for Christian Workers, 130
Truth, Sojourner, 8, 79, 87
    early life, 80–81
    political work, 97
    religious influences, 84–85
    and Quakerism, 88–90
Twelfth Street Meeting, 51

Underground Railroad, 58, 108
Uncle Tom's Cabin, 103, 108, 110–11, 115, 148
    See also Stowe, Harriet Beecher

Union, the, 18, 26–27, 204
    See also American Civil War
Unitarians, 200, 205
University of Birmingham, 245

Valiant Sixty, 126
Van Wagenen, Isaac, 80
Verdé-Delisle, Gaston, 251
Victoria and Albert Museum, 238
Village Album, 103

Wakefield, Priscilla Bell, 169–71, 201
Walton, Margaretta, 20
Ward, Samuel Ringgold, 92
Washington, Margaret, 90
Waterhouse, Mary, 206
Waterloo Yearly Meeting, 24–26
wealth, of Quaker families, 4, 12, 60, 106, 240
Webb, Benjamin, 22–23
Webster, Sarah, 19
Wells, Ida B., 115
Western Quarterly Meeting, 22
Westtown Boarding School, 62, 66–68
Wetherald, Thomas, 52
Whipper, William, 69
White, George Fox, 23–24
White supremacists, 88, 90, 92, 95
whiteness, constructions of, 8, 52, 95, 128
Whitson, Elizabeth Taylor, 58, 63–66
Whitson, Moses, 58
Whitson, Thomas, 58
Whittier, John Greenleaf, 18
Wigham, Eliza, 202–4, 206, 213
Wigham, John Jr., 204
Wilberforce, William, 203

Wilbur, John, 5
Willis, Phebe, 18
Withy, George, 39
Woman's Christian Temperance Union, 30–31
Woman's Wrongs, 210
Women's International League for Peace and Freedom, 30, 202, 260
Women's Liberal Federation, 246
women's rights, 10, 18, 22–25, 28–32
    activism for, 210–13
    opposition to, 24
    property rights, 212
    See also suffrage
Women's Social and Political Union, 247, 257
Woolman, John, 66, 96, 236
workhouses, 201, 208, 209, 254
World Anti-Slavery Convention, 25, 203, 215
World War I, 6, 10, 30, 247
    Battle of the Marne, 251–52
    outbreak of, 249–50
    refugees, 254–55
World War II, 260
World Woman's Christian Temperance Union, 206
working men's movement, 22
Wright, Frances, 23
Wright, Henry C., 89
Wright, Martha, 25
Wybrow, Caroline, 213

Yarnall, Sarah, 19
Young Englishwoman, 238
Young Women's Christian Association, 205

www.ingramcontent.com/pod-product-compliance
Lightning Source LLC
Chambersburg PA
CBHW022037290426
44109CB00014B/886